Pan-Africanism

ADEKUNLE AJALA

Pan-Africanism:
Evolution, Progress and Prospects

ADEKUNLE AJALA

St. Martin's Press New York

AFFILIATED PUBLISHERS: Macmillan Limited, London
—also at Bombay, Calcutta, Madras and Melbourne

To all those who have striven or still strive for
African unity and the advancement of African
people all over the world.

Contents

Contents

Part Three: Any Need for Pan-Africanism?

Appendixes
Documents:

Acknowledgements

I am grateful to Miss Catherine Hoskyns, who read part of the manuscript.

The staff of the British Museum, the British Museum Newspaper Library and the Commonwealth Institute Library, Kensington, have been very helpful.

Miss Judy de Mendonça typed the first draft. The final manuscript would, however, not have been ready for the publishers without the devoted and dedicated service of Mrs Jacqueline De Val.

Special thanks are due to both Lord Brockway and Mr D. F. C. De Val for their interest and ever-ready assistance.

Needless to say, the opinions expressed in the book, and any errors that remain, are my responsibility alone.

ADEKUNLE AJALA
London
February 1972

List of Maps and Tables

Part One: Evolution

I. History of the Movement: 1900–1962

We are related – you and I
You from the West Indies,
I from Kentucky
We are related – you and I
You from Africa
I from these States.
We are brothers – you and I.

LANGSTON HUGHES*

There are three phases in the evolution of Pan-Africanism. The first of these was the gathering of 'exiles' in Europe and the United States of America. During this period Africans, West Indians and Americans of African descent more or less 'discovered' one another. Sharing common disabilities and increasingly aware of many common elements in their heritage, they convened conferences on an ad hoc basis, organized student groups and cultural associations, and in the later stages turned to explicit political agitation for African independence. The second phase was the nationalization of Pan-Africanism. During this period there was a progressive shift in the focus of political agitation to individual territories in Africa; this followed upon the formation of territorial nationalist movements. With the attainment of independence by many African states, the second phase gradually gave way to the contemporary one, which is characterized by two lines of activity. The first of these is the political action within and among independent African states, in close collaboration with nationalist movements from the remaining colonial territories, and having as its aim the complete liberation of all Africa from alien rule. The second aim is the achievement of genuine African unity, which is the precondition for the much-needed economic development of the African continent as well as for making the African voice in world politics both respected and effective.

*Harold Isaacs, 'Five Writers and Their African Ancestors', *Plydon*, 3rd quarter, 1960.

(a) The Origin of Pan-Africanism

The common experience of discrimination based on skin colour, and flagrant injustices and degradation, combined to make people of African descent in both the United States and the West Indies realize that they faced the same problems and must therefore unite in order to find a solution. This realization led to an awareness of their common heritage and to a desire for some link with their African origins. It brought about, too, the wish to redeem Africa from the scourge of imperialism and colonialism. Out of this grew the ideals of Pan-Africanism.

The first attempt towards the attainment of the Pan-Africanist objective was made in 1900, when Henry Sylvester-Williams, a West Indian barrister practising in London, organized a Pan-African conference. This conference, which took place in London between 23 and 25 July, was attended by thirty delegates, mostly from America and the West Indies. Its aims included the following: to act as a forum of protest against the aggressiveness of white colonists; to bring people of African descent throughout the world into closer touch with one another; and to start a movement which would secure to all African races living in civilized countries their full rights and would promote their business interest.

The conference addressed a petition to Queen Victoria through the British Government, complaining about the treatment of Africans in both South Africa and Rhodesia.

(b) Pan-Africanism between the two World Wars

With the death of Henry Sylvester-Williams shortly after the conference of 1900, the organizational aspect of Pan-Africanism was put in cold storage for some time. But the driving force behind it never died. The discrimination, injustice and degradation experienced by Americans of African descent continued unabated and led to the formation, in 1905, of the Niagra Movement, which spearheaded protests against the treatment inflicted upon the American Negroes. By 1910 an interracial

4

organization was formed under the leadership and influence of white American liberals to fight for Negro rights by 'peaceful means'. The organization, the National Association for the Advancement of Coloured People (NAACP), appointed Dr W. E. B. DuBois as director of publicity and research, with the primary function of editing its monthly magazine, *Crisis*. Although the NAACP embarked upon 'a publicity campaign to point out the injustices and abuses of American race relations',[1] nothing of significance was achieved in those years before the First World War.

As this was continued and America became involved, American Negroes joined the army to fight for a 'better world'. Their experience immediately after the war, however, made them realize that their dream of a better world was not going to materialize. In 1919, for example, 'eighty-three Negro Americans, many of them returning [war] veterans, had been lynched – eleven of them being burned alive'.[2] At the same time the living conditions of the American Negroes worsened, while the outbreak of mass intolerance (as evidenced in the violence of the race riots and the resurgence of the Ku Klux Klan) seemed to prove the need for a new approach to the race problem.[3] This new situation led to the revival of Pan-Africanism between the world wars. At this time, however, it was approached from three different angles: that of Marcus Garvey's 'conventions' or 'parliaments'; that of the DuBoisian Pan-African congresses; and through the efforts of the African intelligentsia.

(i) Marcus Garvey and the Universal Negro Improvement Association

Faced with the enormous problems confronting those of African descent in the Americas, and realizing the ineffectiveness of the tactics adopted so far by the NAACP, Marcus Garvey organized a branch of his Jamaica-based Universal Negro Improvement Association in New York in 1917. In spite of the efforts of certain Negro politicians to destroy the organization from the outset, it grew in strength and became the best-organized mass Negro association in America.

5

Evolution

As Marcus Garvey explained in New York shortly afterwards, the UNIA aimed at uniting all people of African descent as well as Africans 'for their own industrial, political, social and religious emancipation'. It was concerned to achieve 'political freedom on the continent of Africa, the land of our fathers'.[4] The series of 'conventions' or 'parliaments' organized by the UNIA in pursuit of its objectives were attended by Africans as well as people of African descent in the United States, West Indies, South and Central America; and the first of them, held in New York in August 1920, was attended by delegates from twenty-five countries.[5] This first convention not only served as a milestone in the efforts to unite Africans and their brethren all over the world, but also achieved two significant purposes. Firstly, it adopted a comprehensive guideline for Pan-Africanism, under the title, 'Declaration of Rights of the Negro Peoples of the World'. (See Appendix 1.) Secondly, it spurred Africans and peoples of African descent into action and gave them confidence in their ability to stand up and work towards their unity and the political emancipation of the African continent. For the first time ever, a gathering of international status was able forthrightly to declare: 'We shall ask, demand, and expect of the world a free Africa.'[6]

Seven other such conventions were held by the UNIA between the world wars and at each one the unity of the African people and the freedom of their homeland were the declared objectives, along with a determination to advance the status of Africans and people of African descent.

(ii) The DuBoisian Pan-African Congresses

While Marcus Garvey and the UNIA maintained that Africans and people of African descent would achieve equality only through personal endeavour, DuBois thought that cooperation with the American and European liberals was essential in the struggle to achieve that goal. As a result, DuBois not only cooperated with the white-dominated NAACP, but sought that organization's advice and support before embarking on his Pan-African congresses.[7]

6

The first DuBoisian Pan-African congress was held in Paris in 1919. It was due largely to Blaise Diagne, the Senegalese deputy in the French National Assembly, that this congress took place at all, for the American Government both openly and covertly (by putting pressure on the French Government) did everything possible to sabotage it.[8] In spite of American efforts, however, the congress, attended by fifty-seven delegates, opened in February. It 'drafted various proposals, though nothing much came out of them'.[9]

Three more DuBoisian Pan-African congresses took place before the world was plunged into another war. The first such congress, which took place in London in 1921, adopted a 'Declaration to the World' including an assertion that 'the absolute equality of races, physical, political and social, is the founding stone of the world and human achievement'.[10]

(iii) The African Effort

With Pan-Africanism split into the 'radical' (Marcus Garvey and the UNIA) and the 'moderate' (DuBois, under the umbrella of the NAACP) groups in America, African intellectuals too were advocating African unity. The cause was championed by Professor Adeoye Deniga of Nigeria, Joseph Casely-Hayford of the Gold Coast (now Ghana), and Ladipo Solanke of Nigeria.

Professor Adeoye Deniga put forward his ideas for African unity (confined to West Africa at that time) in a pamphlet entitled *The Need for West African Federation*.

Joseph Casely-Hayford founded the National Congress of British West Africa at Accra in March 1920. Its inaugural meeting was attended by delegates from Nigeria, Sierra Leone, Gambia and the Gold Coast. In his opening speech at that inaugural meeting, Casely-Hayford declared:

We desire . . . as the intelligentsia of British West Africa, to promote unity among our people. You all know the importance of unity, and you remember the parable of the man who, when dying, called his sons together, and when they were come asked them to bring him a bundle of wood. You all know how he asked them to loose the bundle and how each of them was taken out and could be easily broken and how they were put together and could not be broken. It is in the same manner that our people are learning the importance of unity. Nigeria has joined hands with Gambia and Gambia with Sierra Leone and Sierra Leone with the Gold Coast, etc. and it is our hope, by this combination, to express our views in a way that can be effective.[11]

Shortly after the meeting, a delegation of the National Congress of British West Africa, under the leadership of Casely-Hayford, and with two delegates from each of the territories concerned, went to London, where they submitted a memorandum to the Colonial Office demanding increased representation in the legislative councils of each of the four territories, and the establishment of both a West African court of appeal and a West African university.

Although the delegation achieved nothing, the National Congress of British West Africa did succeed in promoting cooperation among Africans in the four British West African colonies during the next decade.

While the National Congress of British West Africa was fostering the spirit of unity and cooperation in West Africa, West African students in London played their part too. Led by Ladipo Solanke, they formed the West African Students' Union in 1924 with, among others, the following aims:

(1) to provide and maintain a hostel (or residential club) for students of African descent and others approved by the Hostel Board of Management;

(2) to act as a bureau of information on African history, customs and institutions;

(3) to act as a centre for research on all subjects appertaining to Africa and its development;

(4) to provide self-help, unity, cooperation and the spirit of true leadership among members;

(5) to promote, through regular contacts, the spirit of goodwill, better understanding and brotherhood between all persons of African descent and other races of mankind;

8

(6) to present to the world a true picture of African life and philosophy, thereby making a definitely African contribution towards the progress of civilization;

(7) to foster a spirit of national consciousness and racial pride among all African peoples.

The WASU hostel 'became a centre where students from all over Africa met people of African descent from the Antilles and America'[12] to discuss their ideas. With the death of Casely-Hayford in 1930 and the subsequent decline of the National Congress of British West Africa, WASU in fact took over the latter's role and provided most of the future West African leaders.

All these efforts notwithstanding, European rule in Africa seemed totally unaffected and Africans on the continent remained passive. But the situation suddenly changed when Italy invaded Ethiopia in 1935. This invasion roused many Africans and stirred people of African descent throughout the world. A mass meeting in Lagos protested against the Italian aggression, and called upon the British Government to act decisively to restrain Italy. Many prominent Nigerians even formed an Abyssinian association to support the Ethiopian cause. As a result of the invasion, the International African Friends of Abyssinia was formed by Africans and their sympathizers in London. This organization joined forces with others to become the International African Service Bureau in 1937. The new organization's aim was to promote the well-being and unity of African peoples and peoples of African descent throughout the world and also 'to co-operate between [*sic*] African peoples and others who share our aspirations'.[13]

(c) Pan-Africanism 1945–62

(i) *The Beginning of a New Era*

In 1944 the International African Service Bureau and twelve other active welfare, students' and political organizations came

9

together in Manchester to form the Pan-African Federation.[14] The Federation had the following objectives:

(1) to promote the well-being and unity of African peoples and peoples of African descent throughout the world;

(2) to demand the self-determination and independence of African peoples and other subject races from the domination of powers proclaiming sovereignty and trusteeship over them;

(3) to secure equality of rights for African peoples and the total abolition of all forms of racial discrimination.

In that same year the British Trades Union Congress held a conference at which representatives of labour from Africa and the West Indies were present, and it was decided there to hold a conference of the World Federation of Trade Unions in the following year.[15] As this plan became known, the Pan-African Federation decided to seize its opportunity and organize a Pan-African congress, which would coincide with the meeting of the World Federation of Trade Unions. Preparations were immediately undertaken by the specially constituted 'Special International Conference Secretariat'. The members of this special secretariat included the following: Dr Peter Milliard of British Guiana as Chairman; R. T. Makonnen (formerly known as Peter Griffiths) of (now) Ethiopia, treasurer; George Padmore of Trinidad and Kwame Nkrumah of the Gold Coast, joint secretaries; Peter Abrahams of South Africa, publicity secretary. Jomo Kenyatta of Kenya was assistant secretary. By August 1945, all was set.

When the congress finally assembled at Chorlton town hall, Manchester, in October 1945, it was attended by over two hundred delegates from all over the 'coloured world'. The chair was jointly occupied by DuBois and Dr Milliard on the first day of the conference.[16] On subsequent sittings, however, DuBois alone chaired the meeting.

The congress was significant in many ways. For the first time in the history of Pan-Africanism, Africa was well represented. The Africans who took a leading part in it, besides those already mentioned, included Chief H. O. Davies, Magnus Williams and the late Chief S. L. Akintola (Nigeria), Wallace Johnson (Sierra Leone) and Dr Raphael Armattoe from Togo.[17] For the first time Pan-Africanism and African nationalism were fully discussed; and, for the first time also, the necessity for well-organized, firmly-knit movements, as a primary condition for the success of the national liberation struggle in Africa, was stressed.

The congress adopted a number of resolutions, many of which aimed at the abolition of exploitation in the colonies and the injustices of colonialism. One of these declared that, since the advent of British, French, Belgian and other Europeans in Africa, 'there has been regression instead of progress as a result of systematic exploitation by these alien imperialist powers'. In the 'Declaration to the Colonial Powers', the delegates expressed their belief in peace, but made it abundantly clear that 'if the Western world is still determined to rule mankind by force, then Africans, as a last resort, may have to appeal to force in the effort to achieve freedom'. The congress demanded for Africa 'autonomy and independence, so far and no further than it is possible in this One World for groups and peoples to rule themselves subject to inevitable world unity and federation'. It affirmed the right of all colonial peoples to control their own destiny. It expressed the conviction that 'all colonies must be free from foreign imperialist control, whether political or economic'. And after emphasizing that the struggle for political power by colonial and subject peoples was 'the first step towards, and the necessary prerequisite to, complete social, economic and political emancipation', it called on the workers and farmers, the intellectuals and professional classes to awaken to their responsibilities and organize themselves effectively so that independence might be won.

By the end of the congress, it had become clear that Pan-Africanism was growing from a protest movement by people of African descent in the West Indies and United States into an instrument of African nationalist movements fighting colonial rule. The congress 'provided the outlet for African nationalism and brought about the awakening of African political consciousness'.[18] Pan-Africanism was becoming a mass movement of Africa for the Africans.

The congress set up a working committee, with DuBois as president and Nkrumah as secretary, to promote the objectives and plans that had been adopted. And the committee, at a meeting held in London shortly after the congress, chose London as their headquarters and took upon themselves to act as a kind of clearing-house for the various political movements that were emerging in the colonies – a decision which, however, for financial reasons had to be abandoned.

Accordingly, West African students in London examined the possibility of setting up a West African national secretariat. After a meeting of Ashie Nikoe, Wallace Johnson, Bankole Akpata, Awooner Renner, Kojo Botsio and Kwame Nkrumah, that plan went ahead, in order to put the new Pan-African nationalism, with particular reference to West Africa, into action. It was also agreed to call a West African national congress. The secretariat was expected to be the nerve-centre for directing the programme of self-government for the West African colonies. When the West African national congress was called in August 1946, it pledged itself to promote the concept of a West African federation as a stepping-stone to the ultimate achievement of a United States of Africa.

(ii) Pan-Africanism 1958–60

After the West African National Congress of August 1946 no serious organizational developments on an international basis took place until 1958. There were two main reasons. The first of these centred on Kwame Nkrumah, who had been the energetic secretary of the West African National Secretariat in London, and was now invited by the leaders of the United Gold Coast Convention to become the general secretary of the party. He left London for the Gold Coast on 14 November 1947. The second reason resulted from the decision of the Manchester Congress to organize political parties in the different colonies so that independence might be won. Efforts were therefore concentrated in the colonies, and these activities prevented any significant international Pan-African conference.

In December 1953, shortly after Kwame Nkrumah had become prime minister of the Gold Coast, he organized a conference in Kumasi, which was attended by representatives of the nationalist movements from both the English-speaking and French-speaking territories in West Africa, including independent Liberia. The conference recommended the establishment of a national congress of West Africa to promote West African unity. Periodic conferences of the congress were to be held alternatively in an English-speaking and a French-speaking territory of West Africa.[19] Although no such conferences were, in fact, held, the congress was used by African leaders in British and French colonies as a means of keeping in touch with one another.

In March 1957 Ghana became independent; and during the independence celebrations, Kwame Nkrumah announced his intention to convene a conference of the independent African states at a later date. Its aims would be to discuss problems of common interest to all independent African states; to explore ways and means of consolidating and safeguarding the independence of these states; to decide on workable arrangements for helping fellow Africans still under colonial rule; and to examine other world problems. Shortly afterwards, Nkrumah sent out invitations to the leaders of the other independent African states, for a conference to be held at Accra, Ghana, in April 1958. Preliminary discussions on the proposed conference then took place in London among the African ambassadors. Subsequent to these discussions a three-man mission, consisting of Ako Adjei, the minister of justice, Kofi Baako, minister of defence and external affairs, and George Padmore, prime minister's adviser on African affairs, visited the capitals of the independent African states.[20]

Although the proposed conference was intended solely for the independent African states, Nkrumah's request to consult with the Nigerian leaders personally met with a friendly response only from Dr Nnamdi Azikiwe, who was then the premier of the Eastern Region. The prime minister of the Federation, Abubakar Tafawa Balewa, and the premiers of the Northern and Western Regions, Ahmadu Bello and Obafemi Awolowo respectively, claimed that 'because of existing commitments' they would not 'find it convenient to receive Doctor Nkrumah'.[21] So, when a Ghanaian delegation finally went to Nigeria, it was received only by Dr Azikiwe. This episode is significant in view of the Pan-African developments between 1960 and 1962.

THE FIRST CONFERENCE OF INDEPENDENT AFRICAN STATES: ACCRA, 1958

The first Conference of Independent African States was held in Accra from 15 to 22 April 1958. It marked the formal launching of the Pan-African movement on African soil. The conference, which was attended by African leaders from Ethiopia, Liberia, Libya, Morocco, Sudan, Tunisia, the United Arab Republic and Ghana the host country, dispelled the fear that religion and the Sahara would constitute a barrier between the Arabs and other Africans.

During the preparations, Ghana had taken pains to produce a draft memorandum which was submitted in advance to the invited States. In it Ghana suggested that the aims of the conference should be as follows: to bring the African independent states together in order to discuss problems of mutual interest, and to consider, formulate and coordinate schemes and methods aimed at speeding up mutual understanding; to consider ways and means of safeguarding the independence and sovereignty of the participating countries; and to discuss and plan cultural exchanges and schemes of mutual assistance. In addition, the draft memorandum proposed that the conference should set up permanent machinery for cooperation and consultation among the African states, in order to implement its decisions and to provide the machinery for the prompt exchange of views on African and international problems, so that an African personality in international affairs might emerge. The following agenda was then agreed upon:

(1) exchange of views on foreign policy, especially in relation to the African continent; the future of African dependent territories; the Algerian problem; the racial problem; steps to be taken to safeguard the independence, sovereignty, and territorial integrity of the independent African states;

(2) examination of ways and means to promote economic co-

operation among the African states, based on the exchange of technical, scientific, and educational information with special regard to industrial planning and development;

(3) formulation of concrete proposals for the exchange of visiting governmental and non-governmental cultural missions among the various countries, leading to first-hand mutual knowledge and appreciation of one another's cultures;

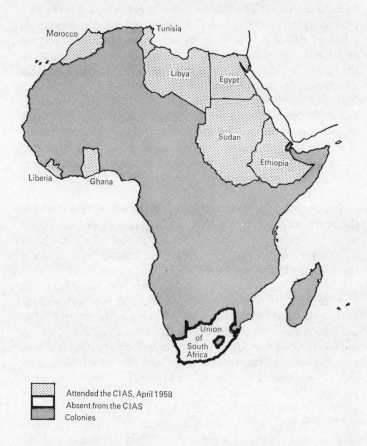

Attended the CIAS, April 1958
Absent from the CIAS
Colonies

1. Independent States in Africa on 1 January 1958

(4) consideration of the problem of international peace and of conformity with the Charter of the United Nations; and re-affirmation of the principles of the Bandung Asian-African Conference;

(5) establishment, after the conference, of permanent machinery for consultation on foreign policy.[22]

When the conference finally began Nkrumah declared in his opening address: 'This is a memorable gathering. It is the first time in history that representatives of independent sovereign states in Africa are meeting together with the aim of forging closer links of friendship, brotherhood and solidarity between them,' reminded the delegates that Africa had for too long been a victim of foreign domination, and continued: 'If we can, as independent African states, show by our own efforts that we can settle our own problems in Africa, then we shall be setting an example to others.' In conclusion, he said: 'Today we are one. If in the past the Sahara divided us, now it unites us. And an injury to one is an injury to all of us. From this conference must go out a new message: "Hands off Africa! Africa must be free."'[23]

Significantly, the conference accorded a non-voting status to the representatives of the Algerian National Liberation Front, which was engaged in armed struggle against the French for Algeria's independence. This action was later to become one of the sources of friction in the Pan-African movement.

The conference demonstrated, however, that Pan-Africanism had emerged from idealism into the field of practical politics. It showed clearly that there were African leaders determined to see Africa not only free but also united. The leaders of the independent African states set a precedent by asserting and proclaiming unity among themselves as well as their solidarity with the still-dependent peoples of the continent. They resolved to preserve their unity of purpose and action in international affairs and also expressed their determination to establish an 'African personality' in world affairs through the cooperation of their countries in foreign policy. They committed all the independent African states to direct involvement in securing the emancipation of the continent, declared war on colonialism and on South Africa's apartheid policy, and also gave their full support to the Algerian people in their struggle for independence. Furthermore, they agreed to coordinate their countries' economic and industrial planning in order to raise the living standard of the African people.

The conference decided to set up permanent machinery for coordinating all matters of common concern to the African states; for examining and making recommendations on concrete, practical steps for implementing conference decisions, and for preparing the ground for future conferences. It agreed that meetings of foreign ministers, other ministers or experts should be convened from time to time, to study and deal with particular problems of common concern to the African states. The Conference of Independent African States was to be held every two years; and it thus came about that the Second Conference of Independent African States was held, at Addis Ababa, Ethiopia, in 1960.

THE ALL AFRICAN PEOPLES' ORGANIZATION: ACCRA, 1958
Before the end of 1958 Ghana acted as host to another Pan-African Conference: this time, of the African political parties. Apart from the conspicuous absence of the Nigerian Northern Peoples' Congress (NPC) and the ruling political parties in French Africa excluding Guinea, the conference was attended by all African political parties from Cairo to Cape Town.

The conference was opened at Accra on 5 December by Kwame Nkrumah, in his capacity as life chairman of the Convention Peoples' Party of Ghana (CPP). In his address Nkrumah said: 'Never before has it been possible for so representative a gathering of African Freedom Fighters to assemble in a free independent African state for the purpose of planning for a final assault upon imperialism and colonialism.' Declaring that the assembly marked the opening of a new epoch in African history, he called on the delegates to remember always that before the final objective of Pan-Africanism could be achieved, four stages had to occur. These were: the attainment of freedom and independence; the consolidation of that freedom and independence; the creation of unity and community between the African states; and the economic and social reconstruction of Africa. He reminded the delegates that the liberation of Africa was the task of all Africans, and in conclusion said: 'Fighters for African freedom, I appeal to you in the sacred name of Mother Africa to leave this Conference resolved to rededicate yourselves to the task of forming among the political parties in your respective countries a broad united front, based upon one common fundamental aim and object: the speedy liberation of your territories.'[24]

After Nkrumah's opening address the conference elected Tom Mboya of Kenya as chairman, with J. K. Tetteh of Ghana and F. S. McEwen of Nigeria as joint secretaries. Speaking after his election, Mboya said: 'The time and hour have now come . . . especially for some very few people in this Conference, this is the climax of a life-long dream. A dream that for many years had been dreamt, wishing that it were to be translated into realities [*sic*] . . . The significance of this Conference is that whereas seventy-two years ago in Berlin, the scramble for Africa, to-day in Accra, we announce to the whole world that these same powers that met to decide the partitioning of Africa will now decide with one firm voice to scram from Africa.'[25]

The conference was divided into the following five main committees:

First Committee	to deal with colonialism and imperialism;
Second Committee	to discuss racialism, discriminatory laws and practices;
Third Committee	to handle the question of lands, implementation of the Universal Declaration of Human Rights of the United Nations; tribalism and human religious separation and other traditional institutions;
Fourth Committee	to concern itself with the progressive federation or confederation of geographical regional state groupings into an ultimate Pan-African Commonwealth of free independent united states of Africa;

Fifth Committee   to consider the setting-up of a permanent
                     secretariat of the Conference.

Publicity, resolutions and credentials were to be dealt with by
three other committees.

Apart from the presence of so many major African political
parties, the conference itself was significant in many ways. For
the first time in the history of Pan-Africanism, a resolution was
adopted by a substantial representative gathering to promote a
commonwealth of united free African states. This read that the
conference:

'(a) endorses Pan-Africanism and the desire for unity among
African peoples;
(b) declares that its ultimate objective is the evolution of a
Commonwealth of Free African States;
(c) calls upon the Independent States of Africa to lead the
peoples of Africa towards the attainment of this objective; and
(d) expresses the hope that the day will dawn when the first
loyalty of African States will be to an African Commonwealth.'[26]

The conference also raised the question of violence, at the
insistence of the Algerian FLN, still engaged in armed struggle
for independence. Recognizing that in certain territories national
independence could be gained without violence, the conference
nonetheless pledged support to those who 'in order to meet the
violent means by which they are subjected and exploited, are
obliged to retaliate'.[27]

Another aspect of the AAPO Conference was its manifesta-
tion of the faith that Pan-Africanism was not based on racialism.
White South Africans representing the South African Liberal
Party and the African National Congress of South Africa, as
well as Indians from East Africa, participated in the deliberations.

1959: THE YEAR OF DECLARATIONS

1959 marked a significant step forward in the Pan-African objective of a commonwealth of free African states. Concrete efforts
were made in West Africa towards achieving that goal, first by

Ghana and Guinea, and later by Ghana, Guinea and Liberia. They led to two important declarations: the Conakry Declaration of 1 May 1959; and the Sanniquellie Declaration of 19 July 1959. These declarations, coupled with the outcome of the Monrovia Conference of foreign ministers held between 4 and 8 August, made 1959 a significant year in the move towards establishing a union of African States.

THE CONAKRY DECLARATION: 1 MAY 1959

Guinea became independent in September 1958 after casting its vote in the referendum of the same year, which gave the French African colonies the opportunity to declare whether or not they intended to remain in the French community. A 'No' vote was to lead to immediate independence which would entail almost inevitable economic disaster. In spite of this ill-concealed blackmail, Guinea, unlike the other French territories, opted out of the French community, thus gaining her independence. French reaction was vicious and Guinea's economic structure was badly affected.

In response to the strangulation policy adopted by France, assisted by some of her NATO partners, Ghana came to Guinea's side. Sékou Touré of Guinea and Nkrumah of Ghana held a series of talks in Accra from 21 to 23 November 1958, at the end of which it was announced that the two countries had decided to constitute themselves into a union of West African states. After a Ghanaian mission had visited Guinea, both countries agreed to appoint two commissions: the first to prepare a draft constitution for the proposed union; the second to study the economic and financial problems facing the two countries. The governments also discussed measures for coordinating their foreign policy, and for improving inter-radio, air and sea communications.[28]

Proposing a motion in the Ghana parliament for the ratification of the Ghana–Guinea Union agreement of 23 November 1958, Kwame Nkrumah said that both Ghana and Guinea had agreed to exchange resident ministers. A joint economic commission was to be set up to study economic and financial affairs, including currency arrangements. The commission would consist of three members from each state. Communications between the states would be greatly improved. A constitutional commission comprising three members from each would also be appointed.[29] At the same time, however, the whole idea of a union of West African states 'predetermined by Ghana and Guinea' came under strong criticism from Chief Anthony Enahoro of Nigeria.[30]

The constitutional commission continued with its work; and when it had reported back to both governments, these solemnly agreed 'to seal the Ghana–Guinea Union in practice'. Since the union was meant to be the nucleus of a union of independent African states, membership was open to all other independent African states. The union was expected 'to build up a free and prosperous African community in the interest of its people and world peace'. It would have a common economic, foreign and defence policy, although each member was expected to have its own army. In order to bring Africans closer together, the union would take the necessary measures to coordinate historical research, teaching of languages, and cultural activities designed to promote the harmonious development of African civilizations.

THE SANNIQUELLIE DECLARATION: 19 JULY 1959

On the initiative of President Tubman of Liberia, a conference was held at Sanniquellie, a small Liberian village, in July 1959, between the heads of state of Ghana, Guinea and Liberia. The Sanniquellie Conference fitted well into the Pan-African structure, despite President Tubman's reservations.

The president suggested in his welcoming address that the conference should discuss African unity, African freedom, the independence of the Cameroons, racial discrimination in South Africa, nuclear tests in the Sahara, and a future conference of independent African states. He was of the opinion that all discussions on African unity should at that time be only of an exploratory nature. He therefore wanted 'no final decision or agreement on such far-reaching, intricate and delicate matters' to be taken until other African territories with fixed dates for independence had become independent. He thought that other independent states should then be consulted, so that they could

fully participate as foundation members in a meeting or conference 'to decide the specific form that unity should take which
will be satisfactory to all and spontaneously supported by all'.[31]
This view was shared by neither Nkrumah nor Sékou Touré.
Nkrumah for his part said: 'Let us not postpone the talks [*sic*]
of laying the foundation of West African Unity. We, the leaders
and representatives of Liberia, Guinea and Ghana, the three
independent nations in this part of the continent, must make the
beginning now. We cannot delay. Time passes. We must start
with what we have.'[32] Sékou Touré explained that any decisions
taken at the conference would not be made merely by the 'three
heads of state, but by the African peoples'. He therefore wanted
the conference to get down to business; to do something constructive which would produce such results as would be a source
of inspiration to the African people, who wanted a lead from
their leaders.

In spite of these exhortations and pleadings for immediate
action, the three heads of state deferred any decision on the
form, method and timing of concrete measures towards African
unity and cooperation until Nigeria and the other African
countries became independent. But they did agree to form 'the
Community of Independent African States' with a view to
achieving unity among independent African states. Each
member state of the community was to maintain its national
identity and constitutional structure. Each member state
accepted the principle of non-interference in the internal affairs
of any other member. The community was to set up an economic
council, a cultural council, and a scientific and research council.
Membership would be open to all independent African states.

The conference also passed several resolutions, among them
one deprecating France's insistence on carrying out nuclear tests
in Africa. It appealed to all Africans, including those in the
French community, and all members of the United Nations, to
associate themselves with Ghana, Guinea and Liberia in their
endeavour to dissuade France from embarking upon such a
devastating course.[33] The conference also agreed to convene a
special conference of the foreign ministers of the independent
African states which would concern itself with the projected

French nuclear tests in the Sahara as well as with other problems of common concern to the African states.

THE MONROVIA CONFERENCE OF FOREIGN MINISTERS OF INDEPENDENT AFRICAN STATES 4–8 AUGUST 1959

Represented at the special conference were the nine independent African states – Ethiopia, Ghana, Guinea, Liberia, Libya, Morocco, Sudan, Tunisia and the United Arab Republic – and the provisional government of Algeria. But apart from passing a somewhat stronger resolution on nuclear tests in the Sahara, this conference achieved nothing new.

Before we leave the year 1959, however, it is worth noting that there were certain other developments in the Pan-African movement that were later to have far-reaching consequences on the course of Pan-Africanism. It has already been pointed out that the attempt to form a Ghana–Guinea union as a prelude to the formation of a union of West African states came under severe criticism from Nigeria and found no favour with the Liberian government either. And the proceedings of the Sanni-quellie Conference underlined the emergence of two different approaches to the achievement of African unity.

During a press conference in America in July 1959, another eminent African leader, Dr Nnamdi Azikiwe of Nigeria, said that 'certain practical steps' should be taken before any African unity could be achieved. He added that 'if for many years certain parties have fought for their sovereignty, it is unlikely that they will surrender that sovereignty to a nebulous organisation simply because we feel it necessary to work together'.[34] In other words he was not in favour of any supranational organization to achieve African unity. Such considerations later formed the basis of the Nigerian approach to African unity.

(iii) Pan-Africanism 1960–62

Yet 1960 started well for Pan-Africanists. It had already been consecrated by no less a person than the secretary-general of the United Nations, Dag Hammarskjöld, as 'Africa Year', for in that year seventeen African territories were expected to become

23

independent – an achievement which was to be a milestone in the history of Pan-Africanism. But before the year ended, the hopes and expectations had somewhat faded. Seeds of division, sown over the years, seemed to be germinating.

THE SECOND ALL AFRICAN PEOPLES' CONFERENCE

The first Pan-African activity of 1960 was the Second All African Peoples' Conference, which took place at Tunis between 25 and 30 January 1960. Like the first AAPO Conference, it was attended by African political parties and trade unions, but it differed from its predecessor in that it not only paid attention to the political, economic and cultural aspects of Pan-Africanism, but also laid rather more emphasis on African unity. In the amended Constitution for the AAPO the objectives of Pan-Africanism were defined as follows:

(a) to promote understanding and unity among the peoples of Africa;

(b) to develop a feeling of one community among the African people;

(c) to accelerate the liberation of Africa from imperialism and colonialism;

(d) to mobilize world opinion in support of African liberation;

(e) to work for the emergence of the United States of Africa;

(f) to work for the economic, social and cultural development of Africa;

(g) to formulate concrete means and methods of achieving these objectives.

In order that the objectives might be achieved, the conference decided to establish a permanent secretariat at Accra with Abdoulaye Diallo of Guinea as the secretary-general.

The conference also dealt with another growing African problem – the affiliation of African trade unions to international trade-union bodies. As both the International Confederation of Free Trade Unions (ICFTU) and the World Federation of Trade Unions (WFTU) were associated with the two camps in the cold war, it was agreed at the Tunis Conference that, in order to preserve an 'African personality', an All-African Trade Union Federation (AATUF) should be established.

On another topic – the Algerian struggle for independence – which was going to become one of the causes of division in the Pan-African movement, the conference made the following recommendations:

(1) that all independent African states should recognize the provisional government of the Algerian Republic;

(2) that all these states should make an annual financial contribution towards financing the Algerian struggle for independence;

(3) that all soldiers from other French African territories fighting alongside the French against the Algerian Nationalists should be withdrawn from Algeria; and

(4) that an international brigade of African volunteers should be set up to assist the Algerian Nationalists in their struggle for independence.

THE SECOND CONFERENCE OF INDEPENDENT AFRICAN STATES

In accordance with the decision taken at the First Conference of Independent African States in April 1958, the Second CIAS was due to take place in 1960. Besides, the proceedings of the Sanniquellie Conference of July 1959 had specifically called for another conference of independent African states to be held in 1960, and it had additionally been agreed at that conference that the proposed CIAS of 1960 was to be attended not only by the independent states but also by those with fixed dates for independence. In view of this it was expected that the next CIAS would be attended not only by the eleven African States already independent[35] – Cameroon, Ethiopia, Ghana, Guinea, Liberia, Libya, Morocco, Sudan, Togo, Tunisia and the United Arab Republic – but also by Congo-Leopoldville (as Congo-Kinshasa was then known), Madagascar (now the Malagasy Republic), the Mali Federation,[36] Nigeria and Somalia. Algeria, which had been enjoying special treatment since 1958, was also expected to take part in the conference. Accordingly invitations

25

were sent to all these countries. But when the conference opened
at Addis Ababa on 15 June 1960, only the Algerian provisional
government, Cameroon, Ethiopia, Ghana, Guinea, Liberia,
Libya, Nigeria, Somalia, Sudan, Tunisia and the United Arab
Republic were represented. The absence of the others, especially
of Madagascar, the Mali Federation and Togo, all from the
former French African empire, was an indication of things to
come. Up till now the African leaders in the French community
had shown little or no interest in Pan-Africanism. As pointed
out above, the political parties they led did not attend either of
the two AAPO conferences. And it can be assumed that their
absence was at least partly due to the presence of the provisional
government of Algeria at the conference.[37] Morocco and Congo
stayed away because of the internal political situation at the time.

Emperor Haile Selassie, in his opening address, emphasized
the importance of stimulating greater cooperation between
African states especially in the spheres of trade and transport.
He advocated the establishment of an African development bank.
While agreeing with the emperor on the need for the establishment of such a bank, Ako Adjei, the leader of the Ghanaian
delegation, proposed the setting-up of a council for economic
cooperation and development to coordinate the economic
policies of African countries and work with the United Nations
Economic Commission for Africa, as well as a cultural council
and a scientific and research council for African affairs. He
strongly pleaded for an African customs-union and the removal
of trade barriers between African countries. A consensus was
reached on the need for more economic cooperation.

Agreement was also easily reached on such topics as the liberation of the remaining dependencies in Africa, the war in Algeria
and the apartheid policy of the South African government. The
most controversial topic was African unity. Although each
delegation realized the need for African unity, there was a substantial disagreement on how that unity should be achieved and
what form it should take. While Ghana, supported by Guinea,
advocated political union and urged the conference to make use
of the Sanniquellie Declaration as a basis for the achievement
of a union of African states, Nigeria took the lead in opposing

such suggestions. The leader of the Nigerian delegation, Maitama Sule, pointed out that 'at this moment the idea of forming a union of African states is premature'. He went on: 'At the moment we in Nigeria cannot afford to form union by government with any African States by surrendering our sovereignty.'[38] Advocating the gradual, functional approach to African unity, he wanted all artificial barriers between African countries to be dismantled, international roads to be built and the exchange of information to be promoted first, before any union of African states could be contemplated. And so began the great debate on which approach would better lead to the Pan-African ideal of African unity.

The Second CIAS was therefore significant in two main ways. First it portended the lukewarm attitude developed towards Pan-Africanism by African leaders in the French community. Secondly it marked the beginning of open controversy on the approach towards African unity. Moreover, other African events of 1960 revealed a dangerous drift. A few days after the conference ended, the Belgian Congo became independent – and almost immediately plunged headlong into a crisis which not only deepened the gulf in the Pan-African movement, but brought the United Nations dangerously near to collapse.

The Congolese national army (ANC) mutinied; the Congolese government of Patrice Lumumba was in grave difficulties; and open rebellion was being encouraged by foreign forces who, because of Congolese mineral wealth, would have preferred the 'wind of change' to blow somewhere else. Worried by the sinister role of certain foreign powers whose nationals had vested interests in the Congo and who were all out to undermine the very existence of the new republic, and also by the somewhat ambiguous role of some UN officials in the crisis, the Congolese prime minister called on independent African states to hold an emergency conference. It took place in Leopoldville (now Kinshasa) between 25 and 31 August 1960, attended by representatives of Congo (Leopoldville), Ethiopia, Ghana, Guinea, Liberia, Libya, Morocco, Sudan, Togo, Tunisia, the United Arab Republic and the Algerian provisional government. Nigeria, who, in spite of the fact that she had not yet become independent, was

27

championing a 'Conservative' approach to African unity, was not invited.

The conference failed to achieve much. By praising the role of certain UN officials in the Congo in particular and the United Nations itself in general, it only added to Lumumba's disillusionment. (This later led him to go it alone in seeking aid from Russia, when the UN came to seem more of a liability than an asset.) And apart from Guinea, no other African country openly supported Lumumba in his desire for the immediate overthrow of the secessionist government of Moise Tshombe.[39]

THE BRAZZAVILLE CONFERENCE

Even if certain African leaders in the French community were unenthusiastic about Pan-Africanism, they realized that some of its objectives were not altogether undesirable. They realized, for example, that the Pan-African goal of national independence as a prelude to the ultimate achievement of African unity was worthwhile. When it became clear towards the end of 1959 that Cameroon, Togo, Mali and Madagascar would achieve independence in the following year, the leaders of the remaining African colonies in the French community also expressed the desire to achieve independence for their countries.[40] Consequently, by the autumn of 1960, all the member states of French West Africa and French Equatorial Africa had become independent.

The responsibilities of independence soon made the new states realize that they could not isolate themselves. They must join forces with fellow states in order to find solutions to the problems facing them. Apart from the Congo situation, the Algerian war of independence was still raging, at immense human cost. Moroccan claims to certain African territories, including Mauritania, prefigured further frontier conflicts. With such burning problems unsolved, no African state could ignore the Pan-African movement. An awareness of this situation led to the Brazzaville Conference of December 1960.

The UN approach towards both the Congo crisis and the Algerian situation had led to a meeting of various African states at Abidjan in October 1960 when the opportunity was also seized to discuss Morocco's claim to Mauritania. At the end of that conference it was revealed that the African leaders participating had undertaken 'a searching examination of the major African problems, especially those of Algeria, the Congo and Mauritania'. They had unanimously reached agreement 'on the most effective methods for finding a solution to each of these problems'. But as it later turned out, during the 1960 session of the United Nations General Assembly, these 'effective methods' centred on either voting against the majority of the other African states or at best abstaining on such controversial and burning issues as the Congo crisis[41] and Algeria. At last the division among independent African states over the Congo crisis had been demonstrated in the arena of world politics. But instead of trying to find an acceptable formula for a united African action, these states not only caused a split in the Africa group at the UN but also decided to prepare their own strategy of attack. And so the way was paved for the Brazzaville Conference.

Before we consider the conference itself it would be useful to have an idea of the Congo situation in December 1960. The Katanga secession, aided and abetted by foreign powers with vested interests in the Congo, was being consolidated. Although UN troops had moved into Katanga they were given orders by the then UN secretary-general, Dag Hammarskjöld, to do nothing which could end Katanga's secession. The Congolese government had been overthrown by Mobutu, and Lumumba had been placed under virtual house arrest, pending his eventual transfer to that arch-enemy of the Congo's unity, Moise Tshombe of the secessionist Katanga province. The overthrow of Lumumba's government and the inaction of the UN forces in the face of this development had led not only to a crisis of confidence in the UN secretary-general, but also to the setting-up of a pro-Lumumba government in Stanleyville (now Kisangani). The disunity within the African group was further deepened by the fact that certain African states wanted immediate UN action, while others blindly supported the UN secretary-general.

Abbé Fulbert Youlou of Congo (Brazzaville) took the initiative in calling for a meeting of the French-speaking states to discuss, among other things, the Congo situation. In the communiqué issued after the Brazzaville Conference, which took place between 15 and 19 December 1960, the heads of these states[42] 'saluted the effort undertaken by UNO to save the Congo (Leopoldville) from chaos and anarchy. They render thanks to Hammarskjöld, Secretary-General of UNO, who, respecting the spirit of the Charter, has striven to stop the Cold War extending to this part of the Continent . . .'[43] The conference therefore served as another lever of disunity within the Pan-African movement.

Other topics considered included Morocco's claim to Mauritania, and economic cooperation. The conference maintained Mauritania's right to independence, thus rejecting Morocco's dubious claim. Also it agreed to set up a commission which would study and recommend ways of facilitating economic cooperation between their countries.

If lack of unity among the African states over the Congo crisis presented Pan-Africanists with a macabre Christmas present in 1960, it would continue to bedevil Pan-Africanism as long as the crisis itself remained unsolved. It did not therefore come as a surprise that certain other African states, unlike the Brazzaville group, preferred action to praises of the passive UN. The desire among these states for a solution led to the next Pan-African conference, which took place at Casablanca in January 1961.

THE CASABLANCA CONFERENCE*

The Casablanca Conference of January 1961 was, in a way, a sequel to the Brazzaville Conference. It acted as a rallying-point for those African states whose leaders were strongly convinced that if the Congo crisis was to be contained and an acceptable solution found, the United Nations must be urged to change its by then ambiguous and unrealistic policy.

Attended by the heads of state of Ghana, Guinea, Mali, Morocco and the United Arab Republic, the prime minister of the Algerian provisional government and the foreign minister of Libya, the conference not only concerned itself with the Congo crisis but tried to find a practical way of achieving African unity.

* See Appendix 2.

King Mohammed V of Morocco, in his opening address about the Congo crisis, stated that the failure of the United Nations in the Congo placed its future existence in doubt. He then went on to outline the following five-point plan for restoring order and the legal authority of Patrice Lumumba's government:

(a) a permanent Congo committee to be appointed by the General Assembly of the United Nations. This committee would advise the U N on all measures to be taken in the Congo;
(b) a conciliation conference of the leaders of all Congolese political parties;
(c) a political truce in the troubled country;
(d) increased United Nations material and technical aid;
(e) an appeal to all African States to act together and give a lead in the Congo.

But it was difficult for the delegates to reach an immediate consensus on how the crisis could best be solved. After a series of talks, the delegates agreed to withdraw their countries' troops and other military personnel from the United Nations Operational Command in the Congo if the U N connivance at Katangan secession continued. (In spite of this decision, Ghana, which had all along come out against such a drastic measure, never withdrew her troops or other personnel from the Congo.)

On African unity the delegates expressed their determination to do their utmost to establish an effective form of cooperation in the economic, social and cultural field. With this in mind they decided to create an African consultative assembly, which would be composed of the representatives of every African state, have a permanent seat and hold periodical sessions. The following committees were also to be set up:

(1) *African Political Committee:* comprising heads of state or their duly accredited representatives, which would meet periodically in order to coordinate and unify the general policy of the various African states;
(2) *African Economic Committee:* consisting of the ministers of economic affairs of the independent African states, which would

meet periodically to take decisions on African economic co-
operation, and would be responsible for the establishment of
postal and telecommunication links among the various African
capitals;

(3) *African Cultural Committee:* to be composed of the
ministers of education of the independent African states, which
would also meet periodically, with a view to preserving and
developing African culture and civilization as well as intensifying
African cultural cooperation and assistance;

(4) *Joint African High Command:* made up of the chiefs of
staff of the independent African states, which would ensure the
common defence of Africa in case of aggression against any part
of the continent, thereby safeguarding the independence of
African states.

In order to ensure effective cooperation among the various
institutions mentioned above, a liaison office was established;
and this was entrusted with organizing a meeting of experts, to
define the practical procedure for the functioning of the institutions in question.

Paradoxically, however, the apparent success of this conference
only promoted further disunity in the already divided Pan-
African camp. The enemies of African unity saw their chance
and started to talk of the 'Casablanca' and 'Brazzaville'
'Powers'. But there were other African countries which could
not be labelled either 'Casablanca' or 'Brazzaville'. It was therefore realized by all Africans that not only must these divisions
be contained; they must be eradicated.

THE GHANA–GUINEA–MALI UNION

The move to form the Ghana–Guinea–Mali Union was announced on 24 December 1960, after a series of talks which took
place at Conakry, Guinea, between presidents Kwame Nkrumah
of Ghana, Sékou Touré of Guinea and Modibo Keita of Mali.

On the Congo crisis the three presidents regretted 'the inability of the United Nations to enforce the resolutions of the
Security Council in regard to the maintenance of the political
independence of the Congo, its territorial integrity and the

normal functioning of its democratic institutions'.[44] They deplored the decisions of the Brazzaville Conference, which they thought was 'likely to jeopardize the unity of Africa and strengthen neo-colonialism'. Condemning 'all forms of African regroupment based on languages of the colonial powers', they also appealed to the heads of states which attended the Brazzaville Conference 'to follow a higher and more healthy conception of African unity'.

As a demonstration of what they meant by this last, the three heads of state agreed to form the Ghana–Guinea–Mali Union. The union would enable them to harmonize and coordinate their policies on all important African and international problems, as well as promote cooperation in the economic and monetary fields. Two special committees were set up to examine practical methods for achieving their objectives. A quarterly meeting of the heads of state was to take place at the capital of each member state in turn.

The reports of the special committees set up at the Conakry meeting led to the 'Charter for the Union of African States', published after the Accra meeting of the three heads of state held from 27 to 29 April 1961. The charter renamed the Ghana–Guinea–Mali Union 'the Union of African States'. Regarded as 'the nucleus of the United States of Africa', the union was an improvement on the Ghana–Guinea Union of 1959. The charter contained sections dealing with political institutions, diplomacy, joint defence, economy and culture.

THE MONROVIA CONFERENCE*

The situation within the Pan-African movement had, by the end of the Casablanca Conference, become intolerable. There were now two distinct and antagonistic camps – 'the Brazzaville group' and 'the Casablanca group'. Between them stood the uncommitted African states such as Ethiopia, Liberia, Nigeria, Sierra Leone, Somalia, the Sudan, Togo and Tunisia. It had become clear that every effort must be made to bring these three groups within the Pan-African movement together and work out an acceptable formula for their collaboration. (See Map 2.)

*See Appendix 3.

33

Evolution

The initiative to convene a conference at which all independent African states in the Pan-African movement would be present came from president Senghor of Senegal, who contacted president Sylvanus Olympio of Togo. After consultations with president Tubman of Liberia and prime minister Abubakar

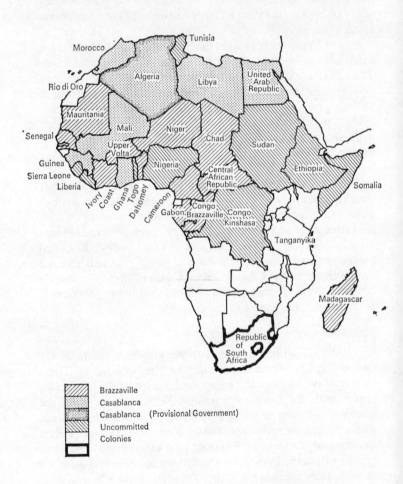

2. Divisions within Pan-Africa: April 1961

Tafawa Balewa of Nigeria, Togo, Liberia and Nigeria agreed to act as sponsors for such a conference. When it became clear that it would be advisable to have six sponsors – two from each of the three groups within the Pan-African movement – the three leaders agreed to let both Liberia and Nigeria represent the un-committed group. The other two groups – 'Brazzaville' and 'Casablanca' – were approached. Cameroon and the Ivory Coast from the Brazzaville group and Guinea and Mali from the Casablanca group agreed to sponsor such a move. Thus it came about that all independent African states were invited to a conference scheduled to start on 8 May 1961, at Monrovia, capital of Liberia.

Everything seemed to be going smoothly until it became obvious, after a series of consultations, that not all the independ-ent African states would attend the proposed Monrovia confer-ence after all. While Ghana, Guinea and Mali called for a post-ponement at the eleventh hour, on the ground that preparations had been inadequate, Morocco refused to attend because of the presence of Mauritania, whose territory she claimed to be part of the old Great Moroccan Kingdom.[45] The Sudan and the United Arab Republic also declined to attend. Behind all this was the refusal to invite the Algerian Provisional Government, which had, until then, taken part in most Pan-African confer-ences.

When the conference therefore opened at Monrovia on 8 May 1961, the seats of Ghana, Guinea, Mali, Morocco, the Sudan and the United Arab Republic remained empty.[46] (See Map 3.) Nevertheless the conference settled down to business. President Tubman, in his opening address, emphasized the need for economic cooperation among African states as a step towards 'unity in Africa'. In the speech delivered on behalf of the French-speaking states, president Senghor of Senegal declared: 'If we wish to succeed we must put the stress on cultural, technical and economic co-operation, rather than on the co-operation of political parties. We must progress step by step, keeping our feet firmly on the ground. This is the essential condition for our success.'[47] Speaking on behalf of the English-speaking states the prime minister of Sierra Leone, Sir Milton A. S. Margai, reiterated 'the principle of African unity which respects the territorial integrity of each state, the free choice of political ideology and form of government'. He went on: 'We pledge co-operation in the defence of the territorial integrity and sovereignty of all freedom loving states in Africa, particularly with a view to curbing any internal subversion against the lawfully constituted government of any friendly state, and are pre-

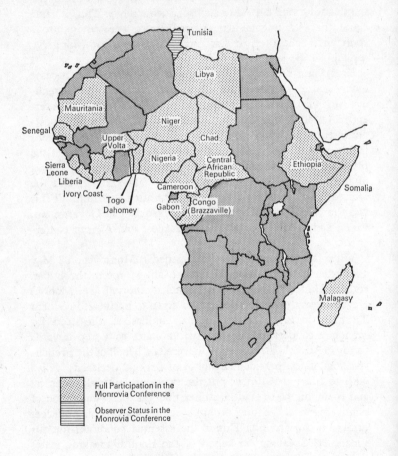

3. Monrovia Group: May 1961

pared at the same time to do everything in our power to safe-guard the territorial integrity and the sovereignty of any African state which might be threatened from without or outside the African Continent.'[48]

The conference passed a series of resolutions, among which was one on the means of 'promoting better understanding and co-operation towards achieving unity in Africa and Malagasy'. In it the conference adopted certain principles which would help promote 'henceforth a full and brotherly co-operation between Independent African and Malagasy States'. They included:

(a) absolute equality of African and Malagasy states irrespective of their size, the density of their populations or their national wealth;

(b) non-interference in the internal affairs of other states;

(c) respect for the sovereignty of each state and its inalienable right to existence and development of its personality;

(d) unqualified condemnation of outside subversive action by neighbouring states;

(e) promotion of cooperation, based upon tolerance, solidarity and good-neighbourliness, periodical exchange of views and non-acceptance of any leadership.

The delegates then declared that 'the unity that is aimed to be achieved at the moment is not the political integration of sovereign African States, but unity of aspirations and of action considered from the point of view of African social solidarity and political identity'.[49] They urged all states to refrain from encouraging subversion directed at others in their ranks. They agreed, in principle, to establish 'an inter-African and Malagasy Advisory Organisation', with a view to putting the above-mentioned principles into effect. A technical commission of experts was established to work out 'detailed plans for economic, educational, cultural, scientific and technical co-operation, as well as for communications and transportation among African and Malagasy States'.[50]

Other Pan-African issues tackled by the conference included

37

the Algerian war of independence, the Congo crisis, decolonization and apartheid. On Algeria the conference welcomed the
impending negotiations between Algeria and France. It appealed
to the French and the Algerian provisional governments to
'conclude at the earliest moment an agreement putting an end
to the war and accord to Algeria its independence and territorial
integrity'.[51]

With reference to the Congo crisis the conference reaffirmed
its faith in the capability of the United Nations, despite its 'past
weaknesses and mistakes', to achieve a real solution.

The delegates expressed the hope that it would be possible
for the absent 'sister states' to attend the next meeting, scheduled to take place at Lagos, Nigeria, in January 1962.

THE LAGOS CONFERENCE

As delegates to the Monrovia Conference were getting ready to
return home, the foreign ministers of the Casablanca group were
meeting in Cairo to examine the recommendations made by the
committee of experts appointed during the January conference.
This foreign ministers' conference produced the significant
Protocol of the African Charter (Appendix 4), which we shall
examine subsequently.

The dynamic, businesslike and fervent approach of the
Casablanca group which was able to produce such a far-reaching
document was more of a challenge to the Monrovia group. The
commission of experts set up at Monrovia, therefore, unwilling
to be left behind, embarked on its work with enthusiasm. Soon
it had finished its job and produced sixteen recommendations
which later formed the basis of the Lagos Charter.

Meanwhile preparations for the Lagos Conference continued.
Once more all independent African states were invited to attend.
The Algerian provisional government was, however, still left
out. In an effort to secure an invitation for the Algerians,
president Sékou Touré discussed the forthcoming Lagos Conference with president Tubman of Liberia when both met late
in 1961. But in spite of this move, the question remained un-
answered. When the foreign ministers of the Casablanca group
met at Accra, a few days before the Lagos Conference, they

considered their position in this light. On 21 January 1962, they announced that, under the circumstances, they found it impossible to attend the Lagos Conference.[52] Although this announcement caused much annoyance and anxiety, it was, in view of the situation, unavoidable and therefore not unexpected. The Algerian issue, however, did not end there.

The conference was preceded by a stormy conference of foreign ministers. Whether Algeria should be invited to the conference had become so controversial a question that it even caused divergencies among the twelve French-speaking states.[53] Six delegations expressed themselves strongly in favour of inviting the Algerian provisional government. A motion demanding an immediate invitation to that government, and supported by Ethiopia, Liberia, Nigeria, Sierra Leone, Somalia, Sudan and Tanganyika, was rejected; upon which the Sudan withdrew from attending the conference.[54]

All these commotions notwithstanding, the conference opened on 25 January 1962. The Dakar recommendations of the commission set up at Monrovia, as well as proposals submitted by Ethiopia, Liberia and Nigeria[55] for a functional approach to African unity, were considered. After much deliberation, the conference agreed in principle to set up an inter-African and Malagasy organization for the purpose of 'promoting a better life for the peoples of Africa', by enlisting the efforts of member states through cooperative and joint actions: in order to 'accelerate economic and social intercourse and promote the pooling and effective utilization of their resources; provide better and broader educational opportunities for its people; raise the level of health and well-being of its people; and concert, as far as possible, political actions and initiate new means of establishing relationships in which the interests of the continent will be better defined and served'.[56] That all these objectives might be achieved, the member states of the organization would cooperate in commerce and industry, education and culture, health and nutrition, politics and diplomacy, science, technology and defence.

The proposed organization would have the following organs: an assembly of heads of state and governments, a council of

ministers, a general secretariat and commissions. The assembly
would be the supreme organ, meet at least once every two years,
and be empowered to consider all matters affecting relations
between the member states. The council of ministers would meet
at least once a year, and when occasion arose, hold emergency
sessions. It would be responsible for working out all areas of
cooperation. The general secretariat was to be the organization's
central administrative organ.

A draft charter, endorsed at the conference, was to be submitted to all the governments for detailed comment and subsequently considered by a committee of representatives from the
governments concerned. The committee was to meet within
three months and incorporate all comments into a revised charter,
to be submitted to the next conference. The work of that
committee became known as the Lagos Charter.

By this time there were two distinct camps within the Pan-
African movement – 'Casablanca' and 'Monrovia'. Each had
produced a charter stating its own approach to African unity.
But before we consider these, to see their similarities and
divergencies, we must examine a very significant development:
the Pan-African Freedom Movement of Eastern, Central and
Southern Africa (PAFMECSA).

(iv) From PAFMECA to PAFMECSA

The Pan-African Freedom Movement of East and Central
Africa (PAFMECA) came into existence at the end of a three-
day conference of twenty-one representatives of political parties
from East and Central Africa, held at Mwanza, Tanzania, in
September 1958 (see Map 4) and conceived in 1957. At that
time it was suggested in Kenya that all legislative council
members from Kenya, Tanganyika and Uganda should meet to
discuss matters of common interest. The meeting had to be
postponed because of unforeseen circumstances. During the
anniversary celebrations of Ghana's independence in March
1958 some leaders of East and Central Africa visited Ghana,
where it was decided to hold an African conference before the
end of the year (this was the 1958 AAPO Conference). As a

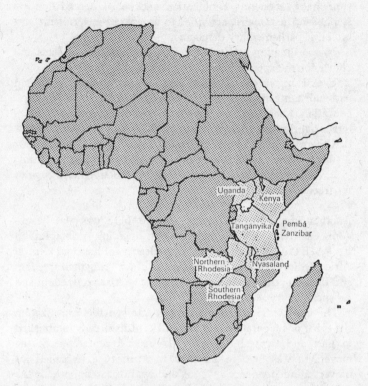

4. PAFMECA: 1958

result of this, the issue of an East and Central African leaders' conference was again discussed. Julius Nyerere, now president of Tanzania, was mandated to convene the conference at Mwanza before the AAPO Conference was to take place in December 1958. It was this conference, which took place between 17 and 20 September 1958, that founded PAFMECA.

The constitution of PAFMECA, approved at the conference, stipulated the following as its aims and objects:

(a) fostering the spirit of Pan-Africanism in order to rid the East and Central African territories of imperialism, white

41

supremacy, economic exploitation and social degradation by stepped-up nationalist activities to attain self-government and establish parliamentary democracy;

(b) coordinating nationalist programmes, tactics, projects and efforts for the speedy liberation of the said territories;

(c) assisting in the establishment and organization of united nationalist movements in African territories through political education, periodic conferences, encouragement of inter-territorial African endeavours in all fields and any other means that the movement might determine;

(d) establishing a joint East and Central African freedom fund;

(e) championing non-violence in African nationalist struggles for freedom and prosperity.

Another important document adopted here was the 'Freedom Charter' which contained the guiding principles in PAFMECA's activities. In this the leaders of East and Central Africa dedicated themselves to the task of restoring their freedom and devoting their energies to the cause of African freedom and prosperity.

The first conference helped to put into concrete organization the spirit of cooperation and Pan-Africanism already established in East and Central Africa.[57] The second conference of the movement was held in Zanzibar in April 1959. It called for universal independence by 1965 and reaffirmed support for the principles of non-violence. At its annual meeting held at Moshi, Tanzania, in September 1959 there were delegates from Congo-Leopoldville and Rwanda-Urundi.

The third annual conference, which was held at Mbale, Uganda, in October 1960, considered plans for an East African Federation (an idea put forward in June 1960 by Julius Nyerere) comprising Kenya, Tanganyika, Uganda and Zanzibar. Both Ethiopia and Somalia joined the movement in February 1962. There were also delegates from African parties in Basutoland (now Lesotho), Bechuanaland (now Botswana), South Africa, South West Africa (Namibia) and Swaziland. It was at this conference that PAFMECA became PAFMECSA (Pan-African Freedom Movement of Eastern, Central and Southern

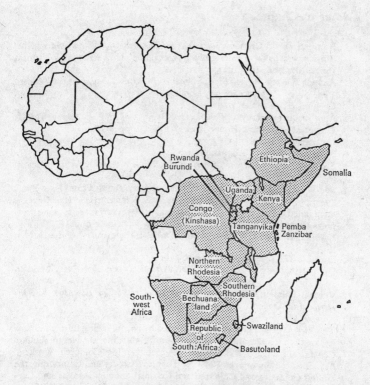

5. PAFMECSA: December 1962

Africa. See Map 5). The conference agreed that an East African Federation should be established when Kenya, Uganda and Zanzibar became independent. The federation was to be regarded as a first and logical step towards the final objective of total African unity. An administering body – the Co-ordinating Freedom Council – was established, with two members from each member country and a permanent secretariat with head-quarters in Dar es Salaam.

The movement was disbanded in 1963 after the Organization of African Unity had been founded. By then it had become 'a unique organisation in the annals of Pan-Africanism'.[58]

43

Evolution

Notes to Chapter 1

1. Edmund David Cronon, *Black Moses: The Story of Marcus Garvey and the Universal Negro Improvement Association*, University of Wisconsin Press, Madison, 1955, p. 35.
2. Russell Warren Howe, *Black Africa – from the Colonial Era to Modern Times*, New African Library, London, 1967, p. 171.
3. Cronon, *Black Moses*, p. 37.
4. Amy Jacques-Garvey, *Philosophy and Opinions of Marcus Garvey*, Vol. II, Universal Publishing House, New York, 1926, p. 95.
5. Cronon, *Black Moses*, p. 62.
6. *New York Times*, 3 August 1920.
7. See Francis L. Broderick, *W. E. B. DuBois – Negro Leader in a Time of Crisis*, Stanford, California, 1959, pp. 123–40.
8. See W. E. B. DuBois, *The World and Africa*, Viking Press, New York, 1947, pp. 8–10; Howe, *Black Africa*, p. 171. When the American Government failed to stop the Congress from taking place, it refused to issue passports to American Negroes who wanted to participate in it.
9. Kwame Nkrumah, *Africa Must Unite*, Heinemann, London, 1963, p. 132.
10. DuBois, *The World and Africa*, p. 238.
11. Quoted in Magnus Sampson, *West African Leadership*, Cass, London, 1949, pp. 62–3.
12. Vincent Bakpetu Thompson, *Africa and Unity: The Evolution of Pan-Africanism*, Longmans, London, 1969, p. 31.
13. Kwame Nkrumah, *Africa Must Unite*, p. 134.
14. The Pan-African Federation was formed by the following thirteen organizations: the International African Service Bureau; the Negro Welfare Centre; the Negro Association, Manchester; the Coloured Workers' Association, London; the Coloured Peoples' Association, Edinburgh; the United Committee of Coloured and Colonial Peoples' Association, Cardiff; the African Union, Glasgow; the Association of Students of African Descent, Dublin; the West African Students' Union of Great Britain and Ireland; the Kikuyu Central Association (Kenya); the African Progressive Association, London; Sierra Leone Section, African Youth League; the Friends of African Freedom Society (Gold Coast).
15. DuBois, *The World and Africa*, pp. 243–4.
16. By this time Marcus Garvey had been dead for five years (see Chapter 3).
17. For a full list of the African participants see *West Africa*, 7 September 1963, p. 999.
18. Kwame Nkrumah, *Ghana – the Autobiography of Kwame Nkrumah*, Nelson, London, 1959, p. 44.
19. *Pan-Africanism*, Central Office of Information, London, 1965, p. 5.
20. Thomas Hovet, Jr, *Africa in the United Nations*, Faber & Faber, London, 1963, p. 26.
21. *Ghana Daily Graphic* (Accra), 5 April 1958.
22. Hovet, *Africa in the United Nations*, pp. 28–9; *New York Times*, 16 April 1958.

44

23. *Ghana Daily Graphic*, 16 April 1958.

24. *Ghana Daily Graphic*, 9 December 1958.

25. ibid.

26. See 'Resolutions Adopted by the All-African Peoples' Conference, Accra, December 5–13, 1958' in Colin Legum, *Pan-Africanism*, Pall Mall Press, London, 1962, p. 230.

27. ibid.

28. *Ghana Daily Graphic*, 8 December 1958.

29. For the full text of Nkrumah's speech, see *Ghana Daily Graphic*, 13 December 1958.

30. *Ghana Daily Graphic*, 12 December 1958.

31. *Ghana Daily Graphic*, 18 July 1959.

32. ibid.

33. *Ghana Daily Graphic*, 21 July 1959.

34. *Ghana Daily Graphic*, 22 July 1959.

35. The increase in the number of independent African states between the First Conference of Independent African States of April 1958 and the Second was due to the attainment of independence by Guinea on 2 October 1958, Cameroon on 1 January 1960 and Togo on 27 April 1960.

36. The Mali Federation was made up of both Senegal and French Sudan. When the Federation disintegrated in September 1960 its components became the Senegal and Mali Republics respectively.

37. The presence of the provisional government of Algeria amounted to a more or less *de facto* recognition of the 'rebel' government. Since any recognition was regarded by France as an unfriendly act these French Community members would not like to displease De Gaulle's Government. The French ambassador to Ethiopia refused to attend the opening session of the conference because of the presence and flag of the Algerian provisional government.

38. Compare this statement with the utterances of Dr Nnamdi Azikiwe at his New York press conference, referred to on p. 23.

39. Vincent Bakpetu Thompson, *Africa and Unity*, p. 150.

40. See I. William Zartman, *International Relations in the New Africa*, Englewood Cliffs, New Jersey, 1966, pp. 13–26.

41. See Catherine Hoskyns, 'The Part Played by the Independent African States in the Congo Crisis, July 1960–December 1961', in *Inter-State Relations in Africa*; edited by Dennis Austin and Hans Weiler, Freiburg, 1965.

42. The states which attended the conference were Cameroon, the Central African Republic, Chad, Congo (Brazzaville), Dahomey, Gabon, Ivory Coast, Madagascar, Mauritania, Niger and Senegal.

43. Colin Legum, *Pan-Africanism*, p. 180.

44. Legum, *Pan-Africanism*, p. 175. The resolutions of the Security Council referred to included S/4387 of 14 July 1960; S/4405 of 22 July 1960 and S/4426 of 9 August 1960.

45. This claim had been responsible for Morocco's alignment with much more progressive African states such as Ghana, Guinea, Mali and the United Arab Republic in the Casablanca group.

46. Although Tunisia was represented she chose merely an observer status.

47. *African Summit in Monrovia*, published on behalf of the Federal Government of Nigeria by the Federal Ministry of Information, Lagos, 1961, p. 13.
48. ibid., p. 15.
49. ibid., p. 17.
50. ibid., p. 19.
51. ibid.
52. *West African Pilot* (Lagos), 22 January 1962.
53. ibid., 23 January 1962.
54. ibid., 24 January 1962.
55. ibid., 26 January 1962.
56. ibid., 1 February 1962.
57. The spirit of cooperation and Pan-Africanism had already taken root; in April 1958 TANU sent £250 to Kenya to help pay for legal expenses of seven accused members of the legislative council. The party also paid for the return air ticket to Britain for a delegate from the Nyasaland African Congress. Earlier the Kenya African Elected Members' Organization had sent £200 to TANU for Nyerere's defence, while the Nyasaland African Congress sent £50 for the same purpose. The Afro-Shirazi Party and the Nationalist Party of Zanzibar sent £300 and £110 respectively to Kenya as legal aid during the seven African elected members' trial.
58. Richard Cox, *Pan-Africanism in Practice*, Oxford University Press, London, 1964, p. 1.

2. The Organization of African Unity

'Only with unity can we ensure that
 Africa really governs Africa. Only
 with unity can we be sure that African
 resources will be used for the benefit
 of Africa.'*

JULIUS NYERERE

(a) The Road to Addis Ababa: 1962–April 1963

We have already noted that the Casablanca and the Monrovia
groups had each produced a charter. The signatories of the
African Charter of Casablanca and its protocol affirmed their
will to intensify their efforts 'for the creation of an effective form
of cooperation among the African states in the economic, social
and cultural domains': while those of the Lagos Charter expressed determination 'to promote henceforth a full and
brotherly cooperation between independent African and Malagasy states'. Both set up committees of experts to consider
detailed plans for economic cooperation among their respective
members and the recommendations of these committees aimed
at the same objectives.

The experts of the Casablanca group recommended the ending
of customs barriers over a period of five years from 1 January
1962, as well as the abolition of quota systems and preferential
treatment, from the same date. They also proposed the establishment of a council of African economic unity and an African
development bank. They suggested the formation of joint air
and shipping lines. The Monrovia group seemed determined
not to be left behind: their experts discussed the setting-up of
an African development bank and recommended the promotion
of trade between African countries through regional customs
unions and the progressive establishment of common external
tariffs. They also suggested the harmonization of development
policies, including investment codes and conventions on investment and guarantee funds, the exchange of economic information

*Africa's Freedom, Allen and Unwin, London, p. 90.

and the coordination of research programmes. In addition they agreed that a network of roads and railways should be built to link the African countries; and that joint shipping and air lines should be formed.[1]

What was needed then was to bring both groups together and, although those forces outside Africa which had something to gain from the division made much of the differences between the groups, Pan-Africanists everywhere emphasized the similarities between them.

Three significant events occurred during the Lagos Conference which augured well. The first was the speech delivered by Emperor Haile Selassie of Ethiopia at the conference. He said: 'We are told that Africa has been split into competing groups and that this is inhibiting co-operation among the African states and severely retarding African progress. One hears of the Casablanca group and the Monrovia group, of the Conakry and Dakar Declarations, and we are warned that the views and policies of these so-called groups are so antithetical as to make it impossible for them to work together as partners in an enterprise to which all are mutually devoted. But do such hard-and-fast groupings really exist? And if certain nations sharing similar views have taken measures to co-ordinate their policies, does this mean that, as between these nations and others, there is no possibility of free and mutually beneficial co-operation?' Continuing, he declared: 'Ethiopia considers herself a member of one group only – the African group. When we Africans have been misled into pigeonholing one another, into attributing rigid and inflexible views to States which were present at one conference but not at another, then we shall, without reason or justification, have limited our freedom of action and rendered immeasurably more difficult the task of joining our efforts, in harmony and brotherhood, in the common cause of Africa . . . No wide and unbridgeable gulf exists between the various groupings which have been created . . . We urge that this conference use this as its starting point, that we emphasize and lay stress on the areas of similarity and agreement rather than upon whatever disagreements and differences may exist among us.'[2]

At the same time as these wise words were being spoken, both

Guinea and Ghana came out strongly in support of a united front. In a broadcast on the 'Voice of Revolution', Guinea called on all African states to come together. The broadcast went on: 'There is not one African State, not one African statesman, who does not realise that the countries of our continent must unite to build after sharing common sufferings for centuries.'[3] A few days later Radio Ghana declared: 'That there is now need for African Unity is a basic question among all African States. That this need is imperative and urgent seems to be appreciated by not a few. What now remains is a sober and constructive approach in order to bring together the countries of the Casablanca charter and the Monrovia group.'[4]

Efforts were intensified, in the course of the year 1962, to make such a conference possible. Negotiations were carried out both formally and informally – through diplomatic channels, at various international conferences attended by African delegations, and in the lobby halls of the United Nations. State visits by heads of state or governments became more frequent: president Abdulla Osman of Somalia was in Ghana in October 1961, the Nigerian prime minister, the late Sir Abubakar Tafawa Balewa, visited Guinea in December 1961; and, at about the same time, president Ould Daddah of Mauritania went to Ghana. Presidents Houphouet-Boigny of the Ivory Coast and Léopold Senghor of Senegal also paid official visits to Guinea, while president Sékou Touré of Guinea and Emperor Haile Selassie of Ethiopia met at Asmara in Ethiopia on 28 June 1962.[5] Although during these diplomatic visits African unity was always high on the agenda there were other factors that contributed greatly towards the attainment of the goal. Algeria, which had been a major issue of separation between the two groups, became independent on 3 July 1962. Congo (Kinshasa) – another divisive factor – had a new government which was neither Gizenga's nor Tshombe's. The heads of state of the Casablanca group, meeting at Cairo in June 1962, supported the Guinean proposal for a continental conference. The Ghanaian president, Dr Nkrumah, also called for a preparatory meeting of African foreign ministers at Addis Ababa.

In February 1963, an agreement was signed between Senegal

Evolution

and Mali on the disposition of assets of the former Mali Federation. Meanwhile, the Ethiopian Government continued with its efforts to convene a conference of all independent African states at Addis Ababa in 1963.[6] It had invited these states to a conference and sent the foreign minister, Ato Ketema Yifru, on a mission to all their countries, with the sole aim of thrashing out the important details of the proposed conference. As a result, it became clear by the beginning of March 1963 that a conference

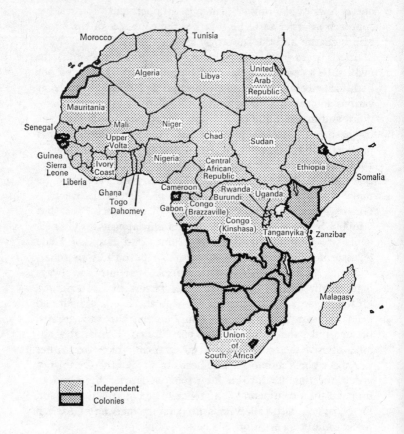

6. Independent States in Africa on 31 December 1962

of the African heads of state and governments would be held at Addis Ababa in May 1963.

Speaking at a press conference at Addis Ababa in April 1963, Emperor Haile Selassie stated that the proposed conference would 'lay for the first time in the Continent's history the basic foundation for unity'. He was convinced that the meeting would also 'formulate a general charter, bringing together all desiring unity'. He expressed his satisfaction at the agreement by all African states to attend the conference and stated that 'this proved the heads of states' strong desire for unity and solidarity on the continent'.[7]

All the thirty-two independent African states under indigenous African rule, invited to attend the Addis Ababa Conference, agreed to take part in the conferences proposed. The summit conference, to be preceded by a meeting of the foreign ministers, was scheduled to start on 22 May 1963. A preparatory secretariat was set up in Addis Ababa to carry out detailed preparations.

(b) The Addis Ababa Conference: May 1963

THE FOREIGN MINISTERS' CONFERENCE

The foreign ministers' meeting began on 15 May 1963 at Addis Ababa. The ministers were to prepare an agenda for the conference of heads of state and government of independent African states. Nine separate agendas, submitted by various countries, were put forward before the meeting; the contents were, however, almost identical.

The foreign ministers' meeting started off very well but because of the assassination of Togo's president Sylvanus Olympio in January 1963, there was an acrimonious discussion on whether or not Togo should be admitted to the conference. Guinea, supported by Nigeria, resented Togo's admission most strongly, whilst Ghana took the lead in urging it. In the end the question was left to the summit conference.

There was some argument about the name of the proposed new continental organization. The Ghanaian foreign minister, Mr Botsio, aptly drew attention to the undesirable association

51

in the initial letters O A S – the Organization of African States.[8] Others argued that what mattered most was the content, rather than the name, of the organization. In the end the views of Ethiopia, the host country, were accepted as the basis for discussion. Discussions on the draft charter submitted by Ethiopia were cordial. Some delegates, however, demanded more time for a thorough study of this document and Ghana's proposal for a union of African states. The foreign ministers ended their discussions on this topic by appointing a sub-committee composed of Algeria, Cameroon, Ethiopia, Ghana, Guinea, Madagascar, Nigeria, Tanzania and Tunisia, to draw up an acceptable charter. This sub-committee, however, only shifted the task of drawing up the charter to the heads of state. The foreign ministers recommended that the summit conference should accept the Ethiopian draft charter as a basis for discussion, with a view to drawing up the charter for an all-African organization. They suggested that the document should be 'transmitted to all member governments to enable them to submit their comments and amendments before the meeting of the foreign ministers' conference, to be held before the end of the year 1963 at Dakar'. They also requested the provisional secretariat to assemble all documents such as the African Charter of Casablanca, the Lagos Charter and the Ghanaian proposals for the Union of African States, along with any amendments and comments, for submission to the next foreign ministers' conference.

While the foreign ministers' decision on the issue of African unity was not very encouraging, their deliberations achieved better results in other fields. A comprehensive agenda was agreed, to include:

1. basic principles and structure of African Unity;
   (a) Declaration of basic principles
   (b) Charter and draft resolution
   (c) Secretariat
2. decolonization, apartheid and racial discrimination;
3. Africa, non-alignment and the United Nations;
4. various fields of cooperation
   (a) Economic problems

(b) Education, science and culture
(c) Public health and social questions
(d) Future of the CCTA.

The Conference of the Foreign Ministers also forwarded to the Heads of State Conference nine resolutions dealing with African unity and the charter, economic problems, decolonization, apartheid, general disarmament, the United Nations and Africa, as well as technical, educational, health and scientific institutions.

THE SUMMIT CONFERENCE

The Summit Conference of all independent African states under indigenous African rule began at Addis Ababa, the capital of Ethiopia, on 22 May 1963. All the thirty-two countries, except Togo and Morocco, were represented either by their heads of state or heads of government. Never in the annals of history have so many leaders of any continent assembled in an effort to achieve continental unity.[9] Also for the first time the leaders of the previous two African groups sat together to work out the best formula for achieving African unity.

In his opening address, Emperor Haile Selassie dealt a death-blow to the discouraging recommendation of the foreign ministers on the charter of African unity. After reminding the delegates that the chief purpose of their conference was to lay the basis for African unity, he urged them to agree, there and then, upon the basic instrument for the growth in peace and harmony of continental unity. He went on: 'This conference cannot close without adopting a single African charter. We cannot leave here without having created a single African organisation . . . If we fail in this, we will have shirked our responsibility to Africa and to the peoples we lead. If we succeed, then, and only then, will we have justified our presence here.'

The emperor went on to describe the type of organization that he thought would be suitable for the achievement of African unity. His opinion was that the proposed organization should possess a well-articulated framework with a permanent headquarters and an adequate secretariat which would provide

53

the necessary continuity between meetings. The organization should have specialized bodies. He stressed the importance of a conciliation commission which would be responsible for settling disputes between African states.[10]

The general debate followed the emperor's speech. All the heads of state and government had the opportunity to state their approach towards the achievement of African unity through the establishment of a continental organization.

President Ahidjo of Cameroon held the view that the proposed organization for African unity should be a highly flexible one. He thought that it would be premature at this stage for the African leaders to agree either on a federation or a confederation. He wanted the periodic meetings of all the African leaders to be institutionalized. The conference of the heads of state and government should weigh up experiences, decide upon alternatives, harmonize policies, and standardize decisions on the main issues of continental importance or requiring a common stand before international opinion. He considered that, if the organization was to be durable, the African leaders had to agree upon certain basic principles. Equality of states, irrespective of size and population, was one of these. The sovereignty of each member state and its right to existence in accordance with the wishes of its inhabitants was another. President Ahidjo supported the emperor's proposal for the establishment of a conciliation commission as well.

President Abbé Fulbert Youlou of Congo (Brazzaville) wanted there to be an African consultative assembly, an African executive, a conference of African heads of state, and a permanent secretariat. The African consultative assembly, he said, should consist of two members from each state on the model of the American Senate: with the members designated by the national assemblies or parliaments of the member states. This method appeared to him preferable to the fusion of the already existing Monrovia and Casablanca groups, because it was better to bring together the independent African states on a new footing, setting aside everything that would recall their former divisions. An authoritative institutional base would constitute the first step towards organizing the institutions of a united Africa.

The African executive's outline would be delineated by the Conference of African Heads of State. These heads of state would meet periodically, having at their disposal in the interval between sessions a permanent secretariat-general. The presidency of the conference of heads of state should be rotated on a yearly basis.

The permanent secretary-general, to be appointed by the conference, was to be assisted by three deputy secretaries-general. The secretary-general and his three deputies were to be chosen according to geographical distribution, so that the four parts of the continent might be equally represented.

The president of the Conference of the Heads of State and the permanent secretary-general should never be allowed to belong to the same geographical region.

The charter of the United African States should be the first task of the conference. This charter should be subject to ratification by the national assemblies or parliaments of the African countries.

The president was of the opinion that the capital of the United African States should 'be located in an extra-territorial area, independent of any African state'. It should be clearly demarcated, if possible, by natural boundaries, and should be situated in 'a central part of the African continent'.[11]

After expressing his opinion that African unity could not be achieved in one full sweep, President Hubert Maga of Dahomey stated that it was a task to be approached and carried out 'progressively if not immediately, by concrete and positive actions, the basis of which we can find here and now'.

President Sékou Touré started his speech by reminding the heads of state and government of the fact that African unity had become an aspiration common to all Africans. He continued: 'The conditions for the rapid achievement of this aim have demanded the attention and mobilized massively the energies and abilities of our various states, our parties, our trade unions, our associations of intellectuals, of women, of young people, and all the organisations grouping serious-thinking men in Africa.' He then went on to enumerate reasons why Africa should be united. He dismissed any idea that there were insurmountable barriers to the achievement of unity. He called on the delegates

55

to 'elaborate and adopt a Charter, lay down its principles and its fundamental objectives and set up an executive secretariat responsible for co-ordinating the activities of our States'. He stressed the point that the African Charter of Casablanca and the Lagos Charter were only two attempts at African unity, and means of accelerating the historic process of Africa. He then urged the conference to adopt a new charter – the Charter of United Africa. He went on: 'It would be harmful to African honour and to the success of our Pan-African enterprises if the Conference confined itself to preparing motions, resolutions and declarations without also clearly defining the practical means whereby they will succeed in suitable conditions. It is not enough to know and say what the African peoples want: henceforth we must achieve the objective of our States' options; bring about the success, through an effective organisation and dynamic action, of the deep aspirations and just causes which our people defend.' He spoke of his conviction that 'African Unity will grow a little more every day from now on; it will be a continuous creation, an irreversible work which will bind together all future generations to the generation which laid the foundation stone of unity at Addis Ababa'.[12]

While agreeing with other speakers on the desirability for African unity, President Houphouet-Boigny of the Ivory Coast wanted the Africans to proceed by 'progressive stages'. He went on to enumerate the basic principles which should guide African states in their quest for unity. These included non-interference in the internal affairs of other states; the recognized equality of all states; condemnation of subversive activities organized against one member state by another; and abhorrence of political assassination.

President Tsiranana of the Malagasy Republic told the delegates that it would be unrealistic for them to think that a continental government and parliament could be achieved in the near future. He went on to state what his country envisaged as the fundamental institutions of an all-African and Malagasy Co-operation. These included a conference of heads of state and government; a council of ministers; a general-secretariat; an African and Malagasy group at the United Nations; a permanent conciliation commission; and an African and Malagasy organization for economic cooperation. He elaborated thus:

The Conference of Heads of State should be convened at intervals, possibly once a year. As the supreme authority of the organization, it might take decisions for immediate implementation. Its decisions should be unanimous. Each member state would have only one vote.

The Council of Ministers should meet twice a year. It would examine matters on which the ministers were competent; superintend meetings of experts; and also prepare the ground for the conference of heads of state and government.

The General Secretariat would be the administrative organ of the organization. It would arrange the meetings of experts and those of the council of ministers, and also be responsible for the execution of decisions reached by the heads of state and government or by the council of ministers, as directed.

The African and Malagasy Group at the United Nations, composed of the permanent representatives of member states, should constitute the permanent instrument for Africa's policy towards the countries or groups of countries in other continents.

The Permanent Conciliation Commission would be responsible for peaceful settlement of disputes among member states. Appeals to the International Court of Justice should be made only when all the means of conciliation in Africa had been exhausted.

The Organization for Economic and Social Co-operation would facilitate economic, social and cultural development of the continent.

President Hamani Diori of the Niger Republic wanted the conference to adopt an inter-African charter whose basic principles would be as follows:

Evolution

(1) respect for the sovereignty of each state and non-interference in the domestic affairs of other independent states;

(2) the establishment of advisory and coordinating political institutions, with a permanent secretariat;

(3) the organization of a collective defence and security system;

(4) the establishment of a conciliation commission.

He also wanted a body responsible for coordinating and harmonizing the economic development efforts of African states to be established.

After advising the delegates against the immediate setting-up of a federation or confederation on a continental basis, President Senghor of Senegal urged them to create an organization of African and Malagasy states before the end of the conference. He suggested the following institutions for the proposed organization: a conference of heads of state and government; conferences of ministers; a general secretariat; and an African group at the UN.

The Conference of Heads of State and Government would be the supreme institution of the organization. Its decisions alone would be binding. It would meet yearly or once every two years to consider, on the one hand, the organization's activities during the previous period; and, on the other, define new objectives for it. Each member state would have one vote.

The Conference of Ministers would be composed of ministers nominated by states according to the problems to be examined. The ministers would study these problems in the different fields of cooperation; and draw up drafts for discussion by, or make recommendations to, the Conference of Heads of State and Government.

The General Secretariat would be an administrative and not a political body. As such, it would only implement and not make decisions. The secretary-general, appointed by the conference, would have assistants and as many directors as were required by the number of specialized agencies in the organization. These assistants and directors should be chosen in such a way that all the regions and all the linguistic groups might be represented.

The African Group at the United Nations should be reorganized so that its deliberations would be representative of all African states.

President Senghor also advocated the setting-up of an economic committee for Africa. He wanted all this to be achieved 'step by step and stage by stage'.

President Nkrumah of Ghana, however, was against a gradual approach; instead he wanted delegates to 'agree here and now to the establishment of a union of African States'. He went on to put his proposals for such a union before the conference. A declaration of principles for African unity should be made, and these principles clearly set down. An all-African committee of foreign ministers should be created forthwith. He wanted this committee to establish on behalf of the heads 'of our Governments' a permanent body of officials and experts with the aim of working out a machinery for the Union Government of Africa. This body was to be composed of two nationals from each independent African state. The conference should empower the committee of foreign ministers, officials and experts to establish:

(1) a commission to frame a constitution for a union government of African states;

(2) a commission to work out a continent-wide plan for a unified or common economic and industrial programme for Africa. This programme should include proposals for:

  (i) a common market for Africa
  (ii) an African currency
  (iii) an African monetary zone
  (iv) an African central bank
  (v) a continental communications system;

(3) a commission to draw up details for a common foreign policy and diplomacy;

(4) a commission to produce plans for a common system of defence;

(5) a commission to make proposals for a common African citizenship.

He suggested that the African Charter of Casablanca, the Lagos Charter, and other relevant documents should be submitted to the committee of officials and experts.

A presidium, consisting of all African heads of government, should also be set up. It would be called upon to adopt a constitution and other recommendations in connection with the launching of the Union Government of Africa, which would have its capital at a central place in Africa.

In concluding, Nkrumah declared: 'Let us return to our people of Africa not with empty hands and with high sounding resolutions, but with the firm hope and assurance that at long last African Unity has become a reality. We shall thus begin the triumphant march to the kingdom of the African Personality, and to a continent of prosperity and progress, of equality and justice and of work and happiness . . .'

Supporting the move for African unity, the president of the Somali Republic, Mr Aden Abdullah Osman, stated three different ways by which this could be achieved:

(1) developing a system of periodic consultations among African governments for the purposes of concerting their foreign and military policies and raising the economic and social level of the African people;

(2) establishing an inter-African organization dedicated to the same purposes, and having its own budget and legal personality;

(3) creating an African union or federation, with a single foreign policy and diplomacy, a common defence system, a common economic planning and a unified currency.

He regarded the vision of an African union, speaking with a single voice in the councils of the world, as noble, but wondered whether the African states would be prepared to surrender their recently-acquired sovereignty to a continental government. The common desire for greater unity among African states would,

at the present stage of their development, in his opinion, best
be expressed by the formation of a new Pan-African organization
with the following four organs: a Pan-African assembly; a
council (of ministers); a permanent conciliation and arbitration
commission; and a secretariat. Giving details he said that:

The Pan-African Assembly should normally meet once a year to
decide the general action and policy of the organization.

The Council (of Ministers) should meet whenever necessary to
deal with urgent matters and also be responsible for the implementation of the policies laid down by the assembly.

The Permanent Conciliation and Arbitration Commission should
be responsible for the settlement of territorial and other disputes
between African states, and should, he added, be made up of a
panel of highly qualified Africans.

The Secretariat should be responsible to the organization, and
should be entrusted with the performance of the administrative
and technical services.

Such an organization, he claimed, would provide a forum for
periodic contacts among African leaders; serve to reach a peaceful settlement of controversies and disputes among African
countries; help to coordinate the policies of the African states at
meetings of the United Nations and other organizations; and
promote the economic and social progress of the African
continent.

The prime minister of Uganda, Dr Milton Obote, started his
speech by calling on the assembled heads of state and government to agree on concrete proposals for the achievement of
African unity there and then. He urged the independent African
states to surrender some of their sovereignty in favour of an
African central legislature and executive body with specific
powers over the establishment of an African common market,
economic planning on a continent-wide basis, collective defence,
common foreign policy, a common development bank and a
common monetary zone among others. He wanted a committee

61

of experts to be set up to investigate the matter of closer economic union among independent African states. His stand was supported, to a certain extent, by presidents Ben Bella of Algeria, Modibo Keita of Mali and Julius Nyerere of Tanzania.

President Gamel Abdel Nasser of the United Arab Republic recommended the establishment of an African common market. He urged cooperation in the scientific and cultural fields, and expressed his desire for the setting up of an inter-African organization at the conference. His speech concluded in an assertion that African unity could not be accomplished overnight.

President Habib Bourguiba of Tunisia and several other heads of delegations spoke in favour of an organization which would allow limited forms of cooperation between member states.

The Nigerian prime minister, Sir Abubakar Tafawa Balewa, spoke on the last day of the general debate, assuming the role of spokesman for the signatories of the Lagos Charter, and spelling out what had emerged as the majority opinion of the conference on the proposed organization for African unity.[13] After reviewing other delegates' previous suggestions on how African unity could be achieved, he stated that his country stood for the practical approach to the unity of the continent. Then he went on:

Nigeria's stand is that if we want this unity in Africa we must first agree to certain essential things: the first is that African States must respect one another. There must be acceptance of equality by all the states. No matter whether they are big or small, they are all sovereign, and their sovereignty is sovereignty. The size of a State, its population or its wealth should not be a criterion.

He spoke of the necessity for recognizing existing boundaries and, consequently, the existence of all the countries in Africa. He condemned subversion because

we cannot achieve this African Unity as long as some African countries continue to carry on subversive activities in other African countries.

On the establishment of an African common market, he said:

This is a very good idea, but I must say that we in Nigeria feel that it is a very complicated matter. We want an African Common Market but can we do it by taking the Continent as a whole? Or can we do it by certain groupings in Africa? What appears to us to be more practical is that we should have an African Common Market based on certain groupings. We are thinking of a North African grouping, which will include the Sudan; a West African grouping which will extend to the River Congo; and an East African grouping, which will include almost all the Central African countries. If we base our examination on these groupings, I think we will arrive at a very successful establishment of an African Common Market, because I think it is good for the trade of Africa.

He ended his speech by expressing the hope that the conference would pave the way for the unity and solidarity of the African continent.

The general debate, which was conducted on the United Nations pattern, lasted two and a half days. Thereafter the conference went into closed session. The closed session was largely confined to canvassing for the unanimous adoption of the charter for an all-African organization. The delegates agreed, among other things, to call their organization the Organization of African Unity and also to include a defence commission among the specialized commissions. The plea for the establishment of a political union of Africa, advocated by Ghana, was rejected.[14]

At an exciting, solemn and impressive ceremony the charter, rightly described by Emperor Haile Selassie as the 'Covenant of Unity', was signed by the heads of state and government of thirty-one independent African states on 25 May 1963. A new chapter in the political history of the African continent was thus opened. The Organization of African Unity came into being. In a speech marking this unique occasion, Emperor Haile Selassie said:

When all of you decided to meet here, you came with the determination to succeed. And succeed we did. For together we have cleared the grounds for concerted action on all our common problems ... Experience has taught us that no matter how much one would sustain hardship and struggle by oneself, one would not survive or solve one's problems alone. Only in the determination of our purpose and our will to solve it together can we discover strength and wisdom to guide us beyond the horizon wherein lies a better life for our peoples ...

President Nkrumah of Ghana, while still hoping that a union government would one day be a possibility, remarked that the decisions taken during this 'historic and momentous Conference' had made African unity a reality. He continued:

The resolutions we have made here are a symbol of our determination to become united and to remain united in an African community with common aspirations and common objectives. We shall, from now on, think, plan and work together for the progress and development of our great Continent.

Commenting on the conference, President Sékou Touré of Guinea started by reviewing African history from 1885 when Africa was divided by European powers in Berlin, to the beginning of the conference. He was happy that

in May 1963, at Addis Ababa, city of freedom, the qualified representatives, the authentic and worthy sons of the African people, met, under the banner of their awareness of their common destiny and fidelity to their personality, and to the original character of their homeland, Africa . . . to undertake, legally and legitimately, the reunification of their States in a single and unique Charter, the Charter of their brotherhood, of their rights and interests to be defended and developed, the charter of their solidarity henceforth indomitable, the Charter of freedom and peace, justice and progress in Africa.

On his return to Nigeria, the Nigerian prime minister, Sir Abubakar Tafawa Balewa, made a broadcast on the conference to the nation. In it he expressed his satisfaction at the adoption of the Charter of African Unity. He was particularly happy that the decisions of the conference vindicated the stand of the Nigerian Federal Government. He expressed his confidence in the future of the continent

because all the Heads of State and Government who attended the Conference were dedicated to the Unity, the progress and the happiness of the entire peoples of the African continent . . . [15]

Other leaders also expressed their satisfaction at the outcome of the historic conference. The conference was hailed by the Press as a great success.

(c) The OAU: Aims, Membership and Structure

The Preamble to the Charter of the Organization for African Unity allows that the founding fathers were motivated by the common determination to promote understanding among Africans as well as cooperation among all African states in accordance with the wishes and aspirations of the entire African people for brotherhood and solidarity throughout the continent. Having realized that before this could be achieved conditions for peace and unity must be established and maintained, they expressed their determination to safeguard and consolidate the independence, the sovereignty and territorial integrity of the African states, and also to fight neo-colonialism in all its forms. In their desire to unite all African states, so that the welfare and well-being of the Africans might be assured, they resolved to set up the Organization of African Unity.

AIMS AND PRINCIPLES

The charter provides for an organization to bring about: promotion of unity and solidarity among African states; co-ordination and intensification of cooperation between the states in their efforts to achieve a better life for the peoples of Africa; defence of the sovereignty, territorial integrity and independence of African states; eradication of all forms of colonialism from the continent; and promotion of international cooperation in accordance with the Charter of the United Nations and the Universal Declaration of Human Rights. Although there is nothing to indicate which of these purposes are primary and which are secondary, there is no doubt that the promotion of unity and solidarity among African states takes precedence over all others. This is not just because it has the pride of place among the listed purposes. It is the motivating force behind the forma-tion of the organization, as is clearly expressed in the preamble too.

The member states pledge themselves to coordinate and harmonize their general policies, especially in the following fields: politics and diplomacy; economics, including transport and communications; education and culture; health sanitation

Evolution

and nutrition; scientific and technical activity; and defence and security.

During the Conference of Heads of State and Government, at which the organization was founded, several speakers advocated laying down certain principles which would not only help to make the proposed organization a lasting one, but also guide member states in their relations with one another. In order that the purposes for which the organization was founded might be achieved, the member states should solemnly affirm and declare their adherence to the following principles: the sovereign equality of all member states; non-interference in internal affairs; respect for the sovereignty and territorial integrity of each state and for its inalienable right to independent existence; peaceful settlement of disputes by negotiations, mediation, conciliation or arbitration; unreserved condemnation of political assassination, as well as of subversive activities on the part of neighbouring states or any other state; absolute dedication to the total emancipation of the African territories which are still dependent; and affirmation of a policy of non-alignment with regard to all international blocs.

A close look at these principles will show that they can be classified into three groups. The first group, consisting of the first five principles, was directed at achieving 'unity and solidarity' between member states. The sixth principle committed all member states to mutual cooperation in their efforts to end colonialism in Africa. There is no doubt that there was a consensus of opinion on this topic among all Africans. The last principle, if properly observed by all member states, would make cooperation in the political and diplomatic field possible. With the cold war easing off, the policy of non-alignment could soon lose its importance in world affairs. Nevertheless, it remains very significant.

MEMBERSHIP

Each independent sovereign African state is entitled to become a member of the organization.[16] This does not mean that a country like South Africa, as long as she is still under a racist minority régime and practises the policy of apartheid, will ever be eligible for admission. Only independent African states under African majority rule have the right to become members. Any state qualified for membership may, at any time, notify the administrative secretary-general of its intention to become a member. But the state must be prepared to adhere or accede to the charter. On receipt of such notification, the administrative secretary-general circulates a copy of it to all members, to enable them to come to a decision. The response of each member state is transmitted to the administrative secretary-general, who, upon receipt of the required number of votes, communicates the decision to the state concerned. Admission is by a simple majority of member states.[17]

Thirty-one African states were foundation members. Togo, whose admission to the conference in May 1963 was refused after the assassination that January of president Sylvanus Olympio, was admitted later in the year.[18] All other African countries which became independent after 1963, with the exception of Lesotho, were admitted on a unanimous vote. Lesotho's admission was at first questioned by Sudan, on the grounds that the new state depended too heavily on South Africa and had been absent during the vote on the United Nations Resolution on Rhodesia on 22 October 1966, at the General Assembly of the UN.[19] She was admitted to the organization nonetheless.

Any member state desiring to renounce its membership is requested to send a written notification to that effect to the administrative secretary-general, and its membership lapses after a year, provided that it does not withdraw the notification within this period.[20] No provision is made for either the suspension or dismissal of member states.

In accordance with the first of the principles to which the member states have solemnly affirmed their adherence,[21] Article V of the charter guarantees that 'all member States shall enjoy equal rights and have equal duties'. As a result, each member state is entitled to be represented on all principal institutions of the organization and also to stand for election to all ad hoc committees which may be set up by any of these institutions, as well as to the Commission of Mediation, Conciliation and Arbitration. Each member state has the right to request

67

an extraordinary session of both the Assembly of Heads of State
and Government and of the Council of Ministers, provided that
such a request wins support from a two-thirds majority of the
member states.[22] This right was exercised by Tanzania following
the army mutinies of January 1964 in East Africa; by Mali and
Algeria in August 1964, because of the worsening situation in
the Congo; by Nigeria in June 1965, for the purpose of persuad-

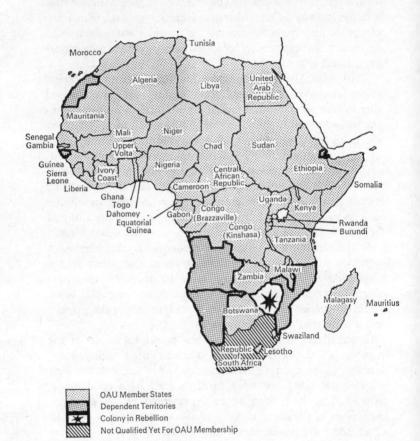

OAU Member States
Dependent Territories
Colony in Rebellion
Not Qualified Yet For OAU Membership

7. Pan-Africa: December 1971

---

ing all members to attend the Conference of Heads of State and Government in Accra later that year; and jointly by Ethiopia, Kenya and Uganda over Rhodesia's unilateral declaration of independence in 1965.

In addition, each member state is entitled to nominate its nationals to any function within the framework of the organization and its general secretariat; receive certified copies of ratifications of member states from the government of Ethiopia (designated as the depository of the charter) and the communications from the administrative secretary general; and make a request for the amendment or revision of the charter. Each member enjoys the right of one vote in each of the organs of the organization as well.

Each member state is equally expected scrupulously to observe the principles to which it has solemnly declared its adherence; refrain from exercising any influence or pressure upon any member of the staff of the general secretariat; agree to settle disputes with any other member state or states by peaceful means through the Commission of Mediation, Conciliation and Arbitration; pay regularly its contributions towards the upkeep of the organization; and contribute its quota towards the attainment of complete cooperation in all fields.

THE STRUCTURE OF THE OAU

To facilitate the achievement of the declared aims of the Organization for African Unity, the charter provides for the establishment of specialized commissions and four principal organs, *viz.*, the Assembly of Heads of State and Government; the Council of Ministers; the General Secretariat; and the Commission of Mediation, Conciliation and Arbitration.

(i) The Assembly of Heads of State and Government

The Assembly of Heads of State and Government is the supreme organ of the Organization. It is composed of the heads of state and government of all independent African States, or their duly accredited representatives.

Meetings: The assembly normally meets once a year. It was proposed by Tunisia in 1967 to make the meetings biennial: but the proposal was rejected at the summit conference of the following year. An extraordinary meeting of the assembly may be held at the request of a member state, subject to approval by a two-thirds majority of all member states. It has become usual since 1965 to limit the number of prepared speeches delivered at the summit to two: one by the host, and the other by the spokesman of the rest. The proposal to this effect, made by Morocco, was accepted at the 1964 summit conference held in Cairo.

Attendance at these conferences by the heads of state and government, or their accredited representatives, has been good. There have been few occasions when a member state has not taken part. Guinea boycotted the 1966 summit, after the arrest by Ghanaian police at Accra of the Guinean foreign minister and members of his delegation, while they were on their way to attend the meeting of the foreign ministers in Addis Ababa. In 1967 Malawi was absent.

There is nothing in the charter to indicate where the yearly summit should be held. When the organization was founded at Addis Ababa in May 1963, it was agreed that the next summit conference should be held at Cairo. The place of meeting, however, became an issue that almost wrecked the annual meeting of the assembly in 1965. Members of the Conseil de l'Entente – the Ivory Coast, Niger, Dahomey and the Upper Volta – refused to attend the meeting at Accra. They alleged that Ghana not only harboured dissident political groups from their countries, but that she encouraged their subversive activities. As a result, Nigeria, seconded by Liberia and Ethiopia, requested an extraordinary session of the Council of Ministers. The foreign ministers met at Lagos from 10 to 13 June, in an effort to mediate between Ghana and the entente states. After Ghana had made a number of concessions and promised to clear the country of 'undesirables' before the opening date of the summit, a seven-point resolution was passed, urging all members to attend the summit and do everything possible to make it a success. Also, in an effort by Nkrumah to placate the entente states, a meeting was arranged at his request with Houphouet-Boigny of the Ivory Coast, Hamani Diori of Niger, and Yameogo of the Upper Volta, at Bamako on 13 October. At the end of the closed-door discussions, Nkrumah agreed to ban political refugees and their families from Ghana. But, in spite of all these efforts, the entente states, joined by Togo, Gabon, Chad and Madagascar, reiterated on 19 October their decision to boycott the Accra summit. When the conference finally opened on 21 October 1965, these eight member states were absent. To avoid any further such incidents, the assembly decided that all future meetings should be held at Addis Ababa, though the summit conferences of 1967 and 1968 were, in fact, held at Kinshasa and Algiers respectively.

The assembly adopted its rules of procedure during its meeting at Cairo in 1964. At the beginning of every meeting, a chairman and eight vice-chairmen are elected; and these hold office for a whole year. The chairman opens and closes the meetings; submits for approval the records of the meetings; directs the debates; grants the use of the floor; submits to a vote matters under discussion; and announces the result of the vote taken – rules on points of order in accordance with the charter and the rules of procedure. Only in exceptional cases are public meetings held. Proposals to hold public meetings are usually put to the vote and decided by a simple majority.

The final decision on agenda items rests with the assembly, although the Council of Ministers is charged with the duty of preparing the agenda for the summit conference. The assembly may not only disregard any recommendation of the council but also decide on the insertion of a new item not considered by the council. The most striking example of this was the discussion on the Nigerian crisis during the Kinshasa Summit Conference of 1967. Thus the eleventh rule of procedure states that the provisional agenda of an ordinary session of the assembly shall comprise: items which the assembly decides to place on its agenda; items proposed by the Council of Ministers; items proposed by a member state as well as other business. In the case of an extraordinary session, however, the agenda is limited to the items which prompted it.

71

Evolution

A two-thirds majority of the entire membership constitutes a quorum. Each member state has one vote. Secret voting is conducted for elections and also in such special circumstances as the assembly may determine by simple majority. Decisions on all except procedural matters are taken by a two-thirds majority of the membership. As a result, it may be quite difficult for the assembly to reach a decision on matters that are somewhat controversial. Though this might suggest a tendency for the assembly to gloss over or even skirt controversial issues, there is nothing to indicate any move in this direction.

Functions and Powers: The assembly has a wide range of functions. It discusses matters of common concern to Africa with a view to coordinating and harmonizing general policy. It appoints the administrative secretary-general of the organization and his assistants. It approves the regulations governing the functions and conditions of service of the administrative secretary-general, his assistants and the staff; the protocol of the Commission of Mediation, Conciliation and Arbitration; and amendments to the charter in conformity with the procedure stipulated in Article XXXIII. It also establishes the specialized commissions.

The assembly has power not only to discuss but also to make recommendations on matters of common concern to Africa. By the terms of Article VIII of the charter it has power to 'review the structure, functions and acts of all the organs and any specialized agencies which may be created in accordance with the present charter'. It is empowered to determine its own rules of procedure. The power to decide questions arising in connection with the interpretation of the charter is vested in the assembly. Amendments to the charter can come into effect only with its approval.

(ii) The Council of Ministers

The Council of Ministers is composed of the foreign ministers or such other ministers as are designated by the governments of member states. It is responsible to the Assembly of Heads of State and Government.

The functioning of the council is not easily definable, however, for though it is charged with the responsibility of implementing the decision of the Assembly of Heads of State and Government, thus acting as 'the executive branch of the Organization of African Unity', the council has no machinery to execute policy. On the other hand, it is, according to the charter and the rules adopted by the other OAU organs, in a supervisory position over the general secretariat and the various specialized commissions – both of which have power to execute policy. It is also not clearly a decision-making body, for this is the function of the assembly itself. Yet it does make decisions in a wide variety of matters, some of which are of great importance. For instance, it was the council which committed all OAU member states to a diplomatic break with Great Britain in 1965; and the council which called for a boycott of the Mexico Olympic Games unless South Africa was barred from taking part. Most of the council's decisions are 'retroactively and summarily' approved by the assembly.

Meetings: The Council of Ministers meets at least twice a year – usually in February and August. The February meeting is the ordinary annual session, while the August one is confined to the preparation of the agenda for the assembly. The February meeting takes place with steady regularity, whilst the second one is always adjusted so as to precede the assembly meeting, the date of which varies from year to year. With the approval of two thirds of the entire membership of the organization, the council can meet in extraordinary session at the request of any of its members, and in fact the council has invoked this provision several times. The first extraordinary session of the council was held in November 1963 to consider the Algeria–Morocco dispute. The second took place in February 1964, to examine the situation in Tanzania following the army mutiny in the previous month as well as the Somalia–Kenya and Somalia–Ethiopia territorial disputes. The council held an extraordinary session at Addis Ababa in September 1964 and another at the UN headquarters the same December, in connection with the situation in the Congo (Kinshasa). Subsequent extraordinary sessions were held in June 1965 to persuade all member states to attend the 1965 Accra summit; in December 1965 to deal with the situation which arose after the Rhodesian Unilateral Declaration of Independence; and in December 1970 to deal with the abortive Portuguese invasion of Guinea.

There is no specific location for the council meetings. The place of the next meeting is usually decided by simple majority at the end of each ordinary session. In the case of extraordinary sessions, the place of meeting is given when the request for such sessions is made.

As a rule the meetings of the council are held in private. Decisions to hold any public meetings are taken by a simple majority. A chairman, two vice-chairmen and a rapporteur are elected by secret ballot and simple majority at the beginning of each session. These officers are not eligible for re-election until the representatives of other member states have held office. The council is divided into political as well as technical and economic committees.

The administrative secretary-general draws up the provisional agenda of the council and communicates this to member states at least one month before the opening of an ordinary session. The provisional agenda usually comprises:

(a) the report of the administrative secretary-general;

(b) items which the assembly decides to place on the agenda of the council;

(c) items which the council has decided at a preceding session to place on its agenda;

(d) items proposed by the specialized commissions of the organization;

(e) items proposed by member states;

(f) other business.

Functions and Powers: The council prepares the conference of the assembly and implements its decisions. It is responsible for the bringing about of inter-African cooperation in accordance with the instructions of the assembly. It approves the regulations of the specialized commissions, the annual budget, and gifts, bequests and other donations made to the OAU, and is empowered to decide on the privileges and immunities to be accorded to the personnel of the secretariat in the territories of the member states.

The council has been a very active body within the Organization of African Unity. It performs its role as the one body within the organization that immediately responds to emergencies. Its customary procedure over matters such as border disputes or general relations between member states is to hear the parties immediately involved; draft resolutions reflecting the consensus of the members; and, usually, appoint a committee to carry out whatever practical action is indicated. It prepares resolutions on the same topic for submission to the assembly if need be, and always gives directives to the general secretariat and other OAU institutions, when action on their part is deemed necessary. The greatest value of the council in such emergencies is that it offers a ready meeting-place for all concerned, as well as a forum for the swift exchange of African opinion. It also provides the means for the official expression of whatever measure of consensus is obtainable on any issue among all the member states of the organization. In a few cases of this kind the council has been instrumental in promoting a solution, as in the case of the Algeria–Morocco border dispute. In others, such as the Ethiopia–Somali territorial dispute, it has managed to persuade the two sides to moderate their attitudes, if not to reconcile their claims. In some cases, such as the Congo crisis, the relations between Ghana and the entente states which almost wrecked the 1965 Accra summit, and the Rhodesian crisis, political antagonism and conflicting interests among OAU members have prevented significant decisions from being made; or condemned to futility whatever decisions have been taken. The resolutions on the Congo passed by the council at Addis Ababa in September 1964 and the ad hoc committee set up to mediate in the Congolese conflict failed to achieve the desired goal. Nor did the extraordinary session held at Lagos in June 1965, for the purpose of persuading all OAU members to attend the summit meeting in Accra later that year, achieve its objective. The most spectacular failure was the fate of the resolution passed by the council at an emergency session held in Addis Ababa early in December 1965, requesting all OAU members to break off diplomatic relations with Britain. It should, however, be noted that all this happened early on in the development of the organization. If such a tendency had persisted, the organization would have become 'a sort of diplomatic tautology' – an organization which functions only when harmony exists, rather than as a force which creates, or at least fosters, good relations among its members.

Also at an early stage of the organization, the council indulged in putting aside major decisions and passing them on to the Assembly of the Heads of State. But this practice, which scarcely promoted the development of the OAU as an active instrument of cooperation, has been abandoned. The change for the better not only reflects well on the council but also augurs well for the organization. It is, however, still not clear as to how binding council resolutions, which have not been approved by the assembly, are upon the member governments. The council resolution of December 1965, calling on all-African governments to break diplomatic relations with Great Britain over Rhodesia, highlighted this issue. At that time two heads of government – the late Sir Abubakar Tafawa Balewa of Nigeria and Alphon Masamba-Debat of Congo (Brazzaville) – declared that the only council resolutions which bind African governments are those approved by the assembly.

(iii) The Administrative Secretary-General and the Secretariat

The Charter of the Organization of African Unity provides for the appointment of an *administrative* secretary-general as head of the organization's secretariat – which clearly shows that the founding fathers were concerned to curb the powers of this crucial functionary by laying great emphasis on the non-political nature of his status. Fear that the secretary-general might, with the passage of time, choose to make, rather than merely implement, policies must have played a significant role in choosing his title. The functions assigned to him as well as to the general secretariat of the organization bring this vividly to light.

According to the charter and 'Functions and Regulations of the General Secretariat', adopted by the Council of Ministers at Dakar in August 1963, the general secretariat is the central and permanent organ of the Organization of African Unity, expected to carry out the functions assigned to it by the charter, as well as any others which might be specified in other treaties and agreements among member states and those enumerated in the Regulations.[23] The general secretariat is charged with supervising the implementation of the decisions made by the Council of Ministers concerning all economic, social, legal and cultural exchanges of member states.[24] Apart from this, it keeps in custody the documents and files of meetings of the assembly, of the Council of Ministers, of the specialized commissions, and of other organs of the organization. It is expected, as far as possible, to place at the disposal of the specialized commissions the technical and administrative services they require. Should a session of a specialized commission be held outside the headquarters of the organization, at the request of a member state, the general secretariat concludes agreements or contracts with the government of the member state in whose territory the session is being held, to guarantee adequate compensation and reimbursement of expenses incurred by the general secretariat. It receives notice of the ratification of any agreements entered upon between states, and it prepares an annual report on the activities of the organization and a report on the activities carried out by the specialized commissions for submission to the Council of Ministers. It also prepares the programmes and annual budget of the organization for consideration and approval by the Council of Ministers. Finally, it prepares the agenda for the meetings of the Council of Ministers, the specialized commissions and other OAU subordinate bodies.

The administrative secretary-general directs the activities of the general secretariat and is its legal representative.[25] He calls ordinary as well as extraordinary sessions of the Council of Ministers and of the assembly, is the accounting officer of the organization, and is also responsible for the proper administration of the budget.[26] He submits a quarterly statement on contributions, paid and outstanding, to member states.[27] He

77

submits reports requested by the assembly, the Council of Ministers and the specialized commissions: in particular, on any matter relating to the financial situation of the organization to the Council of Ministers. He may establish fiduciary funds, reserve funds and special funds with the approval of the Council of Ministers, and may accept, on behalf of the organization, gifts, bequests and other donations made to the organization, provided that such donations are consistent with its objectives and purposes and are approved by the Council of Ministers. He has the right to designate the African banks or banking institutions in which the funds are to be deposited.[28] He draws up the provisional agenda and communicates it to the member states thirty days before an ordinary session and fifteen days before an extraordinary session. He receives notification of adherence or accession to the charter or of renunciation of membership, and communicates this information to member states. He also communicates written requests from member states for amendments or revisions of the charter. With the approval of the Council of Ministers, he establishes or abolishes, as the case may be, such branches and administrative and technical offices as may be deemed necessary for the adequate functioning of the general secretariat. Although there is no mention of his participation in the deliberations of the assembly, of the council or of the commissions in the rules of procedures governing these bodies, his attendance at such meetings has become routine. The present administrative secretary-general was present at all the meetings of the OAU Consultative Committee (set up to mediate in the Nigerian crisis) so as to give expert advice when required. Besides this, he represents the OAU at the conferences of some of the regional groupings.

When the Organization of African Unity was founded in May 1963 at Addis Ababa, no secretary-general was appointed, and no permanent secretariat headquarters was agreed. Instead a committee, composed of Ethiopia, Congo (Brazzaville), Ghana, Niger, Nigeria, Uganda and the United Arab Republic, was set up to act as the provisional general secretariat in accordance with a special resolution passed at the conference, and Dr Tesfaye Gebre-Egzy of Ethiopia became the Administrative

Secretary-General ad interim.[29] The provisional general
secretariat carried on the duties of the general secretariat until
an administrative secretary-general was appointed at the summit
conference held at Cairo in July 1964.

When the Council of Ministers held its first meeting at Dakar
in August 1963, the choice of the permanent headquarters of the
organization was among the items on the agenda. Lagos, Dakar,
Kinshasa and Addis Ababa were all suggested. The council
agreed upon Addis Ababa. The secretariat, however, has not
yet settled in a building of its own. It occupies a complex of four
modern buildings constructed to house the Ethiopian Police
Academy, and now re-named African Unity House. The site
is made available to the OAU by Emperor Haile Selassie at a
nominal rent of one dollar per annum. The conferences of the
organization held in Addis Ababa take place in Africa Hall, the
home of the United Nations Economic Commission for Africa.

The administrative secretary-general and his staff form the only
purely African international civil service. There was much controversy surrounding the election of the administrative secretary-
general during the Dakar meeting of the Council of Ministers
held in August 1963. Although the charter categorically states
that the administrative secretary-general and his assistants shall
be appointed only by the Assembly of Heads of State and
Government, an attempt was none the less made by some states
to elect the administrative secretary-general at the Dakar meeting. Others maintained that the council was only competent to
consider nominations, proceed to actual voting and submit the
outcome to the assembly for endorsement. Still others declared
that the council was not even competent to consider nominations,
much less to recommend a particular candidate for ratification
by the assembly. In the event, the only nominee for the office –
Diallo Telli of Guinea, proposed by the United Arab Republic –
secured less than 50 per cent of the votes. The Nigerian foreign
minister, Jaja Wachuku, pointed out that since the appointment
would have to be approved by a two-thirds majority of the heads
of state, it would be better to leave the choice to the assembly;
and the council, therefore, refused to ratify the nomination.

When the Council of Ministers met again towards the end of February 1964 at Lagos, the headquarters of the organization was again an issue. Ethiopia maintained that the foreign ministers had already chosen Addis Ababa as the permanent headquarters. Nigeria refuted this. At the end of the conference, it was suggested that 'in fact Addis Ababa would be the OAU capital, and Nigeria would have the Secretary-General'.[30]

There were two candidates for the post of administrative secretary-general at the Cairo Summit Conference: Diallo Telli of Guinea; and Dr Zinsou, the foreign minister of Dahomey. After much lobbying and behind-the-scene manoeuvres, Diallo Telli was appointed for a four-year term from 21 July 1964. He was to be assisted by Bognon Gracien of Dahomey, M. Shanoun of Algeria, M. Membolayo of Kenya, and Joe Iyalla of Nigeria.

Diallo Telli had been Guinea's ambassador to the United Nations since 1958 and by the time of his appointment as administrative secretary-general of the OAU, he was one of the senior African diplomats at the United Nations. His views on African unity, his personal stand on the overthrow of Nkrumah and on the 'ineffectiveness' of the Committee of Liberation, as well as on the Middle East crisis, did not subsequently enhance his popularity among all OAU member states. As a result, it took six ballots at the Algiers Summit Conference of 1968 before he was elected for another four-year term. His chief opponent was the general-secretary at Rwanda's Ministry for International Co-operation, Mr F. Nkundabagenzi. Also elected at the Algiers Summit Conference were four assistant secretaries-general: S. U. Yolah of Nigeria, M. Shanoun of Algeria, Joshua Buliro of Kenya and M. Augustin Pognon of Dahomey.

In the early days of the organization, the permanent personnel employed at the general secretariat numbered about seventy, including clerical as well as administrative staff. The staff has grown considerably since then. Almost all member states are represented at the general secretariat and there is a quota system allowing no state more than ten nationals at one time. Recruitment used to be the direct responsibility of the administrative secretary-general, but this has changed. There is now a recruitment board consisting of the administrative secretary-general, his four assistant secretaries-general, and the heads of the four main departments: political; economic and social; administrative and cultural; science, education and research. A notice of any vacancy is usually sent direct to the foreign office of member governments through the embassies in Addis Ababa. The governments then submit candidates for recruitment to the secretariat.

The administrative secretary-general, the four assistant secretaries-general and all other members of staff are requested not to seek or receive instructions from any government, or from any other authority external to the organization, in the performance of their duties. They must also refrain from any action which may reflect on their position as international officials responsible only to the organization. They enjoy diplomatic privileges and immunities. The administrative secretary-general has precedence over even the doyen of the diplomatic corps at Addis Ababa. At official receptions, for instance, he is first as head of the OAU General Secretariat; then come the doyens of the diplomatic corps; they are followed by the four assistant secretaries-general of the OAU, in order of length of service; and after them come the other ambassadors.

(iv) The Commission of Mediation, Conciliation and Arbitration

The Commission of Mediation, Conciliation and Arbitration is the organ set up with the sole objective of settling all disputes among the member states of the OAU. It was decided at the Addis Ababa Summit Conference of 1963 that a separate protocol, defining its composition and conditions of service, should be worked out. The protocol, to be approved by the assembly and regarded as an integral part of the OAU Charter, was endorsed at the 1964 summit conference held in Cairo.

The protocol provides for a president, two vice-presidents and eighteen other commissioners. They must all possess recognized professional qualifications. They hold office for five years and are eligible for re-election. The president and both vice-presidents, elected by the assembly, are appointed on a full-time basis, while the other commissioners are part-time. Together they constitute the Bureau of the Commission and are responsible for consulting with the parties to any dispute over the appropriate mode of a settlement. The commission appoints a registrar and such other officers as may be deemed necessary. Its office, too, is located in Addis Ababa.

The current members of the commission include eminent jurists from Burundi, Cameroon, Congo (Brazzaville), Ethiopia, Ghana, Guinea, Kenya, Liberia, Libya, Mali, Morocco, Nigeria, Rwanda, Senegal, Sierra Leone, Somalia, Sudan, Tanzania, Uganda, the United Arab Republic and Zambia. The commission is at present headed by Justice M. A. Odesanya of Nigeria, while Congo (Brazzaville) and Ghana nationals are the two vice-presidents. As we shall see later on, the commission has become almost entirely redundant: not because there have been no conflicts between OAU members, nor because the commissioners have proved incompetent; but rather because disputes have come to be handled direct by the OAU heads of state and government. The new approach, which more than anything reflects the traditional African way of tackling such problems, has been so successful that the European system of arbitration, conciliation or mediation has been unable to compete with it. In view of the effectiveness of this traditional African approach, whereby elders sit together, hear the parties to a dispute and bring any misunderstanding to an end in the most congenial atmosphere, there seems no reason why the Commission of Mediation, Conciliation and Arbitration should not be disbanded.

(v) The Specialized Commissions

The charter of the OAU empowers the assembly to establish such specialized commissions as it may deem necessary: these include the economic and social; educational and cultural; health, sanitation and nutrition; defence; and scientific, technical and research. Two other commissions – on transport and communications, and the Commission of African Jurists – were added subsequently. The first meeting of each commission was devoted to adopting the rules of procedure. These rules, prepared by a committee of experts and recommended to the commissions by the general secretariat, are similar for each commission. When some of the commissions departed from the recom-. mendations, the Council of Ministers, which had to approve the rules, rejected the changes.[31]

According to the rules, membership of each commission is made up of the appropriate ministers or plenipotentiaries designated by the governments of the member states. The relationship of the commissions to the Council of Ministers was initially a source of some friction. Since the charter simply states that the functions of the commissions should be carried out in accordance with the provisions of the charter and of the regulations approved by the council,[32] many delegations to the first meetings of the commissions felt that the council was not empowered to control the commissions. They argued that one group of ministers could not be responsible to another, since they were all of equal rank.[33] They also pointed out that the Council of Ministers, being composed of the ministers of foreign affairs, could not be expected to supervise the work of ministers in other fields. As a result, the various commissions adopted different rules on this issue. When the Council of Ministers met at Lagos in February 1964, however, the foreign ministers ruled that each commission should submit the result of its work to them for discussion and approval.

The commissions also defined their terms of reference at their constituent meetings. These terms closely followed the relevant resolutions adopted by the Addis Ababa Summit Conference of 1963. At their second meeting most of the commissions adopted numerous resolutions, some purely declamatory in character, others intended to create some of the machinery, and set in motion some of the processes, that would assist the commissions in the fulfilment of their various functions. Most resolutions involved requests and instructions to the administrative secretary-general to perform tasks which, in view of the facilities available to him at that time, seemed bewildering in variety and staggering in volume.

We shall now examine the workings of each commission in turn.

83

Evolution

The Economic and Social Commission held its first meeting at Niamey in December 1963. It adopted for its work detailed terms of reference which became the guiding principles for the economic cooperation policy of the OAU. The commission recognized the need for joint action by all OAU members and resolved to set up a free-trade area among member states; standardize an external tariff; organize African fairs and exhibitions for member states; establish African internal conventions on transport and communications by land, sea and air; set up an African telecommunications union; study the problems of payment agreements among African countries, with a view to establishing an African payments and clearing union; set up a monetary zone; and coordinate and harmonize national development plans. It decided that the United Nations Economic Commission for Africa (ECA) and the Organization of African Unity should work closely together.

It also dealt with the issues to be raised by African countries at the UNCTAD conference held in Geneva in March 1964. It adopted a resolution calling upon the industrialized states to meet the demands of the African countries as well as those of the other developing countries in the world. In it the commission appealed to the developed countries to reduce barriers to trade and give priority to the trade needs of the developing states; to reject the principle of reciprocity in their trade with developing countries, and also adjust the 'most favoured nations' clause; to accord developing countries preferential treatment, particularly in the protection of infant industries; to use to the maximum, as raw materials, natural rather than synthetic products; and to avoid any acts which might have an adverse effect on the economies of the developing states.

It recommended that the developing states should liberalize and strengthen their trade and monetary relationships among themselves, with a view to establishing mutually beneficial trade agencies within the framework of integrated and coordinated programmes of action or development schemes. Another recommendation was the coordination of plans for the development of transport and communications aimed at expanding continental and inter-continental trade. Finally, the commission appealed to the world conference on trade and development to take measures for the improvement of the terms of trade of the developing countries, and secure the maintenance at equitable and remunerative levels of the relationships between prices of primary commodities and industrial goods.[34]

The Education and Cultural Commission held its first session at Kinshasa in January 1964. It resolved to set up an inter-African news agency which would collect and disseminate 'fruitful, objective and impartial news about Africa to the African and world press, radio and television'. The commission also considered a proposal for an institute for African studies to form part of a Pan-African university,[35] and suggested creating a programming committee to draw up a phased work-programme for the commission covering at least three years. This was to include permanent and emergency measures for breaking down the language barrier; coordination of university education by the economic use of scarce resources; budgeting for manpower needs at the higher, intermediate and skilled levels; accelerated development of scientific and technological education; comprehensive planning of educational development; comparative study of the national education system of member states, with a view to harmonizing, rationalizing and standardizing the systems; a rational policy in the use of external aid and the promotion of cultural and literary activities through the exchange of artists and of exhibitions and the organization of seminars and festivals.[36]

The Health, Sanitation and Nutrition Commission met for the first time at Alexandria in January 1964. It considered endemic and epidemic diseases in Africa and the means of controlling them,[37] and recommended the setting up of a public health division within the secretariat of the OAU. It suggested the establishment of a bureau of documentation and information, and also a pool of experts.

The Bureau of Documentation and Information was to be responsible for the coordination and dissemination of information on

85

public health matters. The bureau would facilitate a system of standardization in the education of personnel for medical and public health activities; and in terminology, statistics and health legislation.

The Pool of Experts were to be appointed by their respective governments. They would be charged with the responsibility of carrying out studies on particular matters which would include the exchange of experts and recruitment of personnel for various public health programmes, and of personnel in medical, pre-medical, social and technical fields; the possibility of coordination and cooperation in the fight against endemic, epidemic and nutritional diseases affecting several neighbouring African states, whose operational programmes must be harmonized in order to work efficiently; cooperation in training and upgrading the skills of personnel in the various categories of public health service and research, as well as the possibility of exploiting, to the maximum, the human and material resources available to member states of the OAU, for the benefit of all the people of Africa, especially in times of emergency and epidemics.

The Defence Commission held its first session at Accra in December 1963. It was decided that the commission would act as an organ for consultation, preparation and recommendation for the collective and/ori ndividual self-defence of member states against any act or threat of aggression. The commission was also to promote inter-African cooperation on all defence matters, in accordance with directives from the Assembly of Heads of State and Government or the Council of Ministers. The commission also aimed at promoting unified defence plans, and standardizing of military training and procedures, military production and the supply of equipment.[38]

The Scientific, Technical and Research Commission decided at its first meeting in Algiers in February 1964 to take charge of: all scientific and technical matters affecting the general development of member states, including matters which might be referred to it by the Assembly of Heads of State and the Council of Ministers; formation of scientific policies, and execution, on request, of joint programmes of scientific and technological research; promotion of the training and exchange of scientific, technical and research personnel; promotion of an effective usage of the results of research, with a view to accelerating the economic and social development of member states; handling of external aid for projects of common interest sponsored by the commission; providing facilities for the dissemination of information to workers in the fields of science and technology in Africa, and conducting scientific surveys into the natural resources of the continent.

To facilitate the achievement of these functions, the commission was empowered to establish its own advisory and executive organs; prepare its scientific and technological plans and programmes; organize scientific and technological conferences and seminars; establish training and research institutes and information centres; and to collaborate with international scientific and technological organizations on matters of mutual interest.

The Commission of Jurists was added to the other specialized commissions at the Cairo Summit Conference of 1964, when the Assembly of Heads of State and Government approved the recommendation of the Council of Ministers that the new body be incorporated as one of the OAU specialized commissions.

The commission had its origins in the Conference of African Jurists which took place at Lagos in August 1963. In December of that year the jurists met again at Addis Ababa and drafted a convention and a statute for a proposed Commission of African Jurists.[39] The drafts were later submitted to all African governments for study. They proposed that the commission should be inaugurated at Abidjan in January of the following year and expected that it would become a commission of the Organization of African Unity. The statute of the commission sets out to promote and develop understanding and cooperation among African jurists; promote the development of the concept of justice; consider legal problems of common interest and those that may be referred to it by any of the members as well as by the OAU, and to make recommendations thereon; encourage the study of African law, especially African customary law in the universities and institutions of legal studies in Africa and elsewhere, and its progressive codification by African governments; as well as consider and study international law in its relation to the problems of African states.

The Transport and Communications Commission was established by the Assembly of Heads of State and Government during the 1964 Summit Conference at Cairo. It was charged with the responsibility of drawing up plans and coordinating action for telecommunications and postal services as well as for air and maritime transport.[40]

In spite of the enthusiasm and fervour shown by these commissions at their first series of meetings, many of them were short-lived. Most had no permanent headquarters. They usually met at the OAU headquarters in Addis Ababa, or at such other places as each commission decided by simple majority. With the exception of the scientific, technical and research commission, which, in January 1965, absorbed the CCTA with its staff of about one hundred, most commissions had no staff of their own. They relied solely on the general secretariat of the OAU.

As a result of the numerous meetings of the commissions and their committees, the budget of the OAU soared. There was also considerable overlapping and duplication in their programmes, both among the commissions themselves and with the United Nations activities in Africa. During the 1966 OAU Summit Conference, a proposal was made to amend Article XX of the charter so that the existing commissions might be rearranged to produce only three: an economic and social commission; a commission on education, science and culture; and a defence commission. The new Economic and Social Commission was to absorb the former commission bearing its name, as well as the former commission on Transport and Communications. The former Health, Sanitation and Nutrition Commission and the former Scientific, Technical and Research Commission were to be merged to form the new Commission on Education, Science and Culture. The Defence Commission was to remain un-

changed. In 1967 Tunisia proposed that the commissions should
be abolished altogether. Approval was, however, given to their
regrouping at the 1968 Algiers Summit Conference, while the
Commission of Jurists was asked to revert to the status it had
held before becoming an OAU special commission.

Notes to Chapter 2

1. Doudou Thiam, *The Foreign Policy of African States*, Phoenix House, London, 1965, pp. 68–70; Kwame Nkrumah, *Africa Must Unite*, Heinemann, London, 1963, pp. 144–7.
2. '*Addis Ababa Summit 1963*', Publications and Foreign Language Press Dept, Ministry of Information, Addis Ababa. See also Nkrumah, *Africa Must Unite*, p. 147.
3. *West African Pilo t*(Lagos), 25 January 1962.
4. *West African Pilot*, 30 January 1962.
5. See William I. Zartman, *International Relations in the New Africa*, Englewood Cliffs, New Jersey, 1966, p. 32.
6. The proposal to hold a CIAS in Tunis in April 1962 had run into difficulties.
7. *West Africa*, 27 April 1963, p. 477.
8. The initials OAS also stand for the Organization of American States.
9. Marcus Timmler, 'Das grosse Palaver von Addis Abeba', in *Aussenpolitik*, Jahrgang XIV, pp. 524–32; *West Africa*, 1 June 1963, p. 597.
10. *Addis Ababa Summit*, p. 24, 1963.
11. ibid., p. 39.
12. ibid., pp. 50–53.
13. Timmler, 'Das grosse Palaver von Addis Abeba', loc. cit.
14. T. O. Elias, 'The Charter of the Organization of African Unity', in the *American Journal of International Law*, 1965, p. 245.
15. 'Mr Prime Minister' – a selection of speeches made by Alhaji the Right Honourable Sir Abubakar Tafawa Balewa, K.B.E., M.P., prime minister of the Federal Republic of Nigeria, published by the Nigerian Ministry of Information, Lagos, 1964, p. 103.
16. Article IV of the charter.
17. Article XXVIII of the charter.
18. Togo took part in the foreign ministers' conference held in Dakar in August 1963.
19. Malawi and Botswana were also absent when the vote was taken at the General Assembly of the United Nations.
20. Article XXXII.
21. Article III.
22. Article XIV.
23. 'Functions and Regulations of the General Secretariat', Rule 1.
24. ibid., Rule 2.
25. ibid., Rule 6.

26. ibid., Rule 20.
27. ibid., Rules 18, 19 and 21.
28. ibid., Rules 23, 24 and 26.
29. Resolution CIAS (RES. 1) REV. 1.
30. *West Africa*, 7 March 1964, p. 255.
31. John Markakis, 'The Organization of African Unity: a Progress Report', in the *Journal of Modern African Studies*, Cambridge, Vol. 4, No. 2, 1966, p. 139.
32. Article XXII.
33. Markakis, 'Organization of African Unity', pp. 138–9.
34. *West Africa*, 28 December 1963, p. 1459.
35. The idea of a Pan-African university was first put forward by Emperor Haile Selassie during his opening address to the 1963 Addis Ababa Summit Conference.
36. *West Africa*, 18 January 1964, p. 63.
37. ibid., p. 82.
38. *West Africa*, 9 November 1963, p. 1275.
39. *West Africa*, 14 December 1963, p. 1422.
40. Assembly of Heads of State and Government Resolution, AHG/Res. 20(I), 1964.

3. Men and Ideas that Shaped the Course of Pan-Africanism

In the fight to reach the top the oppressed have always been encumbered by the traitors of their own race, made up of those of little faith and those who are generally susceptible to bribery for the selling out of the rights of their own people.

MARCUS GARVEY*

The ideas of visionaries have had immense influence. They have shaped religion, built empires, produced disastrous wars – and liberated men from bigotry and oppression. When such ideas are first propagated, they are usually regarded as eccentric. Those who produce them have a hard fight when they attempt to explain and to make others see their point of view. The reasons for the opposition they encounter in the task range from inability to grasp the new ideas to downright petty jealousy of an original mind and other human failings . But a visionary who perseveres may change the course of history.

Many people have helped to mould Pan-Africanist commitment. They include Dr Martin Delany, probably the first to use the expression 'Africa for the Africans'; Dr Edward W. Blyden, who first pleaded for an 'African personality'; Marcus Garvey, who first put forward the idea of a United States of Africa; George Padmore, Kwame Nkrumah and those others considered in this chapter, who have influenced the course of Pan-Africanism in different ways. But it is their combined ideas that have made Pan-Africanism what it is today.

(a) The Torchbearers

The ideas which finally led to Pan-Africanism had their origins in both the United States of America and the West Indies even before Marcus Garvey and William E. B. DuBois came on the stage, yet these two men can conveniently be described as the

*Philosophy and Opinions of Marcus Garvey, or Africa for the Africans, Vol. I, p. 29.

torchbearers of the movement. Their approach was not the same – understandable considering their different backgrounds and experiences which produced different personalities in each. Yet they were united in advocating: the 'redemption' and unity of Africa.

(i) Marcus Garvey

Marcus Garvey was born in the little town of St Ann's Bay, on the northern coast of Jamaica, on 17 August 1887. As a result of his family's financial hardship he had to leave school at the age of fourteen to learn the printing trade. During the course of his apprenticeship he read a considerable amount and absorbed journalistic techniques, and after two years, he became a qualified printer. With further rapid progress, he had become a master printer and a foreman at one of the largest Jamaican printing firms by the time he was twenty years old.

Garvey had his first experience of leadership early in 1907. That January a large part of Kingston was destroyed by an earthquake and fire. The wages of the workers were low; and, owing to the scarcity of commodities, prices rocketed. The Printers Union came out on strike for higher wages; and although he had not been party to this decision, he joined in and was elected to lead the strike. He did his best to advance the printers' cause 'in spite of the promise by his employers of a personal salary increase if he would abandon the struggle'.[1] Then, when the strike was finally broken, he found himself blacklisted, while other printers returned to their jobs. Unable to find a private job as a printer he took an appointment in the government Press. Despite this experience, however, he remained convinced of the need for organized action to improve the lot of workers and others.

While working in the government printing office, Garvey tried his hand at editing some periodicals. When this venture proved unsuccessful, he left to travel extensively in Central America, taking all sorts of jobs and studying the conditions of people of African descent in all the countries he visited. He went to London in 1912 in order to learn about the condition of

Africans and peoples of African descent in other parts of the British Empire. During his stay he read Booker T. Washington's autobiography, a book which had such a profound effect on him that he later declared:

> I read *Up from Slavery* by Booker T. Washington, and then my doom – if I may so call it – of being a race leader dawned upon me . . . I asked: 'Where is the black man's Government? Where is his King and his Kingdom? Where is his President, his country, and his ambassador, his army, his navy, his men of big affairs?' I could not find them, and then I declared, I will help to make them.[2]

Consequently he worked out plans and considered the possibilities of uniting all the Negro peoples of the world into one great organization with a 'government absolutely their own'. He was determined to set in motion ways and means to improve the lot of the black man throughout the world. His ultimate aim was 'a new world of black men, not peons, serfs, dogs, slaves, but a new nation of sturdy men making their impress upon civilisation and casting a new light upon the human race'.[3] Armed with this strong determination, Garvey returned to Jamaica in the summer of 1914.

On 1 August 1914 Garvey founded the Universal Negro Improvement and Conservation Association and African Communities League, in order to draw 'the peoples of the race together'. In its manifesto the organization warned against 'the universal disunity existing among the people of the Negro or African race' and also called upon all people of African descent to join in a great crusade to rehabilitate the race. The UNIA, as the organization was later called, not only pledged themselves 'to work for the general uplift of the Negro peoples of the world' but also worked out a concrete 'plan of action for Negro betterment in Jamaica'[4] as a first step towards their world-wide objective. In an effort to gain wider support for the UNIA programme, Garvey went to the United States in March 1916 and made an extensive tour of the country for several months. He discovered during that tour that the leaders of the American Negroes were 'mere opportunists who were living off their so-called leadership while the poor people were groping in the dark'.[5] Disgusted at such an apparent gross inefficiency he

93

started to make plans for the establishment of a UNIA branch in New York. In spite of the initial difficulties, caused mostly by certain Negro politicians who wanted to use the new organization for their own ends, the UNIA quickly gained support throughout the US, from headquarters at 114 West 138 Street in New York.

As the UNIA grew from strength to strength, Garvey decided to call an international convention of delegates representing the entire Negro race. The first of these conventions, held at New York in August 1920,[6] adopted the Declaration of Rights of the Negro Peoples of the World which stated among other things: 'We believe in the freedom of Africa for the Negro people of the world, and by the principle of Europe for the Europeans and Asia for the Asiatics, we also demand Africa for the Africans at home and abroad.' At the end of that first convention Garvey was appointed the provisional president of the African Republic. Having lived among peoples of African descent in Central America, the USA, the West Indies and Britain, Garvey realized the immensity of their problems. He therefore planned not merely to bring them together in the UNIA, but also to ensure that they improved their economic situation through their combined efforts and, if necessary, allowed themselves to be restored to the land of their fathers with a view to setting up an African republic.

His first plan centred on the improvement of the UNIA members in the economic field. In order to achieve this objective he infused in them a sense of confidence and determination. At one of their meetings he declared: 'Up you mighty race, you can accomplish what you will'; the people responded with 'an enthusiastic determination'. He laid before them a plan to own a shipping company which they would manage and run entirely by themselves, and whose ships would facilitate contact between them and their brethren in other parts of the world. The project was endorsed, members bought shares in the projected scheme, and by September 1919 the shipping company, named the Black Star Line, was founded. It was authorized to own, charter, operate and navigate ships of various types in any part of the world and to carry passengers, freight and mails. Its charter of incorporation also authorized the company 'to do any and all things and to exercise any and all powers necessary or advisable to accomplish one or more purposes of the corporation or which shall at any time appear to be conducive to, or for the benefit of, the said corporation in connection therewith'. In the same year, Garvey established the Negro Factories Corporation 'to build and operate factories in the big industrial centres of the United States, Central America, the West Indies and Africa to manu-facture every marketable commodity'.[7] This corporation later provided steady and profitable employment for many previously exploited Negroes in its chain of cooperative grocery stores, its restaurant, steam laundry, tailor and dressmaking shop, millinery store and publishing house. By and large these ventures proved successful, and immensely popularized the UNIA.

At the beginning Garvey and the UNIA were either ignored or belittled by many American Negro intellectuals. However, when the UNIA rapidly developed into a well-organized mass movement and made equal headway in business enterprises, these people changed their tactics. Their resentment of the 'upstart' from the West Indies led them to start a witch-hunt campaign against Garvey. Their opposition gained momentum at an opportune time for the American Government, which had all along viewed the UNIA and its Negro improvement schemes with dismay. In January 1922 the US postal authorities claimed that Garvey and the Black Star Line were using the mails to defraud. Garvey and three of his Black Star Line associates were consequently indicted in February on conspiracy charges. Those Negroes who were opposed to Garveyism quickly joined forces. While the UNIA was holding its Third Convention in New York in August 1922, they organized their anti-Garvey meetings, also in New York, under the auspices of a group called the Friends of Negro Freedom. With the slogan, 'Garvey must go!' they called for his immediate deportation from the United States. A so-called 'Committee of Eight' made up of Harry H. Pace, Robert S. Abbot, John E. Nail, Dr Julia P. Coleman, William Pickens, Chandler Owen, Robert W. Bagnall and George W. Harris – most of them NAACP members – even sent an open letter to the US attorney-general, Harry M.

Daugherty, protesting at the delay in putting Garvey and his associates on trial and condemning the UNIA in the most vicious manner. When in September 1923 the case was heard, an extraordinary judgment was passed. In spite of the fact that three others along with Garvey were being charged for conspiracy, he alone was convicted! He was sentenced to a fine of 1,000 US dollars and to the 'maximum term of five years'. This drastic action was meant to be the death-blow of the UNIA.[8] But an appeal was lodged, and the UNIA members arranged for Garvey's release from the Tomb's prison in New York on a bail of $25,000 on 10 September 1923.

Garvey's project for a return of people of African descent to Africa made more enemies than were made through any other UNIA activity and they ranged from those who feared the loss of their cheap labour supply to those who, while black themselves, despised the Africans as 'uncivilized'. Garvey's motives were dual: respect for human dignity and for Africa's 'redemption'.

The experience of the American Negroes over the ages convinced Garvey beyond any reasonable doubt that as long as they remained in America they would continue to be subjected to all forms of racial discrimination and therefore denied the elementary ingredients of human dignity. He was firmly convinced that 'the white man of America will not, to any organized extent, assimilate the Negro'. But Garvey did not stop at the American situation. He was concerned with the entire Negro world. He was disgusted with 'the problem of lynching, peonage and dis-enfranchisement' in America, and that 'of peonage, serfdom, industrial and political government inequality' in the West Indies, and in South and Central America. The African situation, which he described as 'not only peonage and serfdom, but outright slavery, racial exploitation and alien political monopoly', also infuriated him. He wanted to bring 'these crimes against our race' to an end. Since he realized that this could only be achieved by the united effort of all concerned, he wanted all Africans and people of African descent to live together and improve their lot. The question of where they should live did not worry him, for he had earlier declared that

'Nature intended a place for each and every one' in the world. Consequently, he believed that 'if Europe is for the white man, if Asia is for brown and yellow men, then surely Africa is for the black man'.[9] He felt accordingly justified in raising the cry of 'Africa for the Africans'. His first objective was to 'redeem' Africa 'from the hands of alien exploiters'.

Garvey envisaged a free United States of Africa with 'a government' as 'a nation of our own, strong enough to lend protection to the members of the race scattered all over the world, and to compel the respect of the nations and races of the earth'.[10] The first step taken by Garvey was to get in touch with the Liberian Government, since Liberia was the only independent African state known to most Americans at that time. Early in 1920 he sent a UNIA delegation there to confer with the government over the possibility of transferring the headquarters of the movement to that country. Following their discussions, the Liberian Government gave the assurance that it would 'afford the association every facility legally possible in effectuating in Liberia its industrial, agricultural and business projects'.[11] In November 1920, Garvey launched a drive for $2 million of development aid to Liberia. This was meant to be used for 'construction work in Liberia, where colleges, universities, industrial plants and railroad tracks will be erected; where men will be sent to make roads, and where artisans and craftsmen will be sent to develop industries'.[12] Early in 1921 Garvey sent a group of experts to Liberia 'to start work immediately'. On 22 March 1921, the Liberian cabinet held discussions with a UNIA delegation on the possibility of obtaining sites for further UNIA activities in that country. At the end of that meeting the Liberian acting president, Edwin J. Barclay, personally assured the delegation of the country's implicit support for the UNIA projects.[13] Encouraged by so forthcoming and positive an attitude, the UNIA sent another delegation in December 1923. By then the Liberian Government had set up a local advisory committee, and the delegation was therefore even more warmly welcomed. It returned to the US in May 1924 with a letter from the Liberian chief justice, James J. Dossen, informing Garvey that the Liberian Government and people would 'stand ready to co-operate with you on this side, in putting over the enterprise successfully'.[14]

All these comings and goings were viewed with great anxiety by the colonial powers. Both the British and French governments and the American administration decided to strike back, but in a subtle way. The method whereby inducements are offered at governmental level, and 'moderate' Africans and/or people of African descent are sought and encouraged in an effort to counteract the so-called 'radical' approach to Pan-African ideals originated here. It was used immensely in the 1960s and is still being used now. The effect was immediate then as now. Garvey and the UNIA scheme for Africa's 'redemption' were subjected to a barrage of attacks, and in the forefront of the attackers were Africans and people of African descent!

Blaise Diagne, the Senegalese member of the French Chamber of Deputies, not only attacked Garvey but also declared that 'we French natives wish to remain French, since France has given us every liberty and since she has unreservedly accepted us upon the same basis as her own European children'. He went on to state that 'none of us aspires to see French Africa delivered exclusively to the Africans . . .'[15] It is worth noting that the African member states of the French community translated this declaration into being between 1960 and 1963. It still, in a modified form, affects many of them in their approach to Pan-Africanism! The American Negro intelligentsia, which pinned its hopes on the NAACP, also used the organization's magazine, *Crisis*, to attack the project vehemently and incessantly. This pleased the American administration, so much so that the magazine's editor, W. E. B. DuBois, to whose Pan-African congress of 1919 it had been hostile, suddenly became someone to be honoured! He was chosen in 1924 to be the US Envoy Extraordinary and Minister Plenipotentiary during the second inauguration ceremony of President King of Liberia.[16]

As the 'moderates' of his day were denouncing and bitterly attacking Garvey, his project was also being undermined at governmental level. The Liberian Government, previously so cooperative, suddenly did an about-face. The very government which in May 1924 had undertaken to 'stand ready to cooperate' had by the end of the following month made it known that it would have nothing more to do with the UNIA. Consequently when the UNIA technical experts who were already on their way arrived in Monrovia, they were ignominiously arrested and held for immediate deportation. The Liberian Government also took the unusual step of assuring the US Government that Liberia was 'irrevocably opposed both in principle and fact to the ... policy of the UNIA, headed by Marcus Garvey'.[17] This new policy was adopted as a gesture to Liberia's 'friends'![18] It is significant that the Liberian Government immediately leased the very land which had been apportioned for the UNIA project to the Firestone Rubber Company.[19]

While the 'moderates' were attacking Garvey, and the Liberian Government was switching direction, plans to deal with Garvey were also being considered by the US authorities. We have already noted that he had been sentenced for conspiracy and that only the efforts of the UNIA members secured his release on bail pending the hearing of his appeal. As the Liberian Government was drafting its diplomatic note to the US Government, denouncing Garvey and the UNIA, the US Government was preparing prosecution papers. This time Garvey was accused of 'perjury and tax evasion'. Just as the UNIA convention of August 1924 was about to begin its deliberations, a federal grand jury returned an indictment against him for perjury and income tax evasion.[20] A few months later, his appeal against the conspiracy conviction was also rejected by the US Circuit Court of Appeals. Following this not unexpected decision, Garvey was taken to prison on 8 February 1925.[21] With this achieved, the US authority saw no reason for keeping him in America any longer. The unexpected result was that his sentence was suddenly commuted, and he was deported in December 1927.

In spite of his American experience, Garvey never ceased from any act which he thought might lead to an improvement in the status of the African peoples. In 1928, he organized the European headquarters of the UNIA in London and also established a branch in Paris. In September 1928 he went to

Geneva, where he presented a petition to the League of Nations. He listed the many grievances of the Negro peoples and urged the world organization to support the move for the independence of Africa, which would then be constituted into a United Commonwealth of Nations with a government chosen by the Africans themselves.[22] By 1935 he had moved the headquarters of the UNIA to London. There, never ceasing to advocate Africa's redemption from alien powers, he died on 10 June 1940.

Thus Garvey never lived to see the outcome of his efforts. But one must agree with his declaration on 2 September 1928, that he was 'only the forerunner of an awakened Africa that shall never go back to sleep'. Even his enemies, as far back as 1925, acknowledged his contributions. The *New York Evening Bulletin* of 7 February 1925 admitted that he 'performed many fine acts' and went on to state that, 'had the man been given half a fair deal' he would have accomplished greater things. Another newspaper which had always opposed him admitted that he had 'awakened the race consciousness and race pride of the masses of Africans everywhere as no man ever did . . . He made them think, he made them cooperate, he organized and marshalled their forces'. 'For these things,' the paper went on, 'his service will be historic and epoch-making.'[23] After his deportation from the US, even *Crisis*, the NAACP magazine which had previously attacked both him and the UNIA, now found words of praise for Garvey himself.[24]

Garvey was a controversial figure. His integrity was questioned; charges of corruption and even embezzlement had been levelled against him. Certainly his own appeal to the wretched of the earth was somewhat compromised by his love of flamboyant dress and the extravagance of his personal entourage, which were rich in uniforms and titles. Yet those who attacked him for these weaknesses failed to understand the complexity of his character. If he was indeed corrupt, he was only mirroring an aspect of American society and of white America. It was, too, the desire to establish an African government, which led him to imitate the courts of the European powers. His chief fault was precisely that he wanted to create a new Africa in the image of the existing white world.

Nonetheless it is indisputable that Garvey's idea of a united Africa has become the cardinal point of Pan-Africanism. The resolution adopted at the 1963 Summit Conference of Independent African States which expressed 'the deep concern aroused in all African peoples and governments by the measures of racial discrimination taken against communities of African origin living outside the continent and particularly in the United States of America', may well be the beginning of efforts 'to lend protection to the members of our race scattered all over the world' that Garvey had advocated earlier.

(ii) William E. Burghardt DuBois

DuBois was born at Great Barrington, Massachusetts, USA, on 23 February 1868. He studied at Berlin and Harvard, and received a doctorate. He was professor of Greek and Latin at Wilberforce University from 1894 to 1896; professor of economics and history at Atlanta University from 1897 to 1910. He became the head of the department of sociology of Atlanta University between 1933 and 1944. He was the editor of *Crisis*, the official magazine of the NAACP, from 1910 to 1932, and editor-in-chief of the *Encyclopedia of the Negro* between 1933 and 1945. He was made the director of *Encyclopedia Africana* in 1961 by the government of Ghana under Kwame Nkrumah.

DuBois had his first experience of racial discrimination in America at an early age, but he was to have more later in life. In spite of this, however, he still believed that the Americans would one day see reason and treat people of African origin as equals. He also believed that it would be achieved gradually and by peaceful means. He was convinced that, if the majority of the American people were made aware of the injustices suffered by Negroes, an evolutionary change would take place by which Negroes would receive a fair deal. Cooperation with American 'liberals' seemed to him essential to bring the envisaged evolution about. Since his convictions did not follow logically from the hard realities of American society, however, they were bound to lead him to nothing but a blind alley.

The injustices suffered by people of African descent in

America as a result of racially discriminatory measures led to the ideas of unity and solidarity among them. The move in this direction given by the Negro intelligentsia resulted in the formation in 1897 of the American Negro Academy, succeeded in 1906 by the Niagra Movement. DuBois took an active part in the work of these organizations, and edited their periodical, *Horizon*.

Despite the activities of these organizations, racial discrimination, lynchings, the various activities of the Ku Klux Klan and the denial of constitutional rights continued. It was in this climate that the notorious and horrible Springfield lynching of 1908 took place. Outraged at the incident, a group of American liberals formed the National Association for the Advancement of Coloured People (NAACP) in 1909. It aimed at the eradication of all forms of discrimination and injustice in American society, and for this purpose it 'proposed education, legal action and organization: education of the American people in their abuses of Negro rights; appeals to courts and legislatures to remove obstacles blocking Negro progress; and organization into a single articulate group of those Americans, white and black, whose democratic faith abhorred the color line'.[25] DuBois, who readily supported this programme, was made the director of the organization's publications and the editor of its magazine *Crisis* in 1910. In September 1911, he appealed to many prominent Negroes in the US to join the NAACP, which he thought would speed 'the arrival of democratic justice'. This belief later earned him resentment on two fronts: from the Negroes who soon became disillusioned with the organization's efforts; and the whites (in the majority) who disapproved of attempts to use the organization to bring about a speedy change in the treatment of American Negroes. An uncomfortable tension developed within the NAACP. It was at this stage that DuBois started to have doubts about his previous belief, and consequently to work on 'The Immediate Program of the American Negro', published in 1915.[26]

DuBois realized that the Negroes should work out their own projects for moving ahead and not continue to assume that 'God or his vice regent the white man' would do it for them. He laid emphasis on 'conscious self-realization and self-direction', which he regarded as 'the watchword of modern man'. Declaring that the first article in the programme of any group that was to survive should be the great aim of 'equality and power among men', he wanted the Negroes to plan their own building and loan associations, cooperatives for production and distribution, and blue-prints for systematic charity. He advocated the need for organizations to be controlled entirely by the Negroes and dedicated to 'our objects, our aims and ideals' as distinct from 'the shared goals of a bi-racial group fighting for democratic equality'.[27] When expanding this theme two years later, he declared:

> We see more and more clearly that economic survival for the Negro in America means ... that he must employ labor, that he must organise industry, that he must enter American industrial development as a group capable of offensive and defensive action, and not simply as an individual liable to be made the victim of the white employer and of such of the white labor unions as dare.

He reiterated that American Negroes were well able to work out efficient industrial cooperation.[28] In spite of all these assertions and in spite of his statement that 'the problem of the twentieth century is the problem of the colour-line', DuBois vacillated between Negro self-reliance and cooperation of both races in order to secure 'the arrival of democratic justice' for American Negroes. The latter policy proved the stronger, as his Pan-African congresses clearly showed.

As DuBois became disillusioned with the attitude of the white American liberals over the issue of Negro rights in America, he began to turn his attention to the colonial problem. Being of African origin he was concerned with the African situation and wanted American Negroes to stand up and speak for Africa. Since he still needed the financial and moral backing of the NAACP, he submitted a plan for Africa in 1917 to the organization for approval. This plan envisaged 'the internationalization of Africa', and a Pan-African congress to be held simultaneously with the peace conference after the First World War.[29] While 'the internationalized Africa', to be made up of German colonies, was to be prepared for self-government 'under the guidance of an international organization', the Pan-African congress was to 'focus the attention of the peace delegates and the civilized world on the just claims of the Negro everywhere'. DuBois claimed to have regarded Pan-Africanism as 'the centralization of race effort and the recognition of a racial fount'. But if he really meant this, why did he not cooperate with the UNIA of Marcus Garvey to achieve that end? The reasons are various.

Marcus Garvey was a realist rather than a dreamer. He was firmly convinced that the Negroes would continue to be denied their rights, and subjected to all forms of racial discrimination, even lynchings, as long as they did not rely on their own efforts to improve the situation; DuBois, on the other hand, equally firmly believed that the 'arrival of democratic justice' would be brought about only through the combined efforts of both blacks and whites. This belief was carried by DuBois to the international arena when he started on the Pan-African congresses. There is, however, much more to it than that, for DuBois, the intellectual, seemed to have little or no regard for others who were not as educated and therefore as 'civilized' as he was.[30] Obsession with this idea made it impossible for him to be a real Negro leader in America. Even his own account of the Pan-African congresses between 1919 and 1939 clearly showed that he was much more interested in his association with the many Europeans at those conferences than with what the latter actually achieved.[31] All this made DuBois the 'moderate' of his day in relation to the development of Pan-Africanism. His constant attacks on the UNIA and its leadership plainly confirmed his to be 'the voice of reason among his race' – an expression used in the 1960s to describe the most reactionary African leaders by those powers opposed to Pan-Africanism. But his attacks on the economic and industrial projects of the UNIA, which were more or less in line with what he himself had proposed between 1915 and 1917 but which he lacked the ability to turn into reality, demonstrated that other considerations must have motivated him. One must still, however, regard him as 'the connecting link' between Pan-Africanism in its earliest form and as we know it today. After belatedly realizing his mistakes, DuBois abandoned his previous stand, repudiated his previous attacks on Marcus Garvey's 'return to Africa' project, and became a citizen of Ghana in 1961. By the time of his death in 1963 he had been acclaimed the 'father of Pan-Africanism' – a title merited by the uncompromising nature of his views as contrasted with those of many 'moderate' African leaders.

(b) The 'Progressives'

All efforts made between the two world wars failed to arouse significant African participation in Pan-Africanism. This was due mainly to the political, economic and social situation, which resulted from the colonization of the continent and its repressive impact on the Africans themselves. The Second World War, however, changed the whole situation radically, not only in Africa but throughout the colonial world. It was under these changed conditions that the Pan-African Congress of 1945 was held. That conference, as we have already noted, called for the organization of political parties in all African territories, in order to speed up the liquidation of colonialism throughout Africa. The independence of these territories was regarded as the first step towards a united Africa.

It is one thing to propound theories, however, and another to be prepared to turn those theories into reality. It is also one thing to organize political parties, but another for such parties to have a leadership willing to work courageously towards the attainment of the professed objectives. Political parties shot up like mushrooms in some parts of Africa after the Second World War but many of them lacked the dedicated leadership essential to the struggle for independence. Many of the new leaders had either been nominated members of the Legislative Councils in the British Colonies or were glory-seeking intellectuals who were either interested mainly in their own private enterprises or concerned only with imitating the colonialists. Many soon became agents of colonialism, or turned into unprincipled opportunists who would arouse the masses but in fact did nothing for them. As a result parties became unsuitable to the independence struggle. It was at about this time that Kwame

Evolution

Nkrumah became the secretary of the United Gold Coast Convention – a political party which was in favour of the moderate approach to independence as long as its leaders were allowed to hob-nob with the colonialists. The arrival of Nkrumah in the African political arena marked the beginning of a new era of African politics in general and Pan-Africanism in particular. He more than any African before him set the pace for an independent and united Africa. Nkrumah was joined by Sékou Touré soon afterwards. The two of them became the unrivalled champions of Pan-Africanism. Both showed dauntless courage and unflagging determination in their efforts not only to popularize but also to achieve Pan-African ideals against all odds and both have left so lasting a mark on the course of Pan-Africanism that they may almost be said to personify it. They infused it with new vigour, purpose and determination and made it a positive policy, accepted as a factor in the national politics of all African states. They gave new meaning to the idea of an 'African personality', made Africans feel a sense of pride in their Africanness, and lent impetus to the determination of Africans to speak for themselves in international forums on issues that affected them all. Nkrumah and Sékou Touré were later joined by such able men as Ben Bella, Julius Nyerere, Patrice Lumumba and Ahmed Boumédienne, but at this point we shall concern ourselves only with the two pioneers.

(i) Kwame Nkrumah

Kwame Nkrumah was born at Nkroful, Nzima, Ghana, in September 1909. He taught as a pupil-teacher for a year after elementary school, before going to the government training college in Accra (later incorporated into Achimota College), where he studied to become a qualified teacher. After teaching at various schools he left for the United States in 1935 to pursue further studies. He graduated from Lincoln University with a major in economics and sociology in 1939. He was appointed lecturer in philosophy at Lincoln and enrolled immediately to study theology. He also did postgraduate courses in both education and philosophy at the university of Pennsylvania.

Nkrumah was elected president of the African Students' Association of America and Canada while studying at Lincoln, and helped to organize an African students' section at the university of Pennsylvania. It was during his student days in America that he conceived the idea of a West African federation as a basis for a united Africa, and Marcus Garvey's *Philosophy and Opinions* which he came across at this time added more fuel to the fire of his enthusiasm for African emancipation and unity.[32]

He left the USA in May 1945 for London, where he hoped to study law and complete his thesis for a doctorate in philosophy. These plans, however, he abandoned, having become totally engrossed in student politics.

Soon after his arrival in London he joined the West African Students' Union and was elected vice-president. He played a leading part in organizing the Pan-African congress of 1945 and later acted as one of its secretaries. He became the general secretary of the working committee set up after the congress, and secretary of the West African secretariat. Shortly after becoming secretary of the West African secretariat he went to Paris, where he met the African members of the French National Assembly – Sourous Apithy, Léopold Senghor, Lamine Gueye, Houphouet-Boigny, among them – with whom he discussed the establishment of a movement for a union of West African socialist republics. On his return to London he embarked on organizing the Coloured Workers' Association of Great Britain. Apart from all these activities, he devoted much of his time to assisting African students who for one reason or another found themselves in trouble. While thus occupied, he received a letter from a former colleague, Ako Adjei, asking him to return to the Gold Coast (now Ghana) and take up a post as general secretary of the United Gold Coast Convention. After receiving an official invitation from the party's chairman, Dr J. B. Danquah, Nkrumah finally left London on 14 November 1947 for Accra.

It did not take him long to realize that the methods of the party leaders would not bring self-government about quickly. All his efforts to stimulate other members of the party's working committee to action proved abortive and the split between him and his colleagues persistently widened. He founded the *Accra Evening News* and also organized the Committee on Youth Organization in September 1948. That committee, which was affiliated to the UGCC, soon became disillusioned with the latter and broke away from it on 12 June 1949 – an event which was to bring about the creation of the Convention People's Party (CPP).

The CPP, under the able and energetic leadership of Nkrumah, soon became a country-wide mass organization, destined to play a very important role in securing Ghana's independence. It convened on 20 November 1949 a Ghana People's Representative Assembly of all organizations to consider the constitutional reforms recommended in the Coussey Report published in October. The assembly rejected the reforms as being too moderate. The attitude of the colonial government soon led to disturbances, which gave it the opportunity to declare a state of emergency and arrest the leaders of the CPP. But the popularity of these only increased and the party gained sweeping victories at the municipal elections in Accra, Kumasi and Cape Coast. It then achieved a resounding victory at the general elections of February 1951. The Governor had no real alternative but to release the CPP leaders from prison and call upon Kwame Nkrumah to form a government.

Nkrumah therefore 'graduated from prison' on 12 February 1951 to become the first African leader of government business and prime minister in March 1952. He was elected life chairman and leader of the CPP during the 1953 annual conference of the party; and his motion for independence was carried unanimously by the Gold Coast National Assembly on 11 July 1953. In spite of strong opposition campaigns to produce further delay, Nkrumah was able to lead the Gold Coast to independence on 6 March 1957, thus becoming the first African prime minister of an independent sovereign state. He was Ghana's president from 1960 till February 1966, when he was overthrown by an army coup.

Although Nkrumah was preoccupied with the Gold Coast independence struggle when he became the head of government, he never forgot the idea of a West African union as a first step

to a united Africa. With this in mind, he paid a visit to Liberia
in January 1953. After discussing the issue with president
Tubman he addressed the Liberian legislature, and declared:
'The ideal nearest my heart is the union of all peoples of West
Africa. To this end I am dedicated.'[33] In an effort to revive the
idea which he had already discussed with the African members
of the French National Assembly during his London days, he
called a meeting of all West African nationalist movements at
Kumasi in December 1953. Delegates from the English-speaking
and French-speaking territories as well as Liberia agreed to
establish a national congress of West Africa, with the aim of
promoting West African unity.

During the anniversary celebrations of the CPP in 1955,
Nkrumah thanked all nations which had helped Africa so far
and spoken on her behalf. He went on to declare: 'I firmly
believe that only the African can speak for the African and only
the African can be the spokesman of this great continent.'[34] He
viewed Ghana's independence as the beginning of a new era in
African political history and he entreated his countrymen to
conduct themselves in a befitting manner. At one point he
declared:

How we conduct ourselves when we become independent will affect
not only Ghana but the whole of Africa. We have a duty not only to the
people of this country, but to the peoples everywhere in Africa who are
striving towards independence. If we can make a success of our independence, we shall have made an incalculable contribution towards
freedom and progress throughout Africa.

He continued:

History has entrusted us with a duty, and upon how we carry out
that duty will depend not only the fate of the people of this country but
the fate of many other peoples throughout the whole of Africa. We
must show that it is possible for Africans to rule themselves, to establish a progressive and independent state and to preserve their national
unity.[35]

It was not, however, until the last few hours of colonial rule
in the Gold Coast that Kwame Nkrumah could spell out in
unmistakable terms his ideas of Pan-Africanism. Making a policy

statement in Parliament just a few minutes before the birth of an independent Ghana, he declared:

> The Government of Ghana will direct its efforts to promote the interests and advancement of all African peoples in their pursuit of freedom and social progress. The sacrifices made by the people of Ghana in their struggle for independence are only the first stage in the common advancement of their brothers all over Africa. The Government hopes that, as a free, sovereign and independent state, Ghana can become the centre for the discussion of African problems as a whole and that, with the co-operation of all other African territories, we shall be able to foster a common attitude to local problems and world problems which will ensure that problems peculiar to Africa will receive the attention which they have not had for so long. Our aim is to work with others to achieve an African personality in international affairs.[36]

As the colonial flag was being replaced by Ghana's national flag at midnight of 5 March 1957, Nkrumah reiterated that Ghana's independence would be meaningless 'unless it is linked up with the total liberation of the African continent'.[37]

The policy statement was immediately followed by action. On the very next day Nkrumah informed representatives of the other independent African states of his desire to convene a conference at which they would work out ways and means whereby all independent African states would coordinate their policy at international level, concert their efforts and give assistance to those territories still under colonial rule. That was how the CIAS which began in April 1958 originated. During the first anniversary celebrations of Ghana's independence, Nkrumah put forward the idea of an All-African Peoples' Conference in which the nationalist movements and trade unions throughout the continent would take part. As well as these organizational initiatives, Nkrumah gave moral and financial support to all nationalists, especially those from racist-ruled territories, in the struggle for their birthright. Ghana had become the centre of Pan-Africanism.

But Nkrumah's determination to rid Africa of colonialism, and the strength of his desire to achieve a united Africa, soon brought him enemies both inside and outside Africa. Those people who were incapable of grasping the idea of a liberated

Africa – let alone a united Africa – or who were frightened of losing the 'potential protection' of colonial rule, not only dissociated themselves from his call for a free Africa, but allowed themselves to be used by the colonialists to sabotage Nkrumah's noble aim. Those outside Africa who feared the challenge to their power-base in the colonies and also realized that a united independent Africa would no longer allow itself to be pushed around, fought vigorously to maintain the status quo, and accused Nkrumah of 'inordinate ambition'. They found many ready allies among African leaders. Nevertheless, Pan-Africanism grew from strength to strength, for it appealed to the young and to those educated Africans who were still capable of thinking for themselves. As a result of this those who wanted to fight Pan-Africanism began to back down and a degree of compromise was reached which left Pan-Africanism somewhat emasculated. Hence the OAU was founded in opposition to the idea of a united Africa with a central government put forward by Kwame Nkrumah during the African summit of May 1963.

Nkrumah was fallible, like all men.[38] Perhaps his greatest perennial fault was his propensity to surround himself with flatterers and opportunists, who not only stood between him and the masses, but also fed him with half-truths or downright falsehood in order to please him. Many of these people did not scruple to condemn him at the first opportunity after his overthrow. The lesson to future African leaders is clear. Nkrumah's greatest political fault, however, was his inflexibility. He rejected many of those who were not as immediately enthusiastic as he was on the Pan-African issue, failing to realize that he was almost a century ahead of most of his contemporaries. Had he realized it he would probably have behaved differently, and the course of Pan-Africanism might itself have been somewhat changed. But even if this failing made him many enemies among contemporary African heads of state, it also made him a hero to the young who regarded other leaders, often with justification, as agents of imperialists.

The overthrow of Nkrumah – a result of many forces within and without Africa, as well as of his own mistakes – has robbed Pan-Africanism of one of its most dynamic, charming and dedicated proponents. It will be a long time before anyone can take his place as the symbol of African unity, the chief advocate of a United States of Africa.

(ii) Sékou Touré

Sékou Touré was born at Faranah near the source of the River Niger in January 1922. He began his studies at a Koranic school before going to the primary school. In 1936 he entered the French technical school at Conakry only to be expelled the following year for leading a food strike. Nevertheless, he continued to educate himself, and successfully completed his secondary school education by correspondence. Although not university-trained, he is one of the foremost African intellectuals, eloquent, imaginative, with a clear-cut, coherent and original philosophy.

Sékou Touré started his career in 1940 as an employee of a commercial firm – the Compagnie du Niger Français. In 1941 he passed an examination qualifying him for work in the post and telecommunications organization. His considerable ability and vigorous interest in the labour movement soon earned him the post of secretary-general of the Post, Telegraph and Telephone Workers' Union. He helped to form the Union Cégétiste des Syndicats de Guinée and became its secretary-general in 1946. He joined Guinea's treasury department that same year and was elected secretary-general of the Treasury Employees' Union. His political activities soon brought him into conflict with the French colonial administration, with the result that he not only lost his job but had to spend a brief period in prison in 1947.

After his 'graduation' from prison, Sékou Touré turned his full energies to the trade-union struggle. In 1948 he became secretary-general of Guinea's CGT (General Confederation of Workers) and in 1950 secretary-general of the coordinating committee of the CGT in French Africa and Togoland. He emerged in 1953 as the idol of the Guinean workers after a general strike which lasted seventy-three days. The capitulation of the colonial administration at the end of the strike so pleased youth throughout French Africa that they began to look to

Sékou Touré for a more radical leadership than the RDA had hitherto provided. He founded the Confédération Générale du Travail Africain (CGTA) in April 1956.

Sékou Touré soon became prominent in a wider political field. He was a founder member of the Rassemblement Démocratique Africain (RDA), formed at Bamako in 1946 under the leadership of Félix Houphouet-Boigny, and became in 1952 secretary-general of the Parti Démocratique de Guinée (PDG), the Guinean section of the RDA. He was elected a territorial counsellor for Beyla, Guinea, in 1953; mayor of Conakry in 1955; and a deputy in the French Assembly in January 1956. While a deputy in France he did not hesitate to enter into conflict with the French CGT and the Communist party in order to affirm his Africanism. Unlike some of his colleagues, who spent as much time as they could in Paris, Sékou Touré spent most of his time in Guinea organizing the PDG, advancing the cause of the trade unions, and attacking the feudal system which lent its support to the colonial administration.

At about this time, he was becoming increasingly critical of the RDA leadership, its lukewarm attitude towards African unity and its too pro-French policies which found their expression in the *loi-cadre* of 1956. He spearheaded the call for African unity and for autonomy from French political parties, trade unions, youth organizations, etc. This crusade led to the birth of the Union Générale des Travailleurs d'Afrique Noire (UGTAN) in January 1957 at Cotonou. The UGTAN was meant from the outset to be free of French and international affiliations. It planned 'to unite and organize the workers of black Africa, to co-ordinate their trade union activities in the struggle against the colonial regime and all other forms of exploitation ... and to affirm the personality of African trade unionism'.[39] Such action did not find favour with the RDA leadership, and a crisis within the party resulted. The Bamako Conference of the party held in September 1957 failed to arrive at any clear decision on the issue of African unity. While Sékou Touré, the trade unions and the young people called for the formation of federal executives in both French West and French Equatorial Africa, Houphouet-Boigny advocated the separate

113

political development of these territories. The compromise reached at the Bamako conference only postponed a parting of the ways for the two factions.

On 5 April 1958 the Grand Conseil of French West Africa, under pressure from Sékou Touré, passed a resolution recommending the creation of a federal executive. During the annual congress of the Parti Démocratique de Guinée – the Guinea section of the RDA – held at Conakry in June 1958, Sékou Touré once again advocated that the existing grand conseils of AOF and AEF should be transformed into real legislative assemblies: that both the AOF and AEF should have responsible federal cabinets, which would take over all the functions then exercised by the French high commissioners, and also that the Afro-French Community should unite its component parts under a federal government. Meanwhile, General de Gaulle was occupied with the constitution for the Fifth Republic. This constitution, released in August, ignored the call for the transformation of the existing AOF and AEF into self-governing federations, and instead offered French territories in Africa a choice between total independence (which involved economic rupture) and membership of a French Community. The constitution was severely criticized by Sékou Touré, and de Gaulle was forced to make a few amendments. He offered French African territories, formally balkanized, the option to vote for either autonomy within a new French community or complete independence (with, of course, serious economic consequences).

If by August 1958, when de Gaulle's constitution was released, the line of division within the RDA on the question of African unity and independence had not been clearly drawn, the referendum campaign gave an indication of things to come. While a great many French African leaders were whipping up enthusiasm among their people in order to remain colonial subjects for ever in a nebulous French community, Sékou Touré remained unimpressed by the promise of milk and honey to those choosing to remain French *asimilados*. In contrast to the stage-managed enthusiasm for General de Gaulle in other French African territories during the campaign tour, Guinea showed him the cold shoulder.[40] Speaking in the Territorial

Assembly Sékou Touré made it abundantly clear to the general that nothing short of total decolonization in Africa would satisfy the Guineans, informing him further that 'We prefer poverty in liberty to riches in slavery.' Sékou Touré's determination paid off, and Guinea gained her independence on 2 October 1958. France's subsequent retaliatory measures, intended to cripple the economy of the new state, angered many Africans while Guinea's brave and lonely struggle for survival became an admirable source of inspiration to many Africans.

Decolonization is for Sékou Touré an article of faith. He does not regard independence as an end in itself, but as a means to elevate society materially, spiritually and culturally. He declared in January 1961, after his election as president of Guinea, that Africa could not give up its fight for independence until the continent had been freed of all foreign influences and all foreign armies. He ridiculed those African leaders who collaborated or compromised with the colonial powers.

As a strong advocate of a United States of Africa, he regards the total liberation of Africa as only a first step towards that objective. He has high regard for African culture, expecting it not just to stimulate Africans but also to determine their future course. He is opposed to such Eur-African organizations as seek to perpetuate 'the master and servant mentality', but he favours the establishment of friendly relations between African states and foreign countries, provided, of course, such friendships do not preclude or compromise the development of closer and more friendly relations among African peoples.

Sékou Touré has become perhaps the most influential of contemporary Pan-Africanists. He is a man of dynamic personality and relentless determination, who not only believes that he knows what is good for Africa, but is prepared to pursue his belief, regardless of obstacles. He is selfless, imaginative and energetic, a living example of the type of man Pan-Africa most needs.

(c) The 'Moderates'

The different approaches of African leaders towards Pan-African-ism have made it possible for the foreign powers to label them as 'radicals' or 'moderates', according to the degree of their enthusiasm and involvement. It is nevertheless a fact that the 'moderates' have not all been equally active and the degree of their 'moderation' varies from person to person. For this reason it is worthwhile examining the role of the four leaders – Léopold Senghor, Félix Houphouet-Boigny, Emperor Haile Selassie and Abubakar Tafawa Balewa – who, in their own different ways, have contributed most effectively to the final shaping of Pan-Africanism.

(i) *Léopold Senghor*

Léopold Sédas Senghor was born at Joal, Senegal, on 9 October 1906. He received his primary education at the Catholic school in N'Gesobil, then proceeded to the Lycée in Dakar, where he did brilliantly. After completing his studies there he went to Paris, where he studied at the Lycée Louis-le-Grand, and became the first African to win *agrégation* at the Sorbonne. As a result of this achievement, which qualified him to teach at a lycée, he began his teaching career in Tours in 1935, later transferred to a lycée in Paris and subsequently studied African Languages at the École des Hautes Études. Senghor is a poet of considerable repute. He is passionately interested in African culture and constantly focuses attention on the great accomplish-ments and continuing energy of African art, underlining in his own poetry the beauty of image and rhythm that is so much a part of Africa's literary heritage. In 1947 he joined with Aliounde Diop to establish *Présence africaine*, the magazine which serves as a common African front against cultural colonialism. *Négritude* is one of the concepts he helped forge. He later became Professor of Negro African Languages and Civilization in Paris.

Senghor formed the Bloc Africain with Lamine Gueye in 1945, as the Senegalese section of the French Socialist party

(SFIO). He was elected to the First and Second Constituent Assemblies and played an important part in the framing of the constitutional changes which resulted. Re-elected to the French National Assembly in November 1946, he soon became dissatisfied with the policies of the French Socialist party, and finally left in October 1948 to form his own party, the Bloc Démocratique Sénégalais (BDS). He joined and later became the undisputed leader of the Indépendents d'Outre Mer (IOM), formed by deputies from France's overseas territories who rejected affiliation to any metropolitan political party. He was elected mayor of Thiès in November 1956 and became the president of Senegal after the break-up of the Mali Federation in August 1960.

His advocacy of the transformation of both the AOF and AEF into self-governing federations was strong but unsuccessful. He bitterly opposed the *loi-cadre* of 1956 which finally balkanized French Africa. His opposition to the *loi-cadre* and his belief in federalism were responsible for Senegal's uniting with the Sudanese leaders to form the Mali Federation.

Yet Senghor's approach to Pan-Africanism has been very strange. Apart from the fact that he advocates a 'step by step' approach to what he terms a 'union' of Africans rather than a United States of Africa, it is difficult to connect him with any specific policy. While he passionately advocates *Négritude*, he is wary of any step towards the achievement of African unity. He stands midway between the progressive approach of both Nkrumah and Sékou Touré, and the downright reactionary stand of certain other African leaders. Yet he led Senegal into the Brazzaville camp in 1960. He has never come out boldly in support of any Pan-African move which could have an adverse effect on French interests; but neither has he ever championed any foreign power whose interests have run counter to Pan-Africanism. All in all, Senghor remains something of an enigma and it will not be from following his lead that Pan-Africanism will most surely thrive.

(ii) *Félix Houphouet-Boigny*

Houphouet-Boigny was born at Yamoussokro in the Ivory Coast, in October 1905. He went to school at Bingerville and enrolled at the École de Médicine in Dakar in 1918. Later he served as a medical assistant before becoming a chief in 1940. He also became a plantation owner and made sure that the African planters who were discriminated against received a better deal from the French. He founded and became president of the Syndicat Agricole Africain – a sort of agricultural trade union – of the Ivory Coast in 1944 and led a campaign against forced labour.

He formed the Parti Démocratique de la Côte d'Ivoire (PDCI) in 1945. He was elected president of the Rassemblement Démocratique Africain (RDA) during its inauguration in 1946 and, holding this post, he was, for a long time, to play a significant role in French Africa.

Houphouet-Boigny was elected in November 1945 and June 1946 to the French constituent assemblies. He became a deputy in the French National Assembly after the 1951 general elections. By then he had caused the RDA to sever all its links with the French Communist party. This enhanced the RDA's prestige and it won nine seats to the French National Assembly during the elections of January 1956. Houphouet-Boigny himself became mayor of Abidjan in November 1956. He was also made, as president of the RDA, a cabinet minister in the French Government in 1956, and he remained a member of successive French cabinets until April 1959. As a minister he played a significant role in the framing of the *loi-cadre* of 1956 which gave universal suffrage but laid the foundation for a balkanized Africa. He became, during this period, more French than many Frenchmen and has remained so ever since. Since 1960 he has been president of the Ivory Coast.

Houphouet-Boigny has been an opponent of real decolonization and a strong proponent of a continuing association with France. But he was not strong enough to counter the forces of Pan-Africanism, and circumstances even forced him to demand independence for the Ivory Coast.[41]

In a speech to the French Academy in 1958, made when he was French minister of health, he was happy to declare, in his capacity as president of the RDA, French Africa's decision not to seek 'sterile independence' but continued collaboration with France. He regarded such renunciation of independence as an 'historic choice'.[42] There was widespread yearning for unity in French Africa at that time, however, and this unity was meant to be achieved by transforming both AOF and AEF into real self-governing federations instead of the balkanization projected by the *loi-cadre*. But he was opposed to any such yearning and used his influence in the French Government to thwart it.[43] His first step in this direction was the mobilization of the Ivory Coast against the motion adopted by the Grand Conseil of the AOF on 5 April 1958 demanding the setting-up of a federal executive. He achieved this only a few days afterwards, when the Ivory Coast territorial assembly unanimously rejected the Grand Conseil motion and declared in a motion of its own that the Ivory Coast would never join any federal government set up at Dakar. The motion went on to declare that the Ivory Coast would continue to press for an Afro-French federation whose constituent members would comprise France and individual African territories. Shortly afterwards, Houphouet-Boigny declared in Paris that 'he was delighted that the Ivory Coast had decided to unite its culture and economy with France its colonizing country'.[44] As soon as the constitution submitted by General de Gaulle for a referendum was released in 1958 Houphouet-Boigny made sure that not only the Ivory Coast but other French territories also should vote for it. When Guinea voted against it and automatically became independent, its leaders were summarily expelled from the RDA, of which Félix Houphouet-Boigny was still the president.[45]

Houphouet-Boigny has also been antagonistic to the idea of African unity. He has claimed that a United States of Africa will never materialize. It could, according to him, only lead to communism.[46] During the three-day special congress of the RDA held at Abidjan in September 1959, he strongly attacked Pan-Africanism, but spoke warmly in favour of Franco-African solidarity. He claimed that it was more fruitful to support an

Evolution

Afro-French community – a 'multi-national and inter-continental grouping with a parliament' – than Pan-Africanism.[47]
His disregard for Pan-Africanism was demonstrated again in
November 1959. Leading the French delegation to the UN in
that year, he was received by both President Eisenhower and
the US Secretary of State, Mr Christian Herter, and was
reported to have assured the US Government that all the
member states of the French Community approved the proposed
French explosion of an atomic bomb in the Sahara. That was
just a few months after the foreign ministers of the independent
African states had condemned the proposed French test at their
Monrovia Conference of August 1959. During that very tour of
America he reiterated to the American Press his belief that
African unity would never be achieved.[48]

He was the brain behind the formation of the Brazzaville bloc
which formed its own caucus at the UN during the sixteenth
session of the UNGA and refused to support other African
states in their moves at the UN during the Congo crisis. Besides,
its member states 'shared a desire to remain on the friendliest
terms with France ... were seeking compromise solutions to
both the Congo and Algerian crises'. They were also 'united in
their opposition to political unions among independent African
states, and though they favoured the closest co-operation with
each other, they all favoured Houphouet's lead in claiming that
common political institutions in independent Africa were both
risky and reckless'.[49] The bloc dominated the Monrovia Conference of May 1961, which resolved that 'the unity that is aimed
to be achieved at the moment is not the political integration of
sovereign African states, but unity of aspirations ...' and
endorsed what later became the cardinal points of all subsequent
African gatherings: absolute equality of African states, respect
for the sovereignty of each state, and so on.[50] The attempt to
bring the Monrovia and the Casablanca groups together at the
Lagos African summit of January 1962 failed because the
Brazzaville group led by the Ivory Coast refused to allow the
admission of the Algerian provisional government.[51]

Houphouet-Boigny's attitude towards Pan-Africanism is
succinctly summarized thus by Guy de Lusignan:

During this period [1961–2], Houphouet-Boigny showed his lack of concern for all the discussions and conferences about African Unity. Sometimes he attended and paid lip-service to the cause, thus reinforcing it for such was his prestige. However, he would not commit himself and was less active on the international stage than several of his colleagues.[52]

Even after the OAU had been founded, Houphouet-Boigny did not abandon his belief that African unity would never be achieved. He has recently made himself the champion of what he terms a 'dialogue' with South Africa on the apartheid issue, knowing full well that such a course can only prove futile and will also cause disunity within Pan-Africa.

(iii) Emperor Haile Selassie

Emperor Haile Selassie, formerly known as Lij Tafari Makonnen, was born on 23 July 1893 at Harar. He began his education in Amharic and the Coptic Christian faith before going on to the French Roman Catholic mission school in Harar at the age of five. He started learning French at the age of seven and then went on to learn English. When Emperor Menelik II of Ethiopia heard about the boy's remarkable gifts, he ordered that Lij Tafari Makonnen be brought to Addis Ababa in order to continue his education there.

Before long, at the age of fourteen, he was appointed governor of Gara Huleta in Harar Province. He was summoned to the imperial court in 1906 when his father died, and was made governor of Sidamo province, where he displayed an administrative ability that was to prove an asset to him when he became the governor of his home province, Harar, in 1910. He became the chief adviser, regent and heir apparent, when Princess Zauditu became empress in 1916 after a coup d'état had deposed Lij Yasu, who succeeded Menelik II in 1913. As chief adviser to the empress, he reorganized the country, building more schools and hospitals, and seeing that many young Ethiopians were sent to study abroad. Through his efforts Ethiopia became a member of the League of Nations in 1923 and abolished the slave trade the following year. He became king in October 1928 and was crowned in April 1930. In 1931 he introduced a written constitution establishing a parliament with advisory powers.

When Italy suddenly attacked Ethiopia in 1935 the emperor directed the military resistance personally, and with great courage, for a whole year before going into exile in 1936. He returned to Ethiopia in May 1941.

Although the emperor had not taken the initiative on Pan-Africanism, once he embraced it he did his utmost to reconcile the most enthusiastic and the most conservative wings of the movement. He put forward in June 1960 the proposals for setting up an African development bank, and told the Lagos Conference of January 1962 that the gulf between the Casablanca and Monrovia groups was not as wide as some people thought, for both were aiming at the same thing: African unity. From then on he personally ascertained that all African heads of state would attend the next African summit. His efforts resulted in the Addis Ababa summit of May 1963.

Addressing that summit, Emperor Haile Selassie declared:

> Through all that has been said and written and done in these years there runs a common theme. Unity is the accepted goal. We argue about means; we discuss tactics. But when semantics are stripped away, there is little argument among us. We are determined to create a union of Africans. In a very real sense, our continent is unmade; it still awaits its creation and its creators. It is our duty and privilege to rouse the slumbering giant of Africa, not to the nationalism of Europe of the nineteenth century, not to regional consciousness but to the vision of a single African brotherhood bending its united efforts toward the achievement of a greater and nobler goal ... But while we agree that the ultimate destiny of the continent lies in political union, we must, at the same time, recognise that the obstacles to be overcome in its achievement are at once numerous and formidable.[53]

It was largely owing to his efforts that the summit was able to adopt the Charter of the Organization of African Unity. He has become in a traditional African way the head of Pan-Africanism, and he has played this role with considerable wisdom and industry.

(iv) *Abubakar Tafawa Balewa*

The late Alhaji Sir Abubakar Tafawa Balewa was born at Bauchi, Nigeria, in 1912. He started his education at the local school before going on to the Bauchi provisional school, where he completed his primary education. From 1928 to 1933 he attended Katsina Teachers Training College, and later became a teacher at the Bauchi middle school. He continued with his studies privately until he had passed the Senior Teachers' Certificate examination. Then, in 1945, he went to London to study for the Teachers' Professional Certificate at the London University Institute of Education. On his return to Nigeria he became a native authority education officer.

Shortly after his return from Britain, Sir Abubakar was appointed a member of the Northern Region House of Assembly, from where he was unanimously elected to the Nigerian legislative council. He played a significant role in the establishment, and was elected vice-president, of the Northern Peoples' Congress. In 1951 he was elected to the Northern House of Assembly and from there to the Federal House of Representatives, becoming the Nigerian Federal minister of works in 1952 and minister of transport in 1955. He was the Federal prime minister from 1957 until 15 January 1966, when he was assassinated during a coup d'état.

Sir Abubakar was by nature a gradualist who believed that 'drastic change makes people unhappy'.[54] This cautious outlook, which characterized his internal politics, also affected his approach to Pan-Africanism. The total failure of the Nigerian leaders to achieve 'unity in diversity' – a failure which led to 'tribal politics' scarcely paralleled on the African continent – also exerted a cautionary effect. Asked once for his opinion on the yearning throughout Africa for a United States of Africa, he replied:

I think we are not yet ready for it. . . We in Nigeria have so many other pressing problems to solve . . . First we have to put our house in order and create prosperity in our own country . . . The recently widely discussed plan for a United States of Africa will only create new problems. Nigeria still needs many decades to attain the level of

123

other countries. Our most pressing problems are here and only here.[55]

This attitude may seem selfish but one must remember that Nigeria was not blessed with a leader of Nkrumah's calibre who could unite the country at home and lead her on to play a dynamic role in Pan-Africanism.

Nevertheless, by virtue of her large population, Nigeria was expected by a great many people all over the world to take an active, indeed a leading, role in the quest for African unity. Torn between this expectation and the actual Nigerian political situation, Sir Abubakar was forced to change his opinion on Pan-Africanism. His first step was to urge Sylvanus Olympio of Togo to act as an intermediary between French-speaking and English-speaking African states, so that they might be brought together to work towards the achievement of Pan-African ideals. This move, albeit a cautious one, led to the Monrovia Conference of May 1961.[56]

Sir Abubakar was always opposed to any demand for immediate political union. He advocated instead a functional approach to African unity. Addressing the African summit of May 1963, he reiterated this approach, thus:

There have been quite a lot of views on what we mean by African Unity. Some of us have suggested that African Unity should be achieved by political fusion of the different states in Africa; some of us feel that African Unity could be achieved by taking practical steps in economic, educational, scientific and cultural co-operation, and by trying first to get the Africans to understand themselves before embarking on the more complicated and more difficult arrangement of political union. *My country stands for the practical approach to the unity of the African continent.*[57]

Notwithstanding the caution of such an approach, Sir Abubakar always took a firm stand on other Pan-African issues. He made Nigeria break off diplomatic relations with France over the French atomic blasts in the Sahara, consistently demanded strong action against the South African racist régime and its apartheid policy, and spoke on several occasions for the total liberation of Africa from colonialism. But his 1965 Lagos Conference on the Rhodesian UDI, after the OAU had called on all its members to sever diplomatic relations with Britiain if she failed to take strong measures to bring the rebel régime to an end, cast some doubts on his integrity with regard to the issue of liberation.

Notes to Chapter 3

1. Edmund D. Cronon, *Black Moses*.
2. Marcus Garvey, *Philosophy and Opinions*, Vol. II, p. 126.
3. ibid.
4. Cronon, *Black Moses*, p. 18.
5. Garvey, *Philosophy and Opinions*, Vol. II, p. 128.
6. The eight UNIA Conventions were held as follows:

First	New York	August 1920
Second	New York	August 1921
Third	New York	August 1922
Fourth	New York	August 1923
Fifth	New York	August 1924
Sixth	Kingston, Jamaica	August 1929
Seventh	Kingston, Jamaica	August 1934
Eighth	Toronto, Canada	August 1938

7. Quoted from Cronon, *Black Moses*, p. 60.
8. The US Government, which, to say the least, had misgivings about the UNIA, lost no time in discrediting the organization. The FBI, for example, could, it was said, easily uncover 'evidence of a nation-wide anarchistic plot' by the organization early in 1923 (see *New York Times*, 20 January 1923). There are resemblances between the case of Angela Davis and that of Marcus Garvey, in many respects.
9. Garvey, *Philosophy and Opinions*, Vol. I, p. 32.
10. ibid., p. 52.
11. Quote from Cronon, *Black Moses*, p. 124.
12. *Negro World*, 6 November 1920.
13. See US State Dept Files 882.00/705, National Archives, for a copy of the Memorandum of an interview between Liberian officials and UNIA delegates, 22 March 1921.
14. Letter of 2 May 1924 from James J. Dossen, Monrovia, to UNIA, New York, reproduced in Garvey, *Philosophy and Opinions*, Vol. II, pp. 378–9.
15. Blaise Diagne to Marcus Garvey, 3 July 1922, quoted in Charpin, 'La Question noire', *Revue indigne*, XVII, p. 281. See also R. L. Buell, *The Native Problem in Africa*, New York, 1928, Vol. II, p. 732.
16. See W. E. B. DuBois, *The World and Africa*, pp. 5–10.
17. See US State Dept Files 682.11253 and also 811.108G191/37 and 38 for

the diplomatic notes of 31 July and 8 August 1924 from the Liberian
authority to the US Government; also Buell, *The Native Problem in
Africa*, Vol. II, p. 732.

18. See 'Message of the President of Liberia', C. D. B. King, quoted in
Buell, *The Native Problem in Africa*, Vol. II, p. 732.
19. For information on the Firestone Concession see *West Africa*, 24 October
1925, pp. 1384–5, *African World*, 28 November 1925, p. 5, ibid., 31
December 1925, p. 5.
20. Cronon, *Black Moses*, p. 133.
21. The circumstances of Garvey's imprisonment tempt one to think about
those surrounding the imprisonment of George Jackson and of his subsequent murder in suspicious circumstances on 21 August 1971 at the San
Quentin jail.
22. Cronon, *Black Moses*, p. 148.
23. *New York Times*, 7 February 1925, quoted from Cronon, *Black Moses*,
p. 136.
24. See *Crisis*, Vol. 20, and Cronon, *Black Moses*, p. 209.
25. Francis L. Broderick, *W. E. B. DuBois – Negro Leader in a Time of Crisis*,
Stanford University Press, Stanford, 1959, p. 91.
26. DuBois, 'The Immediate Program of the American Negro', in *Crisis*,
Vol. 9, April 1915, pp. 310–12.
27. Broderick, *W. E. B. DuBois – Negro Leader in a Time of Crisis*, p. 102.
28. ibid.
29. loc. cit., p. 129. See also DuBois, *Africa and the World*, pp. 8–10.
30. This was manifest in all his comments on Marcus Garvey's UNIAC.
Even DuBois's plan for an 'internationalized Africa' bore testimony to
this; according to him only the 'educated' people were 'civilized', and as
a result of this they should not be confused with the majority of his race.
See DuBois, *The World and Africa*, pp. 8–10.
31. See DuBois, *The World and Africa*; see also DuBois, *Color and Democracy: Colonies and Peace*, pp. 18–25.
32. *Ghana – the Autobiography of Kwame Nkrumah*, p. 37.
33. Nkrumah, *I Speak of Freedom*, Heinemann, London, 1961, p. 29.
34. ibid., p. 48.
35. ibid., p. 71.
36. ibid., p. 98.
37. ibid., p. 107.
38. Many people have accused Nkrumah of being too ruthless with his political opponents in Ghana. But he was forced to introduce strong measures
to curb the excesses of an opposition whose methods included assassination, and one would like to know what else he could have done in the
circumstances. It is also interesting to note that those Western demo-
cracies who have accused him of ruthlessness have turned a blind eye to
the same methods being employed in African countries whose leaders
have made themselves the willing tools of those forces bent on sabotaging
the drive towards African unity.

39. Quoted from Ronald Segal, *African Profiles*, Penguin Books, Harmonds-worth, 1963, p. 310.
40. For a full report on the campaign tour of General de Gaulle in Africa see *West Africa*, 6 September 1958, p. 843.
41. See Segal, *African Profiles*, p. 287; Franz Fanon, *Toward the African Revolution*, Penguin Books, Harmondsworth, 1970, p. 128; I. William Zartman, *International Relations in the New Africa*, Prentice Hall, Engle-wood Cliffs, pp. 13–22.
42. See *West Africa*, 25 January 1958, p. 74.
43. See K. M. Panikkar, *Revolution in Africa*, Asia Books, London, 1961, pp. 48–52.
44. *West Africa*, 19 April 1958, p. 366.
45. See *West Africa*, 18 October 1958, p. 993.
46. See *Tanganyika Standard*, 9 December 1958.
47. *West Africa*, 19 September 1959, p. 706.
48. *West Africa*, 21 November 1959, p. 993.
49. Segal, *African Profiles*, pp. 287–8.
50. See Appendix 3 for the Resolutions of the Monrovia Conference.
51. For Houphouet-Boigny's role during the Algerian War of Independence see Franz Fanon, *Toward the African Revolution*, pp. 128–9.
52. Guy de Lusignan, *French-Speaking Africa since Independence*, Pall Mall Press, London, 1969, pp. 139–40.
53. Quoted from V. B. Thompson, *Africa and Unity*, pp. 182–3.
54. *West Africa*, 16 January 1965, p. 59.
55. Rolf Italiaander, *The New Leaders of Africa*, Prentice-Hall, London, 1961, pp. 196–7.
56. Russell Warren Howe, *Black Africa*, pp. 342–4.
57. *Mr Prime Minister – a Selection of Speeches made by Alhaji the Rt Hon. Sir Abubakar Tafawa Balewa*, pp. 94–5.

Part Two: Progress and Problems

4. Achievements

The dawn is here, my brother, dawn! Look in our faces,
A new morning breaks in our old Africa,
Ours only will now be the land, the water, mighty rivers
Poor Negro was surrendering for a thousand years.
And hard torches of the sun will shine for us again
They'll dry the tears in eyes and spittle on your face.
The moment when you break the chains, the heavy fetters,
The evil, cruel times will go never to come again.

PATRICE LUMUMBA
25 January 1961 *
Leopoldville
Congo

(a) Before 1963

The foremost achievement of Pan-Africanism before 1963 was
the mutual involvement which began to emerge in the political,
social and cultural life of the African continent. There can be
no doubt that Pan-Africanism has engendered a feeling of
African-ness. Anything that affects any part of Africa is looked
upon by a significant number of Africans as affecting them all.
Anyone who finds this hard to believe should look back through
the African newspapers at the time of the murder of Patrice
Lumumba in 1961. Even before that shocking incident, however,
there had been major events which equally aroused African
passion. Among these were the British and French adventure of
1956, which became known as the Suez War; the treatment of
Africans in Kenya, which subsequently led to the 'Mau Mau'
uprising; the imposed Central African Federation, doomed to
failure from the very beginning; and, of course, the Algerian
War of Independence. During all these hard times, Africans
from territories not directly concerned were nonetheless passionately involved. When, as in the case of the Suez crisis, they

*Part of a poem Lumumba composed and sent to a friend in India a few
days before he was assassinated by Moise Tshombe. The poem is reproduced
from *West African Pilot*, Lagos, 6 May 1961.

could not render any tangible assistance, they nevertheless followed the course of the war with the keenest interest and were overjoyed when the imperialist forces met with a reverse. During the trial of the leaders of the 'Mau Mau' uprising, Nigerian lawyers were among those who went to Kenya as defence counsel, and African nationalists from the imposed Central African Federation received moral support from fellow Africans in other parts of the continent. If it had not been for Pan-Africanism there would have been no such support: not because other Africans would have been indifferent, but because the sense of being one people would not have been strong enough.

Ghana's independence and its subsequent avant-garde role in the Pan-African movement became something to be envied, and possibly rivalled. It had an impact on the independence drive of other British colonies in Africa that no leader from any of these territories could honestly deny. And the resolutions of each of the Pan-African conferences after 1957 condemning colonialism had an incalculable bearing on the 'wind of change'.

After both Tunisia and Morocco had become independent, Guinea too chose freedom. Her courage and the fact of her survival, despite the odds against her, had a damaging effect on the French colonial empire in Africa. Guinea's example, followed in the next year by demands for independence from Cameroon, Togo and the Mali Federation, had such an effect that even the stronghold of French Africa in territories like the Ivory Coast gave way before the forces of Pan-Africanism. Where, as in the Belgian Congo, the colony was kept under absolute paternalistic and arbitrary control, the forces of Pan-Africanism compelled the colonial power to abdicate.

The sudden achievement of independence by so many African territories within so short a period of time is quite clearly an achievement of Pan-Africanism and a good augur. No amount of dictatorial decrees can finally suppress the efforts of the forces of Pan-Africanism to liberate the remaining dependent territories in Africa. Equally, no amount of legislation, passed by any group of desperate racist rebels, can prevent Pan-Africanism from ultimately achieving independence in the remaining strong-holds of racism. Everyone is aware that the way will be rough, and realizing this, the forces of Pan-Africanism have adopted the motto 'No Cross, No Crown'.

(b) After 1963

With the establishment of the Organization of African Unity, a new era in the course of Pan-Africanism began. Concrete practical steps were taken in order to achieve the much-needed cooperation. Efforts were concentrated mostly in the economic, political, social and educational fields and we shall now examine the achievements of Pan-Africanism in these areas.

I. ECONOMIC COOPERATION

Africans have had to ask a number of different questions in order to find the most effective way towards an economic co-operation which in itself would accelerate the much-needed economic development of the continent. Should economic co-operation be started at a regional level? How should Africa be planned industrially? How can staff as yet unqualified be quickly trained? What should be done to make the best use of the present meagre qualified manpower? All these questions were asked and more. When the Economic and Social Commission held its first meeting it produced the guidelines whereby most of them could be answered.

(i) African Development Bank

One of the most significant achievements in the economic field has been the establishment of the African Development Bank. The idea of establishing such a bank was first made by Emperor Haile Selassie of Ethiopia during the second Conference of Independent African States in 1960, and subsequently received universal support. The Addis Ababa Summit of 1963 endorsed,

133

therefore, an ECA plan to convene a conference of African ministers of finance at Khartoum in July 1963, with a view to setting up an African development bank. When the meeting was held, detailed proposals on the project were submitted by a committee of nine, consisting of Cameroon, Ethiopia, Guinea, Liberia, Mali, Nigeria, Sudan, Tanganyika and Tunisia. By the end of 1963 the agreement establishing the bank had been ratified by most African states and it came into force on 10 September 1964.[1]

The bank's chief purpose is to contribute to the economic and social development of its member countries, both individually and jointly. In order to achieve this, the bank promotes the investment of public and private capital in Africa; uses its own resources to make or guarantee loans or equity investments; and encourages private investment in member countries. It cooperates with these countries in order to ensure better utilization of their resources, by making their economies increasingly complementary and by providing technical assistance in the preparation, financing and implementation of development plans and projects. The bank, in accordance with its statute, may grant direct or indirect credits; operate alone or in concert with other financial institutions or sources; help formulate projects and loan applications, whether for submission to the bank itself or to other lending agencies.

The initial authorized capital of the bank consists of 25,000 shares, equivalent to $250 million. Half the capital stock is paid-up, while the other half is callable, each member state having to subscribe equally to both. The number of votes on its board of governors for each state is calculated on the basis of each country's capital subscription. Each country has 625 votes, plus one vote for each $10,000 share of capital. By 30 June 1969, out of the subscribed capital, $108 million had been called, and, $59·3 million received in convertible currencies.

In order to avoid a situation in which only those African countries which are comparatively rich can afford to borrow from the bank, it is working on a 'special programme for relatively less developed member countries'. This is closely linked with the real solution to the problem of availability of capital: the establishment of an African development fund, contributions to which will be open to non-members. Discussions were held with the United States on the details of a possible contribution of $60 million over a three-year period, and Britain, the Netherlands, Denmark, Finland, Norway and Sweden also expressed their willingness to contribute.

In addition, the bank is actively promoting a multi-national private finance company which would make capital, entrepreneurship and management expertise available to profitable enterprise in African countries. Interest has already been shown in the project by companies and banks in Britain, Japan and the United States of America.

The bank participated in financing the 1,250-mile-long railway which will run from Kampyo in Zambia to Kidatu and Dar es Salaam in Tanzania. It approved three loans in 1968: for irrigation in Tunisia, for engineering studies of water supply and sewerage schemes in Uganda, and the sum of $408,000 to Société Ivoriène d'Engrais in the Ivory Coast to meet part of the funds required for construction of a fertilizer plant to serve the local market and possibly that of the Upper Volta. Total loans committed by the bank stood at $11 million at the end of 1968: this figure included $120,000 for the Sierra Leone National Development Bank, and $1·35 million for the foreign exchange costs of a gas turbine for the Monrovia electric power system.[2]

The bank organized a conference on insurance and reinsurance at Abidjan in June 1970 which agreed to set up a regional insurance and reinsurance body responsible for developing insurance at national level, encouraging cooperation among national insurers and reinsurers, and increasing the continent's insurance capacity.[3]

(ii) L'Organisation Commune Africaine et Malgache (OCAM)

It took some time before the OAU member states endorsed the establishment of regional economic associations as a step towards the final objective of creating an African common market. The initial controversies on this important step centred on the activities of the Union Africaine et Malgache (UAM), then more or less constituting itself within the OAU as a 'state within a state'. But when this organization of the French-speaking African states had reconstituted itself so as to concern itself only with economic matters, the way was clear. At the summit conference held at Kinshasa in 1967, a resolution was adopted on regional economic groupings,[4] encouraging all OAU member states to form them with the final objective of the economic integration of the continent. Other OAU resolutions, such as the resolution on inter-African cooperation[5] and the resolution on industrialization,[6] were in the same direction. The final go-ahead was given in a resolution on 'regional groupings and market integration' adopted by the council at Algiers in 1968. This resolution declared that the 'widening of regional groups is one of the prerequisites for the economic integration of the continent'.[7]

Since then several regional economic groupings have been formed. The most significant among them are OCAM (L'Organisation Commune Africaine et Malgache); UDEAC (L'Union Douanière et Économique de l'Afrique Centrale; UEAC (L'Union des États d'Afrique Centrale); the East African Economic Community; and OERS (L'Organisation des États Riverains du Sénégal). Among them all, OCAM appears, at the moment, to be the most successful.[8]

FROM UAM TO OCAM
THE UNION AFRICAINE ET MALGACHE (UAM)

In December 1960 twelve of the former French territories in Africa – Cameroon, the Central African Republic, Chad, Congo (Brazzaville), Dahomey, Gabon, the Ivory Coast, Madagascar, Mauritania, Niger, Senegal and the Upper Volta – met at Brazzaville to discuss ways of coordinating their political and economic policies. In September 1961 these states, known as the Brazzaville group, formed the Union Africaine et Malgache (UAM) as an organization for political collaboration. There were three reasons for the Brazzaville grouping. First, these countries felt that unless they joined forces they would not be able to make any impact either in Africa or on the wider international scene against the increasing criticism of the other African states. Secondly, they felt the need to band together in order to negotiate their relationship to France and the European Economic Community (whose associate members they were). Thirdly, there was a certain nostalgia among them, stronger than among the former British territories in West Africa, for a renewal of some of the links which had united them during the colonial régime. As a result, UAM became the first organization in Africa to be formed with mainly defensive aims.

The heads of state, the supreme decision-making organ of the organization, met half-yearly. There was a secretary-general to direct a fairly elaborate secretariat, with publicity, research, cultural and administrative departments. Specialized bodies included the Union Africaine et Malgache de Défense (UAMD) responsible for military matters; the Organization Africaine et Malgache de Co-opération Économique (OAMCE), chiefly concerned with economic matters; the Union Africaine et Malgache des Postes et Télécommunications, in charge of postal services; and Air Afrique.

It may be argued that an organization of this nature should have been encouraged by other OAU members, rather than attacked by them. Various reasons, however, were responsible for the call that it disband. The member states constituted a distinct group in two respects. First, they showed in their relations with non-African countries a marked preference for continuing a close relationship with France – the former colonial power. Although other African countries also retained relations of this kind, those of the UAM states were exceptional 'because of the degree of confidence shown in the former colonial power, the comprehensive character of the agreements with that power, the extent to which these continue previous arrangements, and the relatively few counter-balancing agreements with other outside powers'.[9] Secondly, in their relations with other African states, they insisted that each state must retain its own sovereign independence and act upon its own responsibility. They thus ruled out the possibility of any closer union in the foreseeable future.

To justify their closer association with the former colonial power, the UAM spokesmen argued that the African states could not attain the rapid social and economic development to

which they all aspired without entering into outside commitments; and that, in their case, the former colonial power had
most to offer. They maintained that colonization, for all its evils,
had brought Africa into contact with the techniques and the
resources of Western industrialized society and that, with the
attainment of independence, Africans should not deny themselves contacts which could be exploited for their own material
and cultural benefit. They admitted that the ex-colonial powers
still sought to further their own particular interests and also
that occasions would arise when these conflicted with African
interests. But they wanted each African state to be its own
judge. They claimed that their close association with the former
colonial power was to their advantage and they stressed that this
association in no way adversely affected the interests of other
African states, or belittled African unity. They thought that as
long as African states remained poorly developed, they had in
fact little to offer one another, and they claimed that African
states could best contribute to one another's progress by establishing whatever outside relations would promote their own
internal development, and by concerting their policies whenever
this seemed desirable. In this way, they added, African solidarity
would be expressed without prejudice to social and economic
advancement.

Other African leaders found this unacceptable. They maintained that no African country could afford to be so closely
associated with any outside power, especially the former colonial
power dominated by capitalist interests; for this could only
result in continued dependence and exploitation. Moreover,
they argued, progress towards African unity was impossible for
as long as any African state remained closely aligned with any
outside power, since Africa would thereby be subjected to the
divisions which beset the outside world, notably the struggle
between the communist and capitalist powers. They therefore
felt that African states should emphasize their independence,
their neutrality, their own distinct culture and their unity.[10]

Furthermore, they pointed out that the UAM states had their
own separate group at the United Nations, in spite of the fact
that an African bloc there was already in existence.

In July 1963, the heads of state in the UAM met at Cotonou to discuss the future role of their organization in the light of the establishment of the Organization of African Unity. President Yameogo of the Upper Volta proposed, in his opening address, that the UAM should be dissolved, after he had made it abundantly clear that 'an affirmation of the UAM's solidarity with African Unity' was not enough.[11] But, instead of disbanding the organization, it was decided to admit a new member – Togo. The decision not to wind up the affairs of the organization was severely criticized by President Sékou Touré of Guinea, as well as by the Nigerian minister for foreign affairs, Jaja Wachuku. Sékou Touré said that the UAM tended to drain the Charter of African Unity of its essential dynamic content. At the meeting of the Council of Ministers of the Organization of African Unity held at Dakar in August 1963, the decision of the UAM summit conference not to disband the organization also came under fire. Nigeria, supported by Guinea, proposed a motion calling for its disbandment. The foreign ministers of the UAM states argued that the OAU charter in no way prevented member states from forming regional associations of their own: provided that these respected the objectives laid down in the charter, and were based not on political but on geographical, economic, social and cultural considerations. No agreement was reached on whether or not the organization should remain in existence.[12]

In March 1964 another conference of the heads of state in the UAM took place at Dakar. It was decided at this meeting to dissolve the organization: but, at the same time, to form another organization, known as the UAMCE.

UAMCE

The Union Africaine et Malgache pour la Co-opération Économique (UAMCE) was to pursue those objectives of the old UAM which were not incompatible with and did not duplicate those of the Organization of African Unity. It had its headquarters in Yaounde, Cameroon, where the OAMCE (Organisation Africaine et Malgache de Co-opération Économique) – responsible for economic matters – was already situated. Other specialized bodies of the UAM–UAMPT (Union Africaine et Malgache des Postes et Télécommunications) and Air Afrique – would continue to exist. The UAMD (Union Africaine et Malgache de Défense) was to be 'adapted' to the new situation.

The charter of the new organization was signed in May 1964 at Nouakchott, Mauritania, by the foreign ministers of Cameroon, Chad, Congo (Brazzaville), Dahomey, Gabon, Madagascar, Mauritania, Rwanda, Senegal and Togo. The remaining four member states of the UAM – the Central African Republic, Ivory Coast, Niger and Upper Volta – were not present and did not, therefore, sign. The preamble of the charter underlined the desire of the fourteen member states to assure the solid foundations of the Organization of African Unity in accordance with the principles laid down at the OAU Council of Ministers' conference of August 1963. It also underlined the success of the UAM economic organization – the OAMCE – by evoking the historic, economic and cultural link which bound the fourteen member states. The organization aimed to raise the living standards of member countries and provide close cooperation and coordination of development plans. Its main organs were the conference of heads of state, a council of ministers, a secretariat and seven technical committees.

There was no time to assess the value of this new organization, since it was displaced in the following year by yet another organization, the Organisation Commune Africaine et Malgache (OCAM).

L'ORGANISATION COMMUNE AFRICAINE ET MALGACHE (OCAM)

The heads of state of the Union Africaine et Malgache pour la Co-opération Économique (UAMCE) met at Nouakchott in February 1965. At the end of their conference, they announced that the UAMCE had been transformed into a new organization, to be known as the Organisation Commune Africaine et Malgache (OCAM). According to the final communiqué, OCAM was to be 'an African group whose goal, in the context of the OAU, is to reinforce cooperation and solidarity among the African and Malagasy States, in order to accelerate their development in the political, economic, social, technical and cultural domains'. The charter of OCAM was signed by the fourteen member states – Cameroon, the Central African Republic, Chad, Congo (Brazzaville), Congo (Kinshasa), Dahomey, Gabon, the Ivory Coast, Madagascar, Niger, Rwanda, Senegal, Togo and the Upper Volta – at Tananarive on 27 June 1965.

The charter provides for three institutions: the Conference of Heads of State and Government, the Council of Ministers, and a secretariat. The Conference of Heads of State and Government, which is the supreme institution of the organization, meets in ordinary session once a year. The Council of Ministers, composed of the foreign ministers of member states, is answerable to the conference and responsible for cooperation between member states according to directives received from the conference. It too meets in ordinary session once a year. The secretariat, situated at Yaounde, is responsible for administration. It is headed by a secretary-general who is appointed for two years by the Conference of Heads of State on the advice of the Council of Ministers.

Some members of the Organization of African Unity have severely criticized OCAM for its activities in the political field. Its role in the Congo crisis and the refusal of eight of its members to attend the 1965 Accra Summit Conference of the Organization of African Unity were particularly mentioned. These activities seemed to confirm the fear that the organization was usurping or duplicating the activities of the OAU. Besides this, the decision of the eight OCAM members not to attend the Accra summit indicated that the group was acting rather similarly to the various blocs at the United Nations. OCAM was also criticized on the grounds that its leaders seemed to value it more than they did the Organization of African Unity. The OCAM leaders, particularly Presidents Senghor of Senegal, Hamani Diori of Niger and Ahidjo of Cameroon, insisted that this was not so. They pointed out that OCAM was complementary to the OAU, rather than its rival.

Since then the criticisms have died down, and OCAM itself has concentrated its activities on purely economic matters. It has also contributed greatly to the search for African unity by mediating in disputes among member states. This change has been endorsed by the OAU, whose secretary-general, Diallo Telli, has attended most of OCAM's summit conferences since January 1968. At the summit conference of the OAU held at Algiers in September 1968, OCAM was granted observer status with the OAU. Mauritius was admitted to the organization in January 1969.

The record of OCAM in the economic field is very encouraging. It has a well-organized and well-run postal and telecommunications system. Its air service – Air Afrique – jointly owned by most of its members, cooperates with both Air Congo, owned by Congo (Kinshasa), and Air Madagascar, owned by another member of the organization. It has set up a common market for sugar and meat in order to increase the yield of both products as well as improve their quality, and a veterinary college is to be set up at Fakar. The member states have agreed to the setting-up of joint institutions for technical cooperation and the training of young leaders and they have agreed too on free access for itinerant workers moving between states, as well as on attempts to prevent work accidents. The member states cooperate in fiscal matters, and their statisticians meet regularly. OCAM came out in support of the African Groundnut Council in its efforts to convene a world oil agreement meeting.

2. SETTLEMENT OF BOUNDARY DISPUTES

In the course of international relations, border conflicts and irredentist movements have been causes of friction and even of war between nations. They have, therefore, been major determinants of national attitudes towards alliances and armaments in Europe. The unification of Germany and the subsequent settlement of the Franco–German border in the nineteenth century contributed to the pattern of alliances and the armaments race that led to the First World War.[13] In more recent times, boundary disputes have been the causes of conflict between China and the Soviet Union, China and India, India and Pakistan. It is, therefore, not surprising that such disputes have led to the most explosive conflicts of interest in Africa; particularly as these boundaries are colonial legacies.

There are a number of boundary disputes in Africa, some serious, others less so and they range from those that affect no more than a few metres, to others that cover vast territories. While some, like the Nigerian–Cameroonian border dispute, have been peacefully and quietly settled, others have flared up into armed conflict. The containment and subsequent settlement of such conflicts have been among the most significant achievements of Pan-Africanism in recent years.

Boundary disputes have been among the causes of war between Algeria and Morocco, as well as between Somalia and Ethiopia, and have led to a series of raids along the border area between Somalia and Kenya. It was also a boundary dispute that led to a rupture of relations between Niger and Dahomey. In all these cases, the Organization of African Unity stepped in to mediate between the conflicting parties. Its immediate action led to the cessation of hostilities and, consequently, to the normalization of relations between the parties concerned.

(i) *The Algerian–Moroccan Dispute*

A few months after the Organization of African Unity had been founded in May 1963, war broke out between Algeria and Morocco over a boundary dispute that had been dragging on between these countries for some time. Its origins lay in a Franco–Moroccan judgement, itself descended from the 1845 Treaty of Lalla Maghnia, that there was no need for a border demarcation because 'a country which is found without water is uninhabitable and a delimitation thereof would be superfluous'.[14] Independent Morocco decided after 1956 to await the independence of Algeria before finally drawing a border between the countries, since the bilateral commission set up by Morocco and France had failed to reach any settlement. Indeed, between 1956 and 1960, the commission rarely met. In May 1958 Morocco and France agreed to constitute a no-man's-land in the Algerian–Moroccan frontier region, after an incident involving

Moroccan and French troops in the area. Consultations took place over the border issue between the Algerian provisional government and the Moroccan Government between 1960 and 1962. Then, when Algeria became independent in 1962, the Moroccan troops moved into the disputed area only to find that Algerian troops were already there.[15]

Morocco held that the nineteenth-century Sherifian Empire had been dismembered by French and Spanish colonial conquest at the beginning of the twentieth century; and that the people continued, under foreign rule, to consider themselves subjects of the sultan, and members of the Muslim community under him. In 1956 the French and the Spanish protectorates, as well as Tangier, regarded as the central area, were restored to complete sovereignty, and in 1958 the southern Spanish protectorate – Tarfaya – rejoined the kingdom. However, according to the Moroccan argument, this left 'unredeemed' parts of the empire and nation still under colonial (Spanish), neo-colonial (Mauritanian), or simply neighbouring (Algerian) rule.[16] An attempt to secure the 'unredeemed' part of the nineteenth-century Empire under Algerian rule led to war in October 1963.

THE DISPUTE AND THE OAU

On 8 October 1963, the dispute developed into a full-scale war between Algeria and Morocco and as is usual each side accused the other of starting the fighting. The one certainty is that Africans on both sides were being killed and wounded. The fighting took place between Bechar and Tindouf, that is about ninety-five kilometres south-west of Colomb-Bechar, and tanks, heavy artillery and other modern weapons were used. Within a week Algeria occupied Hassi Beida, Tinjoub and Hassi Mounir. A few days later both Hassi Beida and Tinjoub, which were border posts, were recaptured by the Moroccan army. The two countries mobilized and rushed reinforcements to the border zones, and the war continued with greater ferocity.[17]

The gravity of the situation, occurring at a time when the 'Addis Ababa spirit' was still fresh, led to both parties being implored by other African leaders to stop the fighting and settle their dispute by peaceful means. President Bourguiba of Tunisia sent an urgent message to both President Ben Bella and King Hassan, urging them to end hostilities.[18] President Nkrumah immediately sent Kojo Botsio, Ghana's foreign minister, and Kwesi Armah, to Algiers and Rabat in order to mediate between the conflicting parties. President Sékou Touré of Guinea; Sir Abubakar Tafawa Balewa, prime minister of Nigeria; president Modibo Keita of Mali;[19] and president Abdel Gamel Nasser of the United Arab Republic[20] also urged a peaceful settlement upon the contestants. As a result of all these moves, President Ben Bella sent Mohammed Yazid, the former minister of information, and Major Slimane with a personal message to King Hassan. On the very day that these two special envoys were sent to Rabat, King Hassan declared in a speech, relayed in Morocco on both radio and television, that Morocco was prepared to hold discussions with Algeria in order to achieve a peaceful settlement.[21] Yet, despite the Algerian move and the assurance given by the king in his speech, the countries failed to agree on a basis for settlement. Fighting continued and Algeria called on the Organization of African Unity to intervene.

On 17 October 1963 Emperor Haile Selassie of Ethiopia arrived in Marrakesh on a state visit to Morocco, and started immediately to mediate in the dispute. He had a long discussion with the king and sent Ato Katame Yifrou, the Ethiopian foreign minister, to Algeria with a personal message for President Ben Bella. The Algerian Government also sent Abdelaziz Bouteflika, the foreign minister, back to the Emperor with a message. The emperor himself then flew to Algiers on 21 October 1963, to hold discussions with president Ben Bella[22] and suggested a summit conference at which King Hassan, Ben Bella, and he himself would be present. The conference was to find ways and means of settling the dispute peacefully. Algeria accepted the suggestion on condition that the proposed conference took place in the capital of an African state or a neutral state such as Switzerland or one of the Scandinavian countries. At the same time the Algerian Government instructed its representative at the United Nations to request the provisional secretary-general of the Organization of African Unity to call an emergency session of the Council of Ministers at which the Algerian–Moroccan conflict would be discussed. The emperor was kept informed of this and agreed that the Council of Ministers of the OAU should meet at once.

THE SUMMIT CONFERENCE AT BAMAKO

The emperor went to Tunis from Algiers. While in Tunis his public relations officer announced that both King Hassan and president Ben Bella had agreed to the Emperor's suggestion to meet within the next few days in Libya. On 25 October 1963 – the very day that this was made known – King Hassan sent a message to president Bourguiba requesting him to be present with other heads of state at the proposed summit conference due to take place in Tripoli.[23] At the same time a spokesman of the Algerian Government announced that the summit would take place in Tunis, and also that the following heads of state would participate: King Hassan II of Morocco, president Ben Bella of Algeria, president Modibo Keita of Mali, president Abdel Gamel Nasser of the United Arab Republic, King Idris of Libya, president Sékou Touré of Guinea, Emperor Haile Selassie of Ethiopia and president Bourguiba of Tunisia.[24] Morocco retorted that it was necessary for the summit to be preceded by a conference of the foreign ministers of the participating countries. President Nasser had openly come out in support of Algeria, and had also sent troops to assist the Algerians in the border conflict. In addition, Algeria had moral support from president Sékou Touré.[25] When the government of Mali suggested on the following day – 27 October 1963 – that the proposed summit should take place in Bamako, starting on 29 October 1963, the Moroccan Government readily accepted, without demanding any conference of the foreign ministers. This time, however, it was proposed that only these heads of state should participate: Emperor Haile Selassie, president Modibo Keita, and both president Ben Bella and King Hassan.

After both Algeria and Morocco had agreed to take part in this conference at Bamako, the official invitation was taken to

Haile Selassie, who had flown to Paris on a private trip, by the foreign minister of Mali. The summit conference started on 29 October 1963.

The emperor and President Modibo Keita had a long discussion before both held discussions separately with King Hassan and later with President Ben Bella. The four participants met on 30 October 1963. After a series of talks, an agreement was reached whereby the hostilities would cease by midnight between 1 and 2 November 1963. In a communiqué issued after the talks, and signed by the four heads of state, it was agreed that:

(a) A cease-fire should come into force along the Algerian–Moroccan border with effect from midnight between 1 and 2 November 1963.

(b) A mixed commission, consisting of officers from Algeria, Morocco, Ethiopia and Mali, should be formed. This commission would determine the zone from which the troops would be withdrawn when the cease-fire came into effect. The Ethiopian and Malian members of the commission were to supervise the maintenance of the cease-fire.

(c) The four heads of state agreed that an emergency session of the Council of Ministers of the Organization of African Unity should be convened. The session should appoint a special arbitration commission, to study the disputed frontier problem and recommend concrete means of solving it.

(d) In accordance with the decision reached by the four heads of state at Bamako, the parties to the dispute should cease all attacks through the mass media against each other, with effect from midnight between 31 October and 1 November 1963.[26]

The outcome of the summit conference was hailed as a great success not only by Algeria and Morocco but also by everyone who supported the concept of African unity. It showed that the desire of African leaders to promote such unity, and to settle African problems peacefully and without outside intervention, was not an empty one. It also proved that the Organization of African Unity could play a decisive role. This is made clear by

147

the fact that both Algeria and Morocco preferred OAU mediation to that of the Arab League. Certainly, if the OAU had not
been founded, neither Emperor Haile Selassie nor president
Modibo Keita would have been in a position to settle a dis ute
between Maghreb sister-states. It also proved those to be nis-
taken who had always believed that Africa would be permanently
divided by the Sahara.

THE SETTLEMENT OF THE ALGERIAN–MOROCCAN
BORDER DISPUTE

In accordance with the agreement reached at Bamako, the cease-
fire came into force at midnight between 1 and 2 November 1963.
The mixed military commission came into existence and held its
first meeting at the headquarters of the military command in
Colomb-Bechar on 13 November 1963.

The special session of the Council of Ministers of the Organization of African Unity opened on 16 November 1963. The foreign
ministers endorsed the Bamako agreement. They heard both the
Algerian and the Moroccan views, and set up a special arbitration
commission with representatives of Ethiopia, the Ivory Coast,
Mali, Nigeria, Senegal, Sudan and Tanzania. This was mandated
to continue negotiations with the two contestants until the
border dispute was finally settled. Algeria and Morocco were
called upon to refrain from any action which could compromise
the success of the commission. The ministers praised the efforts
of both Haile Selassie and Modibo Keita in achieving the cease-
fire.

The special arbitration commission held its first meeting at
Abidjan on 5 December 1963; and was addressed by the foreign
ministers of both Algeria and Morocco, who renewed their
confidence in and support of the endeavour to achieve a settlement. By the end of the meeting, on 7 December 1963, the
foreign ministers of Algeria and Morocco had been requested to
submit detailed accounts of their points of view before the next
meeting of the commission, scheduled to take place in January
1964 at Bamako. The meeting duly occurred, was followed by a
further one in April and then convened again in Casablanca and
in Algiers in May of the same year.

While the foreign ministers were holding their special session at Addis Ababa in November 1963, the members of the mixed military commission arrived at Figuig, where fierce fighting took place shortly *after* the cease-fire came into effect. From then on, they supervised the cease-fire. They also worked out a demilitarized zone, in accordance with section (b) of the Bamako agreement. The agreement on this zone was signed between Algeria and Morocco on 20 February 1964 and in accordance with the agreement, the border posts in the central sector were evacuated; Ich and Figuig were returned to Morocco; and the dominating heights over the oases were demilitarized. Tindouf was not mentioned.[27] Algeria and Morocco, as a result of the agreement, proceeded to normalize their diplomatic relations through the exchange of ambassadors. Diplomatic relations between Morocco and the United Arab Republic, broken off during the October clashes between Morocco and Algeria, were also restored.[28]

The agreement of 20 February 1964 did not, however, finally settle the Algeria–Moroccan border dispute. The Moroccans were not entirely satisfied, because of Hassi Beida, which their military command felt very reluctant to evacuate. The Moroccan foreign minister, Ahmed Reda Guedira, would only say that the agreement would make it possible to 'tackle the basic frontier problem itself': but he also maintained that in the shortest possible time he and the Algerian foreign minister, Abdelaziz Bouteflika, would 'apply solutions to secondary problems that became grafted on to this basic problem'.[29] Both countries continued, with the other members of the OAU special arbitration commission, to work towards a final settlement; and in May 1970, this was reached. President Boumédienne of Algeria and King Hassan of Morocco agreed on 28 May to end the long-standing border dispute and to cooperate in exploiting the iron-ore deposits in that area. The two countries would set up a joint company to mine and market the huge ore deposits near Tindouf. Rabat and Algiers agreed to set up a border line as marked on a map drawn up under French rule and kept at the Paris National Geographical Institute.[30]

The final settlement of the dispute between Algeria and

149

Progress and Problems

Morocco is proof of the positive role the OAU can play in settling disputes between African states, no matter how complex such disputes may be. It also shows that the African leaders can settle their conflicts within the African context. This is a great achievement when one considers the present situation in world politics, when any conflict can so easily develop into a confrontation between the super-powers.

(ii) The Somali–Ethiopian Dispute

In 1897 Britain, France and Italy concluded treaties with King Menelik of Ethiopia after the king's unexpected victory over the Italians in the previous year. These treaties formed the basis on which the boundaries between Ethiopia and the possessions of these European powers in the Horn of Africa were settled. In 1908 Ethiopia and Italy, which colonized Somalia, signed a convention whereby their common borders were to be delimited, and in 1911 an Italian–Ethiopian boundary commission delimited the border.

The dispute between Somalia and her neighbours – Ethiopia and Kenya – over their respective boundaries had been brewing even before the Organization of African Unity was founded. Somalia claimed that since Somalians were to be found in the north frontier district of Kenya and the province of Ogaden in Ethiopia, these areas should be merged with the Somali Republic. The issue was raised by the Somali delegation at the Pan-African Summit Conference of May 1963 which founded the Organization of African Unity. They said that they regarded their country as still not fully independent as long as territory inhabited by Somalis was to be found in parts of Kenya and Ethiopia. To support their claim they maintained that all Somalis were

members of a single Somali nation. Somali is our language, spoken from the Gulf of Aden to the Northern Frontier District. Islam is our culture, pastoralism our way of life. We want to reunite with our brothers with whom we can evolve an administration suited to our way of life.[31]

There was a heated debate on the issue in the foreign ministers' meeting, as well as outside. The Ethiopians refrained from entering into any detailed discussions of the Somali case, remaining content with stating that the conference should concentrate on the drive towards African unity and avoid being diverted by other issues. But the Kenya delegation, led by Oginga Odinga, Peter Mbiyu Koinage and Dr J. G. Kiano (given observer status as their country was on the threshold of independence), whilst sharing the Ethiopian attitude, also launched a series of attacks on the Somalis. It argued that

since the notorious days of the scramble for Africa this continent of ours has been broken up into numerous states which must now work together in unison to overcome the evil legacies of Divide and Rule. The trend in New Africa is, therefore, toward unity and toward such co-operation that the boundaries between our separate states are of little consequence.[32]

The relations between Somalia and Ethiopia deteriorated sharply towards the end of 1963. This was due to the increasing activities of Somali 'shiftas', or guerrillas, regarded by the Ethiopians as armed bandits, in the border area between Somalia and the Ethiopian region of Ogaden. Police posts were attacked, and some Ethiopians were killed. The Ethiopians retaliated on 12 October 1963, by attacking the Somali police post at Dabagorialeh. This action, however, only increased the 'shifta' activities which, in turn, led to further reprisals by Ethiopia. On 15 January 1964 the Somali border police posts of Gura Giome and El Maghet in the Upper Juba River region were 'attacked and destroyed'.[33] This led the Somali foreign minister, Abdullah Issa, to send a protest to the Ethiopian ambassador in Somalia, Ato Ahadu Saburu. In the protest note Somalia declared that she held Ethiopia responsible for any consequences of the 'armed aggression and isolation of national territory'. On 17 January there was a clash between the Ethiopian security forces and Somali shiftas, during which twenty-six of the shiftas were killed, and twenty-six others captured. A truck carrying ammunition and other supplies was also captured by the Ethiopian security forces. By the beginning of February, there were reports of 'large scale incursions by "bandits" from Somalia' into the Ethiopian region of Ogaden.[34] This worsening situation led to a series of emergency meetings of the cabinets

151

of both Addis Ababa and Mogadishu. And by 7 February the situation had developed into a state of war. The Somali forces attacked Ethiopia at the border post of Tug Wajale and at the point between Hargeissa (Somalia) and Jijiga (Ethiopia). There were casualties on both sides.[35] From then on the armed conflict worsened rapidly, both sides using mortars, tanks, heavy artillery and planes along their border area. A state of emergency was declared by the Somali and Ethiopian governments.

As soon as the situation developed into actual warfare, Haile Selassie sent urgent messages to all African heads of state and government informing them of what was going on.[36] Meanwhile Somalia, who was unhappy with the OAU ruling on boundary situations in Africa, and for whom the achievement of 'Great Somalia' was the cornerstone of foreign policy, asked her chief representative at the United Nations to request a meeting of the Security Council 'as a matter of urgency', to consider the border conflict with Ethiopia.[37] Both governments also sent telegrams to the secretary-general of the United Nations, U Thant, informing him of the conflict. The Ethiopian Government called, too, for an emergency meeting of the Council of Ministers of the OAU to deal with the situation.[38]

The Organization of African Unity and many African heads of state stepped in immediately to bring peace to the troubled area. The provisional secretary-general of the organization sent messages to both countries urging them to end the armed conflict and settle their dispute by peaceful means. President Abboud of Sudan offered to mediate between them, and other African leaders, including Bourguiba of Tunisia, Nkrumah of Ghana, and Nyerere of Tanzania, also appealed to both countries to settle the dispute by peaceful negotiation. The secretary-general of the United Nations as well as the Soviet premier, Nikita Khrushchev, and the American Government called on Somalia and Ethiopia to settle their border dispute by peaceful means. Through the mediation of the Sudanese president, a cease-fire was agreed on 11 February 1964. But this, unfortunately, lasted for only a few hours.

The conflict was discussed at an emergency session of the OAU Council of Ministers which took place in Dar es Salaam from 12 to 14 February 1964. The Committee of Thirteen, comprising representatives of the Cameroon Republic, Dahomey, Ethiopia, Ghana, Kenya, Liberia, Mauritania, Morocco, Sierra Leone, Somalia, Tunisia, the United Arab Republic and the Upper Volta, was set up to work out a draft resolution calling for an immediate cease-fire. It was also requested to work out a cease-fire agreement. At the end of the conference the cease-fire agreement was signed by both parties and an observer commission, comprising two Somali, two Ethiopian and one other representative, was set up to inspect the cease-fire and report to the next session of the council, due to start later that month in Lagos.[39] Both countries were urged to open negotiations in order to find a peaceful solution to their border dispute, and to stop forthwith provocative and insulting propaganda campaigns against each other. The Ethiopian and Somali delegates pledged that their countries would abide by the council's decisions. It may seem strange that the council failed to set up a special arbitration commission, as was done for the Algerian–Moroccan border dispute. This was deliberate, however, because when the OAU was founded it had been tacitly agreed that the present boundaries, although colonial creations, should not be altered. The Somali wish to alter the existing boundaries had led to the conflict, and was felt to be unwarranted. In the Algerian–Moroccan border dispute, there had never been any legally accepted boundary between the countries. It was, therefore, felt that the conflict between Somalia and Ethiopia should normally not have arisen, and could only be ended by the parties directly involved, and through direct negotiation.

In spite of the pledges given by Ethiopia and Somalia at Dar es Salaam to abide by the decisions of the Council of Ministers, armed conflict started up again a few days later. The Ethiopian village of Ferfer was attacked with artillery fire, and its governor kidnapped by the Somali forces. There was heavy fighting between the Somali and Ethiopian forces at Yet and Dolo. At this juncture the Ethiopian government reported the situation to the Organization of African Unity and to the United Nations. The Ethiopian foreign minister, Ato Ketema Yifrou, received the ambassadors of Ghana, Nigeria, Sudan and the

United Arab Republic in Addis Ababa and informed them of the new developments. On 17 February 1964, a day after Ethiopia had written to the OAU and the UN, the president of Somalia, Aden Abdullah Osman, sent a message to the secretary-general of the United Nations as well as to many African heads of state. In it he accused Ethiopia of failing to observe the cease-fire. And both governments resumed their propaganda campaigns against each other.

In view of these new developments, the OAU Council of Ministers had to deal with the Ethiopian–Somali conflict once more at its ordinary session held in Lagos towards the end of February. It again appealed to both parties to solve their dispute by peaceful means. There was, however, a stumbling-block: Ethiopia maintained that only the long-disputed interpretation of the 1908 Ethiopian–Italian Treaty defining the border should be discussed, while Somalia argued that the treaties delimiting her borders were invalid since Somalia had been a colony at the time they were signed. She therefore insisted that her wider territorial claims should be the subject of the negotiations.[40] President Abboud of Sudan, however, succeeded in convincing both parties of the need for negotiations as recommended by the Council of Ministers; and they agreed to meet at Khartoum, the capital of Sudan, on 24 March 1964.

The direct peace negotiations between the countries were conducted in the presence of President Abboud from 24 to 30 March 1964, while the fighting raged on. The Somali guerrillas – themselves an important factor in the dispute – came out strongly against any peaceful settlement. Their leader, Muktal Dahir, who had been the Ethiopian district commissioner at Daghabur when the rebellion began in Ogaden, declared: 'My people are under no one's jurisdiction and take orders from no one but me. We have no intention of observing any cease-fire.'[41] In spite of all this, the Khartoum talks ended successfully. Both parties agreed to:

(1) respect the cease-fire along their border;
(2) withdraw their troops to a distance of between ten and fifteen kilometres on their respective sides of the border, with

such withdrawal beginning on 1 April and ending at the latest on 6 April;

(3) appoint a joint commission with representatives of both parties, to supervise the aforementioned withdrawal of troops;

(4) end all types of hostile, provocative and insulting propaganda against each other, with effect from midnight on 1 April 1964.[42]

Although there were minor clashes after the Khartoum Agreement had been signed, both parties respected the ceasefire when it finally came into operation.

Since then efforts have been made by both to achieve a final settlement of the dispute through negotiations. President Aden Abdullah Osman of Somalia and Emperor Haile Selassie of Ethiopia set the ball rolling when they met at the Cairo Conference of non-aligned nations in October 1964.[43] A meeting of both parties, scheduled to take place in July 1964, had failed to materialize, owing to a government crisis in Somalia. The talks did not move quickly at first. But with the aid of encouragement and exhortation from other heads of state and government at every OAU summit conference both countries continued to seek ways of settling the dispute peacefully. By September 1967 there were signs of a lessening in the conflict. During the Kinshasa Summit Conference of 1967, talks were held between Haile Selassie and the prime minister of Somalia, Mohammed Ibrahim Egal. As a result, a high-ranking Somali delegation, led by the minister of the interior, Yassin Nur Hassan, arrived in Addis Ababa on 19 September 1967, for exploratory talks aimed at improving relations between the two countries. After two days of talks a communiqué was published simultaneously in Addis Ababa and Mogadishu in which it was made known that they had agreed to eliminate all tension between them; establish a joint military commission to examine complaints by either side; and, in order to achieve perfect cooperation, hold quarterly meetings of their administrative authorities. The situation improved so fast between the two countries in the following year that the prime minister of Somalia, Mohammed Ibrahim Egal, could pay a state visit to Ethiopia. At the end of his visit the Ethiopian Government agreed to suspend the state of emergency along the border region, with effect from 16 September 1968. In addition, the two governments decided to conclude a trade and telecommunications agreement. Although a final settlement has not yet been reached, there is good reason to hope that it soon will be.

(iii) *The Somali–Kenyan Dispute*

The boundary between Somalia and Kenya resulted from a treaty signed by Britain and Italy in 1891. This 'partitioned the Sudan and East Africa from Ethiopia and the Somali plateau into respective zones of British and Italian influence. The Southern part of the boundary followed the Juba river northwards into Ethiopia across the Blue Nile to the shores of the Red Sea'.[44] The Northern Frontier District of Kenya came under British rule in 1919. In 1925 Jubaland was transferred to Italy, while the NFD remained part of Kenya. An Anglo–Italian commission set up to demarcate the boundary between Kenya and Somalia started work in 1929 and led to the signing of an agreement by both Britain and Italy in London on 1 June 1931, whereby the boundary between Kenya and Somalia was finally fixed.

As has already been recorded, at the Pan-African summit conference which founded the Organization of African Unity in May 1963, there was a clash between the Kenya delegation, given observer status, and the Somalia delegation, on the question of the Somali-inhabited region of Kenya. In view of the impending independence of Kenya, an effort was made in August 1963, by Britain, Kenya and the Somali Republic, to iron out the boundary problems. Representatives of these three countries met in Rome to discuss the issue, but nothing was achieved. After the break-down of the Rome Conference, Somalia decided to raise the issue of the Northern Frontier District of Kenya, and the right of the Somali people there to self-determination, at the United Nations General Assembly; but the outcome then too was unsatisfactory to the Somali Republic.

Shortly before Kenya became independent on 12 December

1963, the Somali Government attempted to put the Somali case before the Kenya Government. The Somali foreign minister had a meeting on the border issue with the leader of the Kenya African National Union, Jomo Kenyatta, who was premier of Kenya. But a few days later a military depot near Garissa, in the north-eastern region of Kenya, was attacked by Somali shiftas, who had carried out a series of raids in the regions before then. The Kenya Government proclaimed a state of emergency in the area on 25 December. A police camp near Wajir in the north-eastern region was attacked by Somali raiders on 1 January 1964 and similar raids became more frequent in the following months.[45]

On 15 January 1964, representatives of Kenya and Ethiopia started a series of talks at Addis Ababa on the problem of Somali raids in their respective border areas with Somalia.[46] At the end of the talks a memorandum was submitted to the provisional secretary of the Organization of African Unity accusing Somalia of 'pursuing a policy of territorial expansion at the expense of neighbouring states'.[47] When the emergency session of the OAU Council of Ministers was convened in Dar es Salaam in February 1964, the Kenyan–Somali border issue was discussed. The two countries were called upon by the council to settle their dispute in the spirit of Article III of the OAU charter, and refrain from further provocative actions and propaganda while a peaceful settlement was being sought. The council also agreed to keep the dispute on the agenda of all its subsequent sessions until a final settlement had been achieved.

Kenya and Somalia started in May 1964 to explore ways of settling the dispute through negotiations in accordance with the OAU recommendation of February 1964. Letters were exchanged between the governments but demonstrated only that both were sticking to their original demands: Somalia insisting still on the cession to it of Kenya's Northern Frontier District, Kenya adamant in its refusal. Somalia also claimed that the presence of British troops and planes in the disputed area hindered a settlement and that the state of emergency declared by Kenya in its North-Eastern Region made a favourable atmosphere for talks between the two countries impossible.

President Nyerere acted as a mediator; and on his initiative, both premiers Abdirashid Ali Shermarke of Somalia and Jomo Kenyatta of Kenya met at Arusha, Tanzania, in December 1965. This meeting was a failure, but neither government gave up hope that the dispute could be settled peacefully. This hope, coupled with a determination to succeed, led to the Kinshasa meeting of September 1967 at which President Kaunda of Zambia acted as mediator. At the end of the talks, the following communiqué was issued.

Both governments have expressed their desire to respect each other's sovereignty and territorial integrity in the spirit of Paragraph 3 of Article III of the OAU Charter.

The two governments have further undertaken to resolve any outstanding differences between them in the spirit of Paragraph 4 of Article III of the OAU Charter.

The two governments have pledged to ensure maintenance of security on both sides of the border by preventing destruction of human life and property.

Furthermore, the two governments have agreed to refrain from conducting hostile propaganda through mass media such as radio and the press against each other.

The two governments have accepted the kind invitation of President Kenneth Kaunda of Zambia to meet in Lusaka during the latter part of October, 1967, in order to improve, intensify and consolidate all forms of co-operation.

All the other heads of state and government in the OAU were delighted at this new development in Kenyan–Somali relations. They passed a resolution in which they noted with pleasure the joint declaration reached between the governments of Kenya and Somalia 'as represented by the Vice-President, Daniel Arap Moi, and the Prime Minister, Mohammed Ibrahim Egal, respectively, through the good offices of the President of Zambia'. They expressed their 'sincere gratitude and congratulations to President Kenneth D. Kaunda of Zambia, as well as the governments of Kenya and Somalia, for their positive efforts to overcome differences' in the fraternal manner and requested the three governments 'to submit a progress report' on the proposed meeting to the secretary-general of the OAU.[48]

The proposed meeting between Kenya and Somalia took place

at Arusha, Tanzania, in October 1967 with Kaunda acting as mediator. At the end of the talks a 'memorandum of understanding' was signed by President Kenyatta and Prime Minister Mohammed Ibrahim Egal, with President Kaunda as a witness, on 28 October 1967. In view of its significance it is reproduced here verbatim:

Memorandum of Understanding

Meeting in the Arusha Town Hall, the Kenya President and the Somali Premier expressed their desire to consolidate the Kinshasa declaration on Kenya–Somali relations and recognised the need to restore normal and peaceful relations between Kenya and Somalia.

They have, towards this end, reached agreement on the following points:

1 – Both governments will exert all efforts and do the utmost to maintain good neighbourly relations between Kenya and Somalia in accordance with the O.A.U. Charter.

2 – The two governments agree that the interests of the people of Kenya and Somalia were not served by the continuance of tension between the two countries.

3 – They, therefore, reaffirm their adherence to the declaration of the O.A.U. Conference at Kinshasa, a copy of which is attached to this memorandum of understanding.

4 – In order to facilitate a speedy solution to the development [*sic*] and to ensure maintenance of continued good relations, both governments have agreed to: [*sic*]

    A – the maintenance of peace and security on both sides of the border by preventing the destruction of human life and property;

    B – refrain from conducting hostile propaganda through mass media such as radio and press against each other and encourage propaganda which promotes the development and continuance of friendly relations between the two countries;

    C – The gradual suspension of any emergency regulations imposed on either side of the border;

    D – The re-opening of diplomatic relations between the two countries;

    E – A consideration of measures encouraging the development of economic and trade relations;

    F – The appointment of a working committee consisting of

> Somalia, Kenya and Zambia, which will meet periodic-
> ally to review the implementation by Somalia and Kenya
> of points agreed in this document and also to examine
> ways and means of bringing about a satisfactory solution
> to major and minor differences between Somalia and
> Kenya.[49]

The signing of this 'memorandum of understanding' was a
turning-point in Kenyan-Somali relations and proved, once
again, the usefulness and powerful moral influence of the
OAU.

Most of the main points of the memorandum have been
implemented, and efforts are being made to achieve a lasting
solution to the border dispute. The two countries exchanged
ambassadors early in 1968; and a series of meetings has been
held by representatives of the two governments. At one such
meeting, held in Nairobi, under the chairmanship of Kaunda,
Kenyatta and Egal agreed, on 21 February 1969, to cooperate
in mutual development projects. Kenya undertook to promote
the candidature of Somalia for membership of the East African
Economic Community. The Kenya Government also agreed to
lift the state of emergency in her North-Eastern Province, grant
an amnesty to all political offenders connected with the dispute
between the two countries, and allow refugees from Somalia to
return to their homes.

(iv) The Niger–Dahomey Dispute

The dispute between Niger and Dahomey centred on Lete
Island, an island on the River Niger which constitutes the
frontier between the two countries. But in this instance the
boundary issue was a symptom of deeper troubles.[50] In October
1963, the government of Hubert Maga in Dahomey was overthrown in a military coup led by Colonel Soglo, who subsequently
installed a provisional national unity government. Maga (the
former president) and some of his supporters in the northern
part of Dahomey were then arrested early in December 1963,
on a charge of plotting to restore the old régime. In the process
a number of citizens of the Niger Republic were arrested and

others were killed, while the republic itself was accused of supporting the plot. On 21 December 1963 certain members of the Niger National Assembly alleged that Dahomey was preparing to occupy Lete Island, and on the following day it was announced in Niamey, Niger, that the government of the republic had decided to expel all Dahomeyans living on the northern side of the Niger River. Dahomey retaliated by closing the border and thereby blocking any transit of goods to the land-locked Niger Republic.

Because of these events, Dahomey requested a special meeting of the United Nations Security Council; the request was later, however, withdrawn. Gabon and Togo immediately offered to mediate, while the Nigerian minister of state for foreign affairs, Senator Alhaji Nuhu Bamali, went to Niamey and Cotonou after receiving delegations in Lagos from both countries.[51] After intense diplomatic activity, delegations from both countries met at their border and, according to a communiqué issued after the talks, agreed upon the free circulation of goods and people between them; retreat of their armed forces from their common border and cessation of hostile radio broadcasts. They agreed to settle the border dispute through negotiations.

Their first reconciliation talks broke down over the ownership of the island. Niger refused to accept partition as proposed by Dahomey, since it regarded the island as an integral part of its national territory. Dahomey, on the other hand, maintained that the island had been divided by a French decree of 1938. During the conference of the UAM heads of state in March 1964, both presidents, Diori and Apithy, signed a reconciliation agreement. At a meeting held at Dosso in June 1963 they agreed to restore commercial cooperation between their states and to hold new negotiations later in order to solve the expatriate and border problems. A progress report was submitted to the OAU secretariat before the 1964 OAU summit conference. The dispute was finally settled in January 1965, on the basis that the inhabitants of the island were to enjoy dual citizenship.

THE OAU RULING ON BOUNDARY ISSUES

During the Pan-African summit conference of May 1963 which founded the Organization of African Unity, several delegates spoke of the desirability of leaving the existing frontiers unchanged, despite the fact that these were colonial creations. But apart from the principle of 'respect for the sovereignty and territorial integrity of states', the charter of the Organization of African Unity does not specifically require the acceptance of existing borders. The many border disputes which the OAU had to cope with during the very first year of its existence led the 1964 Cairo summit conference to concern itself with the issue. After an interesting discussion, the conference unanimously adopted a resolution on 'Border Disputes among African States'.[52] Because of its importance, it is reproduced here verbatim:

> The assembly of Heads of State and Government, considering that border problems constitute a grave and permanent factor of dissension, conscious of the existence of extra-African manoeuvres aimed at dividing African States;
> Considering further that the borders of African States, on the day of their independence, constitute a tangible reality;
> Recalling the establishment in the course of the second ordinary session of the Council of the Committee of Eleven charged with studying further measures for strengthening African Unity;
> Recognising the imperious necessity of settling, by peaceful means and within a strictly African framework, all disputes between Member States;
> Recalling further, that all Members have pledged, under Article VI of the Charter of African Unity, to respect scrupulously all principles laid down in paragraph 3 of Article III of the Charter of the Organisation of African Unity;
> (i) Solemnly reaffirms the strict respect by all members of the Organisation for the principles laid down in paragraph 3 of Article III of the Charter of the Organisation of African Unity;
> (ii) Solemnly declares that all Member States pledge themselves to respect the border existing on their achievement of national independence.

Some people have condemned the resolution on the grounds that it merely perpetuates the status quo and is, therefore, more or less detrimental to the cause of African unity. This may sound reasonable but is not in fact realistic in the present-day state of African politics, and those who are opposed to the OAU stand on boundary disputes so far should bear in mind that without it most of the disputes would have been settled not through African mediation, but in foreign ministries outside Africa.

3. MILITARY ASSISTANCE

The security of any state can be endangered from within or from without. Mutiny of the armed forces is one of the commonest ways by which the very existence of a state can be threatened and in spite of the fact that it is a treasonable offence and subject to punishment it is still not uncommon in most parts of the world. An attempt to prevent or control mutiny can necessitate the calling in of outside military assistance and Africa, like the rest of the world, has had to take that action from time to time.

(i) *Tanganyika (now Tanzania)*

On 20 January 1964, the first Battalion of the Tanganyika Africa Rifles mutinied at Tolito, near Dar es Salaam. The immediate cause of the mutiny was two-fold. First, the African members of the Tanganyikan army were worried by a government circular issued during the first week of January, informing all ministries and public bodies that 'discrimination in the recruitment, training and promotion of civil servants must end immediately'. The African soldiers who had hoped to be promoted soon and to take over from their European officers saw their hopes dashed. Secondly, they wanted pay increases. They decided to make representations to the government. Their leaders had a discussion with president Nyerere, but no agreement was reached. When they tried to meet him once more, they failed. Taking the law into their own hands, they then arrested their officers. At this juncture they were joined by their companions in the Second Battalion, stationed at Tabora.

But the mutiny did not stop there. It started a chain of

163

similar events which extended to Uganda on 23 January and to Kenya on 24 January. In view of the seriousness of the situation, the three governments asked Britain for military help. This request was granted, and British troops took over from the soldiers, who were immediately dismissed.

The request for British troops was a source of acute embarrassment to President Nyerere, who clearly grasped the implications of their presence in his country and therefore requested a special session of the OAU Council of Ministers. This was held in Dar es Salaam from 12 to 15 February 1964. After hearing the circumstances leading to the request for British troops and proposals for their replacement, the council adopted a resolution granting the request for African troops to replace the British. Tanganyika was given the option to contact any African country she wished, and both Nigeria and Ethiopia were approached. Nigeria sent a battalion of five hundred Nigerian troops, while Ethiopia contributed airmen: these forces were to be stationed in Tanganyika until a new Tanganyikan army had been trained.

(ii) Sierra Leone

The situation in Sierra Leone was quite different. The country had succumbed to a military coup in 1967. But in April 1968, it returned to civilian rule with a 'National Government' made up of the representatives of both the All Peoples' Congress (APC) led by Dr Siaka Stevens and the Sierra Leone People's Party (SLPP) led by Salia Jusu Sheriff. Then, shortly before the end of the year, the National Government was dissolved and the APC, which had a majority in the house of representatives, formed the government.

The situation deteriorated. There were disturbances all over the country. The government declared a state of emergency, and many people were detained. With control apparently re-established, the state of emergency was lifted at the end of February 1969. But a few weeks later, the situation deteriorated dangerously again in certain parts of the country. The newly formed Koidu-New Sembehun town council appealed to the government for assistance and in particular asked them to 'give urgent priority to take action to rid this area, once and for all, of the organisers and financiers of IDM (Illicit Diamond Mining) and also the strangers who threatened so much destruction to our national heritage, wealth and prosperity as well as the safety, health and development of our people'.[53] At the same time a treason trial was in progress against the leaders of the 1967 coup, many of whom were later sentenced to death.

Efforts to work out an acceptable republican constitution continued. The Republican Constitutional Committee, set up in June 1969, was displaced a year later by the Constitutional Review Commission. But before the commission could finish its work a constitutional crisis had broken out. While the prime minister, Dr Stevens, was attending the non-aligned conference in Zambia in September 1970, two of his ministers – Dr Mohammed Forna (Finance) and Mr Mohammed Bash-Taqi (Development) – resigned from the government. They were immediately expelled from the ruling All Peoples' Congress.

Dr Forna, in his letter of resignation, accused the prime minister of intending to become executive president with full power, after the adoption of the not-yet-released republican constitution. The prime minister countered by claiming that Dr Forna had resigned simply because he had not been made the acting prime minister while Dr Stevens was out of the country.

The two former ministers, together with Dr Sarif Esmon and Dr John Karefa-Smart, immediately formed the Committee of Citizens. They addressed a large gathering at the Queen Elizabeth playing fields, where they gave reasons for their resignation. This meeting, which ended in disorder, triggered off country-wide commotion. The Committee of Citizens was transformed into the United Democratic Party, another state of emergency was declared; and the leaders of the new party (the UDP) were arrested and detained.

A few weeks later, an abortive coup was uncovered at the Wilberforce barracks. Two senior army officers were dismissed from the service, while six junior officers and nine other ranks were detained. The second secretary at the United States embassy in Freetown, Mark Colby, who was seen at the residence of one of the two dismissed officers on the day that the coup was discovered, was expelled from the country. Following a combined army and police operation, it was claimed that £50,000 worth of arms and ammunition had been found at a house in Tengbey Fakai, about three miles from Freetown. The house itself was said to belong to a leader of the banned United Democratic Party.

In view of the explosive internal situation, the Sierra Leone parliament approved, on 22 December 1970, a motion authorizing the prime minister to enter into immediate negotiations with both Guinea and Liberia to set up common defence arrangements.

The negotiations began immediately but before an agreement could be reached, another incident took place. On 22 and 23 March 1971 a double assassination attempt, as part of an intended coup, was made by a section of the Sierra Leone army against the person and government of Siaka Steven. The pace of the negotiations quickened, and on 26 March a defence agreement was signed between Guinea and Sierra Leone; in accordance with its provisions, Guinean troops were sent to assist the remaining loyal members of the Sierra Leone army. This assistance has prevented any further attempt at the overthrow of the Sierra Leone government and has proved that with cooperation among African states, there is no need to request the help of outsiders.

4. IMPROVEMENT OF INTER-STATE RELATIONS IN AFRICA

As long as international relations are conducted by human beings, with all their failings, and as long as nations pursue different objectives in different ways there is bound to be friction.[54] And it is not surprising that there has been conflict among African states. We have already seen how frontier issues have led to actual war. But border issues are just one source of conflict. There are of course others.

Since we are here only concerned with the improvement in inter-state relations due to the influence of Pan-Africanism, and not with African inter-state relations per se, we shall examine just a few cases where relations between the states became bad, only to improve. We shall deal, briefly, with Chad–Sudanese relations, the detention in Ghana of Guinean diplomats and students in 1966, and the relations between Congo (Kinshasa) and her neighbours. We shall also briefly examine one further important cause of friction between African States: the question of refugees.

(i) Chad–Sudanese Relations

In November 1965 there were disturbances in the Mangalme district of the Chad Republic. A member of the national assembly, a high official of the government, and six policemen were killed.[55]

The dissidents formed what they called 'the Islamic Government of Chad in Exile'. The Chad Government accused the Sudanese Government of harbouring their rivals. After an effort had been made by both governments, there was some improvement in relations, but it did not last long.

With a series of incidents in the Ouaddai district of the Chad Republic, relations between Chad and the Sudan deteriorated again, on the grounds that the insurgents were entering Chad from Sudanese territory. On 7 August 1966 President Tombalbaye of Chad alleged in the National Assembly that the Sudanese Government was to blame. The Sudanese Government rejected the allegation, claiming that it could not be held responsible for any incidents occurring within the borders of the Chad Republic. As the incidents continued, it was decided at an extraordinary meeting of the Chad Government and Political Bureau of the governing party (PPT), held during the night of 23–4 August 1966, under the chairmanship of President Tombalbaye, to close the border with the Sudan, and to restrict the movement of Sudanese nationals in Chad to within five kilometres of their homes. The government was authorized to take energetic measures for the security of the national territory; and Chad citizens were called upon to report 'the presence of known or suspect foreign elements' to local authorities.[56]

Dr Jacques Baroum, the minister of foreign affairs, said that these measures were being taken because of the Sudanese Government's reaction to the complaints made by Chad about incursions of 'armed bandits' into her territory from the Sudan. He added that Chad's armed forces stationed in the eastern part of the country had been ordered to open fire on any Sudanese aircraft flying over Chadian military installations. But the Sudanese made it clear that no Sudanese military aircraft had either crossed the border or violated Chad's airspace.

On 12 September the Sudanese Government protested to the Chad ministry of foreign affairs about an alleged attack by members of the Chad armed forces against the Sudanese village of Oum-Tessa near the border with Chad, in which three people had been killed and seven wounded. The protest note warned that Sudan would retaliate if there were any more such incursions into its territory. These accusations were described by Dr Daroum, the Chad minister of foreign affairs, as 'devoid of all foundation'. He accused the Sudanese leaders of ill-will. Demonstrations were held in Chad against the Sudan, and in the Sudan against Chad. On 17 September the Fort Lamy radio declared that the Chad people did not want war, but were prepared to wage it if they were forced to. The Sudanese minister of the interior had earlier announced the Sudanese armed forces to be in a state of alert.

As the dispute gathered momentum, efforts were made to get it settled through negotiations. The final settlement was achieved through the efforts of President Hamani Diori of the Niger Republic, who reported to the summit conference of the Organization of African Unity held at Kinshasa in September 1967.

(ii) The Ghana–Guinea Dispute

On 29 October 1966 the Ghanaian military police arrested the foreign minister of Guinea, Lansana Beavogui (who was leading his country's delegation to the OAU Council of Ministers'

Conference, scheduled to start on 31 October 1966) at Addis
Ababa, together with the other members of his delegation, and
fifteen Guinean students, on their way to Nigeria. The Ghana
authorities then announced these arrests as retaliation for what
they called 'the forceful detention of Ghanaian citizens in
Guinea'.

Relations between Ghana and Guinea had begun to deteriorate immediately after Nkrumah was overthrown by a military
coup in February 1966. Nkrumah, who had been in Peking at
the time of the coup, travelled on to Guinea. On 3 March,
President Sékou Touré said at a rally in Conakry: 'I want to
tell you that our brother, the President of Ghana, Kwame
Nkrumah, is not a stranger here'; he went on to proclaim
Nkrumah equally with himself president of Guinea. Ghana
accused Guinea of planning to send Ghanaian subversive
agents to Ghana with false passports; and also alleged that those
Ghanaians who had been with Nkrumah when he was overthrown wished to return to Ghana but were being prevented
from doing so by the Guinea Government.

Yet even if these allegations were justified, was the Ghanaian
Government right in taking such action as that of 29 October
1966? The very OAU conference which these Guineans were
going to attend when they were arrested was scheduled to discuss the deteriorating relationship between Ghana and Guinea.
And since these people were on their way to an international
conference, they were covered by diplomatic immunity, in
accordance with international law as well as the rules and
regulations of diplomacy.

The arrests caused an uproar throughout Africa, not least
among the other African delegates gathered at Addis Ababa for
the proposed conference. The Ghanaian action was condemned
by Ethiopia, Algeria, Tanzania and many other African states
as both a breach of international law and 'an insult to Africa'.
An emergency meeting was held to discuss the situation. And
the delegates agreed to send a three-state mission to Accra and
Conakry, in order to secure the release of the Guinea diplomats
and at the same time find ways of improving relations between
the two countries. The mission, which consisted of Justin

169

Bomboko of Congo (Kinshasa), John Nelson-Williams of Sierra Leone and Joseph Murumbi of Kenya, was received in both capitals. President Sékou Touré made it known that Guinea would allow any Ghanaian who desired to return home to do so at once. When he met the OAU delegation, he repeated this assurance. But Ghana still refused to release the detained Guinean diplomats and students. The OAU conference continued under the shadow of the dispute.

On 5 November 1966 General Joseph Ankrah, the chairman of Ghana's National Liberation Committee, arrived in Addis Ababa at the head of Ghana's delegation to the OAU summit conference. Haile Selassie of Ethiopia, president William Tubman of Liberia, and president Abdel Gamel Nasser representing the OAU, had a long discussion with him on the Ghana–Guinea dispute; as a result, Ghana agreed to release the Guinean diplomats and students. An OAU mission was subsequently sent to Guinea, to interview the Ghanaians there; and some of these agreed to return home. Since then the hostility between these countries has ceased.

(iii) Congo (Kinshasa) and her Neighbours

The Congo crises have at one time or another led to friction between Congo (Kinshasa) and her neighbours, Congo (Brazzaville), Burundi, Rwanda and Uganda. The reason was partly the activities of Congolese 'rebels' from these territories, and partly the involvement of certain foreign powers in Congolese affairs.

CONGO (KINSHASA)–CONGO (BRAZZAVILLE) RELATIONS

From Katanga's secession onwards, the relations between the two Congos had deteriorated. This was at first due to the support given to Moise Tshombe by the Brazzaville Government under Fulbert Youlou. When Katanga was re-integrated into Congo (Kinshasa) in January 1963, a new era in the relations between the countries began. Youlou had been overthrown; and the new Brazzaville Government was more Pan-African in outlook, more inclined to a united Congo (Kinshasa). But for this reason, too, it supported the Lumumbists. And these last were dissatisfied with the Adoula régime in Kinshasa, which was re-shuffled in April 1963 to include representatives from the newly-tamed Katanga province but left the Lumumbists out in the cold. The already uneasy situation in the Congo deteriorated further. The forces of rebellion had by the summer consolidated their strength, and by the autumn of 1963 Christopher Gbenye, with many other Lumumbists, had settled in Brazzaville, where they set up the National Liberation Committee.

In 1964 forces of the National Liberation Committee defeated the Congolese troops (ANC) at several encounters, and rebellion in the Congo seemed to be gaining support. At this juncture, Tshombe became prime minister of the Kinshasa Government and embarked upon recruiting white mercenaries. This, how-ever, did not have any immediate effect on the fortunes of the Congolese army. Tshombe, therefore, decided to strike at what he regarded as the sole base of rebellion. He accused both Congo (Brazzaville) and Burundi of harbouring and supporting the rebels; and he demanded that they expel them. When the governments refused, he proceeded to expel the citizens of both countries from Congo (Kinshasa) and confiscated their property.

As the OAU commission on the Congo, set up in September 1964, was unable to bring peace to the Congo, because of American and other foreign involvement in the crisis,[57] the friction between the two Congos outlasted the Tshombe régime.

This friction was complicated by another factor, which had until then remained hidden: that of ideology. While the United States was openly supporting Congo (Kinshasa), the Congolese rebels were alleged to be receiving assistance from China. And when peace returned to Congo (Kinshasa), the United States had become Congo (Kinshasa)'s 'best ally', whereas, in Brazza-ville, China had established herself as a source of aid.

One further factor in the worsening of relations between the two Congos was provided by what became known as the 'Mulele affair'. In 1968 Pierre Mulele, one of the rebel leaders, who had been granted political asylum in Brazzaville, was returned to

Kinshasa on the clear understanding that he was to be granted amnesty. Mulele was, however, tried and executed. The Brazzaville authorities regarded this as a betrayal, and broke off diplomatic relations with Congo (Kinshasa). Congo (Brazzaville) thereupon refused to attend the summit meeting of OCAM which took place in Kinshasa early in 1969. When, in November 1969, an attempt was made to overthrow it, the government of Congo (Brazzaville) accused General Mobutu of Congo (Kinshasa), NATO, and the CIA of together organizing the attempted coup. President Mobutu denied this, adding that he was getting tired of such allegations:

> I swear to you that, if we really wanted, it would only take us a couple of hours to silence those people over there. If I decided to put my red beret on, two hours would suffice to occupy most of their territory, and all they could do would be to ask the Security Council to order a withdrawal. If it wasn't all over in a couple of hours, I would resign.[58]

This outburst only increased the tension. The government of Congo (Brazzaville) immediately put the army on alert, tested air raid sirens, closed the frontier, and ordered attacks on any aircraft flying over its territory for which no flight plan had been submitted forty-eight hours in advance. The war of words also mounted.

Immediately after the attempted coup, Congo (Brazzaville) sent emissaries to the OAU, Gabon, Cameroon, the Ivory Coast, Niger and the Central African Republic, with details of the country's complaints against Congo (Kinshasa). Efforts to settle the differences between the two Congos were intensified. By June 1970, President Bokassa of the Central African Republic had succeeded in arranging for a meeting, at which the two Congos, the Central African Republic, Chad, Cameroon and Gabon would try to promote a settlement. And it was as a result of this meeting that an agreement between the Congos was reached on 16 June 1970. President Mobutu of Congo (Kinshasa) and president Marien Ngouabi of Congo (Brazzaville) agreed to open the traffic on the River Congo, restore communications, and set up a permanent commission which would resolve any differences between the countries. Representatives of the

Cameroon, the Central African Republic, Chad and Gabon, as well as of the two Congos, would serve on the commission.

CONGO (KINSHASA)–RWANDA RELATIONS

The deterioration in relations between Congo (Kinshasa) and Rwanda arose out of the question of the white mercenaries. These had been forced on 5 November 1967 to flee to Rwanda, where they were interned in a military camp at Shangugu. Before the OAU could decide what to do with them next, the Congolese president, General Joseph D. Mobutu, demanded their return to Kinshasa to stand trial. Rwanda, which was under pressure from both Belgium and France to allow the mercenaries to be flown immediately to Europe, refused either to repatriate them to the Congo or let them be flown to Europe. Instead, president Kayibanda of Rwanda called on the OAU to arrange their safe evacuation from his country.

The Kinshasa Government broke off diplomatic relations with Rwanda. But when the Congolese authorities agreed in March 1968 that the mercenaries should be allowed to be flown to their countries of origin, efforts to normalize the relations between Congo (Kinshasa) and Rwanda were set in motion. After mediation by President Hamani Diori of Niger, both countries agreed to a resumption of diplomatic relations, and to bring the conflict to an end.

CONGO (KINSHASA)–UGANDA RELATIONS

As in the instances discussed above, the deterioration in relations between Congo (Kinshasa) and Uganda was a by-product of the Congo crisis. It originated in a series of incidents in the border area between both countries in August 1964. When some Congolese 'rebels' were hard-pressed by a combination of Congolese army troops and white mercenaries, they sought refuge in Ugandan territory. The Americans, who by then were taking part in the war against the rebels,[59] thought it their duty to 'teach the Ugandans a lesson'. The Central Intelligence Agency organized what it termed 'Operation Big Bill' under the command of Captain Goffin, a Belgian,[60] to make several incursions into and bomb Ugandan territory as a reprisal.

Progress and Problems

But Tshombe soon realized the implications of these activities by his over-zealous friends. Understanding that he could not continue to antagonize every African sister state, no matter what the views of the Americans were, he decided to demonstrate his 'belief in African unity' by sending a Congolese Government delegation, under the leadership of the Congolese chargé d'affaires in London, J. Kabemba, to meet Milton Obote, the prime minister of Uganda, in May 1965, in an effort to 'normalise relations and resume trade',[61] and the Congolese Government offered to pay compensation for the damage done by the raiders.

(iv) Tackling the Refugee Problem

Every continent has, at one time or another, been confronted with the problem of refugees; Africa is no exception. The refugees in Africa fall roughly into two categories: those from still dependent territories, who are either engaged in political activities with a view to gaining independence for their countries, or looking for jobs or other economic and social means of betterment; and those from other independent African states who, for various reasons, ranging from dissatisfaction with the home government to violent upheaval and civil war, have had to flee. Here we are mainly concerned with the second category.

Refugees from other independent states have been a source of friction between OAU members. All the incidents of this kind that we have examined so far, with the exception of the arrest of Guineans by Ghana, have been caused wholly or partly by the activities of those who had cause to leave their own countries and settle down elsewhere, usually in a neighbouring African state. The question of what to do with this type of refugee is not an easy one, as there are no extradition treaties between African states. Further, the OAU Charter, in Article III, condemns what are termed 'subversive activities on the part of a neighbouring state or any other state'. But this means that a state may all too easily accuse another of harbouring 'dissidents' and thereby supporting 'subversive activities'. At the same time, all African governments recognize the need for humanitarian considerations, and it is the recognition of these considerations that has made it possible for Pan-Africanism to achieve something in this field.

The OAU, at its 1965 summit conference held at Accra, dealt intensively with the issue of 'refugees and subversion'. This came about because of the original refusal of certain OAU member states to attend the summit (in spite of many efforts to dissuade them from boycotting it) on the grounds that Ghana was not only harbouring their dissident nationals, but giving them every assistance and encouragement in 'their subversive activities'. The summit consequently passed a resolution entitled 'the Problem of Refugees in Africa'. This, after reaffirming the desire to give all possible assistance to refugees from any OAU member state on a humanitarian and fraternal basis, requested all member states never to allow the refugee question to become a source of dispute between them.

Before the resolution was passed, refugees had already become an economic burden on certain East African states, especially Uganda and Tanzania. In February 1964, through the efforts of these countries, an OAU commission on refugees was set up; and in November 1964 it visited many refugee centres in Uganda, to acquire first-hand knowledge of the problems facing both the refugees and the countries where they had taken refuge. The first tangible result was an agreement signed between Uganda and the Sudan on 18 December 1964.

The agreement, which has since become a model for solving such problems, was ratified in the following week. Under it, the Sudanese Government made a proclamation through the administrative secretary-general of the Organization of African Unity welcoming the return of the refugees. It also agreed not to try any refugees for offences committed on or before 10 December 1964; to rehabilitate them in the areas and villages from which they had fled and to observe the fundamental human rights embodied in the Universal Declaration adopted by the United Nations. The refugees, on returning to the Sudan, would be entitled to equal treatment with other Sudanese, irrespective of race, religion or political affiliation. The Sudanese Government guaranteed them freedom to receive instruction in their religion, freedom of worship and political opinion, freedom

175

of association and assembly, as well as the right to take part in
the government at all levels. It also pledged that the refugees
would not be liable to either taxation or local rates for at least a
year from the date of their return. The cost of their repatriation,
which would be supervised by a six-man commission of Ugandans and Sudanese, was to be met by the Sudanese Government.
By May 1966 most Sudanese refugees had been repatriated.

5. AFRICA AND THE WORLD

We have so far been examining the achievements of Pan-
Africanism in intra-African affairs. What we have to do now is
to examine what Pan-Africanism has achieved in the field of
relations between Africa and the rest of the world; and it can
be said at once that the African member states of the United
Nations have, since the Organization of African Unity was founded, almost always presented a united front on matters of
common concern in that world body. Whenever a member has
dissented on a matter of particular concern to Africa as a whole,
that member has nearly always either abstained from voting or
retired from the chamber during the vote. Indeed, it has become
routine practice for the OAU member states, whose annual
summit conference takes place before the annual session of the
United Nations, to discuss most topics likely to arise there, and
agree on what policy to adopt and what strategy to follow. A
certain number of foreign ministers are appointed to present the
African point of view to the General Assembly or before the
Security Council, as the case may be. Issues which might be
used to cause disunity among African states, such as the election
of officers to such organs as the Security Council, the Economic
and Social Council, the Trusteeship Council and the General
Committee of the General Assembly, are discussed well in
advance; and candidates to such posts as fall to Africa, adopted.
The same procedure is followed for the specialized agencies of
the UN.

The united front presented at the United Nations Conference
on Trade and Development (UNCTAD) from 1964 onwards

is also important. This unity has emerged not only from the fact that all these African states belong to the 'have-nots', but from the Pan-African ideal of economic cooperation.[62]

Pan-Africanism has not only acted as a stimulus to the achievement of independence, but has been successful in making the world recognize the evils of colonialism. The adoption by all shades of opinion within the Pan-African movement during the last two decades of many resolutions against colonialism, racial discrimination and the apartheid policy has made mankind aware that, as long as such problems remain unsolved, relations between nations and peoples will remain bad. The issues have been constantly discussed at the United Nations: where international recalcitrants such as Portugal, Rhodesia and South Africa, in spite of the assistance they receive from their patrons in the Western world, have been treated in the way they deserve.

The audience granted by the Pope to the leaders of those Africans who were fighting for their birthright in the Portuguese colonies,[63] the World Council of Churches' financial aid to those freedom fighters, the 'Stop the Tour Campaign' against the visit of the South African cricket team to Britain in 1970, the British Churches' reaction to the sale of arms to South Africa by the British Conservative Government,[64] despite the United Nations arms embargo, imposed since 1963; and the private donation made by Queen Juliana of the Netherlands to the World Council of Churches' fund which aids the African freedom fighters[65] are all manifestations of the changed attitude towards African liberation.

Two conclusions emerge. First, over problems of concern to the whole continent Africa has so far been able to present a significantly united front before the world. Secondly, world opinion has been greatly influenced against colonialism and racial discrimination in all its forms in Africa. Both of these are great achievements of Pan-Africanism.

Notes to Chapter 4

1. See 'Agreement Establishing the African Development Bank', E/CN 14/ADB/36, UN, New York, 1964; 'Committee of Nine, African

Development Bank: Its Functions and Purposes', ECA, Addis Ababa, 1964, ADB 1/BG/5, Addis Ababa, 1964.
2. *West Africa*, 6 September 1969, p. 1053.
3. *East African Standard*, 24 June 1970, p. 2.
4. Resolution 125 (1X).
5. CM Resolution 123 (1X).
6. CM Resolution 124 (1X).
7. CM Resolution 159 (1X).
8. The rest are considered in Chapter Six.
9. Keith Panter-Brick, 'The Union Africaine et Malgache', in *Inter-State Relations in Africa*, p. 68.
10. ibid.
11. *West Africa*, 10 August 1963, p. 882; see also Z. Cervenka, *The Organisation of African Unity*, Hurst, London, 1969, p. 143.
12. Keith Panter-Brick, 'The Union Africaine et Malgache', p. 62; *West Africa*, 17 August 1963, p. 909; and Cervenka, *The Organisation of African Unity*, p. 143.
13. Vernon McKay (ed.), *African Diplomacy – Studies in the Determinants of Foreign Policy*, Praeger, New York, 1964, pp. 7–8. For a short but concise appraisal of the role of boundary problems in present-day Europe see 'Gedanken zu einer europäischen Friedensordnung', in *Europa Archiv*, Bonn, No. 17/1969, p. 597.
14. Anthony S. Reuner, 'Morocco's International Boundaries: A Factual Background', in the *Journal of Modern African Studies*, Vol. I, No. 3.
15. Zartman, *International Relations in the New Africa*, p. 110.
16. Zartman, 'The Politics of Boundaries in North and West Africa', in the *Journal of Modern African Studies*, Vol. 3, No. 2, p. 164.
17. *Neue Zürcher Zeitung*, 9–16 October 1963.
18. *Neue Zürcher Zeitung*, 16 October 1963.
19. *West Africa*, 26 October 1963, p. 1219.
20. *Neue Zürcher Zeitung*, 16 October 1963.
21. *Neue Zürcher Zeitung*, 15 October 1963.
22. *Neue Zürcher Zeitung*, 21 October 1963.
23. *Neue Zürcher Zeitung*, 26 October 1963.
24. *Neue Zürcher Zeitung*, 27 October 1963. The Libyan Government informed Emperor Haile Selassie on 25 October 1963 that it was impossible for the government, for 'material reasons', to be host to the proposed summit conference.
25. *Neue Zürcher Zeitung*, 21 October 1963. See also *West Africa*, 2 November 1963. The support given to Algeria by the United Arab Republic led to the breaking-off of diplomatic relations between Morocco and the UAR.
26. *Neue Zürcher Zeitung*, 31 October 1963.
27. Zartman, *International Relations in the New Africa*, p. 89; *Neue Zürcher Zeitung*, 26 February 1964.
28. *Neue Zürcher Zeitung*, 21 February 1964. See also Note 16 above. The troops of the United Arab Republic were withdrawn from Algeria.
29. *New York Times*, 21 February 1964.

30. *The Times*, 29 May 1970.
31. *West Africa*, 1 June 1963, p. 597.
32. ibid.
33. *New York Times*, 17 January 1964.
34. *New York Times*, 7 July 1964.
35. *New York Times*, 8 February 1964 and 9 February 1964; *Neue Zürcher Zeitung*, 10 February 1964.
36. *Neue Zürcher Zeitung*, 10 February 1964.
37. *New York Times*, 11 February 1964. See also *Neue Zürcher Zeitung*, 10 February 1964.
38. ibid.
39. *Neue Zürcher Zeitung*, 16 February 1963.
40. Saadia Touval, 'Africa's Frontiers – Reactions to a Colonial Legacy', in *International Affairs*, Vol. 42, No. 4, p. 646; *Neue Zürcher Zeitung*, 6 March 1964.
41. *New York Times*, 28 March 1964.
42. *Neue Zürcher Zeitung*, 31 March 1964.
43. *New York Times*, 17 October 1964.
44. John Drysdale, *The Somali Dispute*, Pall Mall Press, London, 1964, p. 35.
45. *New York Times*, 2 January 1964.
46. *New York Times*, 16 January 1964; *East African Standard*, 16 January 1964.
47. *East African Standard*, 20 January 1964.
48. *East African Standard*, 18 September 1967.
49. *East African Standard*, 30 October 1967.
50. Zartman, *International Relations in the New Africa*, p. 114; *West Africa*, 11 January 1964, p. 39.
51. ibid.
52. OAU Doc. AHG/Res. 16(1).
53. *West Africa*, 22 March 1969, p. 340.
54. The list is by no means exhaustive here. For an analysis of the factors affecting international relations see Norman J. Padelford and George A. Lincoln, *The Dynamics of International Politics* (second edn), Macmillan, London and New York, 1967; especially Part II.
55. *New York Times*, 20 November 1965.
56. *New York Times*, 25 August 1966.
57. *Neue Zürcher Zeitung*, 1 November 1966; *New York Times*, 1 November 1966; *East African Standard*, 1 November 1966.
58. *West Africa*, 29 November 1969, p. 1454.
59. See *New York Times*, 17 and 18 June 1964. For the reactions of East Africans against the American involvement in the Congolese internal affairs, see *Neue Zürcher Zeitung*, 23 and 24 August 1964.
60. Hans Germani, *Weisse Söldner im schwarzen Land*, Ullstein Verlag, Frankfurt–Berlin, 1966, p. 97.
61. *East African Standard*, 10 May 1965.
62. For corroboration of this point see UN Doc. E/CN 14/WP I (13),

Annex I and the resolution CM/Res. 122 (IX) entitled 'Africa and UNCTAD' adopted by the Council of Ministers at its Ninth Session.
63. See *The Times*, 3 July 1970.
64. See *The Times*, 28 October 1970.
65. See *The Times*, 18 February 1971.

5. Failures

Owing to the vast prospects for progress which it will enable Africa to attain under rapid and effective conditions, African Unity is being resolutely opposed in various ways by all the powers and interest groups hostile to the total liberation of Africa. . .

By subversion, lies, corruption, and pressures of all kinds, the enemies of African progress are directly influencing African life with the aim, if not of preventing the ultimate achievement of African Unity at least of deferring it for as long as possible.

SÉKOU TOURÉ*

(a) Case Studies

Pan-Africanism has had many setbacks and failures. Some are trivial; but the major ones, which have had or still have important effects, are considered here. Such are the break-up of the Mali Federation; the inability of the West African states to form a regional economic grouping; the disunity of the African states during the Congo crisis; the inability of the OAU so far to achieve liberation for the remaining dependencies in Africa; and the apparent lack of unanimity among the African states on how best the South African problem can be solved.

I. THE BREAK-UP OF THE MALI FEDERATION

Immediately after the Second World War, French colonial policy started to undergo a series of changes. Africans became able to form trade unions, youth organizations and political parties. By the end of 1955, two main political parties – the Indépendants d'Outre-Mer (IOM) and the Rassemblement Démocratique Africain (RDA) – had been firmly established in all the French West African territories which formed the Federation of French West Africa (AOF).

One of the main differences between these parties was over the issue of African unity, cloaked under the term 'federation'. The leaders of the IOM had always advocated federation, while the

*Addis Ababa Summit, 1963, pp. 50–51.

leadership of the RDA was opposed to the idea. But within the RDA itself there was support for federation. The divergence of opinion within the RDA over the issue came into the open during the Bamako Conference of the party which took place in September 1957. At that conference, both the Guinean and Sudanese sections came out in support of federation, while the RDA president, Félix Houphouet-Boigny of the Ivory Coast, remained firmly hostile.

Meanwhile, territorial elections had been held, and the RDA emerged victorious. As a result of the constitutional changes in France the leader of the RDA, Félix Houphouet-Boigny, became a member of the French cabinet. He was therefore able to use his position to further his anti-federation campaigns. He collaborated with the French on the *loi-cadre*, which sounded the death-knell of the AOF and caused the ultimate balkanization of French Africa.

In spite of this move, the federalists did not give up. Defeated in Paris, the leader of the Bloc Démocratique Sénégalais (BDS), the Senegalese section of the IOM – Léopold Senghor – carried the fight to Africa. In April 1956 he wrote an article in the party's newspaper reiterating the thesis of a West African primary federation, which would be part of a Federal French Republic.[1] At the congress of the party which took place at Kaolack in May 1956, Senghor and Mamadou Dia denounced 'the confusion and difficulties brought about by . . . Balkanization' of the overseas territories, that threatened to 'cancel out any autonomy that might be acquired'.[2] The congress warmly welcomed the initiative of the African trade union (CGTA) to break its metropolitan ties and work for a common African labour front. It also called for a similar union of all African political parties in French Africa. January 1957 marked the growth in harmony of three existing movements in French West Africa: the Mouvement Socialiste Africain (MSA) in Conakry, the Convention Africain (CA) in Dakar, and the Union Générale des Travailleurs d'Afrique Noire (UGTAN) in Cotonou.

Within the RDA itself matters did not stand still. At the end of the Bamako conference an uneasy compromise, which did no more than adjourn the points at issue, was reached. On 12 November 1958, Gabriel d'Arboussier, as head of the Senegalese section of the RDA, circulated a proposal for a primary federation to all the heads of government in French West Africa. Significantly, his proposals were similar to those already put forward by the Parti du Regroupement Africain (PRA), formed in March 1958 when the Convention Africain (CA) and the Mouvement Socialiste Africain (MSA) merged. As a result of this move, an emergency meeting of the RDA Co-ordinating Committee was hastily called by Félix Houphouet-Boigny. At that meeting, which took place in Abidjan, the federalist position was ably represented by Modibo Keita of Sudan and Doudou Gueye of Senegal. The anti-federalists were represented by Félix Houphouet-Boigny and by Hamani Diori of Niger. Because of deadlock, it was announced that the meeting had not taken place 'officially'.[3]

It was becoming increasingly clear to the leadership of the RDA that the idea of federation had much support among its rank and file. The option to join a federation was therefore agreed upon at the party's October congress, and the assemblies of four French West African territories – Senegal, Sudan, Dahomey and the Upper Volta – in quick succession formally chose to become a 'state member of the Community empowered to join a federation'.

The Bamako Congress, at which the leaders of the four territories discussed the federation issue, took place on 29 and 30 December 1958. It appealed to the political leaders of all parties and groups 'to unite their efforts to bring about political unity within each state, as a guarantee of the Federation's cohesion and development',[4] and dispatched official delegates to the Ivory Coast and to Mauritania in an attempt to make them join the proposed federation. A resolution urging representatives of the four states to meet on 12 January 1959 in a Federal Constituent Conference at Dakar was endorsed.

The Federal Constituent Assembly started immediately the Grand Council of the now defunct AOF was wound up on 10 January 1959. The dominant delegations from Senegal and the Sudan worked smoothly together, and the proceedings were productive. Despite the absence of the Dahomeyan premier,

183

Sourou Migan Apithy, the Dahomeyan delegation was led by convinced federalists – Alexandre Adande and Émile Zinsou. The Voltaic delegation, whose status at the Bamako Congress had been open to doubt, attended this time with full powers; and its hitherto hesitant leader, Maurice Yameogo, declared that the Upper Volta gave its total and unrestricted support to the federation.

The draft constitution of the proposed Federation of Mali, drafted by experts under Gabriel d'Arboussier and Doudou Thiam, was approved by acclamation. At the end of the conference the delegates, led by Modibo Keita, swore three times 'to defend everywhere the Mali Federation, to become tireless pilgrims and preachers of political unity, and to accept the ultimate sacrifice for the realisation of African Unity'.[5]

While the federalists were consolidating their powers, and everything seemed set fair for the establishment of a Mali Federation composed of Senegal, the Sudan, Dahomey and the Upper Volta, there were those inside both French West Africa and France who were determined to wreck the enterprise. The African forces of reaction, led by Félix Houphouet-Boigny and the Ivory Coast section of the RDA, with encouragement from the French, started to bring pressure on both Dahomey and the Upper Volta.[6] The Voltaic Assembly nonetheless approved, on 28 January 1959, the Mali federal constitution without a single dissenting vote, although several important members were absent from the sitting of the National Assembly. Annoyed at the decision, the opposition stepped up its pressure. A hastily-arranged meeting of the Voltaic Assembly was called for at midnight on 28 February. At that meeting, which was reported to have been attended by thirty-nine of the seventy members of the Assembly,[7] a draft constitution, submitted by Yameogo, which made no mention of the Mali Federation, was approved. In a speech to the Assembly, Yameogo said among other things:

The Government of Upper Volta wants African unity and will fight to bring it about. But just as one bloc unites so two blocs divide. Upper Volta does not want to choose between Dakar and Abidjan.[8]

Two weeks later, this draft constitution was also approved in a referendum; and the Upper Volta ceased to belong to the Mali Federation.

Pressure was also brought upon Dahomey – and Dahomey had a ready-made anti-federalist collaborator. The premier, Sourou Migan Apithy, who, after a quick trip to Paris, had refused to attend the Federal Constituent Assembly, immediately resigned from the PRA and joined forces with the Dahomey section of the RDA and other anti-federalist forces. When the Dahomeyan Constituent Assembly met in February under the control of the new political alignment, it endorsed a new constitution; Dahomey, too, thus backed out of the proposed Mali Federation.

In spite of these defections, the Mali Federation was formally launched on 4 April 1959. Modibo Keita of the Sudan was chosen to head the federal government; while Senghor was elected president of both the Federal Assembly and the new federal party, the Parti Fédéraliste Africain (PFA). Mamadou Dia became the federal vice-premier and minister of defence. The ministries were shared equally between the two component territories.

Everything seemed to be going well until the issue of independence arose. For on this issue, the leaders of Senegal and of Sudan held different views. The Senegalese were perfectly satisfied with the constitutional provisions of the Fifth Republic which, in establishing the French Community, granted sovereignty over internal matters to the constituent states, but left foreign affairs, defence and money policy under the exclusive jurisdiction of France. This met the Senegalese desire for 'independence in interdependence'. The Sudanese leaders, on the other hand, looked to the achievement of complete national sovereignty. Yet the issue was resolved peacefully and with a minimum of hard feeling, perhaps because other African territories, too, were yearning for independence.

The Mali Federation was, from the very beginning, faced with the problem of ideological orientation. The Sudanese, who had a well-organized party, came out in April 1959 for a strong unitary government; and, besides, held radical views on economic and foreign policy. The Senegalese, on the other hand, already used to the delicate functioning of their political system, wanted to guarantee what Senghor had called the 'autonomy of the Senegalese soul'; favoured a liberal economic policy; and were far more favourably disposed towards France. This divergence was responsible for the first major clash between the partners in the Mali Federation.

The Sudanese aspired to concentrate supreme political power in the hands of a single officer. This they intended to achieve, once independence was proclaimed, by combining the role of the chief of state with that of the head of government responsible for foreign affairs. The Senegalese were strongly opposed to this on the ground that the principle of parity, as laid down in the agreements signed in April 1959, which divided executive functions between the chief of state and a head of government of different nationalities, would be jeopardized. The issue was so serious that both Gabriel d'Arboussier and Doudou Thiam secretly circulated a proposal in April 1960 urging that Mali be transformed into a loose confederation, with the executive power restricted to an economic and technical role.[9] In an effort to resolve the crisis, a meeting of Mali's political leaders was called for 14 April.

This meeting, behind closed doors, lasted three days.[10] It resolved that the offices of chief of state and head of government should remain separate, with the latter retaining control over foreign affairs. It also agreed that a Senegalese might be chosen as chief of state. A conciliation mission, made up of the Directing Committee of the PFA, was empowered to work out the details of an acceptable formula to end the crisis.

The conciliation mission decided that the president of the Federation should be chosen by a congress composed of an equal number of Senegalese and Sudanese Territorial and Federal Assembly members. This congress was to meet before the opening of the 1960 September session of the United Nations General Assembly, to which the Mali Federation was expected to be admitted. The mission also succeeded in persuading the Sudanese to accept some changes in the federal constitution, so that each territory might have greater control over its own economic planning and taxation. At a meeting of the Mali leaders on 21 and 22 May 1960, the work of the mission was endorsed, and the crisis appeared to have been resolved.

Soon afterwards, however, another major policy matter caused conflict between the constituent parts of the Federation. This time it was the Africanization of the Civil Service. Already, during the constituent congress of the PFA which took place early in July 1959, the Sudanese had made their position on the matter clear. They maintained that the establishment of the Federation required men who were 'politically committed and not primarily technical experts'. The Senegalese, on the other hand, emphasized the need for technical expertise; and in consequence employed many French nationals to man their finance and planning ministries. This policy found no favour with the Senegalese youth, and was, indeed, a source of friction between the main body of the UPS – the Senegalese section of the PFA – and its own youth movement. Even during the party's congress, held in July 1960, both Senghor and Mamadou Dia were obliged to spend hours with the younger delegates, in order to persuade them to approve a party programme which did not include a commitment to rapid and total Africanization. As the congress was coming to an end, Modibo Keita was asked by Senghor to say a few words in his capacity as head of the Sudanese delegation. He took the opportunity to declare that he did not agree with the Senegalese on the Africanization question. And the younger delegates, having just been coaxed into accepting the party programme, now seized the chance to express their disapproval of it. Uproar ensued, and it took Senghor and Dia the better part of the night to re-establish control and get the resolution reapproved.[11]

After this incident, relations between Senghor and Dia on the one hand, and the Sudanese leaders on the other, deteriorated fast. Matters which could have been amicably and simply settled were magnified out of all proportion. It is in this context that the Sudanese hints for a revision of the Franco–Malian agreements, and Senegalese reactions to them, must be viewed.

During a state visit to Liberia, Modibo Keita expressed the view that the establishment of an African monetary zone might advance the cause of African unity. This view was interpreted by the Senegalese as an indication that the Sudanese wanted to take Mali out of the franc zone: a move which the Senegalese, the French commercial interests and the French Government viewed with great concern. At about the same time, some Sudanese vaguely alluded to the desirability of revising the Franco–Malian military pact. Both the French and the Senegalese misinterpreted this as well. While the French thought that the Sudanese were trying to oust them from their Dakar naval and air-force headquarters, the Senegalese premier, Mamadou Dia, who was also the federal vice-premier, regarded such a move as a threat to the ten billion francs which the French military expenditures contributed annually to his economy.

To make a situation that was already defunct even more so, the Mali Federation, in accordance with the Franco–Malian military pact, had to have her own army, which' clearly had to be commanded by someone! The Federation had two colonels with equally distinguished military records, who were separated by a few days in seniority. One was a Senegalese; the other Sudanese. Dia, in his capacity as minister of defence, preferred the Senegalese, although the Sudanese was senior. Modibo Keita, on the other hand, argued that the Sudanese, being senior, should be chosen. Dia refused to sign the nomination documents. The appointment was officially gazetted on 25 July 1960 all the same. Thus alienated, Dia refused to receive Soumare, the appointed chief of staff, and also cut off all communication with Modibo Keita, the Federal premier.

By this time only Senghor, among the Senegalese leaders, remained convinced of the necessity for the further existence of the Mali Federation. And at this stage an incident took place which antagonized him also. A certain Cheikh Tidjane Sy informed the Senegalese premier that he and several other religious leaders had been approached by certain Sudanese leaders, with the suggestion, allegedly, that Mali's evolution along Muslim lines might be better assured if a Muslim, instead of a Catholic (Senghor), were to be made the president of the Mali Federation. When it was later revealed that emissaries of Modibo Keita had actually had contact with Cheikh Tidjane Sy's uncle, and also that Modibo Keita himself had asked to pay a formal call on

Falilou M. Backe, the grand khalif of Senegal's six hundred thousand Mourides, Senghor agreed with Dia that Senegal should pull out of the Mali Federation so long as anyone else outranked him in the federal government.[12] On 8 August Senghor, Mamadou Dia and Gabriel d'Arboussier held a meeting in Paris. They agreed there that unless Senghor got the presidency, and unless it was certain that the Sudanese would 'behave themselves', they would take Senegal out of the Federation.

Events now piled upon one another. The Senegalese leaders remained more or less in permanent contact with the French High Commissioner in Dakar. Outside the capital the UPS political secretary, Ousmane N'Gom, kept the party faithfuls on the alert, for movement to the capital at a moment's notice.

On 16 August Colonel Soumare asked Lieutenant-Colonel Pierre, the French commander of the Mali gendarmerie, what number of platoons were around Dakar; and whether these would be ready for action in case of an emergency. Lt-Col. Pierre, who was aware of the relationship between Dia and Soumare, promptly notified Dia, and informed the French High Commissioner about the discussions between himself and the army chief of staff. Dia immediately promulgated an order placing the gendarmerie under the exclusive order of the governments of the territories in which the units were stationed. At the same time he informed all the Senegalese regional governors to be on the alert in case of trouble.

On 18 August Soumare dispatched two telegrams to the army posts at Podor and Bignona, requesting them to stand ready, as they might soon be needed in Dakar during the presidential elections. Lt-Col. Pierre made sure that Dia was kept fully informed. On the night of 18 August, the Senegalese leaders alerted the rank and file of the UPS, with the information that something was afoot. Local committees were ordered to mobilize many faithfuls, for transport to Dakar immediately.

On 19 August Dia requested Lt-Col. Pierre to have eight platoons of gendarmerie ready to maintain order in Dakar with effect from noon. The Sudanese had been unaware of the Senegalese activities; but now news reached them that several trucks and buses, loaded with Senegalese peasants carrying flintlocks and bows and arrows, were arriving at Rufisque, bound for Dakar. An emergency meeting of the federal cabinet was hastily called. Significantly only one Senegalese member of the cabinet – Boubacor Gueye – attended. But undeflected by the absence of the other Senegalese federal ministers, the cabinet took far-reaching decisions. Mamadou Dia was relieved of his post as defence minister, and his duties were transferred to the federal premier. A national state of emergency was declared. The army was immediately deployed to safeguard all public installations.

Caught unawares by this response, the Senegalese leaders started to seek ways out of the new situation. When Gabriel d'Arboussier saw the troops surrounding the federal parliament building, he immediately roused Senghor, who was having a nap there. They quickly left for Dia's house, where they met Lt-Col. Pierre; Valdiodio N'Diaye, the Senegalese minister of the interior; and others who had also been looking for Dia. D'Arboussier was left behind to alert the loyal Senegalese territorial assembly members, and the others drove to the gendarmerie barracks. While Senghor and Valdiodio N'Diaye were whipping up enthusiasm for their cause, Lt-Col. Pierre lured Soumare to the gendarmerie barracks where, immediately on arrival, he was overpowered and put under house arrest. After the arrest of Soumare the way was clear; and Col. Fall, his rival and next ranking officer, ordered the troops to yield their guard of public installations to the gendarmerie.

At a midnight session of the Senegalese territorial assembly, the sixty-seven members present declared the independence of Senegal from the Mali Federation.

The Sudanese leaders with the Senegalese federalists were put under house arrest. On 22 August 1960, they were sent back to Bamako in a sealed train. The dream of unity had turned into nightmare.

2. INABILITY TO FORM A WEST AFRICAN REGIONAL ECONOMIC COMMUNITY

The UN Economic Commission for Africa has taken the lead in urging African countries to form economic groupings on a regional basis. At its seventh session held in 1965, it recommended by its resolution 142(VII), the early establishment 'of inter-governmental machinery responsible for the harmonization of economic and social development in the sub-regions' of North, West, Eastern and Central Africa.[13] These subdivisions of the continent were regarded as viable economic units, within which economic and particularly industrial development could most productively be planned on an integrated basis. It was also felt that the establishment of regional institutions of economic co-operation would facilitate the establishment of other links between existing integrationist groups and neighbouring countries in the regions concerned. As already pointed out above[14] this policy has been endorsed by the OAU in a series of resolutions.

All the West African countries have recognized the importance of coordinated development, if economic growth is to be accelerated in their region, with diversification, economies of scale, specialization, and greater self-sufficiency.

As Table 1 shows, the fourteen West African countries have a combined population of a little less than 100 million, which is very unevenly spread over an area of approximately six million square kilometres. The three landlocked countries – Mali, Niger and the Upper Volta – together with Mauritania, account for over 60 per cent of the total area but contain only 14 per cent of the population.

The ECA efforts to bring about general coordination began with industrial development, because it was realized that co-operation in this field was crucial, if the very low level of industrialization in the area (see Table 2) was to be raised. Negotiations proceeded, particularly in relation to the iron and steel industry, until October 1965; when representatives of the countries decided that such development should be placed in the context of 'general, industrialized economic co-operation'. As a

191

Table I. West Africa: selected indicators

Country	Area (thousands of square kilometres)	Population (a) (thousands)	Population density (persons per sq. km.)	Gross domestic product (b) (millions of dollars)	Gross domestic product per capita (dollars)	Purchasing power (c) (thousands of dollars per sq. km.)
Dahomey	113	2,300	20·4	177	77	1·6
Gambia	11	324	29·5	26	80	2·4
Ghana	239	7,537	31·5	1,901	252	8·0
Guinea	246	3,420	13·9	275	80	1·1
Ivory Coast	322	3,750	11·6	1,010	269	3·1
Liberia	111	1,041	9·4	280	269	2·5
Mali	1,202	4,485	3·7	305	68	0·3
Mauritania	1,031	1,030	1·0	111	123	0·1
Niger	1,267	3,250	2·6	263	81	0·2
Nigeria	924	56,400	61·0	4,307	76	4·7
Senegal	196	3,400	17·3	674	198	3·4
Sierra Leone ·	72	2,240	31·1	343	156	4·8
Togo	56	1,603	28·6	156	97	2·8
Upper Volta	274	4,750	17·3	229	48	0·8
W.A.E.C.*	6,064	95,500	15·7	10,104	107	1·7

Source: *Economic Co-operation and Integration in Africa: Three Case Studies* (ST/ECA/109, United Nations Publication, Sales No. E.69.II.K.7), New York, 1969

(a) UN mid-year estimate 1964;
(b) at market prices; 1964, except 1963 for Mauritania;
(c) defined as gross domestic product per unit of area.
*Proposed West African Economic Community.

Table 2. Origin of Gross Domestic Product of selected countries in West Africa, 1964 (Percentage)

Country	Primary sector (a)	Secondary sector				Tertiary sector				
		Total industries	Extractive industries	Manufac-turing	Construc-tion	Total	Commerce	Trans-port	Admini-stration (b)	Other services
Ghana	51·4	14·4	2·5	7·5	4·4	34·2	—	—	—	—
Guinea (c)	53·8	24·8	8·9	2·6	13·3	21·4	3·0	3·0	7·8	13·6
Ivory Coast (d)	42·3	16·1	0·5	10·9	4·7	42·3	15·7	8·4	5·7	11·8
Liberia	28·0	36·0	26·0	4·0	6·0	36·0	11·0	6·0	—	—
Mali (e)	54·0	12·0	1·0	6·0	5·0	34·0	17·0	6·0	2·0	9·0
Niger (f)	61·0	11·1	0·4	4·6	6·1	27·9	—	—	—	—
Nigeria (e)	62·6	11·3	1·9	5·4	4·0	26·1	11·8	4·9	5·7	3·7
Senegal (e)	29·4	13·0	1·8	7·4	3·8	57·6	30·2	3·8	8·6	15·0
Sierra Leone (g)	30·2	26·3	17·7	5·5	3·1	43·5	14·0	7·1	17·5	4·9
Togo	54·0	15·2	4·9	6·6	3·7	30·8	11·2	6·3	4·9	8·4
Upper Volta	52·0	13·0	1·0	9·0	3·0	35·0	—	—	—	—

Source: *Economic Co-operation and Integration in Africa: Three Case Studies*

(a) including agriculture, livestock, fishing and forestry;
(b) government, in French-speaking countries, also includes private non-profit services;
(c) 1964–5, estimated;
(d) 1965;
(e) 1962;
(f) 1963;
(g) 1964–5.

result of this decision, further action on a sectoral basis was postponed, and a series of regional meetings on economic co-operation was organized by the ECA.

In November 1966 twelve of the West African states – Dahomey, Ghana, the Ivory Coast, Liberia, Mali, Mauritania, Niger, Nigeria, Senegal, Sierra Leone, Togo and the Upper Volta – took the first major step, under the guidance of the ECA, towards economic integration. Experts from these countries met in Niamey and resolved to promote 'co-ordinated development of their economies, especially in industry, agriculture, transport and communications, trade and payments, manpower and natural resources'. They also agreed to 'further the maximum possible inter-change of goods and services', and to eliminate progressively customs and 'other barriers to the expansion of trade' as well as 'restrictions on current payment transactions and on capital movements'.[15] The Niamey conference was followed by another meeting, held at Accra in April 1967, at the end of which, representatives of the states signed the Articles of Association of a West African Common Market, described as 'a transitional agreement governing the means of co-operation be-tween the Member States prior to the formal establishment of the West African Community'. They also endorsed the Niamey resolution and agreed to set up an Interim Council of Ministers. In order that the envisaged goal might be achieved, the member states pledged themselves to 'endeavour to formulate and adopt common policies, including specific branches of industry and agriculture, the joint operation of specific transport and com-munication services, the development and use in common of sources of energy, joint research training of manpower and the joint implementation of all other projects designed to promote the objectives of the Community, as well as of common trade and payments arrangements'.[16]

The Interim Council of Ministers met in November 1967 at Dakar and considered the preliminary draft of a treaty for the proposed community, which had been prepared by the ECA. A provisional secretariat was set up and requested to prepare a second draft treaty, while bearing in mind a set of specific principles or points of reference put forward by the council.

194

These included the harmonization of policies and cooperation with respect to agricultural production; general coordination of economic policies including industrialization, education, training and research; coordination of development programmes and their financing; the question of compensation for loss of customs revenue arising from trade liberalization under the treaty; and bilateral cooperation between some members of the Community without detriment to the others.[17] The second draft treaty was to be considered by the council not later than November 1968. The council also came to the conclusion that further study was needed on the necessary measures to achieve economic integration of the region, particularly in the agricultural sector; and the secretariat was therefore requested to study the areas of priority for cooperation within the Economic Community.

In April 1968 the first West African Summit Conference was held in Monrovia. Nine of the fourteen West African countries – Gambia, Ghana, Guinea, Liberia, Mali, Mauritania, Nigeria, Senegal and the Upper Volta – were represented: and though the others – Dahomey, the Ivory Coast, Niger, Sierra Leone and Togo – stayed away, the conference adopted a protocol establishing the West African Economic Community. The conference communiqué made known that the Articles of Association signed at Accra on 4 May 1967 formed an integral part of the protocol. The communiqué further stated that:

(a) by signing the protocol, the summit conference had created a conference of heads of state and government as the supreme authority of the West African region, a council of ministers and an executive secretariat;

(b) the protocol empowered these organs to implement programmes of action adopted at the meeting, and gave them a mandate for the future joint development of the region;

(c) the conference adopted a general resolution and programme of action on the substantive measures to be undertaken in the immediate future, covering cooperation in the development of industry, agriculture, transport, telecommunications, energy, health, education, training and research, as well as cultural exchanges;

(d) the protocol declared that the aim of the new regional group should be economic integration of the region;

(e) the conference also decided that barriers standing in the way of increased trade between member countries should be removed, and a West African common market ultimately established.

It was also agreed that the next ministerial meeting of the community and its conference of heads of state and government should take place at Dakar in December 1968 and at Ouagadougou in March 1969 respectively. Neither of these scheduled meetings materialized, however. Indeed, the fact that West Africa was unable to form a regional economic community by the end of 1969 made it the only region in Africa without one. Why then has West Africa, so long in the forefront of the Pan-Africanist cause, lagged behind other regions in this respect? The answer lies chiefly in inter-state relations there. (The dynamic Pan-African policies of president Nkrumah seemed to find no favour with the so-called 'moderate' leaders of West Africa; and it must be noted that there have been many of these. Besides, some leaders of the former French West Africa regarded Ghana as the base for subversive actions directed at their overthrow. So, during the Nkrumah era, the Ghana–Togo, Ghana–Ivory Coast and Ghana–Upper Volta borders remained closed for most of the time, and were opened only after the overthrow of Nkrumah. Apart from this, Nkrumah himself was against the setting up of regional organizations. He was, indeed, responsible for the break-up of common services among the former British territories in West Africa. After his overthrow, the new leaders of Ghana thought it right to expel many West Africans from the country, and this only served to poison inter-state relations in West Africa. The Nigerian civil war and the role played by the Ivory Coast then did not make the climate for cooperation more congenial. And relations between Guinea and most of her other partners in the former French West Africa seemed for a long time at a very low level.)

Despite the ending of the Nigerian civil war, a detente between Guinea and the Ivory Coast, and efforts by the Ghanaian authorities to improve relations with other West African states, the West Africans have still not been able to inaugurate a West African Economic Community. Instead, the Customs Union of West African States (UDEAO), which groups Dahomey, the Ivory Coast, Mali, Mauritania, Niger, Senegal and the Upper Volta, was re-christened the 'West African Economic Community' on 21 May 1970. And one is tempted to regard this as yet another move to prevent real unity from being achieved.

What are the consequences? The most important is that economic cooperation is still not possible in West Africa. On the contrary: there is already an increasingly destructive competition in the industrial field. New factories are established, when existing factories that manufacture the same products in neighbouring countries are operating at less than full capacity. There are, for example, three bicycle-assembly factories in West Africa – in the Ivory Coast, Nigeria and the Upper Volta. The total capacities of the first two are 140,000 bicycles and 30,000 motor cycles; but production was 32,000 and 750 respectively in 1965.[18] In spite of this, new bicycle-assembly plants were planned in other UDEAO countries. Similar examples abound for the manufacture of cigarettes, shoes, soap, nails, matches, etc.

Trade between the West African states is minimal (see Table 3). The main causes are two: the traditional, climatically induced specialization in the production of foodstuffs and certain other agricultural materials; and the existence of preference systems and monetary arrangements among groups of West African countries. About half the intra-regional trade consists of foodstuffs, while another 14 per cent is composed of fats, oils and other crude materials (again see Table 3). Yet despite their relatively large volume of mutual trade in foodstuffs, the West African countries are able to supply one another on the average with only some 7 per cent of total food imports.

Since the development of oil resources in Nigeria, petroleum has become an important item in intra-regional areas. Nigeria already supplies a significant proportion of Ghana's needs. With the establishment of a West African Regional Economic Community on the basis of the ECA proposal, there would be better

Table 3. West Africa: commodity composition(a) of regional imports.(b) 1962–6 average (Percentage)

Commodity	Composition of imports from		Share of intra-regional imports in total imports
	World	West Africa	
Total	100	100	2·7
Food, beverages and tobacco	19·4	49·1	6·9
Inedible crude materials, animal fats and vegetable oils	2·1	14·2	18·3
Mineral fuels	6·2	9·3	4·0
Machinery and transport equipment	26·4	1·9	0·2
Other manufactured goods	45·8	25·5	1·5

Source: Economic Co-operation and Integration in Africa: Three Case Studies
  (a) based on the UN Standard International Trade Classification;
  (b) excluding the imports of Gambia, Guinea and Liberia, for which no data are available.

intra-regional trade, with a combined market of about one hundred million inhabitants. (See Table 1 above.)

3. THE CONGO CRISIS

The affairs of the Belgian Congo (now the Zaire Republic) first came up for discussion at the Conference of Independent African States at Addis Ababa in June 1960. Although invited to attend, Congo herself could not be represented because of her internal situation. The conference called on the rival leaders of the country – Patrice Lumumba and Joseph Kasavubu – to settle their differences and work for unity.

Shortly afterwards the Congo became independent, and was confronted within a few days by an army mutiny. The Belgians, who arrogated to themselves the right to intervene in the internal affairs of the new independent country, returned in force as military and paramilitary personnel. The Congolese central Government appealed to the United Nations for help in getting rid of the Belgian invaders and in sorting things out. This request led to the United Nations intervention, which began with the Security Council resolution of 14 July 1960.[19]

Before the resolution was passed, the secretary-general of the United Nations received offers of troops from Ghana, Guinea, Morocco, Tunisia and Ethiopia. For at this stage there was still cooperation among all African member states of the United Nations.

That year, christened the 'Africa Year', saw the emergence of many African states, which subsequently joined the United Nations. As noted in Chapter One, seventeen African states became UN members before the end of that year. But the influx of these states completely changed the atmosphere within the African group at the United Nations.[20] The new members from the former French Africa – Cameroon, the Central African Republic, Chad, Congo (Brazzaville), Dahomey, Gabon, the Ivory Coast, Madagascar, Niger, Senegal and the Upper Volta – did not join hands with the existing African members, but kept largely aloof. This was due partly to the fact that most leaders of these states had never been very enthusiastic about Pan-Africanism, and partly because of their conservative approach to international affairs, especially with regard to the attitude between newly independent countries and the former colonial powers. Most of them were tied to the apron-strings of France economically, financially and even militarily. By the end of the year, therefore, as we saw in Chapter One, there were three distinct groups within the combined African UN members: Ghana, Guinea, Mali, Morocco and the United Arab Republic composing the first; Ethiopia, Libya, Nigeria, Somalia, Sudan, Togo and Tunisia, forming the second; while all others – the members of the French Community – made up the third. This disunity was later to affect Pan-Africanism badly at the United Nations.

Meanwhile, in the Congo the situation continued to deteriorate. Aided and abetted by Belgium and other powers with vested interests in the province, Moise Tshombe had declared the secession of Katanga from the rest of the Congo, as 'the Republic of Katanga'. Although the United Nations forces (ONUC) sent to assist the Congolese Central Government were standing by, they were ordered not to give any assistance in bringing the Katangan secession to an end.[21] Disillusioned by the UN attitude, the Congolese premier, Patrice Lumumba, turned to the independent African states. The result was the Conference of Independent African States which took place in Leopoldville between 25 and 31 August 1960. The conference came out in support of the UN, but regretted the lack of cooperation between the latter and the Congolese Central Government. It insisted that all aid to the Congo should be chanelled through the UN. No unanimity was reached on the issue of Katangan secession. Only Guinea supported Lumumba in his desire to take immediate steps for the overthrow of Tshombe's secessionist government. Disillusioned and desperate, without consulting President Kasavubu, Lumumba then appealed to the Russians for aid in ending the Katangan secession. This led to an estrangement between the leaders, and the subsequent dismissal from office of each by the other. The Congolese Senate stepped in and confirmed both leaders in their posts. The African states, supporting the Senate's move, insisted that no Congolese government without both Lumumba as prime minister and Kasavubu as president could be regarded as legitimate.

In the meantime, Kasavubu had appointed Joseph Ileo as Congolese prime minister on 5 September 1960, after dismissing Lumumba. After the Senate decision it appeared as if there were two governments in the Congo: one led by Lumumba, the other by Kasavubu and Ileo. On 20 September the Congo was formally admitted to the UN. The arena of conflict was transferred to New York, where both sent delegates to attend the Fifteenth Session of the UN General Assembly.

On 10 October, Guinea submitted a draft resolution to the General Assembly requesting that the Lumumba delegation be seated, pending the report of the Assembly's Credentials Committee. This move was supported by Ghana and Morocco, and a revised version of the draft resolution was submitted by the three countries on 12 October. With more support forthcoming from other members of this group (called the 'first group' above),[22] the resolution was further revised, and was re-submitted on 28 October. The final draft resolution not only sought to seat the

Lumumba delegation but also called on the UN secretary-general to take steps to promote and ensure the security of a meeting of the Congolese parliament.[23] Other African groups refused to co-sponsor this resolution, on the grounds that a decision to seat the Lumumba delegation would constitute an insult to Kasavubu.[24] While the draft resolution was undergoing revisions, Kasavubu continued to bombard the Assembly president with cables claiming that his own delegation should be accorded recognition.[25] On 8 November he addressed the General Assembly. He announced a new delegation, headed by himself, and asked that its credentials be examined immediately, claiming that he, as chief of state, was the sole authority entitled to designate representatives to the Assembly. Efforts to prevent the seating of either delegation were made by the African states in the first and second groups, after Kasavubu's speech. The states of the third group, however, came out in support of Kasavubu, and, with backing from the Western powers, succeeded. The Assembly admitted the Kasavubu delegation to the Fifteenth Session of the UNGA.[26]

Meanwhile, on 14 September 1960, Mobutu had announced assumption of authority. And this later turned out to have been a well-managed manoeuvre. Mobutu, who had received money from the CIA with which to pay his troops, was only carrying out a CIA plan to get rid of Lumumba. A government under Joseph Ileo, with a 'college of commissioners', was established. Lumumbists under the leadership of Antoine Gizenga gathered themselves in Stanleyville. On 27 November, Lumumba escaped and made for Stanleyville. Since he took no precautions and stopped at almost every village en route to address the people, he was caught on 1 December and flown back to Leopoldville, from where he was sent to Moise Tshombe on 17 January 1961.

By the end of the year there were three main centres of power in the Congo: Leopoldville, where the Kasavubu–Mobutu–Ileo trio was in control; Stanleyville, the Lumumbist stronghold; and Elisabethville, the seat of Tshombe's secessionist government.

On the Pan-African front, the division which had become apparent at the UN over the seating of the Kasavubu delegation deepened. In December the supporters of Kasavubu met to plan their new strategy at a conference in Brazzaville. This meeting led to the Casablanca conference of January 1961, attended by those states which were inclined towards the Lumumbist camp.

At the beginning of 1961 there seemed to be some understanding between the states of the first and second groups; both thought that something should be done very urgently in order to save the Congo from further disaster. When it became clear that Lumumba had been transferred to Elisabethville, they called for a meeting of the Security Council. During the Security Council meetings of 1, 2 and 7 February 1961, they called for urgent measures to release Lumumba and the two comrades who had been transferred with him to Elizabethville. In an effort to prevent the Security Council from taking any immediate action on the issue, the states of the third group – now known as the Brazzaville group, after their 1960 December conference – bombarded the Security Council with representations, requesting a postponement of the debates until they had time to consider their position.[27] On 13 February 1961 the world learnt that Patrice Lumumba and his two companions were dead.

While the Brazzaville states were engaged in protestations, the states of the first and second groups had started to negotiate over what kind of resolution should be submitted to the Security Council.[28] A draft resolution[29] submitted on 17 February received the support of all African states in the first and second groups and, as usual, many Asian UN members. The Brazzaville group refused to support the resolution. Nevertheless, it was adopted by the Security Council at its 942nd meeting, on 20–21 February 1961, by nine votes to nil with two abstentions. Significantly, France was one of the two abstaining members. In view of the significance of this resolution (S/4741) it is reproduced here verbatim:

[A]

The Security Council,
Having considered the situation in the Congo,
Having learnt with deep regret the announcement of the killing of the Congolese leaders, Mr Patrice Lumumba, Mr Maurice Mpolo and Mr Joseph Okito,
Deeply concerned at the grave repercussions of these crimes and the

danger of widespread civil war and bloodshed in the Congo and the
threat to international peace and security,

Noting the Report of the Secretary-General's Special Representative
(S/4691) dated 12 February 1961 bringing to light the development of
a serious civil war situation and preparations therefore,

1. *Urges* that the United Nations take immediately all appropriate
measures to prevent the occurrence of civil war in the Congo, including
arrangements for cease-fires, the halting of all military operations, the
prevention of clashes, and the use of force, if necessary, in the last
resort;

2. *Urges* that measures be taken for the immediate withdrawal and
evacuation from the Congo of all Belgian and other military and para-
military personnel and political advisers not under the United
Nations Command, and mercenaries;

3. *Calls* upon all states to take immediate and energetic measures to
prevent the departure of such personnel for the Congo from their
territories, and for the denial of transit and other facilities to them;

4. *Decides* that an immediate and impartial investigation be held in
order to ascertain the circumstances of the death of Mr Lumumba and
his colleagues and that the perpetrators of these crimes be punished;

5. *Reaffirms* the Security Council resolutions of 14 July, 22 July and
9 August, 1960, and the General Assembly resolution 1474(ES-IV) of
20 September 1960 and reminds all States of their obligation under
these resolutions.

[B]

The Security Council,
Gravely concerned at the continuing deterioration in the Congo, and the
prevalence of conditions which seriously imperil peace and order, and
the unity and territorial integrity of the Congo, and threaten international peace and security,

Noting with deep regret and concern the systematic violations of human
rights and fundamental freedoms and the general absence of rule of
law in the Congo,

Recognizing the imperative necessity of the restoration of parliamentary
institutions in the Congo in accordance with the fundamental law of
the country, so that the will of the people should be reflected through
the freely elected Parliament,

Convinced that the solution of the problem of the Congo lies in the
hands of the Congolese people themselves without any interference
from outside and that there can be no solution without conciliation,

Convinced further that the imposition of any solution, including the formation of any government not based on genuine conciliation would, far from settling any issues, greatly enhance the dangers of conflict within the Congo and the threat to international peace and security,

1. *Urges* the convening of the Parliament and the taking of necessary protective measures in that connection;

2. *Urges* that Congolese armed units and personnel should be reorganized and brought under discipline and control, and arrangements be made on impartial and equitable bases to that end and with a view to the elimination of any possibility of interference by such units and personnel in the political life of the Congo;

3. *Calls upon* all States to extend their full cooperation and assistance and take such measures as may be necessary on their part, for the implementation of this resolution.

The public exhibition of disunity among the African states over the Security Council resolution of 21 February 1961 was the last of its type over the Congo crisis in New York. This, however, did not mean that the states sank their differences and became united in that assembly. Far from it. By the beginning of the Sixteenth Session of the General Assembly, which started in September 1961, the Brazzaville group had formally launched their own bloc at the UN.[30] The Congo crisis continued until the ONUC was given a mandate by the Security Council resolution of 24 November 1961 to use force in order to bring the recalcitrant secessionist Katanga back into the Congolese Republic. This was achieved early in 1963. A few months afterwards, the OAU was founded. It received a few months' breathing space before having to concern itself with the still unresolved Congo crisis.

THE OAU AND THE CONGO CRISIS

The Katangan secession was ended by the United Nations force (ONUC) in January 1963. In April 1963 the Congolese premier, Cyrille Adoula, proclaimed a 'government of national reconciliation', which included representatives of the newly-tamed Katanga Province. But those who were excluded from this new government were more important than those inside it. The former included Antoine Gizenga, who was in jail; Christopher Gbenye, expelled from the previous Adoula government;

Sendwe and many other former supporters of the first Congolese premier, Patrice Lumumba. That meant that the newly-formed 'government of national reconciliation' excluded the real opposition in the country. But, apart from this, Adoula had given in to the forces of regionalism and tribalism, and had divided the country into twenty-four provinces. It soon became clear that, in too many provinces, the only real power lay with the tribal chiefs; and this led to tribal clashes. The provincial governments became powerless, while the central government's authority evaporated further. The economy was in terrible shape, and the central government fast losing control over its army. There was increasing discontent throughout the country.

Towards the latter part of the summer in 1963, Gbenye and many supporters of the murdered Lumumba fled to Brazzaville, where a new government, more radical, had displaced the rule of Abbé Youlou, and where they set up the National Liberation Committee. In the autumn they were joined by discontented army officers. Already guerrilla training-camps had been established deep in the forest by Pierre Mulele, an aide of Gizenga. Towards the end of the year there were signs of rebellion in the country. A state of emergency in Kwilu province was declared on 21 January 1964. The rebellion spread to the Kivu province, where the rebels captured Uvira on 15 May, proclaiming their own government and going on to rout the Congolese National troops (ANC) at Bukavu, the provincial capital. On 27 May, Albertville, in northern Katanga, fell to a group of rebel youths. By the end of June the rebels controlled Kwilu, Kivu and northern Katanga. While the strength of the 'rebels' was growing and the ANC proving itself unfit, Adoula's prestige was falling. The people had no faith in his government, and with each passing day the fear of rebellion in Leopoldville itself grew stronger. Moise Tshombe said in an interview that premier Adoula was 'a finished man' because he had 'brought complete disorder' to the Congo.[31]

On 7 July 1964, Moise Tshombe became prime minister of the Congolese Central Government. Those who brought him back to head the new government thought that he was the only man who could end unrest in the country. Tshombe, an old hand at recruiting white mercenaries, started afresh to recruit them in large numbers, not only from Europe but also from South Africa and Southern Rhodesia. By the end of August more than one thousand of them were fighting with the Congolese national army.[32]

At about the same time as Tshombe formed his régime, the rebels proclaimed a provisional government of the National Liberation Committee, headed by Craston Soumialot. By 5 August they had won control of Kisangani, known then as Stanleyville. Besides this, the National Liberation Committee was firmly established in Bujumbura, capital of Burundi. So, as the rebels became more confident, the Tshombe régime continued to recruit more mercenaries. The fighting became bloodier, and the whole country was sinking deeper into chaos every day.

The relations between Congo (Leopoldville) and her two neighbours – Congo (Brazzaville) and Burundi – deteriorated rapidly. Tshombe, who during the heyday of his rebellion against the Congolese nation had received assistance from Congo (Brazzaville), now accused both countries of supporting the rebels. He expelled their citizens living in Congo (Leopoldville); and then said that he was prepared to cancel the expulsion orders if the rebels were expelled from Brazzaville and Bujumbura!

The annual summit conference of the OAU took place in August 1964. The new Congolese premier, Moise Tshombe, was not allowed to attend, since several heads of state and government had made it clear that they would never sit at the same table with him. Considering Tshombe's role in the Congo crisis, and the murder of Patrice Lumumba, such an attitude seemed to be justified. But the member states of the organization soon found out that they could not just stand by doing nothing while the Congolese were busy slaughtering one another; the Tshombe régime continued to recruit more and more white mercenaries; it became clear that South Africa was giving open support to Tshombe; and, at the same time, the relations between the Congo and her neighbours were getting worse every day. At the end of his state visit to Algeria, President Modibo Keita of Mali joined President Ben Bella of Algeria in calling for an emergency

session of the OAU Council of Ministers to examine the situation in the Congo and its repercussions on other African states.
The leaders of Guinea, the Ivory Coast, Liberia and Sierra
Leone – Sékou Touré, Félix Houphouet-Boigny, William Tubman and Sir Milton Margai – added their voices to the call. The
request for the session was endorsed by other member states, and
the emergency session convened at Addis Ababa.

Tshombe represented Congo (Leopoldville) at the meeting of
the Council of Ministers, held from 5 to 10 September 1964.
Among the plans discussed was one submitted by Kenya. This
proposed a round-table conference of all Congolese political
groupings under the auspices of the OAU, in order to achieve a
reconciliation; the establishment of an OAU peace-keeping
force; and the appointment of a commission to settle the differences between the Congo and her neighbours. The Ghanaian
foreign minister, Kojo Botsio, called on the assembled ministers
to 'make a solemn appeal to the United States to cease their
intervention in the affairs of the Congolese Republic'. Both
Belgium and China were to be approached similarly.[33] The
following proposals emerged after much discussion: that the
Congo should expel immediately all foreign mercenaries and
ensure the withdrawal of all foreign military forces; that all the
parties concerned in the Congo should agree to a cease-fire and
scrupulously obey its conditions; that all political leaders in the
Congo should seek national reconciliation by setting up a government of national unity to ensure the maintenance of law and
order and the holding of free elections; that a commission should
be appointed to restore normal relations between the Congo and
her neighbours; and that all mercenaries should be replaced by
an OAU police force. A Committee of Seven, consisting of the
Central African Republic, Ghana, Mali, Nigeria, Tanzania,
Tunisia and the United Arab Republic, was set up to draft a
resolution which would be put before the plenary meeting of the
Council. Sitting all night, the committee submitted several draft
resolutions to the Congolese delegation for approval, and only
then offered its suggestions to the Council. The final resolution
called upon the Congolese Government to stop recruiting mercenaries and work for national reconciliation. It also appealed to

Progress and Problems

foreign powers to cease intervention in Congolese internal affairs, and requested all OAU member states to refrain from any action which might aggravate the Congolese situation. A special conciliation commission, to be headed by Jomo Kenyatta, and comprising Cameroon, Ethiopia, Ghana, Guinea, Kenya, Nigeria, Somalia, Tunisia, the United Arab Republic and the Upper Volta, was set up to work for the ending of hostilities and the restoration of normal relations between the Congo and her two neighbours.

THE EFFORTS OF THE SPECIAL CONCILIATION COMMISSION

The meeting of the OAU Special Conciliation Commission for the Congo was convened on 18 September 1964 at Nairobi. After consultations with representatives of Congo (Brazzaville) and Burundi, it was agreed that the commission should make an on-the-spot appraisal of the situation in the three countries before finding ways of restoring normal relations between them and bringing about a reconciliation in the Congo. The Congolese premier, Moise Tshombe, and the representatives of both Congo (Brazzaville) and Burundi agreed to cooperate fully with the commission on its trip and scrupulously respect their pledges of assistance. They promised to provide the necessary facilities to help the commission make contact with the Congolese rebels, as well as to provide any further facilities to assist the commission in its dual tasks of trying to achieve national reconciliation within the Congo and normalize relations between the Congo and her neighbours. Congo (Leopoldville) was asked by the commission to submit a report with specific proposals; as were Congo (Brazzaville) and Burundi. The reports were to be deposited with the OAU secretariat as soon as possible.

At the subsequent meeting of the commission it was decided that, in order to achieve a lasting reconciliation in the Congo, all foreign intervention should be brought to an end; and that for this purpose a delegation should visit Washington to dissuade the Johnson administration from supplying any further weapons to the Congolese Central Government. The commission made it clear that it did not rule out the possibility of sending such a delegation to any other country deemed involved in the Congolese troubles. Immediately the Congolese Government learnt of the decision to send a mission to Washington, it decided to cease cooperation with the commission. Why did the commission take this step before consulting the Congolese Government? Was the commission empowered to go so far? There is no doubt whatsoever that the American Government was supplying the Congolese Central Government with military equipment and personnel. In addition, the American Central Intelligence Agency (CIA) had recruited anti-Castro Cubans to fly planes and drop bombs on behalf of the Congolese Central Government.[34] There was also conclusive evidence that the American Government had not only participated in the plan to recruit white mercenaries but had also helped to meet the cost.[35] Indeed, the American Government's involvement was the backbone of the Congolese Central Government's operations against the rebels. It followed therefore, that, as long as this continued, the Congolese would continue to slaughter one another, and that it would be impossible to achieve the much-needed reconciliation in the Congo.

What of the other side? There were rumours that the rebels were receiving assistance from the People's Republic of China. Tshombe accused the republic of supplying the Congolese rebels with 'money and arms'.[36] Although this could not be substantiated, it might well have been true.

If, then, both the US and China were involved in the Congolese conflict, why did the commission decide to send a delegation to the United States first and 'to other countries' later? The reason is to be found in the genuine but naïve assumption of certain African politicians who believe that international relations can be conducted on a 'friend–enemy' basis. As Jomo Kenyatta, the chairman of the commission, indicated, it was intended that their 'friends' – the Americans – should first be persuaded, before an approach would be made to those who were not their 'friends'.[37] If, however, the commission had decided to send delegations to Washington and Peking simultaneously, it would have been difficult for the Americans to refuse to receive any OAU delegations. It would have been equally difficult for the Tshombe-Kasavubu régime to react in the way it did.

Thus, the work of the OAU Conciliation Commission, though promisingly begun, was brought to an abrupt and futile end.

4. LIBERATION

The liberation of the remaining dependent territories in Africa presents Pan-Africanism with an immense problem. Four factors are the cause: lack of unity among the nationalist movements of the territories concerned; cooperation with the colonialist die-hards in Southern Africa by some African states; lack of concerted policies or determination among the independent African states; and the support given by the Western powers to the colonial régimes in Southern Africa.

The areas to be liberated include all the Portuguese colonies in Africa – Angola, Mozambique and Guinea (Bissau); Zimbabwe (Rhodesia) and Namibia (South-West Africa).

(i) Portuguese Colonies

Portugal, the most backward state in Western Europe, possesses three colonies in Africa and has consistently refused to grant them independence, because she depends mostly on them for 'her economic strength, strategic potentiality and political dimension'.[38] The colonies were turned overnight in 1951, through a decree of the Portuguese dictator – Salazar – into 'overseas territories'. Portugal claims that all the inhabitants of the colonies enjoy the same privileges as do the Portuguese themselves. But these inhabitants are classified into two categories – the *assimilados* and the *indigenas*. The *assimilados* are those whom Portugal thinks have been 'europeanized', while the *indigenas* are the 'natives'. Most of the colonial population are *indigenas*; they have virtually no rights; are not entitled to vote or be voted for; and constitute the source of 'forced labour'.

The yearnings for independence in the Portuguese colonies gathered momentum in the 1950s. Portugal's refusal to grant independence led to armed struggle in Angola in 1961. And

Angola was followed by both Mozambique and Guinea (Bissau). Portugal, relying on her NATO allies for military support, launched a counter-offensive, killing several thousands of Africans. As a result of these massacres, the Pan-African summit conference of 1963 had to concern itself with the situation. After thorough examination, the conference decided to give every moral support to the nationalists in their struggle for independence; call on the Great Powers to cease lending support or assistance to Portugal; request a meeting of the Security Council to examine the situation in these colonies; and also send a delegation of foreign ministers to speak on behalf of all African states whenever the requested meeting of the Security Council was convened.

The foreign ministers of Liberia, Madagascar, Sierra Leone and Tunisia were sent to attend the meeting. Presenting the OAU case, the Liberian foreign minister, Randolph Grimes, made it clear that the independent African states intended to do what they could to halt the uncivilized and inhumane policies of Portugal. After reciting Portugal's role in the exploration of Africa, he declared that her contention that Angola, or indeed any other Portuguese colony in Africa, was an integral part of her national territory dated back only to certain changes made in 1951. He accused Portugal of deliberately disregarding the United Nations over Angola, and said that the Portuguese exploited the Africans to the point of slavery and massacred them when they resisted. Supporting him, the Tunisian foreign minister, Mongi Slim, told the council that Portugal was applying in her African colonies a nineteenth-century style of colonialism, which was provoking an explosive situation that could eventually menace international peace. The situation in the Portuguese colonies had worsened to such an extent that 'we fear a state of war will grow up not only in Angola and Guinea, but also in Mozambique. For the measures taken by Portugal to procure arms in considerable quantities only show her determination to build up her military force for the repression she is undertaking. This makes even more clear the threat to peace in Africa.'[39]

At the end of the Security Council debates a resolution was

211

passed requesting all UN members to impose an embargo on the sale and supply of arms and military equipment to Portugal.[40] Portuguese allies in NATO – Britain, France and the United States – did not let their ally down. They abstained in the vote. And subsequently they have continued to assist Portugal one way and another in her bid to keep her colonies.

ANGOLA

Angola gave a lead in calling for independence. The UPA, União das Populacaoes de Angola (People's Union of Angola), was set up in 1954 by Holden Roberto in Kinshasa. Conditions in Angola were very difficult; nevertheless, efforts to form a nationalist movement within the territory materialized in December 1956, when the MPLA (Movimento Popular de Libertaçao de Angola) was founded in Luanda. The Portuguese secret police – PIDE (Policia Internacional e de Defesa do Estado) – as ruthless as the Gestapo, soon arrested many of its leaders and followers. In 1956 alone, more than a thousand Africans were arrested for what were described as 'crimes against the state'. The wave of arrests continued until 1960, when the MPLA was forced to set up its headquarters also in exile: first in Conakry and then in Kinshasa.

Both the UPA and MPLA publicized the situation in the Portuguese colonies. They called on Portugal to negotiate for reforms in Angola; but Salazar refused to recognize even their existence. Nevertheless, they persisted in their efforts to bring about reforms in Angola by peaceful means. They wrote articles and protested in London, Paris and New York. When all these failed to move the dictator, they changed their tactics, in 1961. On 3 February of that year, the MPLA staged a peaceful demonstration march to Luanda prison, to demand the release of the thousands of political prisoners held there on the orders of the Salazar régime. The Portuguese authorities in Luanda and the Portuguese settlers seized the opportunity to massacre some three thousand Africans.

The Congolese Government of Patrice Lumumba was very well disposed towards the Angolan nationalists in Kinshasa, who were allowed to establish training-camps. By April 1962, Holden

Roberto's party, the UPA, had joined forces with another Angolan nationalist movement, the Angolan Democratic Party (PDA), to form both the FLNA (National Front for the Liberation of Angola) and the Angolan Revolutionary Government-in-Exile (GRAE). The formation of the Government-in-Exile brought the rivalry between the MPLA and FLNA into the open. But as well as the MPLA and the FLNA, there were other small parties.

The first task of the OAU Liberation Committee set up during the Pan-African Summit Conference of 1963 was to try to reconcile all the Angolan nationalist movements. A good-will mission was sent to Kinshasa in July 1963 in an attempt to settle their differences. After interviewing all the nationalist movements, the Committee came to the following conclusions:

(1) that the fighting force of the FLNA was far larger than any other: the most effective and indeed the only real fighting front in Angola;

(2) that the best channel for extending aid to the fighters for Angolan liberation was through the government of the Republic of Congo (Kinshasa);

(3) that the continued separate existence of another minor front such as the MPLA was detrimental to the rapid achievement of independence by the Angolan peoples;

(4) that it was necessary for the FLNA to continue the leadership which had so far proved effective.

All the other nationalist movements were therefore called upon to cooperate with the FLNA and the Angolan Revolutionary Government-in-Exile under the leadership of Holden Roberto. The Revolutionary Government-in-Exile was to be recognized by all OAU member states.

Shortly after recognition had been accorded to the FLNA and the GRAE, they received the sum of £30,000 from the OAU to enable them to carry on their struggle for Angolan independence. When the OAU Council of Ministers met at Lagos towards the end of February 1964, more aid was voted. At that time the foreign minister of the GRAE, Jonas Savimbi, told a Press conference in Lagos that his movement was reluctant to accept funds from countries involved in the cold war. That was, however, not true; they had already been receiving financial aid from the CIA. By the end of July 1964, when the OAU Summit Conference was held in Cairo, the divisions within the FLNA and the GRAE had come into the open. The foreign minister of the GRAE himself, Jonas Savimbi, declared to the OAU summit that he had resigned, because divisions in the nationalist movement had made any real success against the Portuguese impossible.

The MPLA had moved its headquarters to Brazzaville, where the climate was now more favourable to the Angolans. But Malawi, which preferred the assistance of the 'white fathers'[41] in Portugal, Rhodesia and South Africa, refused to cooperate with the other OAU member states in supporting the Angolan struggle. And though, when he became the Congolese prime minister in 1964, Tshombe publicly pledged himself to follow the previous government's policy of friendship and aid to the Angolan nationalists, he did not keep his word. He confiscated all aid coming into the country for the Angolan struggle.

The OAU continued its efforts to unite the Angolan nationalist movements. These efforts were crowned with success in September 1966 when a merger of the FLNA and the MPLA was achieved. But the merger did not last long. Two factors were responsible. First, Holden Roberto had become too much involved with the CIA and rather more interested in his own personal welfare than in the independence struggle for Angola. It was alleged that 'large sums of money have been paid into Mr Roberto's numbered account in Geneva. They have come from unnamed American sources.'[42]

The MPLA on the other hand rightly felt that the independence of Angola was more important than financial interest, when help was provided only to stifle the aspirations of the Angolan people. The split was inevitable.

When it occurred, the MPLA organized several new guerrilla fronts in Angola. And these new fronts have been responsible for any real fighting against the Portuguese since 1966. As a result of its activities the MPLA was recognized by the OAU as the only

214

effective fighting movement in July 1969. At the same time the
OAU withheld all support from the FLNA of Roberto, until it
dropped its claim to be the Angolan Revolutionary Government-
in-Exile. Recognition was finally withdrawn from Roberto's
GRAE during the OAU Summit Conference held at Addis
Ababa in June 1971.[43]

GUINEA (BISSAU)

The Partido Africano de Independencia de Guiné – Cabo Verde –
PAIGC (African Party for Independence of Portuguese Guinea
and Cape Verde) led by Amilcar Cabral – was founded in 1956.
Other nationalist movements – the Liberation Front for the
National Independence of Portuguese Guinea (Frente Libertação
de l'Independencia Nationale de Guiné) or FLING, and the
Union of Portuguese Guinea Nationals (URGP) led by Pinto
Bull – soon followed.

PAIGC was initially an advance-guard, composed only of a
few determined men and women. In 1961 it broadened its
membership when it was joined by several hundred young volunteers who subsequently acquired experience and leadership in
the field. FLING was founded by exiles in Senegal as a 'moderate alternative' to the PAIGC. It is therefore not unlikely that
it enjoyed a certain favour with the Portuguese. But it has never
grown up. The third movement, URGP, achieved nothing
except negotiations with Portugal: a course condemned to
futility from the onset.[44]

The OAU Liberation Committee also got in touch with the
nationalist movements in Guinea (Bissau) in July 1963, to find
out which of them should be recognized by the OAU. The
committee was impressed by the organization of the PAIGC
(which had already begun operations within the colony), and
recommended that it alone should be recognized. It called on
FLING to join hands with the PAIGC to form a United Action
Front. When these recommendations came up for endorsement
by the OAU Council of Ministers at its meeting at Dakar in
August 1963, however, they were vetoed by Senegal, which
supports FLING. Following this, the Council of Ministers
dispatched a sub-committee of three states to inspect FLING

215

operations inside Guinea (Bissau). The sub-committee was taken on a tour of military establishments, hospitals, schools, etc. operated by FLING. It subsequently recommended to the Council of Ministers that FLING be officially recognized. This recommendation was rejected by the council after a thorough study. As a result, neither group has been officially recognized, but both are receiving aid from the OAU.

The superiority of the PAIGC over FLING has been in increasing evidence since 1964. Its secretary-general, Amilcar Cabral, who addressed the 1964 Summit Conference in Cairo on behalf of all liberation movements in Africa, was the only representative from Guinea (Bissau) who could report any considerable military victories against the colonialists. He claimed that the PAIGC had been able to cut the territory in two and isolate the Portuguese.[45]

In 1964 the PAIGC army – the People's Revolutionary Armed Forces (FARP) – was formed inside Guinea (Bissau) out of various fighting units already in being. These included mobile units on the three fronts, as well as local guerrilla groups. Since then the PAIGC has achieved a considerable amount.[46] On the other hand, FLING remained 'little more than its original handful of "mountain-topists" with the additional comfort that their "mountain-top" was in Dakar, far away from any danger – gaining only from time to time a few individuals for whom the way of PAIGC represented too hard and perilous a sacrifice.'[47]

It is hoped that the OAU will soon recommend again that PAIGC alone be recognized by the OAU or that a United Action Front be formed by both PAIGC and FLING. There are two reasons for this hope. First, the successes of the PAIGC warrant such a move. Secondly, the formation of the Organisation des États Riverains du Sénégal (OERS), of which both Guinea and Senegal are members, may provide an instrument for ironing out differences between the countries. This, coupled with the successes of the PAIGC, may lead Senegal to review her support for FLING and consequently force FLING to join forces with PAIGC, so that the much-desired independence of Guinea (Bissau) might soon be won.[48]

On 22 November 1970, Portugal, joined by certain African

mercenaries, invaded the Republic of Guinea. This act of aggression was a clear indication of Portuguese frustrations in their attempt to hold on at all costs in Guinea (Bissau). A further aspect of the invasion was the involvement of another European country in its planning. But then who doubts that Portugal could hold on to her colonies without the moral and material assistance of certain other powers?

MOZAMBIQUE

In 1949, secondary-school pupils formed the Núcleo dos Estu-dantes Africanos Secundarios de Moçambique (NESAM). Linked with the Centro Associativo dos Negros de Moçambique, it was able to conduct 'among the youth a political campaign to spread the idea of national independence and encourage resist-ance to the cultural subjection which the Portuguese imposed'.[49] The Portuguese Gestapo – PIDE – kept the organization under severe surveillance, and many of its leaders were later arrested. Nevertheless the agitation for independence continued.

On 16 June 1960, at Mueda in the northern part of Mozam-bique, the Portuguese killed about six hundred unarmed African men, women and children without provocation.[50] This action triggered off attempts to form a nation-wide radical nationalist movement. As the long arms of the PIDE reached everywhere in the colonies, the Mozambicans had no alternative but to establish nationalist movements outside the colonies. Con-sequently, the following three movements were formed: UDENAMO (União Nacional Democrática de Moçambique) formed at Salisbury, Rhodesia, in October 1960; MANU (Mozambique African National Union) formed in 1961; and UNAMI (União Africana de Moçambique Independente). When Tanganyika became independent in December 1961, the three nationalist movements established their headquarters in Dar es Salaam.

When the struggle for independence started in Angola in 1961 the Portuguese intensified their repressive measures against the Africans in all the colonies. As a result of these measures many Africans fled into the neighbouring independent countries. Among these exiles were many Mozambicans. Those of them who went to Tanganyika (now Tanzania) did not join any of the existing nationalist movements but exercised heavy pressure for the formation of a single united body.

In October 1961 a Conference of the Nationalist Organizations of the Portuguese Territories (CONCP) was held at Casablanca. The conference made a strong call for the unity of nationalist movements against Portuguese colonialism. In June 1962 leaders of the Mozambique nationalist movements called on president Nkrumah of Ghana, who strongly encouraged them to form a united front. President Nyerere of Tanzania, too, personally exerted his influence on the movements to unite. As a result of all these moves, MANU and UDENAMO agreed on 25 June 1962 to merge and form the Mozambique Liberation Front (Frente de Libertaçao de Moçambique) or FRELIMO.

Several attempts have been made by Portugal, her allies and agents to split FRELIMO; but all have so far proved unsuccessful. A new method was therefore adopted: a few Mozambicans were encouraged to establish other organizations. These organizations, formed by almost the same people, have at different times borne such names as COSERU (Comite Secreto de Restauraçao da UDENAMO); the New UDENAMO; MORECO (Mozambican Revolutionary Council); COREMO; the New UNAMI; the New MANU; and UNAR (União Nacional Africana da Rombézia). UNAR's objective has been to weaken the work of FRELIMO in the area between the Rivers Zambezi and Rovuma. The organization, which enjoys the confidence or sympathy of the Portuguese, significantly has its headquarters in Blantyre, Malawi; and its 'leaders enjoy the protection and cooperation of some influential figures in the Malawi Congress Party'.[51]

The OAU has been able to give considerable assistance to the nationalist movement of Mozambique. And although the final objective – independence – has not yet been attained, FRELIMO has shown itself able to surmount difficulties that might well have crushed a lesser resolve.[52]

(ii) *Zimbabwe (Rhodesia)*

The situation in Zimbabwe is much more complex than in the Portuguese colonies, so it is essential that we trace here the course which Zimbabwe has taken since it became a British colony under the name of Southern Rhodesia. In 1923 it was granted internal self-rule, and in 1953 the three British colonies in Central Africa – Northern Rhodesia, Southern Rhodesia and Nyasaland – were forcibly merged, to form the ill-fated Central African Federation. By 1960 it had become abundantly clear that the Federation could not survive. In 1961 the British Government gave Southern Rhodesia a new constitution which can conveniently be described as a Westminster-mandated magna carta for white dominance. As a camouflage, the British Government laid down the following principles, which they claimed must be fulfilled before Rhodesia could become independent:

(1) unimpeded progress towards majority rule;

(2) guarantees against retrogressive amendment of the constitution;

(3) an immediate improvement in the political status of the Africans;

(4) progress towards ending racial discrimination;

(5) any basis proposed for independence must be acceptable to the people of Rhodesia as a whole.

In 1962 the 'Rhodesian Front' – an amalgamation of right-wing parties, whose members were exclusively white – won the election under the constitution of 1961. The Federation of Rhodesia and Nyasaland which had been imposed was dissolved in 1963, as a result of pressure from the African nationalists in both Northern Rhodesia (now Zambia) and Nyasaland (now Malawi). This event and the impending independence of both Northern Rhodesia and Nyasaland combined to harden the hearts of the already frustrated and disillusioned members of the Rhodesian Front in the colony. By September 1964, indications that the white minority régime might rebel against the British Government and declare independence unilaterally had already been given to Sir Alec Douglas-Home by Ian Smith during the talks on the constitution.

The British Government, which knew how the policy of apartheid had been promoted in South Africa, despite the assurances, guarantees and pledges given by the leaders of all political parties when power was transferred from Westminster to South Africa in 1910, realized what the Rhodesian minority racist régime was likely to do. But, in their concern for their kith and kin, they did nothing to prevent it. So the way was clear for Smith and his fellow-travellers, as a first step towards this objective, to declare the independence of Rhodesia unilaterally on 11 November 1965.

The British Labour Government, in power since October 1964, could have brought down the rebellion in a swift police action, by detaining the members of the minority régime. Instead, it belatedly took the matter to the UN, and asked for sanctions to be applied in the full knowledge that certain UN member states and those states which do not belong to the world organization would not wholeheartedly support such a move. It ruled out the possibility of any military intervention, because Rhodesian defence was 'very strong'. It is, however, worth mentioning that Britain, which was afraid to bring down the Smith régime by military means, can claim to be able to stand up to the Russians in the Indian Ocean! This would, according to the Conservative Government, be achieved by selling arms to South Africa.

After seven years the crisis remains unsolved. The Labour Party, which might have done something worthwhile and honourable when in power, did nothing of the sort. Its leader only talked and talked and talked. The way is once again clear for the Conservatives – anyway more or less responsible for the mess – to allow the success of Rhodesian independence by some policy of malign neglect. Britain will then have launched two states pursuing a policy of apartheid in Africa within half a century. A great achievement! And the sixth principle of NIBMAR (No Independence Before Majority African Rule) – Mr Wilson's only achievement in the Rhodesian impasse – has already been thrown overboard by the Conservatives in their effort to appease the white racist minority régime in Rhodesia as well as to promote what they would presumably call the 'best interests' of Britain.

What about the Africans of Zimbabwe? What have they done to gain their birthright? The Zimbabwe African People's Union (ZAPU) and the Zimbabwe African National Union (ZANU) were in existence before the OAU was founded. Yet although both are fighting for majority African rule in an independent state, they are more interested in cutting each other's throats than in jointly attacking their common enemy. It was therefore easy for the white minority régime to ban their leaders as it thought fit. Several efforts have been made by the OAU to unite them for their common objective; but all these efforts remained un-rewarded. To make matters worse, ZAPU has been torn apart as a result of 'bitter personal feuds and tribal conflicts in the party leadership'.[53]

THE OAU AND UDI

During the Pan-African Summit of May 1963, President Milton Obote of Uganda suggested 'that if the white minority of Southern Rhodesia should be permitted to declare themselves independent, the African States should promptly counter this by severing trade and other relations with the United Kingdom and her fellow travellers'.[54] The situation in Zimbabwe has since then been a staple topic at all meetings of the Assembly of Heads of State and Government and the Council of Ministers. Resolutions were passed by both bodies, warning the United Kingdom that the African states would have to reconsider their diplomatic relations with her, in the event of a unilateral declaration of independence on the part of the white settler government in her colony. The Council of Ministers, at its meeting prior to the summit conference of 1965 held at Accra , considered the possi-bility of a Unilateral Declaration of Independence (UDI) by the white minority régime in Rhodesia, and recommended that an OAU peace-keeping contingent be established. But a proposal to impose economic sanctions against Rhodesia was defeated on the grounds that it was unrealistic. Although President Nkru-mah's assurance, in his opening address at the summit, that, if the UDI were declared, 'the OAU will take whatever steps are necessary', drew an emotional response, the resolution adopted by the summit conference on 22 October was moderate in tone. The summit did not endorse the recommendation of the Council of Ministers. Instead, it adopted a resolution placing the responsibility squarely on Britain and urging her to use force to prevent a unilateral declaration of independence. It also called on the United Nations to do everything possible to prevent such a declaration by the minority settler régime in Zimbabwe. The summit, however, set up a special committee on Zimbabwe, and also prepared a plan for action in case Britain granted negotiated independence to a minority régime in that colony. The plan agreed:

(1) to refuse recognition to such a government;

(2) to recognize a Zimbabwean government in exile;

(3) to hold an emergency meeting of the OAU Council of Ministers, with a view to involving the United Nations more directly in Zimbabwe;

(4) to reconsider relations with Britain;

(5) to treat the white minority government in Zimbabwe on the same footing as that in South Africa.

Three weeks later, the threat of UDI materialized. OAU members were unanimous in condemning the illegal declaration; but while some states felt that all initiative should be left to Britain, others called for African military preparations and requested an emergency conference of the Organization of African Unity. The special committee set up at Accra also met immediately in Dar es Salaam, in the presence of the OAU secretary-general, and decided to recommend to the Council of Ministers a resolution committing the African states to a diplomatic boycott of Britain.

An extraordinary session of the Council of Ministers was convened at Addis Ababa for 3 to 5 December 1965, to tackle the crisis. At the end of the meeting it was announced that if the revolt had not been crushed by 15 December the African states would declare war on Rhodesia; cut all economic exchanges and communication; and, finally, break off diplomatic relations with

Britain. Although the resolution to break off diplomatic relations with Britain if she failed to crush the rebellion was taken unanimously, reports from various African capitals shortly afterwards indicated reservations. First came news from Lusaka on 9 December that the leader of Zambia, Kenneth Kaunda, felt that breaking relations with Britain would pose serious difficulties for his country, and that he was writing to the other heads of government to advise them of this. It was a very significant intervention, since Zambia was the OAU member most affected by the Rhodesian situation, and its cooperation was essential to any move by the organization against the Rhodesian régime.

On 11 December Emperor Haile Selassie of Ethiopia sent a message to the other heads of state and government through the secretary-general of the OAU. In it he stated that an attempt to apply the resolution with less than a united front might fail to bring about the desired results, and might, in fact, become a source of dissension among the members of the Organization. He therefore asked for delay in the implementation of the decision, pending a meeting of the Assembly of Heads of State and Government. Other African governments followed suit, declining to take action and calling for a summit meeting of the OAU. Some even went further, to imply in their statement that they considered the council resolutions not binding on the African states unless approved by the assembly of heads of state and government. On the eve of the deadline, Sir Abubakar Tafawa Balewa, the Nigerian prime minister, in a move to preserve the Commonwealth from the disintegration that the diplomatic rupture would entail, launched a proposal for a Commonwealth meeting at Lagos to discuss the Rhodesian crisis. Kenya, on the other hand, without previously informing other OAU member states, sought to bring the issue before the United Nations Security Council, catching the rest of the African delegations unprepared, and thus forcing them to oppose such a move. As a result of all this dilly-dallying and indecisiveness on the part of many OAU member states, only ten – Algeria, Congo (Brazzaville), Ghana, Guinea, Mali, Mauritania, Somalia, Sudan, Tanzania and the United Arab Republic – finally complied with the resolution of 3 December 1965 on diplomatic rupture. Attempts to call an extraordinary session of the assembly also failed. Proposals to hold another extraordinary session of the Council of Ministers met with protests from the states which had broken off diplomatic relations with Britain. As President Massemba-Debat of Congo (Brazzaville) justifiably put it, in a telegram sent to the OAU secretary-general at the end of December 1965:

The Rhodesian problem has been studied sufficiently and was the object of unanimous decisions at Accra and at Addis Ababa. By calling a new 'Summit' Africa would show that it does not know what it wants. Before seeking new decisions, it would be best to apply courageously those that have already been pronounced.

The question of reconstituting unanimity on the Rhodesian question was therefore postponed until the sixth ordinary session of the Council of Ministers, scheduled to take place at Addis Ababa from 28 February 1966. The session opened, however, under the shadow of the coup in Ghana, which had taken place just four days before. The meeting tried unsuccessfully to reach agreement on the seating of the Ghanaian delegation. The eventual decision to recognize the delegation led to a series of walk-outs.

Earlier, Haile Selassie had said in his opening address that Ethiopia would support any decision which the OAU member states might collectively consider appropriate to help resolve the question of the diplomatic break with Britain. He went on:

We wish to recall the sad experience which Africa passed through as a result of the diverse positions taken by African states on the implementation of the decision you took on Rhodesia during your extraordinary session last December. At that meeting, in our opening address, we . . . expressed that all decisions taken in the name of our 'Organisation' would be effective only if implemented unanimously by all Member States. Unfortunately such unanimity did not materialise . . . The stand taken by Member States concerning the last OAU decision on Rhodesia has been subjected to unexpected interpretations. Nonetheless, it still remains within the power of us Africans to determine a common approach to this problem. The policy which we consistently maintained with regard to the crucial problem of Rhodesia remains unchanged. We are prepared to support any decision which the Member States may collectively consider will help to bring a solution to the question of Rhodesia. However, it is imperative that we ensure peace and stability within our respective countries in order to prevent the rise of events which would distract our attention from the problem of Rhodesia. The rebellious régime of Ian Smith has not yet been overthrown. And, we emphasize, his downfall will come about only if our decisions are carried out unanimously.[55]

Two resolutions were put before the session on Rhodesia. The first, moved by Algeria, called for intensified training of the Zimbabwean nationalists, and the recognition of the Zimbabwe African People's Union (ZAPU) as the only liberation movement. It also requested all African countries, and especially those neighbouring Rhodesia, to do their utmost to facilitate the organization of the armed struggle, the transport of fighters, the transit of material and the establishment of training-camps. The second, put forward by Tunisia and seventeen others (among them Ethiopia, the Ivory Coast, Kenya, Senegal, Sierra Leone, Sudan and Zambia), did not refer to the recognition of the Zimbabwe African People's Union (ZAPU) or mention specifically the role of Rhodesia's neighbours. It repeated the OAU's call for effective measures, including the use of force, to bring about the immediate downfall of the Smith régime. It also included the setting-up of a committee of solidarity for Zambia, composed of Ethiopia, Kenya, Sudan, Tanzania and the United Arab Republic, to help with economic and technical assistance, and urged all necessary aid to the Zimbabwean nationalists willing to fight for the liberation of their country. When the two motions were finally put to the vote, the first was rejected in favour of the second. This led to another series of walk-outs, on the grounds that the resolution was too weak. Once again the OAU failed to establish a consensus on Rhodesia; and this severely hampered African efforts to work for a swift overthrow of the illegal Smith régime.

The Rhodesian crisis has come up at all subsequent meetings of both the Council of Ministers and the Assembly of Heads of State and Government. In November 1966 the summit conference passed a resolution that condemned the Anglo-Rhodesian talks; denounced countries aiding Rhodesia; and called on Britain to use all means, including force if necessary, to end the

Smith régime. At the preparatory meeting of the Council of Ministers for the 1968 Summit Conference in Algiers, some of the foreign ministers favoured a new call for the use of force by Britain. But a memorandum from ZAPU made it clear enough that this would be useless. It called instead for more aid to the guerilla commitment.

Note: Since this section was written there have been new developments in the Zimbabwe question. On 24 November 1971, Sir Alec Douglas-Home, the British foreign secretary, and Ian Smith, the head of the illegal régime, signed, in Salisbury, an agreement to end the crisis. In accordance with the fifth of the principles mentioned above, the agreement was to be submitted to the Zimbabweans of all races for approval. The agreement contained the usual so-called 'entrenched clauses', which everybody knew would never be honoured when a final settlement had been reached. In order that African approval might be gained the Africans were promised development aid of £50 million, to be made available over a period of ten years; with this sum, of course, controlled by the illegal racist minority régime.

The British Conservative Government had two objectives in making the deal. First it wanted to wash its hands of the Zimbabwe question by means of a political manoeuvre. Secondly, it intended to legalize UDI, thus securing international recognition for the illegal régime. Faced with this challenge, the Africans reacted spontaneously and vigorously against the deal. Indeed, the deal achieved what the OAU had so far failed to do: a united front of ZAPU, ZANU, and other Zimbabwe nationalists in the struggle for Zimbabwe's independence.

(iii) Namibia (South-West Africa)

The question of Namibia is not merely a Pan-African predicament, but an international problem of the greatest magnitude. Namibia (known then as South-West Africa), a former German colony, was mandated as a trust territory, in accordance with Article 22 of the Versailles Treaty of 1919, to South Africa, by a resolution of the Council of the League of Nations on 17 December 1920. Indeed, for many years, South Africa reported regularly on the administration of the territory to the Mandates Commission of the League. Then, in 1946, the United Nations superseded the League of Nations, and all other former trust territories came under the United Nations trusteeship system. But South Africa, with the support of Britain, the United States and a few other Western powers, refused to place South-West Africa under the UN trusteeship system. Instead she attempted to incorporate the trust territory into the Union of South Africa. This met with hostile reaction from the United Nations, and from 1949 South Africa bluntly refused to submit any report to the UN on the administration of the territory. This refusal led the General Assembly of the UN to ask for an advisory opinion on the legal status of the territory from the International Court of Justice.

The International Court, in its judgement of 11 June 1950, ruled that South-West Africa was still under the international mandate assumed by the Union of South Africa on 17 December 1920; so rejecting South Africa's contention that the mandate had lapsed with the demise of the League. South Africa was, therefore, under a legal obligation to accept international supervision and provide reports to the UN General Assembly, which was declared qualified to exercise the necessary supervisory functions. In spite of this ruling, however, South Africa has refused to recognize the norms of international law, and has continued to abuse the trust once put in her by the international community. To make matters worse, she has continued to promote the despicable 'apartheid policy' in the territory. In view of this, efforts have been made to bring South-West Africa under UN direct control. Several UN resolutions to that effect have been passed; and advisory opinions of the International Court of Justice have been sought. But still South Africa has refused to honour her obligations.

Her refusal to comply with the mandate and her promotion of the apartheid in the territory have caused widespread anger, especially, of course, in Africa. One response was the institution of legal proceedings against South Africa before the International Court of Justice, for violating the terms of the 1920 mandate by pursuing policies of racial discrimination in the trust territory. Both Liberia and Ethiopia brought these charges in

November 1960; and on 21 December 1962, the World Court ruled that it had jurisdiction to adjudicate on the merits of the case. In its final judgement of 18 June 1966, however, the Court claimed that neither Ethiopia nor Liberia could be considered to have established any legal right or interest in the case.

The UN has, since then, resolved to terminate South Africa's mandate and bring Namibia under direct UN control. But South Africa once again failed to comply with the UN decision. Because of this intransigence, the Security Council brought another action against South Africa before the World Court. The Court, in its ruling of 21 June 1971 – with only the judges from Britain and France against – declared:

'The continued presence of South Africa in Namibia being illegal, South Africa is under an obligation to withdraw its administration immediately and thus put an end to its occupation of the territory.'[56]

This does not mean that the problem has been solved. But there is a ray of hope. All the big powers with the exception of Britain and France – which both busily supply arms to South Africa, in defiance of the UN embargo – support the termination of the mandate. The more that South Africa contemptuously refuses to comply, the stronger grows the case of those who advocate UN armed intervention.

(iv) Cooperation between and support for the colonial régimes

Portugal, Rhodesia and South Africa have joined hands in thwarting so far the aspirations of the African nationalists in the remaining dependent territories. They have formed an unholy alliance, called 'ASPRO' by the Portuguese and nicknamed the South African Treaty Organization by others. It is on the basis of this unholy alliance that South Africa has sent security forces into Rhodesia and gives so much assistance to the Portuguese in their attempts to liquidate the African freedom fighters. Joint military exercises have, on several occasions, been held.

Yet without the support given directly and indirectly to these countries by certain powers, the three régimes would find it far less easy to continue their operations against the nationalists.

NATO countries have been responsible for the supply of arms and other military equipment used by Portugal in her colonial wars. Britain, France, West Germany and the United States are the chief sources of supply.[57] Financial and industrial institutions in these countries are also responsible for the construction of the infamous Cabora-Bassa dam in Mozambique.[58] And a West German spy ring was discovered in Guinea shortly after the Portuguese invasion of that country in November 1970.[59]

As regards Rhodesia, the United States and Britain (especially under the Conservative Government) have even gone to the extent of using their vetoes at the UN Security Council to block measures which could have helped to bring down the illegal racist minority régime of Ian Smith.[60]

Over Namibia, the chief supporters of the South African presence have been Britain and France. Britain, even under a Labour Government, made a deal with the South African régime over the newly-found uranium deposits of Namibia.[61] The United States has, at least, come out strongly in support of the UN decision to terminate the South African mandate over Namibia. It is, however, too early to say whether or not this apparent shift in policy is only a diplomatic manoeuvre. Certainly US companies continue their profitable operations in the territory.

The cooperation between the three racist régimes in Southern Africa, coupled with the support given them by Western powers, and the consequent threat to other neighbouring independent African states, forced these states in East and Central Africa to come closer together within the Pan-African movement. When they started a series of what have become known as the 'good-neighbourliness' meetings in April 1966, it was made abundantly plain that they did not wish their conferences to develop into a new regional organization. In a communiqué issued during the conference, attended by the heads of state and government of Burundi, Congo (Kinshasa), Ethiopia, Kenya, Malawi, Rwanda, Somalia, Sudan, Tanzania, Uganda and Zambia, they declared:

It was agreed that the nature and purpose of the conference should be made clear from the outset so as to avoid misunderstanding and any possible misinterpretation. The conference must not be regarded as an attempt to usurp the functions of the OAU or an attempt to set up a regional organisation. On the contrary, all the states present re-affirmed full loyalty and support for the OAU. The conference provided the opportunity for the first time since the illegal declaration of independence by whites in Rhodesia for President Kaunda of Zambia to confer with his neighbours.[62]

At the end of the conference it was announced that all partici-pants had agreed to strengthen the OAU and support it in its efforts to liberate the remaining dependent territories in Africa.

Meetings have continued since then. And that of April 1969, which took place at Lusaka in Zambia, was of especial signifi-cance. Attended by fourteen (instead of the original eleven) East and Central African States – Burundi, the Central African Republic, Chad, Congo (Brazzaville), Congo (Kinshasa), Ethi-opia, Kenya, Malawi, Rwanda, Somalia, Tanzania, Uganda and Zambia – as well as the OAU secretary-general, Diallo Telli, and the secretary of the UN Economic Commission for Africa, Robert Gardiner, it produced what has now become popularly known as the Lusaka Manifesto.

This manifesto, which has since been endorsed by the OAU, the non-aligned nations and the UN, declares that Africans have always preferred and still prefer to achieve the liberation of the remaining dependent territories without physical violence. It goes on: 'If peaceful progress to emancipation were possible, or if changed circumstances were to make it possible in the future, we would urge our brothers in the resistance movements to use peaceful methods of struggle even at the cost of some com-promise on the timing of change.' It emphasized, however, that as long as the colonial oppressors showed no change of heart, policy or both, Africans would continue to give to the peoples of those territories 'all the support of which we are capable in their struggle against their oppressors'.

5. SOUTH AFRICA

South Africa, which, in view of her economic and industrial development, might well have taken the lead in the search for

African unity, had she had the right leadership and followed the right policy, has become instead the arch-enemy of Pan-Africanism. Since so much has already been written and said about the apartheid policy of her white minority racist régime, it would be superfluous to explain its implications in this book. It is worth mentioning only that the worldwide indignation over this policy continues unabated, and will so continue until South Africa herself changes direction. No 'certificate of respectability' given by any British Conservative Government, or any other government for that matter, will affect the issue.

The need to bring about a reversal of policy in South Africa has caused the United Nations since 1946 to concern itself with the inhumane discriminatory policies of the South African régime. Pan-Africanists have not lagged behind. But up till now, nothing substantial has been achieved.

The questions remain. Should South Africa be totally excommunicated from the rest of the world? What purpose would such isolation serve? Would it be better to leave her in the world community, so that incessant pressure could be brought upon her to change? Is she not a threat even to the very existence of the other independent African states; not least for as as long as she continues to assist both Portugal and Rhodesia in their repressive measures against the nationalist movements in Africa? Could a change be brought about in South Africa through peaceful negotiation? What has the UN been able to achieve in this field so far? Such are the questions that have been asked not only by Pan-Africanists, but also by all those who have more respect for human dignity than for business interests and personal gain. As long as no satisfactory answer has been found and there is no change of policy, South Africa will continue to top the list of Pan-African predicaments.

In an effort to find a solution, the Pan-African summit of May 1963 intensively concerned itself with the problem of South Africa. At the end of the discussions, a resolution on 'Apartheid and Racial Discrimination' was adopted. It expressed in unmistakable terms a unanimous conviction 'of the imperious and urgent necessity of co-ordinating and intensifying' the efforts of all the independent African states 'to put an end to the South

African Government's criminal policy of apartheid and wipe out racial discrimination in all its forms'. As a result, the heads of state and government agreed to coordinate their efforts; and decided on the following measures:

(1) creation of a fund for concerted financial assistance to the anti-apartheid movement in South Africa;

(2) effective assistance of every kind to anti-apartheid movements in South Africa to help them carry out their struggle for freedom;

(3) granting of scholarships, educational facilities and possibilities of employment in African government service to refugees from South Africa;

(4) supporting the recommendations presented to the Security Council of the General Assembly by the special committee of the United Nations on the apartheid policies of the South African Government;

(5) coordination of concrete measures of sanction against the government of South Africa;

(6) condemnation of racial discrimination in all its forms in Africa and all over the world.

Furthermore, the heads of state and government called for the immediate release of Nelson Mandela, Sobukwe, and all other political prisoners in South Africa. They appealed 'to all states, and more particularly to those which have traditional relations and cooperate with the Government of South Africa, strictly to apply United Nations Resolution 1761 of 6 November 1962, concerning apartheid'.[63] They also appealed to all governments who still had diplomatic and economic relations with the Government of South Africa to break off relations and cease any other form of encouragement for the policy of apartheid. They finally decided to send a delegation of foreign ministers to impress upon the Security Council that an explosive situation existed in South Africa.

The problem of apartheid and racial discrimination has since then become a regular item on the agenda of both the Council of Ministers and the Assembly of Heads of State and Government. At its second ordinary session held at Lagos early in March 1964, the Council of Ministers adopted a strongly worded resolution on apartheid. Another resolution called on all OAU member states to take necessary steps to refuse any plane or ship going to or coming from South Africa the right to fly over their territories or utilize their ports or other facilities. It also urged an end to the encouragement of investment in and commercial relations with South Africa. The summit conference of that year adopted a resolution calling on all African states to implement forthwith the decision taken at Addis Ababa in May 1963 to boycott all South African goods and to cease the supply of minerals and other raw materials to South Africa. It further decided to establish a sanctions bureau within the OAU secretariat. The 1967 summit held at Kinshasa also passed a 'Resolution on Apartheid and Racial Discrimination': which, having considered that 'the continued existence of apartheid and racial discrimination constitutes an odious crime against humanity, and represents a grave menace to peace and security', condemned the political, economic and military collaboration of the Western powers with South Africa. The Council of Ministers, deeply disturbed by the aggressive attitude of the South African régime towards countries such as Zambia and Tanzania, adopted at its session of February 1968 a resolution which showed the growing sense of urgency among OAU member states. It again:

1. draws the attention of the main trading partners of South Africa, in particular the three permanent members of the Security Council, to the fact that their continued refusals to apply economic sanctions in accordance with Chapter VII of the United Nations Charter would only increase the threat of a violent conflict in South Africa and accordingly calls upon them once again to take urgent and concrete steps to sever all ties with South Africa;

2. condemns unreservedly the actions of those States, in particular the United Kingdom, the United States, France, the Federal Republic of Germany and Japan, which through their continued political, economic and military collaboration with the South African regime, are encouraging and strengthening it to persist in its racial policies;

3. deplores the actions of the main trading partners of South Africa who, in defiance of appeals made by the Organisation of African Unity and in violation of United Nations resolutions, have increased their trade with, and their investments in South Africa;

233

4. strongly condemns some members of the North Atlantic Treaty Organisation (NATO), in particular the Federal Republic of Germany, Italy and France, which continue to sell military equipment to South Africa or to assist it in the production of arms, ammunition, and poison gas, in violation of the resolutions of the United Nations General Assembly and the Security Council;

5. strongly condemns the direct and indirect help given to the racist minority regime of Ian Smith by the South African regime;

6. denounces the manoeuvres of the South African regime whereby it seeks to weaken the energetic opposition to apartheid of the independent African States through offers of economic and financial aid, and strongly condemns African States which maintain political and economic relations with the racist regime of Pretoria;

7. calls on all States which still maintain commercial and other ties with South Africa to sever them without delay; and

8. deeply regrets that the Security Council of the United Nations has failed to bring about an end to apartheid in South Africa because of the resistance of the main trading partners of South Africa, including three permanent members of the Security Council.

The council also appealed to all states to observe 21 March, the anniversary of the tragic Sharpeville massacre, as an international day for the abolition of racial discrimination throughout the world.

Yet, immediately after the Conservative Party returned to power in the British General Election of 18 June 1970, the British Government declared its intention of breaking the UN arms embargo against South Africa. (Although the Conservatives were in power when the embargo was imposed in 1963 they do not appear to regard their new policy as an example of what they themselves have always termed 'double standard'.[64]) In spite of the OAU efforts, and those of the African and Asian members of the Commonwealth along with Canada, to dissuade it from such a course, the British Government insisted that it was in the British interest to flout world opinion and arm the apartheid policy-makers of South Africa.

The attitude of both the British Conservative and the French Government on the sale of arms to South Africa is reminiscent of the British and French diplomacy during the Italian–Ethiopian crisis of 1935 and the subsequent notorious Hoare–Laval Pact:

234

by which both Britain and France, although professing to be
Ethiopia's protectors, agreed to appease the Italian fascist leader,
Mussolini, by forcing Ethiopia to cede a large portion of her
territory to Italy.

The Pan-African movement itself appears split over the issue
of South Africa. For reasons outlined on pages 241–2, Ghana, the
Ivory Coast, Gabon and the Malagasy Republic have come out in
support of what they have termed a 'dialogue' with the South
African régime. What they have, however, failed to do is to
explain what form the 'dialogue' should take; how long it
would be carried on; and what objective it would have.

South Africa has already offered to sign peace pacts with
African states. The African states have not absolutely rejected
such a move. They only maintain that if South Africa is really
interested in any peace move, she must follow the adage –
'charity begins at home'. She has now indicated that the 'Bantustans' would be free in 1979.[65] If she *means* this then that is the
first tiny step in the right direction. The 'Bantustans' and the
white and 'coloured' communities could go on to form either a
federation or a confederation, with parliaments where whites and
non-whites would sit together as equals. Pass laws would be
abrogated. Education would not be segregated. Everybody would
have equal rights. The constitution might initially provide that
the whites, the 'coloured' and the Africans would have equal
representation. The cabinet could be composed in the same way.
Such a situation might last for a period of twenty-five years, after
which the constitution could be reviewed by a special panel of
equal representatives from the white, 'coloured' and African
communities. While such changes were clearly in process, every
effort would be made by the other independent African states to
make the experiment a success. Contacts between South Africa
and other African states would be improved. Exchanges of
students, professional people such as lawyers, doctors and pro-
fessors might take place. South Africa might then take part in
Pan-African sports, exhibitions, fairs, etc. Indeed, it might come
about during the last ten years of the twenty-five-year period. At
the end of it all, South Africa would become a full-fledged
member of the Organization of African Unity.

If, however, South Africa and her allies in Europe and America feel that the only way out is to cause disunity within the Pan-African movement by bribing and setting off one section against the other, they will come to realize that they are living in a fool's paradise. If they think that the present leaders can be easily manipulated, what of the next generation? Will *they* be prepared to sell their birthright or betray their degraded brothers in South Africa simply for personal gain?

It would, however, be unrealistic for the African states to fold their arms and hope that South Africa would willingly be prepared to accept the experiment outlined above. In this connection it is worth noting that South Africa, while happy at the 'dialogue' noises coming from some among the African states, has shown no appreciable sign of willingness to bring about a change of policy within her territory. On the contrary: she has made it clear that any détente in her relations with the OAU members would not necessarily affect her abominable apartheid policy. Besides, African states must learn from the experience of history. Perhaps they should bear in mind the circumstances which surrounded the Italo–Ethiopian crisis of 1935–6 which subsequently led to the end of the League of Nations as an organ for the maintenance of international peace and security. It was after the so-called Treaty of Friendship, Conciliation and Arbitration of 2 August 1928 had been signed that Italy started to establish political and intelligence bureaux within Ethiopia. Those bureaux were responsible for creating disaffection and disorder there – a situation exploited and used by Italy as a pretext for exciting the crisis of 1935–6. Anyone who cries for a dialogue with South Africa at all costs without knowing what he aims to achieve by it, apart from financial aid, should learn from the Ethiopian experience.

In view of this the only course left open for the African states is to be well prepared to meet South Africa with force if need be, in order to bring about a change in that country: unless there is concrete evidence to show that she is not only prepared, but has also begun, to implement the stages outlined above in an effort to bring about a peaceful change within her territory.

(b) Factors responsible for the Failures

The failures of Pan-Africanism outlined above are due to certain
factors which result in part from colonialism and the subsequent
process of decolonization, and range from balkanization to the
vanities of human beings. But before we consider them, we must
look at political Africa.

The division of the continent into so many states (Map 7) has
brought in its wake a host of problems to bedevil Pan-Africanism. Many of the states are unviable and even rely on foreign
military assistance for their internal security. This has led to two
weaknesses: first, economic dependence on outside powers; and,
secondly, the signing of military pacts with the former imperial
masters. How far have these, then, been responsible for the
failures of Pan-Africanism?

When any state depends substantially on foreign aid not only
for economic development but even for balancing its annual
budget, that state cannot formulate any foreign policy without
due consideration for the wishes of the aid-giving country. In
such a case, even when the state would wish to advance the
cause of Pan-Africanism it may, in one way or another, be
prevented from taking an active or constructive part in the
promotion of its ideals, if the interests of the aid-giving country
are accordingly to be jeopardized.

Moreover, it is well-known that, as a result of balkanization,
many African states attained independence without the necessary
qualified manpower even to run the civil service. Such states rely
heavily on the nationals of the former imperial power. And since
these foreign nationals are naturally more interested in their own
countries they tend to formulate the policies of the African states
concerned in such a way as to ensure that the interests of their
homelands take precedence. Even if the African leaders in such
states are opposed to such policy, they can act against it only at
the risk of alienating their former imperial masters.

The most dangerous aspect of balkanization is the signing of
defence agreements with the former colonial powers. Facilities
given to these powers by the African states concerned can be used
even against Pan-African ideals. This was evident during the

237

Nigerian crisis. French arms were passed to the Biafrans through the governments of both the Ivory Coast and Gabon. Besides, such agreements make it impossible to have an African high command.

It is easy to conclude that most of the responsibility for Pan-Africanist failures has its origin in the balkanization of the continent as well as in Africa's recent political history. The chief factors involved are: Africa's dependence on foreign aid; membership in certain 'Eur-African' organizations; political instability and foreign manipulations; and what may be ascribed to human shortcomings. Each factor will now be considered in detail.

I. AFRICA'S DEPENDENCE ON OVERSEAS AID

It has become more or less normal practice in international relations for aid-giving countries to influence the foreign policy of aid-receiving states. It is, therefore, not surprising that the aid-giving nations have played a significant role in the formulation and implementation, directly and indirectly, of the foreign policy of the African states, which depend heavily on foreign aid for their economic development. At this stage, in order to understand the necessity for foreign aid to bring about rapid economic development of the African continent, we should consider the economic situation at the point when most African states achieved independence. The most salient feature of the economy bequeathed by colonialism is that most Africans are partly or wholly engaged in agricultural and pastoral activities (see Table 4). These are concerned with low-productivity food and handicraft products intended either for individual use or for sale in local markets. Where economic development of any sort did take place during the colonial era, it was concentrated in sectors almost entirely limited to production for export, the import trade and related services. Over much of the African continent this represented only the visible part of the economic iceberg, and the degree of integration into the money economy varied greatly from place to place. Africans were not encouraged or permitted to achieve anything approaching full development of their own resources. Since education and social services lagged Africans were forced to remain either in the unskilled labour force, or in the traditional sector of the economy. The most important factor

Table 4. Share of agriculture^(a) in Gross Domestic Product of a few African states

Country	Share of agriculture in GDP (per cent)	Year
Somalia	85[b]	1963
Rwanda	80	1964
Ethiopia	69	1963
Uganda	64	1964
Tanzania	58	1964
Malawi	50	1963
Madagascar	42	1963
Kenya	42	1964
Zambia	11	1964
Ghana	51·4	1964
Guinea	53·8[b]	1964–5
Ivory Coast	42·3	1965
Liberia	28	1964
Mali	54	1962
Niger	61	1963
Nigeria	62·6	1962
Senegal	29·4	1962
Sierra Leone	30·2	1964–5
Togo	54	1964
Upper Volta	52	1964

Source: *Economic Co-operation and Integration in Africa: Three Case Studies*
  (a) including crop production, livestock, fishing and forestry;
  (b) estimated.

in economic development – a skilled, educated, highly productive labour force – was not sought and was even avoided. Consequently, when most countries achieved political independence they were very poorly equipped economically. As a result of this economic situation the new states, realizing that if political independence was to have any meaning it had to be matched by economic independence, started to devise ways and means whereby the states would be developed economically. To implement the plans, capital, which most states did not have, was badly needed. They therefore had to rely heavily on foreign aid and to compete with one another for it. So most of them signed all sorts of agreements with the former colonial powers; remained in the organizations devised by the colonial powers; or became associate members of the economic groupings to which the former colonial power was attached. This, in turn, put most of them in a foreign-policy strait-jacket. Their approach to Pan-Africanism has equally been influenced by this desire to secure foreign assistance at whatever cost.

One of the most glaring examples is the attitude of OAU members to apartheid. Even before the OAU was founded, all Africans were united in their opposition to so abominable a policy, as was manifest at the Addis Ababa Conference of May 1963, when all heads of African states came out in strong condemnation of apartheid.[66] In order to demonstrate their utter hostility they unanimously passed the resolution on 'Apartheid and Racial Discrimination' referred to on pages 231–2. They resolved to use any means in order to bring about a change of policy in South Africa. At that time Malawi had not yet become independent and could therefore not participate fully at the conference. She could, however, still have expressed her disapproval of the conference's outlook if she had any misgivings. This she did not do. On attaining independence on 6 July 1964, she could have refused to join the OAU, whose member states are dedicated to an anti-apartheid policy. This, too, she did not do. Instead, in accordance with Article XXVIII of the OAU Charter, Malawi applied to become a member of the organization. That meant, in effect, that she was prepared to abide by the charter, which included the purposes for which the organization was founded. One can therefore assume that all OAU member states were united in their attitude towards South Africa.

The unity of African states against the South African apartheid policy was maintained until the end of 1966. But before the end of that year, Malawi had been having secret contacts with the South African régime in an effort to secure a loan for her development projects, of which the building of a new capital was the most significant and costly item. As there were signs from South Africa that financial aid would be forthcoming if Malawi would openly attack the OAU outlook on South Africa, the walls of unity started to crack. In order to show Malawi that she meant business, South Africa made an offer of a 'trade agreement'. Significantly, when that 'trade agreement' between Malawi and South Africa was signed at Pretoria in March 1967, the Malawi five-man delegation was led not by the country's minister of trade, but by the commissioner for industrial development, Donald Pearson.

The 'trade agreement' of March 1967 was just the beginning. Immediately afterwards South African offered Malawi financial and material aid for installing strong radio transmitters. This time it came as a gift. Malawi decided to open diplomatic relations with South Africa, and this was announced on 10 September 1967, a day before the 1967 OAU summit at Kinshasa began. In order to impress her benefactors, Malawi seized the opportunity to attack the OAU. This apparently achieved its objective. A few months afterwards, the South African régime offered to contribute substantially towards the building of Malawi's proposed capital at Lilongwe. In addition, South Africa's Industrial Development Corporation offered Malawi a loan to build a railway linking Malawi with Northern Mozambique. The project, wholly financed by the corporation, cost £6,400,000. Since then Malawi has repeatedly expressed itself hostile to the OAU stand on South Africa's apartheid policy. And some African countries, dazzled by Malawi's 'achievement', have been tempted to follow the same track. Malawi acted as the middleman between South Africa and two African countries – the Malagasy Republic and Kenya.[67]

Malagasy, excited by South Africa's 'generous offer of financial aid' to Malawi, put out secret feelers to the South African régime in 1968. Encouraged by this and by Malawi's openly accommodating attitude, the South African Government set up a special foreign loans fund to promote economic cooperation with 'well disposed' African states. Initially Malagasy vacillated between her OAU commitment and sacrificing this for South Africa's aid; the vacillation was, however, overcome when the French stepped in and encouraged her to go ahead with a much more 'accommodating and moderate' policy. Talks between

Progress and Problems

Madagascar and South Africa took place through the bad offices of both Paris and Malawi. The first outcome was a financial agreement signed by a South African delegation (led by the foreign minister, Hilgard Muller) and the Malagasy Republic at Tananarive on 20 November 1970. At a welcoming address, the Malagasy foreign minister and vice-president, Jacques Rabemananjara, expressed the hope that 'the agreement ... will constitute a starting point, and I think we should study other areas together. That will be the object of our talks.'[68] Before the talks ended, Malagasy had received concrete assurances of more financial aid from the South African Government, the South African Industrial Development Corporation and the Southern Hotel group.

Gabon for her part has even sent delegations to South Africa. President Bongo has declared his willingness to cooperate with South Africa in economic and medical fields.[69] As a result, the South African millionaire Louis Luyt has taken a share with the French Government and a major French oil company (UTA) in a $7,000,000 hotel projection in the capital, Libreville. The Ivory Coast, too, is said to have 'received significant, but unpublished financial assistance from South Africa'.[70]

Ghana's situation is somewhat different. Her change of policy resulted first from pressure by her creditors to take a much more moderate line on the South African issue, and secondly from a desire to show the world that the new Ghana would be different from Nkrumah's old one.

In relation to the South African issue, we have to remember the Commonwealth Conference of January 1971, at which South Africa featured very prominently. The attitude of African states towards the British decision on the sale of arms to South Africa was largely dictated by the amount of financial aid each received from Britain. Tanzania, Uganda, Zambia and Nigeria made their opposition absolutely clear; but Kenya, Ghana and Malawi acquiesced.[71]

2. MEMBERSHIP IN CERTAIN 'EUR-AFRICAN' ORGANIZATIONS

Membership of certain African states in organizations like the European Economic Community, the French Community and the Commonwealth has not helped Pan-Africanism.

In the case of the European Economic Community, the associate membership of certain African states has not only led to discrimination against others on the continent, but is bound to affect joint economic efforts to develop Africa. The right of a state to choose the role of perpetual 'drawers of waters and hewers of wood' must not be allowed to obstruct economic development of the continent, which Africans agree should be planned jointly. It is common knowledge that most development plans of the African associate member states of the European Economic Community must be submitted to the EEC Commission for approval before they can be implemented.[72] Such a situation cannot but impair cooperation in the economic development of Africa on a continental basis.

Membership of certain African states in the French Community played a significant role in promoting African disunity at the United Nations between July 1960 and December 1962. On 20 September 1960, Cameroon, the Central African Republic, Chad, Congo (Brazzaville), Dahomey, Gabon, the Ivory Coast, Madagascar, Niger and the Upper Volta were admitted to the UN. They were joined by Senegal on 28 September 1960. Under the pretext that French was their official language and that 'they had very small delegations, most of which had had no previous experience in an international organization',[73] they kept aloof from other delegations in the African group which had been inaugurated in 1958. After the Abidjan conference of their heads of state, where it was decided that they would adopt common attitudes on international issues, they started a series of their own informal meetings at the UN headquarters. In this non-cooperative attitude towards other African states, they had the backing and support of the French delegates. Indeed, they consistently supported French policy on Algeria, voting in the

243

General Assembly against most other African states. As we have noted above, they opposed other African states over the Congo crisis as well, when France supported the Belgian policy.

During the Fifteenth Session of UNGA the group was organized on an ad hoc basis. The French delegates not only attended its meetings but, on occasions, took the chair.[74] The group was formally launched at the beginning of the Sixteenth Session of UNGA in September 1961. On 12 June 1962, the secretary-general of the group's organization (the African and Malagasy Union), Albert Tevoedjre, declared: 'We cannot accept the fact that a single tendency of African expression be represented [on the Security Council] alone ... The African and Malagasy Union wishes to take its place in the sun ... We cannot be relegated to the role of those who are set aside and overlooked.'[75] Immediately after this declaration, the group set up a secretariat in New York to coordinate its activities. Thus, unlike other African states which belonged to the Commonwealth but nonetheless cooperated with the African group at the UN, the African member states of the French Community preferred cooperation with France to cooperation with their fellow African states. This situation continued until the OAU was founded in May 1963, when all joined hands to form a strong and united African group at the UN.

Membership in the French Community has also been responsible for misunderstanding in West Africa, hindering economic cooperation between the West African states. Ever since Guinea decided to be free in September 1958, the relationship between Guinea's president, Sékou Touré, and the other heads of state of former French Africa has left much to be desired. Most of them held the view that by leading Guinea out of the proposed French Community he had committed an unpardonable offence. Since Charles de Gaulle also took this line, it was difficult for most of these African leaders to hold an objective view of the situation. After an effort had been made by Sékou Touré, relations between Guinea and the Ivory Coast improved.[76] But when students came out in support of the Guinea Government after the Portuguese invasion of that country in November 1970, president Houphouet-Boigny's Government in the Ivory Coast expelled

244

many African students in Abidjan for demonstrating against 'our friends'. Unfortunately this high-handedness was supported by the presidents of the other entente states at an extraordinary meeting held at Yamoussoukro early in December 1970.[77]

The attitude of the Senegalese Government towards Guinea over the invasion is another example of how membership in the French Community has adversely affected Pan-Africanism. Portugal is a member of the Western Alliance, and the members of this alliance tried to play down the invasion as non-existent, despite UN confirmation of Portuguese involvement. France, like the other members, would naturally have been glad to see the invasion succeed. But since it failed, everything should be done to protect the invaders. It is in this light that the refusal of Senegal, unlike Gambia and Sierra Leone, to extradite the Guineans who took part in this invasion must be viewed.

The attitude of the African French Community member states over the French atom-bomb tests in the Sahara has been another pointer in this direction. While other African states were engaged in diplomatic activities to dissuade France from making the Sahara tests, these states were not merely mute but appeared happy at what they regarded as French achievement. Their venerable leader and spokesman, Houphouet-Boigny of the Ivory Coast, even claimed that it was in the best interests of them all that such tests should take place there.[78]

Their reaction to the French sale of arms to South Africa is yet one more case in point. They fully realize that arming South Africa constitutes a serious threat to the existence of many OAU member states. In spite of this and in spite of the UN arms embargo, imposed since 1963 – a move which resulted from an OAU initiative – they have maintained a conspiracy of silence. When in 1970 the OAU decided to appeal to both France and Britain to stop the sale of arms to South Africa, Houphouet-Boigny came out in support of a 'dialogue' with South Africa. He was promptly supported by both the Malagasy Republic and Gabon, which were already expecting financial aid from South Africa. It is, furthermore, an open secret that their membership of the French Community has facilitated secret dealings between some of them and the South African régime.

The timing of Houphouet-Boigny's call for a 'dialogue' and the immediate support for the call from a few African French Community members was calculated to achieve two objectives. The first was the sabotage of OAU efforts at dissuading France and other Western powers from arming South Africa. The second was closely related: for if the OAU had succeeded, and France, along with other Western powers, had agreed to stop selling arms to South Africa, this would have dried up a lucrative source of French foreign earnings. Houphouet-Boigny and others were thus more concerned with French than with African interests.

The situation within the Commonwealth is not nearly as rigid as that within the French Community. The reactions of nearly all African Commonwealth members to the British sale of arms to South Africa clearly demonstrated this difference.[79] Nevertheless, there has been one particular case in recent years which must be especially condemned. This was the role of Nigeria during the initial stages of the Rhodesian crisis in 1965. Shortly after the minority racist régime in Rhodesia declared that country's independence, an emergent session of the OAU Council of Ministers was held at Addis Ababa on 3 December 1965. The council decided that if the rebellion was not crushed by 15 December all African states should break off diplomatic relations with Britain. In a move to preserve the Commonwealth from the disintegration which such a diplomatic rupture would entail, the Nigerian prime minister, Sir Abubakar Tafawa Balewa, called a Commonwealth conference at Lagos, to discuss the Rhodesian crisis – thereby wrecking the action proposed by the OAU Council of Ministers.

Is it not time that African states renounced their membership in such organizations, if these continue to impede the achievement of Pan-Africanism?

3. POLITICAL INSTABILITY AND FOREIGN MANIPULATIONS

There has been widespread instability in the new African states. A series of coups d'état has taken place during the first decade of their existence. Secessionist aspirations have already led to civil war in the Congo and Nigeria. This political instability makes it much easier for foreign powers to interfere in and manipulate African affairs, with disastrous consequences for Pan-Africanism.

There is no doubt whatsoever about the justification for the overthrow of many African governments. Most of the politicians were more interested in their own personal ambitions than in the welfare of the people they led. They abused their positions, to amass wealth while the living standards of the ordinary citizen deteriorated. Most of them were so corrupt that they earned the nickname 'Mr Ten Per Cent'. They appealed to the civil servants and other citizens to accept austerity measures in the interest of the nation while, at the same time, they indulged in exorbitant living; bought or allowed their wives to present them with the most expensive cars and even golden beds. They gave the most lavish parties, while most ordinary citizens could not be sure of earning £50 in a whole year. They started to create a special class for themselves and their relatives.[80] Nevertheless these coups d'état had unfortunate results. Either the ensuing military régime is very conservative or it becomes a pawn in the power-game of world politics: whether this happens depends mostly on what type of government the military junta succeeds. But most of the military régimes are easily susceptible to foreign manipulations. Only when a country is faced with the gigantic problem of having to fight for its unity and happens to realize the destructive intentions of 'former friends', do such manipulations usually fail.

There have been two recent cases where it is difficult to say categorically whether coups d'état resulted mainly from the failings of the overthrown government or whether foreign influence played the leading role. In Ghana, there is no doubt that Nkrumah made many blunders.[81] But the claim by Major-

247

General Kotoka, in an interview over the West German television network, that the army had decided to overthrow President Nkrumah because he 'wanted to send them to fight in Rhodesia'[82] makes one wonder.

Another example of such dubious circumstances surrounding a coup d'état occurred in Uganda. Attending the Commonwealth Conference in Singapore, president Obote was strongly attacking the sale of arms to South Africa by the British Conservative Government. Before he returned to Uganda the army was in power. (A similarity with Nkrumah's overthrow?) There are, however, indications that the head of the military régime himself was under suspicion of having committed serious crimes against the existence of the state.[83] Did he therefore decide to overthrow the government of president Obote to save his own skin, or was he advised by foreign powers? Or were both these factors involved? What is clear is that: 'General Idi Amin, upon taking over power from Dr Obote in Uganda, cancelled Obote's threat to withdraw from the Commonwealth if Britain were to sell arms to South Africa.'[84] Of course, Britain was the first to recognize the new régime. Such examples do not imply that coups d'état in Africa are necessarily always engineered by foreign powers. The situations within many African states (as mentioned above) are conducive to army take-overs.[85]

Foreign manipulations are mainly directed at changing the course of a country's policy:[86] in Africa, this is achieved by presenting the head of state with a private executive jet, lavish cars and other luxurious articles, or by opening a secret bank account for influential members of government in a foreign country, especially Switzerland. When this has been done, policies are rapidly reformulated as required. In other cases, pressure is brought to bear on different forces within the country, so that a change of policy may be achieved. And manipulation is not employed only by foreign governments against African ones. African governments themselves may practise such techniques for their particular ends. A flagrant example may be found in the circumstances leading to the withdrawal of both the Upper Volta and Dahomey from the proposed Mali Federation in 1959.

We have already noted that in January 1959 Senegal, Sudan,

the Upper Volta and Dahomey agreed to form the Mali Federation, and also that the Voltaic Assembly approved the constitution for the proposed federation on 28 January 1959. The four states took this major decision in spite of opposition from the president of the RDA, Félix Houphouet-Boigny, the Ivory Coast and the French authorities, who feared that federation meant eventual independence from France.

United i n their aim to sabotage the proposed federation, both Félix Houphouet-Boigny and the French administration planned their strategy. Their combined assault was first directed against the Upper Volta, which supplied much of the labour force for the Ivory Coast plantations.[87] The internal political situation in the Upper Volta was conducive to foreign manipulation, since the territory was divided by regional and ethnic differences, mainly between the Mossi and non-Mossi. After the general elections of March 1957, a coalition government had been formed by the RDA and the MVD (Mouvement Démocratique Voltaique). But in December 1957 the MVD and a section of the RDA had broken away from the coalition, leaving the government with a minority of the assembly behind it. The premier, Ouezzin Coulibaly, had refused to resign and even gained a new majority when some of the MVD deputies, led by Yameogo, had agreed to join the RDA themselves. At the end of 1958 Yameogo had himself become the premier after some negotiations; and had formed a coalition government made up of RDA and various opposition parties allied to the PRA.[88] The new coalition government had, however, a majority of only two. The RDA itself depended for its strength on Morho Naba, the 'emperor' of the Mossi, who had fused his personal party with the RDA. For ethnic reasons there was always a difference within the party's official hierarchy on matters of importance. The majority was therefore not a reliable one.

In their strategy, the combined anti-federation forces of Houphouet-Boigny and the French authorities sent a delegation to Morho Naba. And immediately after receiving this, Morho Naba warned against joining the Mali Federation, which, according to him, could become a dangerous weapon in the hands of 'subversive elements'. France quickly made it known that he

supported the anti-federation policy of the Ivory Coast leadership. In order to undermine the federalists further, France
announced the appointment of a new high commissioner to
Ouagadougou (capital of the Upper Volta) without consulting the
Voltaic Government: and this on the very day that Yameogo
arrived in Dakar for the Constituent Assembly of the Mali
Federation! All Voltaic protests against such a move were of no
avail. Shortly afterwards the Voltaic army veterans, who numbered some 17,500 and were extremely loyal to their French
leader as well as to France, started to show anti-federalist sentiments. Yet, despite all these activities, the Voltaic Assembly
approved the federal constitution.

This only provoked the Ivory Coast to increase its pressure. A
delegation of the PDCI (Parti Démocratique de la Côte d'Ivoire)
– the Ivory Coast section of the RDA – went to the Upper
Volta in February 1959 and visited major trading-centres,
where it stressed the importance of Abidjan as a commercial
outlet for the Upper Volta. The delegation also spared no pains
in reminding the Voltaic leaders how important the Ivory Coast
was as a place of employment for Voltaic nations. A delegation
of chiefs from Niger also visited Morho Naba, advising him
strenuously of the dangers to the chieftaincy in the activities of
the Senegalese and Sudanese. To back their anti-federalist
campaign, bribery was employed; and 'it is commonly assumed
that during this period considerable Ivory Coast funds found
their way into Voltaic pockets'.[89] These activities resulted in the
desired goal. On 28 February 1959, as we have noted earlier, the
Voltaic Assembly, by approving a draft constitution at a hastily-
arranged session which took place at midnight, formally withdrew from the Mali Federation.

4. HUMAN AND PSYCHOLOGICAL FACTORS

The most significant human factors are such vanities as the search
for personal glory, and inordinate ambition, which carry clashes
of personality to the level of national politics. In an effort to
achieve personal ends, ethnic ('tribal') or sectional emotions are

irresponsibly, dangerously aroused. There is also indulgence in corrupt practices. And throughout there is the problem of the colonial complex. All these factors have at one time or the other helped to promote the failures of Pan-Africanism.

As a direct result of colonialism, many African leaders still suffer from a sense of cultural inferiority. And this is responsible for the ease with which certain foreign powers can manipulate some of them. The 'complex' manifests itself in many other ways, such as the reliance on imported 'experts' to work out development plans, even where there are qualified nationals who could do as well, if not better. Such 'experts' are all too often inclined to put the interests of their own country above those of the African state; driving wedges between one African state and another, and causing friction, misunderstanding or conflict within the Pan-African movement.

Another source of serious harm is tribalism. One is bound to wonder what observations some African leaders who indulge in tribalism made, when they were students abroad. Britain is made up of Englishmen, Scots, Welsh and Irish. There are considerable differences between the French who live in Brittany, Paris or Lorraine; and at least as different from one another are the Germans who live in Hamburg, Berlin, Westphalia and Bavaria. The same applies to the Russians and, of course, the Americans. Educated Africans know full well that no nation can be built on 'tribal' or ethnic grounds – yet most of them indulge in tribalism. They start by appealing for national unity; but when they fail to achieve their personal ambitions they whip up tribal sentiments instead. Then, either the foreigners who are interested in dividing Africans seize this opportunity to sow dissension between groups within the state, or nepotism flourishes. Such a state of affairs must be eradicated.

The expulsions of many West Africans from Ghana by the government of Kofi Busia in November 1969 should also be viewed in the tribal or sectional context. If Africans cannot live peacefully in other African states, how then can African Unity ever be achieved? The average Ghanaian surely had nothing against his brother from any other African state. The deportation of Africans under very appalling conditions was thus a triumph of sectionalism over Pan-Africanism; and it must not only be condemned, but be prevented from occurring again in any part of Africa.[90]

One other enemy of Pan-Africanism is the use of corrupt practices. This vice is, of course, not confined only to Africa. But its existence elsewhere does not in any way exonerate any African, who would rather obstruct Pan-Africanism than forgo his personal ambition, and is ready to use the most corrupt practices for his end.

Notes to Chapter 5

1. See *Condition Humaine*, 14 April 1956 – 'Confédération et fédération'.
2. See *Le Monde*, 29 May 1956. For the major speeches and resolutions of the congress, see *Condition Humaine*, 31 May 1956.
3. For the unofficial report of this meeting, see *Afrique Nouvelle*, 21 November 1958.
4. Quoted from William J. Foltz, *From French West Africa to the Mali Federation*, Yale University Press, London and New Haven, 1965, p. 100.
5. Agence France Presse, Bulletin, 18–19 January 1959.
6. See section (b) of this chapter – 'Factors responsible for the Failures'.
7. The federalists maintained that only twenty-two members were present and that as a result the decision reached was illegal. See *Le Drame de la Haute Volta* (Paris, Documents Africains, 1960), p. 2.
8. The Upper Volta in fact chose Abidjan. On 4 April 1959, the Upper Volta signed bilateral agreements with the Ivory Coast, setting up a council of the entente.
9. Foltz, op. cit., p. 169.
10. See République du Sénégal, *Livre blanc sur le coup d'état manqué du 19 au 20 août, 1960* (Dakar), 1960), p. 5 and Modibo Keita, 'Communication à l'Assemblée Législative de la République Soudanaise' (Bamako, 29 August 1960, mimeo) for different accounts of this meeting.
11. See *Livre blanc*, p. 8.
12. Foltz, op. cit., p. 177.
13. These sub-regions comprise the following independent states:
   North Africa: Algeria, Libya, Morocco, Sudan, Tunisia and the United Arab Republic;
   West Africa: Dahomey, Gambia, Guinea, the Ivory Coast, Liberia, Mali, Niger, Nigeria, Senegal, Sierra Leone, Togo and Upper Volta;
   East Africa: Botswana, Burundi, Ethiopia, Kenya, Lesotho, Madagascar, Malawi, Mauritius, Rwanda, Somalia, Uganda, Tanzania and Zambia;
   Central Africa: Cameroon, the Central African Republic, Chad, Congo (Brazzaville), Congo (Kinshasa) and Gabon.

14. See Chapter 4, especially pages 136–7.
15. Economic Co-operation in Africa: 'Present situation and proposed programme of activities for 1967–1968' (E/CN.14/386, January 1967).
16. ECA Document E/CN.14/366.
17. For the preliminary draft of the treaty for the West African Economic Community and explanatory notes, see ECA Doc. E/CN.14/WA/EC/5 of October 1967. For the proceedings of the meeting of the Interim Council of Ministers, see West African Economic Community, 'Preliminary report of the first session of the Interim Council of Ministers held at Dakar, 21–7 November 1967'.
18. *Economic Co-operation and Integration in Africa – Three Case Studies* (ST/ECA/109), p. 60.
19. S/4387 of 14 July 1960.
20. For an account of the emergence and workings of the African group at the UN, see Thomas Hovet, Jr, *Africa in the United Nations*, Faber & Faber, London, 1963.
21. See UN Security Council Doc. S/4417/Add.2 of 6 August 1960; the Second Report by the UN secretary-general on the implementation of the Security Council Resolutions S/4387 of 14 July 1960, and S/4405 of 22 July 1960, pp. 2–3; and the Security Council Resolution S/4426 of 9 August 1960.
22. Asian UN members working hand in hand with the group included Ceylon, India and Indonesia.
23. For the text of this draft resolution and its revisions, see UN Doc. A/L.319, A/L.319/Rev.1 and Add.1, 2+A/L.319/Rev.2 of 10, 12 and 28 October 1960, respectively.
24. Catherine Hoskyns, *The Congo since Independence*, Oxford University Press, London, 1965, p. 260.
25. See UN Doc. A/4560 for the exchange of messages between Kasavubu and the UNGA president.
26. For the verbatim records of the session, see GAOR Fifteenth Session, Plenary Meetings 911, 912 917–24. See also UNGA Resolution 1498(XV) of 22 November 1960.
27. See S/4671, 6 February 1961 from Congo (Brazzaville); S/4673, 6 February 1961 from the Malagasy Republic; S/4677 – Note Verbale, 7 February 1961 from Senegal; S/4679 and S/4680, 9 February 1961 from the Malagasy Republic.
28. See *Afrique Action*, 27 February 1961; Hoskyns, op. cit., p. 328.
29. S/4722, 17 February 1961.
30. For further details on the groups at the UN, see Hovet, op. cit., pp. 92–6.
31. *New York Times*, 15 June 1964.
32. See the *Neue Zürcher Zeitung*, 31 August 1964.
33. *East African Standard*, 8 September 1964.
34. See *New York Times*, 5, 7, 17 and 18 June 1964; also *Neue Zürcher Zeitung*, 19 and 21 August 1964.
35. *New York Times*, 25 August 1964.

Progress and Problems

36. *New York Times*, 23 September 1964.
37. ibid.
38. *The Times*, 4 April 1970 – 'Portugal's Fear of Colonization by Europe'.
39. *West Africa*, 27 July 1963, p. 849.
40. UN Security Council Document S/5380, 31 July 1963.
41. This has nothing to do with the missionaries known as the 'White Fathers' whose withdrawal from the Portuguese colonies in Africa in protest against the Portuguese colonial policy of repression and genocide is to be commended.
42. *Sunday Telegraph*, 29 June 1969.
43. See *The Times*, 17 June 1971.
44. It is worth noting that the brother of the leader of URGP called James Pinto Bull was at one time Portugal's right-hand man in Guinea (Bissau). He was the secretary-general of the colonial Portuguese Government there.
45. *West Africa*, 1 August 1964, p. 858.
46. For a detailed account of PAIGC's achievements, see Basil Davidson, *The Liberation of Guiné*, Penguin Books, Harmondsworth, 1969; also the *Financial Times*, 30 June 1971.
47. Davidson, op. cit., p. 87.
48. Senegal's refusal to hand over those who took part in the Portuguese invasion of Guinea in November 1970 does not help the situation.
49. Eduardo Mondlane, *The Struggle for Mozambique*, Penguin Books, Harmondsworth, 1969, p. 113.
50. For a detailed account of the incident, see Mondlane, op. cit., pp. 117–18.
51. ibid., p. 132.
52. For a detailed account of the work done by FRELIMO in the struggle for independence of Mozambique, see Mondlane, op. cit.
53. See the *Observer*, 26 April 1970.
54. *Addis Ababa Summit*, May 1963, p. 86.
55. *West Africa*, 5 March 1966, p. 281.
56. *The Times*, 22 June 1971.
57. Mondlane, op. cit., pp. 197–206.
58. See *The Times*, 3 July 1970.
59. *The Times*, 2 January 1971. For the CIA role in organizing the Portuguese invasion see the *Daily Telegraph Magazine* No. 377.
60. See the Security Council Official Records, 1534th meeting, at which an Afro-Asian draft resolution S/9696 'failed of adoption due to the negative votes of two permanent members (United States and United Kingdom)' on 17 March 1970; also the proceedings of the Council at its 1556th meeting, when, following the negative vote of the United Kingdom, draft resolution S/9976 'failed of adoption'.
61. See the *Observer*, 7 February 1971.
62. *East African Standard*, 1 April 1966.
63. The General Assembly Resolution 1761 (XVII) of 6 November 1962, reads as follows:

The General Assembly

Recalling its previous resolutions on the question of race conflict in South Africa resulting from the policies of apartheid of the Government of the Republic of South Africa,

Further recalling its resolutions 44 (I) of 8 December 1964, 395 (V) of 2 December 1950, 615 (VII), 1302 (XIII) of 10 December 1958, 1460 (XIV) of 10 December 1959, 1597 (XV) of 13 April 1961 and 1662 (XVI) of 28 November 1961, on the question of the treatment of peoples of Indian and Indo-Pakistan origin,

Noting the reports of the Government of India and Pakistan on that subject,

Recalling that the Security Council in its resolution of 1 April 1960 recognised that the situation in South Africa was one that had led to international friction and, if continued, might endanger international peace and security,

Recalling further that the Security Council in its aforesaid resolution called upon the Government of South Africa to initiate measures aimed at bringing about racial harmony based on equality in order to ensure that the present situation does not continue or recur, and to abandon its policies of apartheid and racial discrimination,

Regretting that the actions of some Member States indirectly provide encouragement to the Government of South Africa to perpetuate its policy of racial segregation, which has been rejected by the majority of that country's population,

1. *Deplores* the failure of the Government of the Republic of South Africa to comply with repeated requests and demands of the General Assembly and the Security Council and its flouting of world public opinion by refusing to abandon its racial policies;

2. *Strongly deprecates* the continued and total disregard by the Government of South Africa of its obligations under the Charter of the United Nations and, furthermore, its determined aggravation of racial issues by enforcing measures of increasing ruthlessness involving violence and bloodshed;

3. *Reaffirms* that the continuance of those policies seriously endangers international peace and security;

4. *Requests* Member States to take the following measures, separately or collectively, in conformity with the Charter, to bring about the abandonment of these policies:

(a) Breaking off diplomatic relations with the Government of the Republic of South Africa or refraining from establishing such relations;

(b) Closing their ports to all vessels flying the South African flag;

(c) Enacting legislation prohibiting their ships from entering South African ports;

(d) Boycotting all South African goods and refraining from exporting goods, including all arms and ammunition, to South Africa;

(e) Refusing landing and passage facilities to all aircraft belonging to the Government of South Africa and companies registered under the laws of South Africa;

5. *Decides* to establish a Special Committee consisting of representatives of Member States nominated by the President of the General Assembly, with the following terms of reference:

(a) To keep the racial policies of the Government of South Africa under review when the Assembly is not in session;

(b) To report either to the Assembly or to the Security Council or to both, as may be appropriate from time to time;

6. *Requests* all Member States:

(a) To do everything in their power to help the Special Committee to accomplish its task;

(b) To refrain from any act likely to delay or hinder the implementation of the present resolution;

7. *Invites* Member States to inform the General Assembly at its eighteenth session regarding actions taken, separately or collectively, in dissuading the Government of South Africa from pursuing its policy of *apartheid*;

8. *Requests* the Security Council to take appropriate measures, including sanctions, to secure South Africa's compliance with the resolutions of the General Assembly and of the Security Council on this subject and, if necessary, to consider action under Article 6 of the Charter.

64. For the 'Double Standard' speech delivered by the British foreign secretary, Sir Alec Douglas-Home, see the House of Lords' Debates of 18 December 1961, the *New York Times* and British newspapers of 19 December 1961. Significantly, Sir Alec, now as British foreign secretary once again, is still the champion of arms sales to South Africa.

65. *The Times*, 18 June 1971.

66. For the speech of each and every African head of state on the subject, see *Addis Ababa Summit*, 1963.

67. Kenya started seeking technical and economic aid from South Africa in 1967. A personal secretary of Kenyatta even went to Pretoria, where a series of meetings were held with cabinet ministers. But the project did not materialize.

68. *The Times*, 20 November 1970.

69. See the *Financial Times*, 4 December 1970.

70. ibid.

71. See the *Observer*, 24 January 1971, p. 11: 'Knocking the wealth out of Commonwealth' (last paragraph). Lesotho, Swaziland and Botswana are also heavily dependent on South Africa's financial aid.

72. See the EEC Commission Ordinance No. 62/65 of 25 March 1965 (Verordnung Nr 62/65/EWG der Kommission vom 25 März 1965), pp. 83–9 of DAS ABKOMMEN VON JAUNDE – die Assoziierung der Überseeischen Länder mit der EWG: Dazugehörige Dokumente.

73. Hovet, op. cit., p. 92.

74. ibid., p. 95.

256

75. op. cit., p. 96. See also *Newsday*, 13 June 1962: 'UN African "Bloc" achieves Unity – In small Groups'.
76. *West Africa*, 15 August 1970, p. 948.
77. *West Africa*, 26 December 1970–1 January 1971, p. 1520.
78. See *West Africa*, 19 September 1959, p. 706.
79. For the factors responsible for the lukewarm attitude of Kenya, Malawi, Ghana, etc. on this topic at the Commonwealth Conference of January 1971, see page 242; also note 67 above.
80. For a detailed account of the circumstances which led to coups d'état in most of the African states, see Ruth First, *The Barrel of a Gun: Political Power in Africa and the Coup d'État*, Allen Lane, The Penguin Press, London, 1970; also P. C. Lloyd, *Africa in Social Change*, Penguin Books, Harmondsworth, 1967, and Okoi Arikpo, *The Development of Modern Nigeria*, Penguin Books, Harmondsworth, 1967, especially pp. 112–22.
81. See First, *The Barrel of a Gun*, and W. Scott Thompson, *Ghana's Foreign Policy, 1957–1966*, Princeton University Press, Princeton, New Jersey, 1969.
82. *East African Standard*, 16 March 1966.
83. See *The Times* (London) and the *Financial Times*, 27 January 1971.
84. *The Times*, 24 May 1971.
85. For the role of foreign powers, see First, op. cit., pp. 411–26; also Paul W. Blackstock, *The Strategy of Subversion: Manipulating the Politics of Other Nations*, Quadrangle Books, Chicago, 1964.
86. For an analysis of these means, see Blackstock, op. cit.
87. Foltz, op. cit., p. 107.
88. Ronald Segal, *African Profiles*, Penguin Books, Harmondsworth, 1963, p. 294.
89. Foltz, op. cit., p. 109.
90. See *The Times*, 17 December 1969, p. 11. For the reactions of other West African states to the expulsions, see *West Africa*, 9 May 1970, p. 519.

6. Pan-Africanism in Travail

The ends you serve that are selfish will take you no further than yourself; but the ends you serve that are for all, will take you even into eternity.

MARCUS GARVEY*

Problems are bound to arise in the course of anything worthwhile in life. And Pan-Africanism provides no exception. The experience of the Nigerian civil war, which has proved the greatest test for Pan-Africanism since the establishment of the OAU, has shown that challenges of even such a magnitude may yet be surmounted.

(a) The OAU and the Nigerian Crisis†

Although this section is concerned with the role of the Organization of African Unity in the Nigerian crisis, it is nonetheless desirable to look first at the events which led to the crisis itself. This virtually began on 15 January 1966, when a group of army officers carried out a coup d'état at Lagos, Ibadan and Kaduna. The prime minister of the Federation, Sir Abubakar Tafawa Balewa; a few other federal ministers, including the premiers of the Western and Northern Regions, Chief S. L. Akintola and Sir Ahmadu Bello; and some army officers, were murdered. Following this action, the head of the Nigerian army, Major-General Johnson Thomas Umunakwe Aguiyi-Ironsi, was called upon, by the remaining members of the federal cabinet after a meeting, to assume the reins of government throughout the Federation.[1] Then, on 29 July 1966, Lieutenant-Colonel Yakubu Gowon took over the Nigerian military government, after Aguiyi-Ironsi had been killed in another coup.

In September 1966, many Ibos were killed in Northern Nigeria as a result of tribal revolts. Lieutenant-Colonel C. Odumegwu

*Philosophy and Opinions, Vol. I, p. 2.
† The genesis of the Nigerian crisis is very complex and outside the scope of this book. I am therefore now working on a book to cover the crisis.

Ojukwu, the military governor of Eastern Nigeria, announced on 2 October that the Eastern Region would boycott the constitutional talks scheduled to start at Lagos on 21 October. All efforts to dissuade him proved abortive. In January 1967 all the military governors of the Federation met at Aburi, in Ghana, in an attempt to break the deadlock in the relations between the Eastern Region and the rest of Nigeria. The Aburi Agreement, however, did not achieve the much-desired improvement in relations, since there were serious differences over its interpretation.

In March 1967, Ojukwu decided to cease the payment of all revenues collected in the Eastern Region on behalf of the federal treasury to the Federal Government. As a result of this action, the Government imposed an economic blockade on the Eastern Region. On 16 April, the Eastern Region authority took over the administration of all federal institutions in the East. On 27 May the military government declared a state of emergency throughout the Federation. The 'States (Creation and Transitional Provisions) Decree'[2] was issued, creating twelve states out of the former four regions and the Federal territory of Lagos. Three days later, on 30 May, Ojukwu declared the Eastern Region an independent state, to be called 'the Republic of Biafra'.

On 6 July the Federal Government started a 'police action' against the rebels. It developed into a war, since Ojukwu and his advisers had been preparing for just this since October 1966.[3]

Within the shortest possible time, what was rightly regarded by the Nigerian Federal Military Government as strictly an internal Nigerian affair was internationalized. Both sides purchased arms abroad; and the Churches, the International Red Cross, Caritas and some other European organizations began supporting Biafra.[4]

THE OAU INITIATIVE

The Nigerian crisis was first discussed by the Organization of African Unity at the summit conference held in Kinshasa in September 1967. It had not been submitted as an item for the conference agenda by the Council of Ministers, because Nigeria had always maintained that the crisis was its own internal affair, and that any discussion of it by the OAU would amount to a violation of Article III(2) of the Charter, which prohibits interference in the internal affairs of member states. By this time, however, the well-organized Biafran propaganda movement abroad, especially in Europe, and the suffering of the ordinary people in Biafra as a result of the war, made it impossible for the African heads of state and government to leave Kinshasa without discussing the crisis. Private talks between the head of the Nigerian delegation and a few heads of state cleared the way.

After much discussion, the conference adopted a unanimous resolution which accepted the Nigerian view, in a solemn affirmation of adherence to the principle of respect for the sovereignty and territorial integrity of member states, and in condemnation of secession within any member state. The leaders expressed their concern at the grave and tragic situation in Nigeria; and considered it Nigeria's responsibility to find a solution. But although they reposed their trust and confidence in the Federal Government of Nigeria, they nevertheless expressed their desire to explore the possibilities of placing the services of the Assembly at the disposal of the Federal Government. They therefore resolved to send a consultative mission, composed of the heads of state of Cameroon, Congo (Kinshasa), Ethiopia, Ghana, Liberia and Niger, to the head of the Federal Government, 'to assure him of the Assembly's desire for the territorial integrity and peace of Nigeria'.[5]

Reactions to this resolution from both Lagos and Enugu were not hostile. When Chief Awolowo, the leader of Nigeria's delegation to the OAU summit conference, returned to Lagos, he made it abundantly clear that the mission would assure the Federal Government of the OAU's solidarity in its attempts to solve the Nigerian crisis. The officials in Lagos also repeated the two conditions previously laid down by General Gowon for talks with secessionist Biafra: renunciation of secession, and acceptance of the twelve new States. In Enugu the Biafran authorities promised to cooperate with the OAU mission, provided that they were told what was going on. Enugu Radio described the mission as a 'move to mediate in the Nigerian civil war' and also as a 'victory over Nigeria'.[6]

After several postponements, the OAU consultative committee on Nigeria,[7] headed by Emperor Haile Selassie, finally arrived in Lagos on 23 November 1967. Welcoming the committee, Major-General Yakubu Gowon said, among other things:

I wish to take this opportunity to express formally our appreciation of the brotherly spirit of the O.A.U. Summit in recognising the need for Nigeria to be preserved as one country. It is in the interest of all Africa that Nigeria remains one political and economic entity. The O.A.U. has rightly seen our problem as a purely domestic affair ...

He promised the committee every assistance in its mission. Replying, Haile Selassie said that the committee's cardinal objective was to discuss ways and means

with the help of the Federal Government whereby Nigerian integrity is to be preserved and innocent Nigerian blood saved from flowing needlessly ... We believe a solution needs to be urgently sought to accommodate the varying interests in Nigeria but it must be specific enough to ensure the steady development of the Nigerian State.[8]

After a day of talks in Lagos, the following communiqué was issued by the committee:

The O.A.U. Consultative Commission held consultations with Major-General Yakubu Gowon, Head of the Federal Military Government of Nigeria yesterday, pursuant to the resolution on the Nigerian situation adopted at the fourth session of the O.A.U. Summit Conference in Kinshasa on the 14th September, 1967. The Mission reaffirmed the decision of the O.A.U. Summit embodied in its resolution condemning all secessionist attempts in Africa. The Mission also reaffirmed that any solution of the Nigerian crisis must be in the context of preserving the unity and territorial integrity of Nigeria. The Mission considered the Federal Government's terms for the cessation of military operations. The O.A.U. Consultative Mission agreed that, as a basis for a return to peace and normal conditions in Nigeria, the secessionists should renounce secession and accept the present administrative structure of the Federation of Nigeria laid down by the Federal Military Government of Nigeria in Decree No. 14 of 1967.[9]

General Ankrah of Ghana, who had been responsible for bringing all the Nigerian military governors together at Aburi in January, was given by the committee a mandate to convey the text of the OAU Kinshasa Summit resolution, as well as discussions and conclusions of the first meeting of the committee in Lagos, to the secessionists; and urgently to report their reaction; the Committee would then decide on the next course of action. It was also agreed that the OAU consultative committee would remain in constant touch with the Federal Military Government.

Before leaving Lagos for Kinshasa, to report on the meeting to President Mobutu, who was the current chairman of the OAU Assembly of Heads of State and Government, Diallo Telli, the OAU secretary-general, declared himself happy that a clear understanding between the Federal Government and Africa, represented by the Organization of African Unity, had emerged. It was vital, he said, for the secessionists to realize that they could not stand against all Africa.

The outcome of the Lagos meeting came as a bitter disappointment to the Biafrans, who had often previously emphasized that their sovereignty was not negotiable, and who wanted Biafra to be invited to any peace talks as an independent state. Indeed, an official statement broadcast over Enugu Radio on 24 November 1967 declared that by deciding to consult with only one party to the dispute the OAU committee on Nigeria had demonstrated its lack of objectivity and doomed itself to failure from the start. The statement also claimed that the committee condoned genocide and proved itself a rubber stamp by merely endorsing General Gowon's warning that their own countries would disintegrate if they did not rally to the Federal Government's support. By so doing, the statement ended, the Organization of African Unity had proved itself 'a willing tool of reactionary African leaders and an instrument of imperialist and neo-colonialist intrigue'.[10]

Despite this hostile reaction from the Biafrans, General Ankrah started consultations with their leader, Ojukwu, by telephone immediately he returned to Accra from the Lagos meeting. It was, however, not until July 1968 that the Organization of African Unity could bring the two sides together.

In the meantime, the Organization of African Unity continued with its efforts to bring peace to Nigeria. Answering questions at a Press conference in Freetown in January 1968,

Diallo Telli stressed that the OAU was not seeking to impose any particular constitution on Biafra, but was concerned only to maintain the integrity of Nigeria and so of Africa. He made it clear that the OAU could not regard Biafra's secession as an ordinary domestic matter, because all African states had minority problems, and secession in one affected all, particularly if such secession was based on 'irrational considerations such as tribalism and religion'.[11] In April, further efforts were made by the OAU to get talks between the two sides started. President Mobutu of Congo (Kinshasa), as a member of the OAU consultative committee on Nigeria and also the current chairman of the Organization, went to Accra for talks with General Ankrah, who had been given a mandate by the committee after the Lagos meeting to get in touch with the Biafrans. The secretary-general of the Organization, Diallo Telli, also had talks with the head of the Nigerian Federal Military Government, Major-General Yakubu Gowon. All these efforts were at last crowned with success when both sides met at Niamey in July.

THE NIAMEY TALKS

By the time that the Niamey Talks began on 15 July 1968, the task of the OAU consultative committee on Nigeria had been complicated by Tanzania's recognition of Biafra on 13 April; Gabon on 8 May; Ivory Coast on 14 May; and Zambia on 20 May.[12] Recognition by these four African states only helped to strengthen the Biafran leaders in their hope of being invited to any further peace talks as representatives of a sovereign state.

As the meeting was about to begin, the federal build-up for the final attack on the remnant of Biafra continued; and there was news of Biafran preparations for prolonged guerrilla warfare. Starvation and suffering mounted, and the world pressure for relief to refugees on both sides of the fighting line seemed rather to complicate the politics of the conflict than to make relief effective.

Members of the OAU consultative committee on Nigeria present at Niamey included Presidents Diori of Niger, Tubman of Liberia and Ahidjo of Cameroon; General Ankrah of Ghana, and Emperor Haile Selassie of Ethiopia. President Mobutu of

Congo (Kinshasa) was represented by a delegation under Jean Umba-de-Lutete, the deputy foreign minister; and Diallo Telli, the OAU secretary-general, was also present.

The meeting was addressed by General Gowon on 16 July 1968. Declaring that the Biafrans and their foreign backers were playing politics with the whole question of human suffering, he told the committee that, in military terms, the rebellion was 'virtually suppressed already'. And he added:

A unilateral cease-fire by the Federal Government without any prior commitment by the rebel leaders will give the rebels the opportunity to re-group and re-arm and prepare for a bloodier conflict. It will also give them a diplomatic advantage since such a unilateral cease-fire will guarantee the continued existence of the rebel régime in rebel-held areas, since the rebels will not allow the refugees to return to their homes and villages in Federally controlled parts of the former Eastern Region of Nigeria.

As a result of this, he was convinced that 'a Federal Government decision to order a unilateral cease-fire on humanitarian grounds will not in any way relieve the suffering of the innocent victims of our tragic civil war'.[13]

Continuing, he made it clear that 'the Federal Government has agreed to have an outside observer force to give a sense of security to the Ibos'. The observer force, which could go to Nigeria only at the specific invitation of the Federal Government, would be drawn from friendly governments to witness the reassertion of federal authority in rebel-held areas and bear testimony to the fact that federal troops would not go into rebel-held areas to 'massacre' Ibos. After presenting the federal case to the committee, he returned to Lagos, leaving behind at Niamey a Nigerian delegation led by Mr Allison Ayida.[14]

The committee held private discussions immediately after General Gowon's address. It was agreed that the Biafrans should be invited. The Biafran delegation,[15] led by Colonel Ojukwu, arrived at Niamey on 18 July 1968. After presenting the Biafran case to the committee on 19 July, Colonel Ojukwu proposed two ways of getting food into Biafra. One was a route up the River Niger to the Port of Oguta; the other was for the internationalization of Port Harcourt under neutral control, and for a ten-mile-wide corridor from there up the front-line positions north of the town where the Biafran Red Cross would take over. He also proposed a truce for a limited period. Behind him he left a nine-man delegation, headed by professor Eni Njoku. Commenting on the Niamey meeting at a Press conference in Owerri, Ojukwu said:

Provided the spirit of sincerity and honesty which was so very evident in Niamey continues, provided Africa is left on its own to grapple with the problems posed by our difficulties, I think there is hope. Judging from the way the conference started moving I think there will be permanent peace or at least temporary peace.[16]

Before Ojukwu left Niamey, discussions were held with him by the members of the committee. It was announced afterwards that both Nigeria and Biafra had agreed to hold preliminary discussions in Niamey, preparatory to resuming peace talks in Addis Ababa, under the auspices of the OAU consultative committee on Nigeria, as soon as possible. The following communiqué was also issued:

The Organisation of African Unity Consultative Committee on Nigeria, meeting in Niamey last Friday, July 19:

Having reviewed the present developments in the Nigerian civil war;

Deeply concerned about sufferings of civilians on both sides;

Considering the urgent need for supplies of food, medicine and clothing to be sent quickly to the affected areas;

Considering further the efforts made by various Governments and institutions to convey into the affected areas badly needed supplies of food, medicine and clothing;

Confident that these Governments and international institutions will continue to give assistance to the affected areas;

Mindful of its mandate from the Assembly of Heads of State and Government of the Organisation of African Unity held at Kinshasa;

Taking note of the decision by the Nigerian Federal Military Government to establish a corridor in the territory it controls to enable the despatch of food, medical and clothing supplies to the affected regions; as well as of its decision to guarantee the security of members of international relief organisations entrusted with the task of transporting and distributing these supplies:

(1) Requests the Federal Military Government to implement without delay its decision to establish a 'Mercy' corridor with

appropriate collecting points to facilitate the transportation of essential food and medical supplies to the affected areas; to guarantee the safety and freedom of movement of the agents of international relief organisations within federal controlled territory so as to ensure the effective distribution of these supplies to the needy civilian population in the affected areas; and also to guarantee the safety and security of observers and representatives of international relief agencies who shall inspect supplies at such collecting points.

(2) Appeals to the secessionists to co-operate by accepting relief supplies of food, medicine and clothing transported through the 'Mercy' corridor to the collecting points and to provide facilities to ensure the safety and free movement of the personnel of the international relief agencies and guarantee effective distribution to the needy civilian population in the territory under their control.

(3) Thanks those Governments and Organisations which have so far given assistance for their sympathy and generosity in relieving the sufferings of the civilian population and appeals to these and other Governments and Organisations to assure the continuation of this humanitarian support.

(4) Urgently appeals to all Member States of the OAU to assist in these massive humanitarian relief efforts.

(5) Urgently invites both parties, as a matter of urgency, to resume peace talks as soon as possible in order to achieve a final solution of the crisis prevailing in their country, with the object of preserving Nigeria's territorial integrity and guaranteeing the security of all its inhabitants.

(6) Decides that the Organisation of African Unity Consultative Committee shall remain at the disposal of both parties to help them in this direction. The Consultative Committee will remain in contact with the Federal Government of Nigeria. Colonel Ojukwu or his accredited representatives may at any time contact any of the member Governments of the Organisation of African Unity Consultative Committee.

22 July 1968

The preliminary talks, which began on 20 July under the chairmanship of president Hamani Diori of the Niger Republic, lasted until 26 July. They concentrated chiefly on the supply of relief to the innocent victims of the war. Nigeria agreed to the setting-up of a demilitarized corridor, three to five miles in length, on each side of the road from Enugu to Ogoja. The corridor,

Nigeria maintained, should be supervised by civilian observers from Cameroon, Congo (Kinshasa), Ethiopia, Ghana, Liberia and Niger, the six countries composing the OAU consultative committee on Nigeria. Biafra, on the other hand, wanted these observers to be joined by the representatives of those four countries – Gabon, the Ivory Coast, Tanzania and Zambia – which had recognized Biafra. Biafra also wanted the airport at Enugu to be demilitarized, in order that supplies could be air-lifted from there without having to pass through Nigerian terri-tory. The Nigerian Government, which had broken off diplo-matic relations with Gabon, the Ivory Coast, Tanzania and Zambia when they recognized Biafra, refused to consider an observer from any of these countries. Nigeria also rejected any idea of demilitarizing the Enugu airport, and refused any direct relief flights from Libreville (Gabon) and Abidjan (Ivory Coast) to Biafra. As a result, only a partial agreement was reached at Niamey on relief supplies.

Another topic discussed was the proposed peace negotiations at Addis Ababa. Both parties agreed on the procedure and the starting-date of the peace talks.

On 26 July 1968 the following communiqué was issued:

Preliminary peace talks took place in Niamey from July 20th to July 26th 1968, in accordance with the terms of the final communiqué on July 19th 1968 by the OAU Consultative Committee on Nigeria. During the deliberations the two parties have adopted the following agenda for the Addis Ababa peace negotiations under the auspices of the OAU Consultative Committee:

1. Arrangements for a permanent settlement;
2. Terms for the cessation of hostilities;
3. Concrete proposals for the transport of relief supplies in food and medicine to the civilian victims of the war.

The two parties have examined in detail arrangements for the sending of relief supplies to the civilian victims of the war. No agreement has been reached on certain points in this connection. The two parties, however, agreed to hold additional consultations aimed at taking immediate action which would lead to agreement at Addis Ababa on practical steps on the humanitarian issue whose importance and seriousness has been acknowledged by everyone.

The two parties have agreed on the detailed procedure to be followed at the Addis Ababa peace negotiations. It has been unanimously agreed upon that the peace negotiations should begin in Addis Ababa on August 5th, 1968 at the latest.

THE ADDIS ABABA PEACE NEGOTIATIONS

Before we trace the course of the ensuing peace negotiations, it is necessary to examine the stand of both parties at this stage. In view of the first item on the agenda agreed at Niamey,[17] it would appear as if the Biafrans had dropped their condition that a cease-fire should precede any discussion for a settlement. But in fact they had not. Shortly before the Addis Ababa negotiations started, C. C. Mojekwu, the Biafran minister of internal affairs, declared at a Press conference in London that the main Biafran proposals for a settlement were a cease-fire, withdrawal by federal forces to pre-war boundaries, and lifting of the economic blockade. He maintained that Biafra would never give up her sovereignty.[18] Biafra's insistence on the last point was strengthened by what amounted to France's near-recognition of Biafra at that time.[19]

Nigeria, on the other hand, still maintained that a peace settlement could be achieved only if Biafra renounced secession and accepted the new arrangement of twelve states in Nigeria. Thus, prospects for a negotiated settlement at Addis Ababa did not seem very high. Nevertheless, the peace negotiations started, under the chairmanship of Emperor Haile Selassie, on 5 August 1968.

Opening the conference, the emperor appealed to both sides to take 'this last chance' to find a solution to the crisis. 'You cannot afford to fail; you must succeed.' He was followed by Chief Anthony Enahoro, leader of the Nigerian delegation, who opened his speech with the warning that these talks probably represented the last opportunity for a negotiated settlement of the crisis. He declared, however, that he could not conceive of any mutually acceptable settlement which did not envisage the unity and territorial integrity of Nigeria. In conclusion he appealed personally to the members of the Biafran delegation to seize 'this opportunity to bring the sufferings of the Nigerian people to an end'.[20]

268

Colonel Ojukwu's speech, which came after that of Chief Enahoro, lasted for almost two hours. In it he described at length the history of the conflict. He accused General Gowon of 'aspiring to be the Hitler of Africa'. And he concluded by declaring: 'Against all the background of suspicion, hate, conflict and war, our survival cannot be separated from the sovereign independence of our state.'

The federal delegation, outraged by the tone and content of Ojukwu's speech, asked for time to consider what it described as a 'tirade' and 'a gross violation of protocol which was done in bad taste'.[21] When the session had ended, the Nigerian delegation issued a Press release refuting all the allegations and emphasizing their desire to keep polemics out of the talks.

Emperor Haile Selassie closed the first session with an extempore speech which emphasized that neither the OAU nor himself were present as judges; their sole role was to provide a forum in which he hoped a settlement could be achieved.[22]

Colonel Ojukwu, accompanied by Dr Azikiwe and Messrs M. T. Mbu and A. Akpan, left Addis Ababa on the following day. A Biafran delegation, led by professor Eni Njoku, was left behind.

The conference then went into closed session. The first private meeting could not be held on 6 August because the federal delegation refused to take part in any talks with the Biafran delegation, as long as this included two Gabonese – one an official and the other an army officer – whom they regarded as foreigners. When the first private meeting was held, on 7 August, Chief Enahoro outlined the federal proposals for a peace settlement. He started by saying that no solution to the crisis was possible without Biafran renunciation of secession. This, he suggested, should come in the form of a joint statement, the terms of which could be negotiated by both sides, on the basis that all were from the same country. He added that Nigeria should be reunified according to the Nigerian external frontiers established on 1 October 1963. Second: the declaration and cessation of hostilities should be followed by the disarming of rebel troops; military officers would meet to work out detailed procedures for disarmament. Third: the areas still held by the

Biafrans would be policed by units consisting mostly of persons of Ibo origin. The units would, however, form an integral part of the Nigerian police force. Fourth: the federal army, which would not normally be responsible for policing duties, should be placed at strategic points in the East Central State, as a precautionary measure in case of any threat to peace or a break-down of law and order. Fifth: as a further guarantee of the physical security of Ibos, an external international force drawn from sources acceptable to both sides would be formed. While not ruling out alternative sources acceptable to both, he suggested troops from Canada, Ethiopia and India. Sixth: the East Central State, like the other eleven states of the Federation, would be administered by a military governor assisted by an executive council composed mainly of civilians. The military governor and the members of the executive council would be Ibos. The council would be made up of persons loyal to the Federal Military Government, as well as persons who had supported the Biafran cause. Seventh: a general amnesty would be granted in most cases, whilst other claims for similar treatment would be thoroughly examined. Eighth: Ibo civil servants who had left their posts in other parts of the Federation would be re-absorbed into public employment; and the Ibos would be assured of a fair share of employment in the public service, including federal statutory corporations. A rehabilitation commission would be responsible for the resettlement of all displaced persons. Ninth: arrangements for calling a constitutional conference, at which the Ibos from the East Central State would have the same rights of representation as other ethnic groups and states, should be discussed. Tenth: once the major question of secession and reunification had been resolved, and the war ended, relief supplies would reach all areas by land, sea and air. In the meantime, the Federal Government still stood by the previous offers of land corridors.

When the next meeting was held, Dr Eni Njoku put the Biafran proposals forward. These included:

1. acceptance of Biafra's sovereignty;
2. cooperation between Nigeria and Biafra in the fields of economics and common services;

3. negotiations to be conducted at Addis Ababa on matters such as the sharing of assets and liabilities, following the separation of Biafra from the Federation of Nigeria;

4. an immediate cease-fire should be agreed. The economic blockade should also be ended, and the troops withdrawn behind pre-war boundaries to enable refugees to return home;

5. the cease-fire line should be policed by an international force drawn from the countries which constituted the OAU consultative committee on Nigeria – Cameroon, Congo (Kinshasa), Ethiopia, Ghana, Niger and Liberia – and the countries which had recognized Biafra – Gabon, the Ivory Coast, Tanzania and Zambia – until permanent arrangements could be made;

6. a plebiscite should be held in disputed areas inside and outside Biafra to determine the true wishes of the people;

7. an immediate agreement on the transportation of relief supplies by air, sea and land to civilian victims on both sides should be reached.

After the two delegations had outlined their respective proposals, Emperor Haile Selassie began a series of long private talks with each delegation, urging them to come to some terms of agreement. He tried several times to get the Biafrans to yield some ground on the issue of secession, in the hope that such a move might enable the federals to move towards a compromise. But the Biafrans flatly refused.

The leader of the federal delegation, Chief Enahoro, in reply to the proposals put forward by the leader of the Biafran delegation, made it absolutely clear that if the proposals represented Biafra's final position, there was very little scope for negotiation. He pointed out that since 'secession is the basic issue which divides the two sides to the Nigerian conflict', Dr Njoku's position was totally unrealistic. Since the Biafrans agreed in Niamey to talks under the 'auspices of the OAU Consultative Committee on Nigeria, they should treat with less levity the Mandate of the Committee, which enjoins it to assist in the search for a solution which will preserve the unity and territorial integrity of Nigeria'. He pointed out that the mandate precluded the consultative committee from condoning secession. The Niamey resolution of

Progress and Problems

the OAU consultative committee on Nigeria had urged the two parties to resume peace talks with the sole objective of preserving Nigeria's territorial integrity and guaranteeing the security of all its inhabitants. In conclusion Chief Enahoro said that Dr Njoku's only proposal deserving of any consideration was the appeal for immediate agreement to be reached on the transportation of relief supplies to the civilian victims of the war. He suggested that the details of this agreement should be negotiated under item 3 of the agenda agreed upon at the Niamey talks.[23] Haile Selassie then continued with his private talks, and tried to impress upon both delegations the necessity of a workable agreement for relief supplies to the war-ravaged areas. His efforts, however, failed to achieve much. The talks were, therefore, temporarily adjourned on 14 August 1968.

On 15 August the emperor invited the other members of the OAU consultative committee to attend a meeting in Addis Ababa on 19 August. Replying to the invitation, president Tubman of Liberia suggested that the emperor should propose to both Nigeria and Biafra a conditional renunciation of secession as well as a conditional cease-fire, in order to break the deadlock. He stated in his telegram that he had made the suggestion to Dr Nnamdi Azikiwe, the former Nigerian president, and that it seemed to have been favoured by him.

On 22 August 1968, negotiations were resumed at Addis Ababa by the parties to the dispute. It was announced on 24 August that an agreement had been reached 'in principle' on a compromise proposal for air and land mercy corridors to bring relief supplies to the civilian victims of the war. Details of this compromise proposal put forward by Emperor Haile Selassie were not revealed. Earlier, the federal delegation had requested the Biafrans to put one of their strategic airports at the disposal of the Red Cross. In reply, the Biafran delegation suggested the Umuahia airport, which was already under the Red Cross, since it could receive freighter aircraft. After two more meetings, they failed to agree on any details.

While the negotiations were in process, the war continued unabated. General Gowon announced the launching of a 'final offensive' on 25 August. Aba, one of the few remaining towns in

Biafran hands, fell to federal forces on 4 September. On 9 September, the Addis Ababa talks were declared adjourned indefinitely, after nearly five weeks of negotiations.

Shortly before the adjournment, Haile Selassie addressed a joint private session of the Nigerian and the Biafran delegations. He reviewed the trend of the talks and noted that some progress had been made, particularly with regard to relief supplies. Continuing, he told the two delegations that although 'the conflict in Nigeria has not come to an end, yet I don't despair. A peaceful settlement of the problem can be attained if there is good will from all concerned.' After describing the crisis as a passing convulsion in the evolution of a family, the emperor said: 'I don't abandon my conviction that we will, with God's help, find a satisfactory solution.'

THE OAU SUMMIT AT ALGIERS, SEPTEMBER 1968

Shortly before the secretary-general of the OAU, Diallo Telli, left Addis Ababa for Algiers, to prepare for the summit conference there, he confirmed that the Nigerian crisis was on the agenda. He again made it clear that 'the OAU wants to see the unity and territorial integrity of Nigeria preserved, with a general reconciliation under a just and durable peace, so that Nigeria can continue her important role in the OAU, in Nigeria and the world'.[24]

The Council of Ministers, at its preparatory session shortly before the summit conference, dealt with a motion tabled by Tunisia which requested that both Nigeria and Biafra should be invited to the conference; but this was opposed not only by Nigeria, who continued to insist that the civil war was an internal affair,[25] but also by several other African states. The motion was subsequently withdrawn.

The summit conference opened at the Club des Pins in Algiers on 13 September 1968. In his opening address, president Boumédienne not only fiercely denounced 'plots from all sides directed against Nigeria, aiming to disintegrate and shake to its foundations this great African State, of the unity and cohesion of which we were and are proud', but also the 'political and religious organisations' which were making 'such a concert of

273

lamentations, mixed with humanitarian sentiments which they have not, however, shown before other human dramas affecting whole countries over the years'.[26] When the secretary-general of the United Nations, U Thant, spoke at the conference, he too supported the Nigerian stand. He then called upon the Organization of African Unity to bring about a settlement, and reminded the assembled heads of state and government that the Nigerian conflict was already creating 'difficulties in relations between African States'. He then pointed out that its continuance was bound to affect the badly-needed cooperation and unity among African countries. Having expressed his conviction that the 1967 OAU summit resolution pledging faith in the Nigerian Federal Government and recognizing Nigeria's territorial integrity formed the only basis for solving the problem, he concluded: 'I believe that the Organisation of African Unity should be the most appropriate instrument for the promotion of peace in Nigeria.'

When the Nigerian crisis finally came up for discussion only Tunisia and Sierra Leone appeared wary in their attitude towards the federal position, while the four countries which had recognized Biafra came out openly in the latter's support. The following resolution, introduced by the OAU consultative committee on Nigeria, was passed by thirty-three votes to four: after an Ivory Coast amendment, calling more specifically for a cease-fire, had been withdrawn:

The Assembly of Heads of State and Government of the Organisation of African Unity meeting in its Fifth Session in Algiers from the 13th to the 16th September, 1968, RECALLING the Resolution AHG/Res.51(IV) adopted by the Fourth Session of the Assembly of Heads of State and Government in Kinshasa (Congo):
RECALLING the decisions taken by the Consultative Committee on Nigeria in Lagos and Niamey;
DEEPLY concerned with the continuing sufferings of the civilian population in Nigeria;

1. EXPRESSES its gratitude to all Heads of State who are members of the Consultative Committee, and particularly to his Imperial Majesty Emperor HAILE SELASSIE I, for their invaluable efforts to carry out the mandate entrusted to them by virtue of the KINSHASA resolution;

2. NOTES the Consultative Committee's report on NIGERIA;

3. APPEALS to the secessionist leaders to co-operate with the Federal Authorities in order to restore peace and unity in Nigeria;

4. APPEALS for cessation of hostilities;

5. RECOMMENDS that the above being accomplished, the Federal Military Government of Nigeria declares a general amnesty and co-operates with the Organisation of African Unity in ensuring the physical security of all the people of Nigeria alike until mutual confidence is restored;

6. APPEALS further to all concerned to co-operate in the speedy delivery of humanitarian relief supplies to the needy;

7. CALLS UPON all Member States of the United Nations and the OAU to refrain from any action detrimental to the peace, unity and territorial integrity of Nigeria;

8. INVITES the Consultative Committee, in which it reiterates its confidence, to continue its efforts with a view to putting into effect the KINSHASA and ALGIERS resolution.

THE MONROVIA TALKS

The Monrovia Talks constituted the third and last attempt made by the Organization of African Unity to achieve a peaceful settlement of the Nigeria crisis. Beginning on 18 April 1969, at Monrovia in Liberia, they were attended by all six heads of state composing the OAU consultative committee on Nigeria.

In his opening address, President Tubman of Liberia said that all six heads of state were aware of the progress of the Organization of African Unity in trying to bring the conflict to an end. The crisis, he remarked, could not be settled on the battlefield, but only at the conference table. He went on: 'The fate, not only of Nigeria, but of Africa, is in the balance.' Emperor Haile Selassie, the chairman of the committee, said that he was glad to note that correspondence from both sides showed a disposition to cooperate.

Again, both the federal and the Biafran delegations submitted proposals for ending the civil war. The federal delegation, led by Femi Okunnu, said that theirs included equal rights for Ibos and other Nigerians; an Ibo in the federal cabinet; a predominantly Ibo police force in the East Central State; and a promise that the Ibos would not be treated as defeated persons after Biafra had renounced secession. The Biafrans, who had all along insisted on a cease-fire as a pre-condition for further negotiations, now climbed down on this point. Sir Louis Mbanefo, the leader of the delegation, however, accused the OAU of not demanding seriously enough that the Nigerians stop killing fellow Africans.

After hearing both sides, the committee divided for separate discussions with the two sides. Presidents Tubman of Liberia and Hamani Diori of the Niger Republic were mandated to make contact with the Biafrans; whilst Emperor Haile Selassie and president Mobutu of Congo (Kinshasa) were to hold discussions with the federal delegation. After much discussion and persuasion on 18 and 19 April, the delegations met at a final session on 20 April. In a communiqué issued at the end, the committee called on the parties to 'accept in the supreme interest of Africa a united Nigeria which ensures all forms of security, and guarantees equality of rights and privileges to all its citizens'. Within this context, both sides were asked to agree to 'an immediate end to the fighting and the opening without delay of peace negotiations'. The committee offered its good offices for further negotiations, and appealed to Colonel Ojukwu to accept them so that 'reconciliation, peace and unity may be restored in Nigeria'. The communiqué noted with satisfaction that Nigeria had accepted these proposals – and with regret that Biafra had not.[27]

Sir Louis Mbanefo, commenting on the talks, said that Biafra's fears had not been allayed. He complained that the Organization of African Unity and its secretary-general, Diallo Telli, were supporters of a 'One-Nigeria' policy. He, therefore, was of the opinion that the Organization of African Unity had neither the ability nor the genuine desire to bring the civil war to an end. He therefore called for 'others' to take the initiative.[28]

Diallo Telli, the OAU secretary-general, on the other hand, told newsmen after the talks that 'for the first time we can fix the responsibilities where they belong. We regret that Biafra has rejected the proposals.'[29] He said that contacts would still continue individually and collectively until a peaceful settlement was achieved.

When the OAU summit conference was held at Addis Ababa in September 1969, Emperor Haile Selassie, the chairman of the OAU consultative committee on Nigeria, reported to the heads of state and government on the efforts of the committee to reach a peaceful settlement of the Nigerian crisis during the past year. Discussion began afterwards with a condemnation by the outgoing chairman of the Assembly of Heads of State and Government, president Boumédienne of Algeria, of the greedy colonialism and imperialism which had caused the conflict, 'because they desire to weaken Africa's energies'. Emperor Haile Selassie called for a frank exchange of views on the crisis in order that a satisfactory solution might be found. After this, General Gowon, the leader of the Nigerian delegation, addressed the summit. He emphasized that there could be no compromise over Nigeria's territorial integrity; and he warned that if Biafra failed to accept realistic terms, the federal troops would 'carry on military operations to their logical conclusion, no matter how long it takes'. Earlier, the secretary-general of the United Nations, U Thant, had appealed to the assembled heads of state and government to work for resumption of relief supplies to Biafra, and also for the end of the war. He reiterated that only the acceptance of the OAU recommendations could lead to the cessation of hostilities.

In order to get a frank exchange of views on the crisis, the OAU consultative committee on Nigeria held a series of sittings at which it heard several delegations. Those who had recognized Biafra expressed their views first. President Nyerere, who had earlier issued a twelve-page booklet on the Nigerian civil war, was then able to propound his theory. A meeting was also arranged for both President Nyerere and General Gowon. During the discussions between the leaders, President Nyerere pleaded for peace talks to bring the war to an end. General Gowon did not rule out the possibility, 'on condition that the Biafrans were sincere'. He made it clear to Nyerere that it was his desire to end the crisis peacefully, but only so that Nigeria might remain a united country. Impressed by the sincerity of General Gowon, President Nyerere agreed to withdraw his pamphlet on the crisis which had been so severely criticized by the Nigerian delegation.

After a meeting as well between General Gowon and Samuel Kapwepwe, the leader of the Zambian delegation, the summit passed a resolution by thirty-six votes to nil, with five abstentions (Gabon, the Ivory Coast, Tanzania, Zambia and Sierra Leone). In it, the heads of state and government appealed to both parties in the Nigerian civil war to 'preserve in the overriding interest of Africa the unity of Nigeria and to accept immediately a suspension of hostilities and the opening of negotiations, intended to preserve the unity of Nigeria and restore peace that will assure for the people every form of security and every guarantee of equal rights, prerogatives and obligations'. While Nigeria accepted all the terms of the resolution, Biafra announced that it would accept only that part which called for an immediate cease-fire. It described the idea that the cease-fire should be accepted within the context of 'one Nigeria' as unrealistic and unacceptable.[30]

THE CIVIL WAR ENDS

Since both sides failed to change their stand, in spite of all efforts made by the OAU, the conflict was settled on the battlefield on 10 January 1970. Major-General Philip Effiong became the Biafra leader after Ojukwu had fled to the Ivory Coast, upon the collapse of the Biafran forces. He declared that Biafra was prepared to send a delegation to meet representatives of the Nigerian Federal Government anywhere, so as to negotiate a peace settlement 'on the basis of the OAU resolution'.[31]

The relations between Nigeria and the four African states which recognized Biafra – Gabon, the Ivory Coast, Tanzania and Zambia – were normalized at the 1970 summit conference of the OAU.

THE NIGERIAN CRISIS AND THE FUTURE OF
PAN-AFRICANISM

For some it may appear that as long as the unity of Nigeria was maintained the outcome of the crisis (the greatest test since the founding of the OAU) should be regarded as a victory for Pan-

Africanism. That is true. But questions remain. What will be the after-effects in the internal situation of Nigeria, when the politicians are back at their game? Will things continue as they were before the army take-over of January 1966? What role will a new Nigeria play in Pan-Africanism? Will Nigeria be able to prove to the world that every Nigerian, irrespective of religion or ethnic origin, will be entitled to equal facilities, and really taste the honey of social justice? The way Nigeria answers these questions in her internal politics will have far-reaching effects on other African countries, which may face the same secessionist problems. That is why the Nigerian crisis can hardly be classified yet as an unqualified success for Pan-Africanism.

The crisis was, indeed, brought to an end on the battlefield. Yet despite the inability of the OAU to bring peace, Pan-Africanism was the victor for two reasons.

In the first place, it prevented an escalation of the crisis. Had it not been for the existence of the Organization of African Unity, the Nigerian crisis would certainly have been raised at the United Nations as one coming within the context of East–West confrontation. All those countries, such as France and certain other members of the European Economic Community, and even the United States, which either openly supported the break-up of Nigeria or appeared lukewarm to the idea of a united Nigeria, would then have made use of such an opportunity to pursue their objectives in the name of 'humanity'. Pan-Africanism, however, was able to insulate the Nigerian crisis from the more abrasive pressures of world politics, thus saving Nigeria from balkanization.

Secondly, the stand taken by most African countries on the crisis was a vindication of Pan-Africanism. If Nigeria had been broken up, this would have set a bad and dangerous precedent, which might have turned the African continent into chaos within the next decade. Those very forces which had failed in Nigeria would have been emboldened to encourage secessionist movements elsewhere in Africa. They would have got hold of new, gullible, over-ambitious Africans, willing, for personal greed or ambition, to sell their birthright and the second 'scramble for Africa' would have begun. But with its forces triumphant over those of less worthy causes, Pan-Africanism has emerged stronger and more compelling.

This, however, does not mean that the Biafrans had no case at all. No one should deny that many people of Eastern Nigerian origin suffered a great deal in the North, especially during the outbreaks of violence in May and September 1966. As a result of their sufferings, there were those who concluded that secession would be the only solution. But the events of 1966 were not the real cause of the secession. The plan to secede from the rest of Nigeria had been taken in the East even before the coup d'état of January 1966 which brought the First Republic to an end.[32] Those who glibly argued that the war was conducted by Nigeria mainly because of the newly-discovered oil resources in the East had no proper understanding of the issue. The oil played a very significant role in the crisis as a cause of conflict for both parties; but since we are here concerned only with Pan-Africanism and how it was affected by the Nigerian crisis, we shall not explore the oil issue further.[33]

Although it is too early to judge what role Nigeria will play in the future course of Pan-Africanism, especially when the politicians are back in power, it is to be hoped that she will display a profound commitment to the cause of African unity. She might well even take over the role once played by Nkrumah's Ghana: provided, of course, that tribal politics do not emerge to command the future. For it is in this regard particularly that Nigeria's impact on Pan-Africanism would be measured. If Nigeria does not show the light by her example at home, she may set a precedent whereby all other secessionist movements in the continent will be forced to stay within their own countries, whether or not their governments have respect for human dignity and a sense of social justice. That would be disastrous for Pan-Africanism itself.

(b) Other Secessionist Movements

We have already noted how secessionist aspirations led to civil war in both the Congo and Nigeria. Two other OAU member

states, Ethiopia and the Sudan, are also faced with this problem
that puts Pan-Africanism under serious strain, for as long as an
honourable settlement has not been achieved.

I. ETHIOPIA

Secessionist activities in Ethiopia centre on the province of
Eritrea, where the Eritrean Liberation Front is agitating for
complete independence.

Before the Second World War Eritrea was an Italian colony. It
was occupied by the British early in 1941, and subsequently
administered by Britain. On 2 December 1950, the UN General
Assembly adopted a resolution whereby Eritrea was to constitute
an autonomous unit federated with Ethiopia under the sovereignty of the Ethiopian Crown. An Eritrean government was
organized under the supervision of a UN commissioner, and the
British administration ended on 15 September 1952. From then
on Eritrea became an integral part of Ethiopia, administered on a
federal basis. In 1962 the Eritrean Assembly voted for complete
incorporation of the Eritrean province in the Ethiopian empire.
But since then there have been protests against this decision. Led
by the Eritrean Liberation Front, those who protested aimed at
first at mere reversion to federal status. When this failed, the
Front increased its activities and called for complete secession
from Ethiopia.

The Front turned to guerrilla activities. Villages were attacked,
and many lives lost. As a result, Ethiopia increased its military
presence in the area. The Ethiopian army's retaliation to the
attacks resulted in more lives being lost. Thousands of people
have fled to the neighbouring Sudan.

In December 1970 Ethiopia declared a state of emergency in
Eritrea: claiming that certain foreign countries were arming the
members of the Eritrean Liberation Front in an effort 'to undermine Ethiopia's sovereignty and territorial integrity'.

THE PROBLEM AND PAN-AFRICANISM

We have seen that instability in any OAU member state can
have disruptive effects on Pan-Africanism itself. Secessionist

activities open ways for foreign intervention in African affairs. But in the Eritrean issue, much more is involved. Eritrea is predominantly Muslim. The Eritreans have, therefore, set up their headquarters in Arab countries such as Libya, Iraq, Syria, Kuwait and Saudi Arabia. This naturally leads to the accusation by Ethiopia that the Eritrean Liberation Front is financed by certain Arab states.[34] The effect of an Arab–African confrontation could cause untold harm to the cause of African unity.

There are indications that the Eritrean secessionist moves have already affected relations between two OAU member states: Sudan and Ethiopia. In May 1967, after a series of increased ELF guerrilla actions, the Ethiopian Government intensified its campaigns against the secessionists. As a result, some 20,000 Eritreans fled into the Sudan; and for a time there was a build-up of Ethiopian troops along the borders. In July 1967, armed conflict nearly occurred between the countries, when the Sudanese army was reported to be 'face to face with a large Ethiopian force'. In November the Sudanese National Unionist Party – a partner in the Umma Party in the Sudanese coalition government – adopted a resolution at its annual congress giving absolute support to the ELF in the attempt to secede from Ethiopia. This situation has been tactfully played down by both governments; but there is no doubt that as long as the Eritrean problem resists solution, relations between these OAU member states will be affected – which will undoubtedly affect Pan-Africanism in turn.

What then should be done to spare not only damage to Pan-Africanism but also the horrors of another civil war involving the whole continent? Neither the OAU charter nor the OAU decision on boundary issues offers a satisfactory way of settling the problem. The charter regards the problem as an internal affair of an OAU member state; the OAU decision on boundary issues rejects any change of the present national borders. But the Eritrean problem, like any other secessionist problem, is not merely a legalistic but also a human problem. Any attempt to solve it in military terms will only result, as both the Congo and Nigerian cases have shown, in heavy loss of life and untold human misery. The OAU, which advocates the maintenance of present boundaries, cannot just fold its arms and do nothing to bring about an acceptable and honourable settlement. It must, therefore, disregard any attempt to keep the Eritrean problem a purely 'internal concern' of Ethiopia. Nigeria attempted this at the beginning of its own civil crisis but the OAU had to step in at last; and even if it did not succeed as intended, the final settlement of the conflict was 'on the basis of the OAU resolution'.[35] It would be wrong to allow the Eritrean problem to degenerate further, before action is taken. The OAU must set up a special committee to deal with the issue. This could be composed of Nigeria (because of her experience), one country from North Africa, one from the African French Community members, and one from East Africa. The committee should find a peaceful and honourable solution to the problem. There is no doubt that Ethiopia, whose emperor has become one of Africa's troubleshooters since the OAU was founded, would agree to seek a peaceful solution through OAU mediation. Certainly no other course is open to the OAU, if the organization is to live up to its aims and objectives. For real unity cannot be achieved as long as any secessionist problem afflicts a member state.

2. SUDAN

The secessionist problem facing Sudan is much more complicated and deep-rooted than that of Ethiopia. Sudan became a dependent territory, ruled by Britain, as a result of the Anglo-Egyptian Condominium Agreement of 1899. With Islamic Arab-speaking inhabitants in its north and non-Islamic Negroes in its south, Sudan is actually the 'crossroad of Africa'. Difference between the north and the south has played a major role in the secessionist crisis.

When the British administration took over, it vacillated between creating a united Sudan, and separating the southern provinces from the northern part so as to join them with one of the East African colonies. This vacillation was to have disastrous consequences.

In 1902 the British administration decided to treat the southern part of the Sudan, divided into three provinces, as a separate

entity from the north. The south was opened to various foreign
Christian missionaries; and Northern Sudanese were allowed to
trade there only under licence. This policy was intensified in
1930, when artificial barriers were set up between the two sections of the country: all Moslem colonies were removed from the
southern provinces; the licences of Northern traders were not
renewed; Northern Sudanese were forbidden to enter the south;
Southern Sudanese were equally prevented from visiting the
north. And while Arabic was recognized as a medium of expression in the northern provinces, English was encouraged in the
south.

The Christian missionaries, too, played their part in strengthening the barrier. They significantly succeeded in 'christianizing'
the south, and played upon the suspicions and resentments of the
other Southerners with jogs to their memories of the slave trade.
Within one decade, the desired objective of separating the parts
of the country seemed to have been achieved.

Immediately after the Second World War, however, the
British administration had second thoughts. Probably as a result
of the problems posed by the white settlers in the East African
colonies, the British realized that it would not be advisable to
merge the Southern Sudanese provinces with any of these territories. A new 'Southern policy' was devised, which aimed at
joining north and south Sudan into a single political entity.
Frantic efforts were made to achieve this objective; but the
policy of 'separate development' had taken root. Before the new
policy could become effective, the British were already packing
their bags, and Sudan was nearing independence. When the
British finally departed in 1956, they left behind a Sudan in
many ways dangerously divided.

SUDAN AFTER INDEPENDENCE

After its change of policy, the British administration called to a
conference the leaders of the southern provinces at Juba in 1947.
These agreed to join hands with the Northern Sudanese in
building a united country, as long as their interests were also
taken into account. When the Legislative Assembly was established in 1948, the south was represented by thirteen members.

On 12 February 1953 Britain and Egypt agreed to end the 'Condominium' and give the Sudan self-rule as a first step towards complete independence. By then some political parties had emerged: the most significant being the Umma Party, the National Unionist Party (NUP), and a southern party later called the Liberal Party.

After the constitutional change of 1953, general elections were held. The NUP, which won a majority, formed the government; while the Umma Party and a few southern politicians formed the opposition. In August 1954 the opposition leaders tried to capitalize on the north–south differences; toured the southern provinces and addressed a series of meetings. By the end of the tour the Southerners were calling on those of their politicians who had joined the government party, to resign. The government, in retaliation, issued a warning to the effect that as they were 'fully aware of the conspiracies that are being worked in the south', they would not hesitate to 'use an iron fist in dealing with any southerner who dared or attempted to break the national unity'.[36]

The names of the Sudanese civil servants who were to take over from the British in the senior administrative posts were announced in October 1954. To the disappointment of the Southerners, none of them was among the nominees. Some southern members of the NUP resigned and joined the Liberal Party. A meeting of the Liberal Party was immediately convened to discuss the Sudanization issue. It adopted a resolution calling for a federal constitution and an equitable distribution of posts in the Sudanese civil service.

Before the conference of the Liberal Party took place, however, the Southern politicians who were members of the governing party – the NUP – held a meeting on 25 September 1954, to consider the Southern demands. The meeting not only called for an equitable distribution of civil service posts, but presented the cabinet with a list of what they regarded as 'minimum Southern demands' for the civil service. The meeting agreed that there was great trouble in the south, and recommended that the prime minister should, by legislative means, accelerate promotions and appointments to the higher administrative posts. It asserted:

Progress and Problems

'considering the difficulties both you and ourselves are facing at this critical moment, we feel that we have demanded the absolute minimum; and unless these are met with, there can be no other alternative to solve the southern problem except more chaos and more intrigues by the Opposition and Communists'.[37]

Instead of following the advice of his party members from the south to try to find a formula whereby an acceptable solution to the problem could be found, the prime minister, Ismael El Azhari, together with other NUP members, made a tour of the southern provinces. During the tour, the government announced that the salaries of the prison warders, policemen and clerks in the south would be immediately raised. This move was regarded by the Southerners as a form of bribery. When the government did nothing to meet the southern demands, two NUP cabinet ministers from the south resigned from both the government and the NUP to join the Liberal Party. The government inaction led to the army mutiny and disturbances of August 1955 in the south. Thus, when the Sudan became independent on 1 January 1956, the relations between north and south had been badly impaired.

Barely two years after independence the country came under military rule. This ensued from the coup d'état of 17 November 1958, and ushered in an era of repression throughout the country. The period is well described in an article written by Peter Kilner for *Africa South* (Vol. 5, No. 3, April–June 1961):

For two years now, the ordinary basic liberties have been suppressed in the Sudan. That political parties and demonstrations are not allowed under military rule is natural enough. Repression has, however, become all-pervading. The closing down of newspapers, which have avoided anything but the mildest criticism in any case, the careful watch by the police on opinions expressed in public places, the pressures brought on suspected opponents of the regime, the occasional arrests and trials by military courts, the virtual suspension of the rule of law through the operation of a new all-embracing Act which punishes critical words or actions with heavy sentences, the control of the trade unions, and now, the latest move, the end of Khartoum University's former independence from government control – all these limits on liberty have spread a growing dislike and discontent.[38]

This country-wide repression only helped to worsen the already bad north–south relations. The army activities in the south caused many people to flee into neighbouring countries. The Southerners became more embittered. Agitation for complete separation of the three southern provinces from the rest of the Sudan intensified. By the time that the military régime was overthrown in 1964, the conflict had developed into open rebellion. According to the secretary-general of the Sudan African National Union (SANU), Bona Malwal, during an interview early in 1965: 'The conditions which drove the people away have not yet been removed. Up to 1958 people could talk of one country; but since then things have been so bad that enormous efforts will be needed to bring confidence and goodwill if the Sudan is to stay as one.'[39]

ATTEMPTS TO FIND A SOLUTION

Faced with the repressive measures of the army rule under General Abboud, the southern leaders formed the Sudan African National Union in their exile at Kampala. Meanwhile, guerrilla activities conducted by Anya'nya had become a part of the secessionist campaigns.

When the military régime was overthrown, a caretaker government was formed whose first acts were concentrated on easing the tension between north and south. Efforts were made to persuade the leaders of SANU to attend a round-table conference. The new prime minister, El Khatim El Khalifa, renewed the government offer of an amnesty to the refugees and guerrillas. There was no immediate response from the refugees, who in the course of time had become too embittered and suspicious of any Khartoum government. When they finally responded, the leaders of SANU agreed to take part in talks on two conditions: that such talks should be held outside the Sudan, preferably in Uganda; and that a final decision on the country's future should be taken at them. These two conditions were unacceptable to the Khartoum caretaker government, which felt that any such talks should be held within the Sudan; and also that any final discussion on the country's future should be taken by a new parliament, elected after the talks. Stalemate ceased when both sides agreed to hold talks in Khartoum. The result was a twelve-man commission, with six representatives from each side, to draft a new constitution for the country. Elections were held, though they were boycotted by both the People's Democratic Party and the Southern Front.

The work of the twelve-man constitutional commission proceeded at a snail's pace. After two years it still could not produce a satisfactory constitution. For the south wanted some sort of autonomy; and this was opposed by the Northern representatives. As no solution seemed to be forthcoming, the guerrillas intensified their activities. These were met by army reprisals. It was a vicious circle. Then, on 25 May 1969, the army again took over the government.

Up till now most Sudanese governments seemed to have fallen as a result of their inability to solve the southern problem. Probably with this in mind, the new military ruler, Major-General Jaafer El-Nimeiry, proclaimed immediately after the coup of 25 May the Revolutionary Council's intention to grant local autonomy to the south, in an effort to solve the problem. He also set out the following four-point programme:

(1) continuation of the amnesty for refugees and guerrillas already announced by the previous régimes;
(2) an intensive social, cultural and economic development programme for the southern provinces;
(3) appointment of a minister for southern affairs;
(4) the training of southerners for higher posts in the civil service.

A minister for southern affairs was promptly appointed, and a three-man delegation led by the minister of agriculture, Dr Mohammed Nur, paid a goodwill visit in June 1969 to Tanzania, Kenya and Uganda, in an effort to explain the new policy to the Sudanese refugees there. Many refugees then agreed to go back to the Sudan. Major-General El-Nimeiry himself made an extensive tour of the southern provinces to explain the new government's policy.

But shortly before the military takeover in Khartoum, the

288

exiles had announced, in March 1969, the setting-up of a provisional government of a 'Nile Republic', headed by Gordon M. Mayen, formerly a police officer and minister of works in the caretaker government which replaced the Abboud régime. The decision to proclaim the 'Nile Republic' had been reached in December 1968, at a meeting of the leading exiles; and seems to have arisen out of the deadlock in the constitutional commission's work.

This development affected the efforts of the new Khartoum military government to grapple with the southern problem. Its appeal met with no immediate response from the provisional government-in-exile, now led by Ateny Pajokdit. When the response did come, it contained conditions under which talks for granting autonomy to the southern provinces within a united Sudan could be held, including a round-table conference between the Khartoum Government and the Southern leaders in exile. The conference was to be held in a neutral country under a neutral chairman with observers from the Sudanese neighbouring states, certain unnamed charitable organizations, and the OAU and the UN. A cease-fire was also to come into operation before the conference would take place. No response came from the Khartoum government. By October 1970 the Army started stepping up its operations in the south.

THE OAU AND THE SOUTH SUDAN PROBLEM

The Khartoum Government has maintained all along that it regards the southern problem as an internal affair, which, according to the OAU charter, the organization cannot attempt to solve. One wonders why the African leaders cannot learn from the experiences of the Congo and Nigeria.

There is no doubt that many lives have already been lost. And apart from this, the problem has been responsible for friction between the Sudan and Uganda. The borders between the countries were closed in May 1969: because of constant raids into Uganda by Sudanese troops in their attempt to capture the Anya'nyas, or guerrillas, who after their operations in the Sudan retreat into Ugandan territory for refuge. On 24 May three Ugandans were killed in East Acholi, and Sudanese troops fired on Ugandan soldiers at Unyama. Shortly before, Sudanese troops had conducted a raid into the Kideop National Park.[40]

As the trial of Rolf Steiner, the West German mercenary, has shown, agents of international misunderstanding and enemies of African unity will always try to exploit the situation. They will seize upon the gullibility of Africans only interested in their own personal ambitions. They will play off one section against another, because they are more interested in what divides than in what unites Africans. When they speak with the Arabs of the Sudan, they will remind them of 'the glorious past of the Arabs', as compared with 'the heathens of the south'. When they speak to people from the southern part of the Sudan, they will praise them for their 'valour, their belief in Christianity and their determination to fight oppression'. They have only one objective, and that is to divide and rule. Once any country is beset with civil war, they will arm one side against the other. They will go further: will find allies among the African states and thus cause divisions within the Pan-African movement.

There is one major factor which needs every encouragement. As the *East African Standard* of 4 July 1970 reported:

... even among refugee students at Makerere College, in Kampala, one can now find signs of reconciliation towards the Khartoum Government. The students still consider themselves Sudanese instead of citizens of that Anya'nya demand, 'The Nile Republic'.

The same newspaper had, at the beginning of the same year, cited another such encouraging piece of news. In its edition of 6 January 1970 it reported how the leader of the provisional government-in-exile, Ateny Pajokdit, had thanked 'the southern Sudanese students for their relentless efforts in trying to reconcile the politicians and above all, for their impartiality'. He went on to 'congratulate them for their victory over the forces of tribal, fractional and reactionary interests among our politicians'.

Will the OAU and the Sudanese Government let these youths down? If they do, posterity will never forgive them. These young, determined Pan-Africanists need every encouragement from both the OAU and Khartoum. As Dr Mohammed Nur, the minister of agriculture in the government led by Major-

General El-Nimeiry, explained during a Press conference at Nairobi Airport in June 1969, the southern Sudanese problem is a political one, which can only be settled by political means.[41] No amount of military force can settle it, as has been demonstrated for over a decade now.

What can the OAU do to bring about a peaceful and honourable settlement? The organization should set up a special committee, on which both Libya and the United Arab Republic should be asked to serve: while Nigeria and Congo (Kinshasa), along with all East African countries, should be ready to assist as well.

(c) Regional Economic Groupings

The regional economic groupings considered here – OERS, UDEAC, UEAC and the East African Economic Community – are either for some reason not working in perfect harmony; or, as in the case of both the UDEAC and UEAC, could better advance the cause of Pan-Africanism, if they merged to form a strong and efficient regional economic community, in the interest of the Central African people as distinct from certain non-African vested interests. As long as the causes of disharmony are not removed, and as long as a union of UDEAC and UEAC has not been brought about in Central Africa, there will be only a dissipation or duplication of energy, and Pan-Africanism will continue to be the worse for it.

I. L'ORGANISATION DES ÉTATS RIVERAINS DU SÉNÉGAL (OERS)

The Senegal River Committee, composed of representatives from Guinea, Mali, Mauritania and Senegal, was inaugurated in March 1964. It was entrusted with the responsibility of working out plans for the improvement of the Senegal River both as a waterway and as a source of energy and irrigation. After a series of meetings held at ministerial level, a conference of the heads of the four states was convened at Nouakchott in November 1965. The project was endorsed there, but had then to be temporarily shelved because of a plot to overthrow President Sékou Touré's Government in Guinea discovered that very month. The discovery led to an estrangement in the relations between Guinea and Senegal. By 1967, however, relations had again sufficiently improved for the revival of the project. Another summit conference of the states was therefore held at Bamako in November 1967. This paved the way for the inauguration of the Organisation des États Riverains du Sénégal (OERS) – Organization of Senegal River States – during the next summit conference, which took place at Labe, Guinea, in March 1968.

The Labe summit conference was significant in many ways. The OERS was launched amidst 'a euphoria of a kind not seen since the first days of independence', and seemed to herald a new era of understanding among the four states whose relations had previously been strained following Guinea's vote for independence in September 1958 and the break-up of the Mali Federation in 1960. Before the actual conference, the four presidents – Sékou Touré of Guinea, Modibo Keita of Mali, Moktar Ould Daddah of Mauritania and Léopold Sédar Senghor of Senegal – had made an extensive tour of Guinea together, receiving a rapturous welcome everywhere they went, and all speaking of their desire for unity. The significance of the summit itself was expressed by Senghor, on his departure for Dakar. 'This conference will stand out in the history of Africa, for it is the first time that states are creating a confederation.' He claimed that 'we have all the assets for success.'[42]

The Organization of Senegal River States has the following four principal organs: a conference of heads of state; a council of ministers; an interparliamentary commission; and an executive secretariat. The heads of state conference is convened once a year, and is the supreme organ of the organization. Its decisions have to be unanimous, and each member state is bound by them. The president of the conference is elected for a year, and can always summon an emergency summit. The council of ministers, consisting of the foreign ministers of member states, is the 'organ of conception, execution and control'. It is responsible to the heads of states conference, and meets twice a year. The inter-parliamentary commission, composed of twenty members – five from each member state – also meets twice a year. The secretariat of the OERS, situated in Dakar, is subdivided into three departments: one for the development of the Senegal River; one for planning and development; and the third for education, cultural and social affairs. It is headed by a secretary-general, who is appointed by the heads of state for a three-year term.

Shortly after the inaugural meeting, which also elected the Guinean president, Sékou Touré, as the organization's chairman during the first year of its existence, the secretariat was set up in Dakar. Ahmed Ould Daddah of Mauritania was elected secretary-general: with Oumar Balde of Guinea in charge of planning, and Robert Ndau of Mali in charge of administration, as deputy secretaries-general.

Soon afterwards the trade ministers of the four states met and drew up a draft multilateral trade agreement. They also decided that there would be a settlement of financial balances between their countries before the new trade agreement would become operative. A clearing-house, envisaged as developing into a settlement bank, would also be set up. It was hoped that the agreement would help to remove trade difficulties between the states.

The trade ministers' conference was followed by a health ministers' meeting and a meeting of experts in other fields. While the health ministers agreed to set up an OERS health council, to bring about cooperation in health matters, the experts of member states responsible for planning, industry, mining, geology and energy agreed in October 1968 that a meeting of OERS ministers of planning should be held at Conakry on 21 November. In a communiqué issued after their meeting, the experts said that they had worked out 'a minimum programme of industrial rationalisation and harmonisation in the way of co-operation and integration'.

But before all the above-mentioned projects could come into effect, the OERS had been ground to a halt, mainly because of

293

the overthrow of President Modibo Keita of Mali by the armed forces. Guinea refused to work with the new men in Bamako for two reasons: the removal of Modibo Keita badly upset the political balance within the OERS; and Guinea has always strongly opposed military coups. The new men in Mali, too, were reluctant to go to Guinea.

As time went on, however, Guinea's concern for the success of the organization outweighed all other considerations: while the military régime in Mali was also worried by the impasse. Anxiety on both sides led to a series of diplomatic moves. The Mali head of state, Lt Moussa Traore, visited Dakar and Nouakchott, where he received active support from president Moktar Ould Daddah and the Mauritanian ambassador in Dakar. By July 1969, Lt Traore had agreed to go to Conakry; and in September a Guinean mission went to Bamako. As a result of the thaw in relations between the countries, the way was open for further OERS activities.

The first meeting of the organization after the Guinea–Mali rapprochement took place at Nouakchott towards the end of October. Technical experts from member states considered cattle problems. Then, at long last, an actual summit meeting materialized towards the end of January 1970, preceded by a meeting of the OERS council of ministers. The council meeting took many far-reaching decisions, which would help to coordinate the economic plans of the member states. It agreed to abandon the formerly proposed 300 MW Gouina dam project in Mali, for a smaller one at Manantali, which would still meet the energy, navigation and irrigation needs of members. The ministers also discussed other projects, such as the building of another dam nearer the mouth of River Senegal, for irrigation purposes; the construction of a new port at St Louis; and the improvement of port facilities at river towns such as Rosso, Dagani, Podor, Kaedi and Matam, for which studies were expected to be completed within six months. They also endorsed study plans, concentrated on the upper reaches of the river in both Mali and Guinea, for a system of flood alert, and for research on agronomics and other subjects.

In an effort to elevate the OERS into something much more

comprehensive than an organization meant for river development only, many measures were adopted. The OERS ministers of industry were to meet in June 1970, in order to approve the creation of four industrial projects, one in each country, to be jointly operated. They agreed to produce an OERS development plan with effect from 1975, and to create a council of higher education coordinating scientific research and cooperating educationally in many fields, such as the admission of students to the institutions of member states. A cultural commission was also to be established; while the inter-parliamentary group would be transformed into a consultative commission in which parliamentarians, unionists and other groups would be represented.

All these proposals were endorsed by the four heads of state at their summit; and most of the proposed meetings took place before the end of the year. The first meeting of the newly-formed OERS council for education, training and research was convened in Dakar. At a meeting of the OERS finance ministers, Guinea's representative, Ismael Touré, called on member states to find ways of integrating their economies and setting up a common currency. As a direct result of the meeting, a trade agreement was signed between Mali and Guinea whereby duties on certain goods would be abolished. The four OERS ambassadors in both Washington and Brussels submitted joint requests to the US Government and the EEC for aid in the organization's campaign against pleuro-pneumonia. In June 1970 the ministers of transport adopted a three-stage programme to open up the Senegal River as a navigable waterway. They decided to create an international service for placing navigation buoys in the river and for the warning of floodwaters. They also agreed in principle to set up a transport company, to operate on the river.

The OERS was once again in productive movement. But then, in November 1970, the Portuguese, assisted by certain Guinean mercenaries, made an abortive attempt to overthrow the government of President Sékou Touré. The OAU decided that all Africans who had taken part in this act of aggression, and who had subsequently sought refuge in neighbouring states, should be handed over to the Guinea Government to stand trial. The Gambia and Sierra Leone complied with this request but

Senegal, though an OERS member, refused. And this led to a serious deterioration in the relations between Guinea and Senegal. Guinea (conscious of the need for African unity, and realizing also that, as President Sékou Touré had put it during the 1970 summit conference, 'what unites us is more important and more powerful than that which divides us')[43] took the matter to the OAU summit conference of June 1971 at Addis Ababa. It is hoped that the OAU mediation will prove of assistance and prevent any break-up in the efforts of the OERS to create, as president Senghor himself put it in 1968, 'a model organization' which has 'all the assets for success'.

What the OERS badly needs, and only the four heads of member states can and must provide, is political cooperation at the top. There should be no doubt whatsoever that president Senghor, the advocate and torchbearer of *négritude*, can cooperate with the dedicated Pan-Africanist, Sékou Touré, to achieve this objective. It is only thus that the OERS can achieve the noble aims which the four leaders advocated during their extensive tour of Guinea in 1968, and which led to the enthusiasm for the OERS in the four member states 'because it holds out a hope for better things, and caters for the sentimental desire for African unity'.[44]

2. UDEAC AND UEAC

The ECA, as far back as 1965, had recommended that a regional economic grouping should be established in Central Africa,[45] comprising Cameroon, the Central African Republic, Chad, the Republic of the Congo – now known as The People's Republic of the Congo, or Congo (Brazzaville) – the Democratic Republic of the Congo or Congo (Kinshasa) – now known as Zaire – and Gabon. This recommendation was made on the basis that such a grouping would facilitate economic cooperation and industrial planning on an integrated basis. In spite of this recommendation, made on sound economic reasoning, *two* economic groupings – UDEAC and UEAC – have been established in the area.

L'Union Douanière et Économique de l'Afrique Centrale

(UDEAC). Before independence, French Equatorial Africa was economically united in the Union Douanière Équatoriale (UDE). Then, in 1961, the UDE – Equatorial Customs Union – whose members were the Central African Republic, Chad, Congo (Brazzaville) and Gabon, was expanded to include the Cameroon. In 1963 these countries decided to set up an oil refinery to serve the area; and the problem arose of where such a gigantic investment project should be located. In May 1963 the matter was referred to the UDE mixed commission.[46] Attempts to solve this problem in particular, and the coordination of industry in general, 'sparked off the series of meetings and commissions which finally led to the signing of the UDEAC Treaty'[47] in December 1964.

UDEAC, which came into existence on 1 January 1966, aims at the establishment of a common market, to harmonize the production and planning of the member states in order to promote mutual economic growth. It is envisaged that policies for taxes and investment promotion should be coordinated: as would monetary and fiscal policies, through the existing joint central bank – BCEAEC.

UDEAC has four principal organs: the conference of heads of state; the council of ministers; the committee of direction; and a general secretariat. The conference of heads of state, the supreme policy-making organ of the organization, is convened once every year. Its decisions are taken unanimously and are legally binding on member states. The council of ministers, consisting of the foreign ministers, is responsible to the heads of state. It approves plans for industrialization, which are always prepared by the secretary-general, after consultation with the ministers of member states responsible for economic planning. The secretariat at Bangui, headed by a secretary-general, provides the administrative machinery through which economic cooperation is effected. It includes an economic and financial office and provides statistical services. The committee of direction, with two representatives from each member state, is the principal common-market instrument. Although subordinate to the council of ministers, it is nevertheless responsible for the harmonization of industrial projects, development plans and transport policy. It also has certain consultative functions in matters such as wages and social policy which affect the operation of the common market.

By the end of 1967, UDEAC had effectively developed a common monetary system and a collaborative transport organization – the Transequatorial Communications Agency. There was complete freedom of movement for goods, capital and persons, while a common external tariff had been instituted. A special system for distributing revenues from a production tax (*taxe unique*), between the producing country and the consuming countries, had also come into effect. In order to avoid defining policies for the allocation of industry, as well as to provide the landlocked member states with a net gain from the union, a solidarity fund was paid to both Chad and the Central African Republic (see Table 5).

In spite of the benefits which apparently accrued to both Chad and the Central African Republic from the solidarity fund (as shown in Table 5), neither country was entirely satisfied with UDEAC. UDEAC agreements on industrial allocations only partially met their doubts over the effects of the union on their industrial development. Their dissatisfaction led to a crisis in February 1968, when they decided to leave UDEAC and join hands with Congo (Kinshasa) in establishing the UEAC.

L'Union des États d'Afrique Centrale (UEAC). In February 1968 President Mobutu of Congo (Kinshasa) announced the formation of the *Union des États d'Afrique Centrale* (UEAC) on his return from the Central African Republic, where he had met both president Bokassa of the Republic and President Tombalbaye of Chad. The Central African Republic, Chad and Congo (Kinshasa) were reported to have signed an agreement to this effect. In announcing the birth of UEAC, President Mobutu said that Burundi, Rwanda, and Congo (Brazzaville) would be invited to join the new grouping.

The charter of UEAC was signed at Fort Lamy on 2 April 1968. It envisaged a common customs and tax tariff, as well as the free circulation of people, services and capital, and provided for three organs: a heads-of-state conference to meet at least once a year; a council of ministers; and a secretariat, headed by a secretary-general appointed for a three-year term. Decisions by

298

Table 5. Amount of Solidarity Fund between 1960 and 1968 (to the nearest million CFA francs)

Country	1960	1961	1962	1963	1964	1965	1966	1967	1968
Cameroon									
Paid							300	500	500
Received							—	—	—
Difference							−300	−500	−500
Chad									
Paid	188	207	233	267	316	303	300	300	300
Received	548	651	699	749	805	820	1,175	1,170	1,200
Difference	360	444	466	482	489	517	875	870	900
Gabon									
Paid	15	27	21	43	40	53	500	200	250
Received	1	2	2	2	2	2	3	—	—
Difference	−14	−25	−19	−41	−38	−51	−497	−200	−250
Congo (Brazzaville)									
Paid	510	609	613	608	624	672	500	500	500
Received	26	32	34	36	39	40	57	—	—
Difference	−484	−577	−579	−572	−585	−632	−443	−500	−500
Central African Republic									
Paid	174	211	264	293	321	298	300	300	300
Received	310	369	396	424	455	464	665	630	650
Difference	136	158	132	131	134	166	365	330	350
Fund Total	886	1,053	1,130	1,211	1,301	1,325	1,900	1,800	1,850

Source: *Economic Co-operation and Integration in Africa: Three Case Studies*

both the heads of state and the council of ministers are reached unanimously.

RELATIONS BETWEEN UDEAC AND UEAC

With the inauguration of UEAC, two rival economic groupings existed in Central Africa. When the leaders of the three remaining UDEAC member states – Presidents Ahidjo of the Cameroons, Massemba-Debat of Congo (Brazzaville), and Bongo of Gabon – met at Port Gentil in May 1968, they agreed that UDEAC should continue, despite the defections of the other two foundation members. It was agreed that their headquarters should be transferred from Bangui, capital of the Central African Republic, to Brazzaville.

Before the end of the year, however, a new situation had arisen in Central Africa. President Bokassa of the Central African Republic had decided to withdraw from the UEAC and go back to UDEAC. There is no doubt whatsoever that France, which regarded the establishment of UEAC as an American brainchild and had even sent Jacques Foccart, secretary for African affairs, to persuade Bokassa against joining UEAC, had a hand in the new development. Ever since Foccart's mission to Bangui, the CAR leader had shown signs of indecision. At a meeting of the Cameroon–CAR mixed committee for railway studies held in May 1968, the CAR Government expressed its total unity of viewpoint with the government of Cameroon, and the great interest that it had in the construction of a rail link between Bangui and the Transcam railway. The president, unlike President Tombalbaye of Chad, did not attend the coup anniversary celebrations in Kinshasa on 24 November 1968.

President Bokassa's decision to return to UDEAC, which was announced at the UDEAC summit held in December 1968, led to a deterioration in relations between the CAR and the two remaining UEAC states – Chad and Congo (Kinshasa).[48] At the same time the relations between the two Congos (in UDEAC and UEAC respectively) were at a low ebb as a result of the Mulele affair (see Chapter 4 above). A rapprochement between the economic groupings, therefore, appeared unlikely for some time to come. By June 1970, however, the UDEAC member

Table 6. Main economic indicators(a) in Central Africa

	1	2	3	4	5	6
		Gross domestic product			Share of subsistence sector in GDP percentage	
Country	Population (thousands)	(thousands of millions of CFA francs)	per capita (thousands of CFA francs)	Export as a percentage of imports	1963 (actual)	1970 (planned)
Cameroon	5,060 (1963)	560 (1963–4)	110	110	26	20
Central African Republic	1,430 (1966)	132 (1965)	92	75	33	25
Congo (Brazzaville)	800 (1963)	102 (1963)	127	—	20	13
Gabon	460 (1965)	170 (1963)	360	125	—	—
Chad	3,310 (1965)	214 (1965)	65	67	53	50
Congo (Kinshasa)	15,258 (1965)	1,300 (1959)	90	140	—	—

Source: *Economic Co-operation and Integration in Africa: Three Case Studies*
(a) data in columns 1 to 4 refer to the latest year for which information is available.

states had helped to resolve differences between the Congos, while CAR and Congo (Kinshasa) had improved their relations. Nevertheless, these two separate economic groupings are still operating in Central Africa.

A CASE FOR A MERGER

Table 7 clearly shows that UDEAC (including Chad) provided a market of just a little over eleven million people in 1966. This market was considerably reduced in 1968, with Chad still in the UEAC, which itself, as Table 6 shows, had a market of some

Table 7. The submarkets of UDEAC, 1965–6

Country or area	Total population (thousands)	Urban population (percentage)	Total monetary income (thousands of millions of CFA francs)	Per capita monetary income (CFA francs)
Cameroons:				
Centre–South–East	2,550	23	100	39,000
West	1,100	13	16·5	15,000
North	1,500	7	12·0	8,000
Congo (Brazzaville)	900	28	34·3	38,000
Gabon	470	22	50·5 (a)	107,000 (a)
Central African Republic	1,400	25	28·8	21,000
Chad	3,300	8	32·5	10,000
Total	11,220	16	274·6	24,000

Source: *Economic Co-operation and Integration in Africa: Three Case Studies*
(a) this figure is distorted, since a large part of the income is expatriated.

twenty million people in 1968. Hence UDEAC and UEAC combined would have a market of about thirty million, or sufficient for the development of heavy industries. As it is, the UDEAC area's total gross domestic product by 1965 was less than Congo (Kinshasa)'s in 1959! (1,178 thousand million CFA francs, to 1,300 thousand millions [Table 6]).

Apart from the size of the market in a combined UDEAC–UEAC economic grouping, there are many other advantages.

By 1963, the value added by industry in Congo (Kinshasa) was double that achieved in the UDEAC area: industry met home demand to the extent of 48 per cent, as against 36 per cent in the UDEAC area. The country already had basic and intermediate industries not represented in the UDEAC area at all, such as sulphuric acid, smelting, and general mechanical engineering. In addition, the country was producing large quantities of bicycles, refrigerators, and enamelled articles, among others. UDEAC, on the other hand, had made headway in establishing the first petroleum refinery in Central Africa, and would soon be self-sufficient for cement. The manufacturing and mining activities of Congo (Kinshasa) would be of tremendous benefit to all the UDEAC–UEAC states, if they joined forces to establish a single economic grouping.

What is needed is the right political will among the heads of the six Central African states, who significantly are all associate members of the EEC, to pool their resources and so raise the living standards of their nationals. The fact that there are two different monetary systems is not a hindrance to the achievement of economic unity in Central Africa. (The EEC, whose associate members they all are, does not yet have a unified monetary system.) Once the political determination was there, all other things would follow. A supra-national industrial commission, with powers and staff to work out regionally-orientated proposals, could be established. An industrial complex could be jointly developed around the Inga Dam project. Central Africa, comprising all the UDEAC–UEAC member states, is blessed with 'the co-existence of high-quality metallic ores, such as iron, copper and manganese, with a considerable hydro-electric potential'.[49] The hydro-electric potential of the area has been estimated as follows:

Country	Megawatts
Central African Republic	3,500
Chad	1,600
Gabon	6,000
Cameroon	4,800
Congo (Brazzaville)	3,000
Congo (Kinshasa)	100,000[50]

This augurs well for the building of an industrially strong and economically sound Central Africa, with general living-standards rapidly and significantly raised; but only if micro-nationalism, petty jealousies, and the disruptive favouritism shown to foreign powers at the expense of African Unity are abandoned. Otherwise, it is clear that the Central African states have not learnt from 'the lessons of the last ten years of development', which the UDEAC member states claim have led them 'to take a somewhat pessimistic view of our chances for economic growth'.[51]

As the UDEAC states admitted during the OAU conference of ministers of industry, organized by the ECA in May 1971, 'there is a very wide gap separating us from the affluent countries in the different sectors which constitute the points of comparison between those countries and our own'. They also noted that 'since 1960, not only have our gross national product (GNP), our per capita income, our savings and the consequent accumulation of capital been the lowest of all developing countries, but as yet no means or stimulus has been found to enable us to make up the leeway which has accumulated over the past ten years'.[52] They went on to admit that, 'after independence, each of our countries believed it possible to develop through national self-sufficiency, by banking on its own natural resources and its bilateral alliances with the affluent countries'. But unfortunately experience had turned out differently. They have, accordingly, come to the conclusion that 'the only hope for the harmonized and continuing industrial development of Africa lies in regional development, which, step by step, will bring about the integration of all domestic industries, guarantee the expansion of our markets and of our production factors and consequently ensure a viable economic approach to each of our undertakings'. As they themselves admitted, 'it is through regional development' (much more easily to be facilitated by joint UDEAC–UEAC efforts) that Central Africa 'can achieve the regional and international co-operation which will be beneficial to all our countries'.[53]

What remains lacking is the political will to translate the new-found ideal into reality.

3. THE EAST AFRICAN ECONOMIC COMMUNITY

On 6 June 1967, the East African Co-operation Treaty, which came into effect on 1 December 1967, was signed in Kampala by presidents Jomo Kenyatta of Kenya, Julius Nyerere of Tanzania and Milton Obote of Uganda. It established the East African Economic Community as a successor to the former East African Common Services Organization.

The community, carrying on most of the services of EACSO, has its headquarters at Arusha in Tanzania. The Treaty envisages a split of the East African railways and harbours administration, with the railways headquarters remaining in Nairobi, and the harbours administration moving to Dar es Salaam. Kampala becomes the new headquarters of East African posts and telegraphs, while Nairobi remains the headquarters of East African airways.

The new community has the following institutions: an East African Authority; East African ministers; an East African legislative assembly; a central secretariat; a service commission; and five councils (finance, common market, economic consultative and planning, communications, research and social).

The East African Authority, composed of the heads of the partner states, is responsible for controlling the executive functions of the community. It meets at least three times a year, with chairmanship by rotation.

The East African ministers, made up of the three ministers in the community's central secretariat, assist in executive functions to the extent required by and subject to the control of the authority. They advise the authority generally in respect of the Community's affairs. The ministers, one from each partner state, are appointed by the authority, and are helped by three deputy ministers appointed in the same manner.

The central secretariat, located at Arusha in Tanzania, is composed of three secretariats: finance and administration; common market and economic affairs; and communications, research and social services. Each secretariat is headed by a minister at political level, and a secretary at civil-service level. The secretary-general, appointed by the authority, heads the civil service of the community. He is the secretary to the authority, committee of ministers and all the councils of the community.

The East African legislative assembly which legislates on all matters of the community has a membership of thirty-six, including a chairman, the three East African ministers and their deputies, the secretary-general and the counsel of the community. The other members are appointed nine each from the three partner states. A community service commission, composed of a chairman, two deputy chairmen and three non-resident members, is responsible for employment, including promotion and related duties in the community.

Membership of the five councils is at ministerial level. The three East African ministers are members, and each is chairman of one or other of the councils. National ministers are members of the councils dealing with matters that come under their respective national portfolios. The common market council supervises the functioning and development of the common market. A common market tribunal, with a judicial chairman from outside, and with members from East Africa, has been set up to ensure observance of the law and the terms of the common market treaty. The chairman is appointed by the authority. Each partner state nominates one member for appointment by the authority; and the fourth member is nominated by the chairman and the other three, also for appointment by the authority.

The East African Co-operation Treaty is chiefly concerned with the setting-up of an East African common market. The member states are pledged to maintain a common customs tariff, and to reject any tariff concession agreements with a foreign country unless these concessions are available to all three members. With the exception of a transfer tax system, internal tariffs are to be abolished. The transfer tax system, devised in an effort to correct the inherited serious economic imbalances, especially in the industrial sector, among member states, allows any member which has a deficit in its total trade in manufactured goods with the other two members, to impose transfer taxes on such goods as originate in the partner states. Such tax may only be imposed if the tax-imposing country manufactures similar goods or can reasonably expect to manufacture them within three months; and the tax-protected industry must have a productive capacity equivalent to at least 15 per cent of total domestic consumption of relevant products in the tax-imposing country, or be worth £100,000. The transfer tax cannot be imposed for more than eight years; and the provision for such taxes is to be revoked altogether after fifteen years of the community's existence.

Table 8. The value of inter-state transfers in £1,000 (1966–8)

Year	Kenya		Tanzania		Uganda	
	To Tanzania	To Uganda	To Kenya	To Uganda	To Kenya	To Tanzania
1966	13,282	15,619	3,806	842	7,317	3,120
1967	11,382	14,796	3,288	750	10,165	2,432
1968	13,069	13,265	3,692	855	8,650	2,029

Source: *Fifty Facts about the East African Community* (Information of the EAC)

Other measures agreed upon, in order to counter the existing industrial imbalance among member states, include the establishment of an East African development bank, and a joint initiative to harmonize fiscal incentives offered to industry in each of the partner states. The bank, with an authorized initial capital of £10 million, is to give priority to development in Tanzania and Uganda, as well as to projects designed to make the economies of the member states more complementary in the industrial sector.

THE COMMUNITY 1967–70

Immediately the East African Co-operation Treaty came into force on 1 December 1967, all relevant organs were established.

Nor have the three member states failed to take appropriate joint action whenever experience dictated such action for the maintainance of the common market arrangements: for instance there was an agreement to amend the treaty so that, where goods manufactured in East Africa were subject to excise duty, the total of transfer tax and excise duty would not exceed the external tariff.

The East African committee of planners has split into working

groups to deal with development in the principal economic
sectors: agriculture, commerce, industry and tourism, so as to
achieve greater economic integration. Plans for tourism are now
coordinated on a regional basis, to make maximum use of available resources. The central secretariat of the community has been
asked to prepare comprehensive reports on planned tourist
development, with emphasis on possible areas of cooperation
such as the joint development of adjoining areas and training
facilities.

In transport and communications, studies are conducted to
review and prepare a long-term approach to development. These
also cover the general coordination of policies: enabling member
states to consult on such subjects as dual registration of vehicles
and licensing of road transporters.

The economic consultative and planning council, with the
assistance of the committee of planners, examines the possibility
of establishing large capital-intensive industries requiring the
entire East African market for viability. Such multi-national
industries would speed up the industrialization of East Africa.

The EAC has successfully concluded an agreement to expand
sales of agricultural exports at improved prices in the EEC.

Apart from efforts to preserve and improve the common
market, attention has been directed to the improvement of the
common services, always a symbol of cooperation in East Africa.
The four corporations – railways, airways, post and telecommunications, and harbours – have improved and modernized
their services. Each has had a development plan under which
several important projects are either completed or nearing
completion.

The community runs twelve research stations: five are located
in Kenya, three in Uganda, and four in Tanzania; and to
coordinate research in medicine and natural resources, two
councils have been set up. The research stations include:

The Marine Fisheries Research Organization, in Zanzibar, which
carries out research into all aspects of sea-water fishing, with
particular emphasis on long-lining, to determine the fish potential of East Africa's coast;

The Freshwater Fisheries Research Organization, for research work into freshwater fish in East Africa, with a view to determining population and abundance, so as to assist potential fish-canning industries in EAC member states;

The Institute of Malaria and Vector-Borne Diseases, charged with developing ways of controlling malaria and of insect carriers of the disease:

The Institute of Medical Research, involved in a bilharzia eradication campaign in the Lake Victoria town of Mwanza and surrounding areas:

The Tropical Pesticides Research Institute, engaged in research work on such diseases as coffee berry disease and on pests such as stalk borers and fungus; for human pests it deals with snail vectors of bilharzia, tsetse and mosquitoes, and tests insecticides;

The Industrial Research Organization, carrying out research into the industrial potential of certain East African raw materials, to determine if viable industries based on them can be established, and advising industrialists already in the market or those who intend investing in East Africa;

The Tuberculosis Research Centre;

The Agriculture and Forestry Research Organization, which deals with research into the possibilities of improving production of East Africa's cash and food crops;

The Veterinary Research Organization;

The Leprosy Research Centre;

The Trypanosomiasis Research Organization, which evolves ways of controlling sleeping sickness in man, and nagana in cattle (both caused by the tsetse fly);

The Virus Research Institute, which carries out research on the causes of such widespread diseases as yellow fever, flu, polio, small-pox, chicken-pox, hand cow-pox, and also isolates viruses from diseased animals or humans in order to study them for prevention and eradication purposes.

By the end of 1970, the East African Economic Community had become a model for all Africa – the only truly Pan-African endeavour so far to achieve economic unity. Unlike some other 'regional' economic groupings, it was established with genuine African effort, not prompted into existence by foreign forces. Every Pan-Africanist was proud of its achievements. But in January 1971 the unforeseen happened, affecting the EAC so badly that some even doubt whether it can continue.

THE UGANDA COUP AND ITS AFTER-EFFECTS

In January 1971, while the Commonwealth conference was taking place in Singapore, General Idi Amin, the Ugandan army commander, overthrew the government of President Milton Obote in circumstances which remain ambiguous.[54] President Nyerere of Tanzania made it known immediately that his country would not recognize the new Uganda régime. A series of events have thus been set in motion which are bound to have damaging effects on the effective functioning of the East African Community.

The progress of the East African Community between 1967 and 1970 was a direct result of the effective working relationship among the heads of the three member states. But for as long as Tanzania refuses to recognize the new régime in Uganda, it cannot be expected that President Nyerere and General Amin will be able to sit together at the same table as equals in the EAC authority. This can paralyse the activities of the community, since the authority has general direction and control over executive functions.

To complicate matters, General Amin, whose position seems insecure, embarked on a series of adventures which could only damage Ugandan-Tanzanian relations even further. He started using border incidents as a pretext to consolidate his position at home and unite his dangerously divided army.[55] A few days after coming into power, he accused Tanzania of trying to invade Uganda. This proved, however, to be no more than a flimsy cover-up for internecine warfare within the Uganda army that he headed.[56] In July 1971, he again accused Tanzania, and again this proved false.[57] Amin nonetheless ordered the closing of the border between the countries. Already in April 1971, he had ordered the severance of telephone links between Uganda and Tanzania, as well as the suspension of flights by the East African Airways Corporation between them. Border clashes followed in August 1971.[58] These incidents added fuel to the fire.

Concerned with the future of the EAC, president Nyerere made a number of concessions before General Amin's border incidents of August 1971. He agreed to accept nominations from Amin for community posts, as long as such nominations passed through the proper channels. He even allowed Tanzania to resume attending official meetings of the community; many of which the country had boycotted since the January coup in Uganda. But in reply General Amin refused even to sign the Appropriations Bill of the community.[59]

What emerges is that as long as the relations between two EAC member states are not normalized, the EAC's functions are impaired. This does not augur well for the organization's future. As long as the EAC's activities are thus hampered, the chances of enlarging the community through the admission of other East African applicant states – Zambia, Ethiopia, Somalia and Burundi – remain bleak.

(d) The Middle East Crisis

The cause and course of the Middle East crisis are too well-known for recital here. What is plain is that the crisis has affected Pan-Africanism in many ways. Because of their preoccupation with it, the North African states have appeared more Pan-Arabic than Pan-African in their policies. And this has led most African states 'south of the Sahara' wrongly to conclude that North Africa is not interested in Pan-Africanism. The error has been carefully and systematically nurtured by forces interested in seeing Africa disunited. The role of the North African states in the Pan-African arena, at least since the OAU was founded, should have by now convinced doubters on the other side of the Sahara that Pan-Africanism is embraced by all the African states.

Ever since the North African states have taken active part in Pan-African affairs, however, they have endeavoured to enlist support for their cause in the dispute from other African states. But such endeavours have produced no significant results. During the OAU summit conference of 1964, president Bourguiba of Tunisia passionately appealed to other African heads of state for support, reminding them that they could not continue to advocate continental unity if they ignored the problem facing an important part of the continent. Most African states remained unconvinced. After the 1967 Middle East war, however, there was some small change in their attitude. Although the Somali request for an emergency session of the OAU council of ministers failed to get the necessary two-thirds majority of OAU members, African states began to realize that they could not turn a blind eye to the crisis indefinitely.

The first move was taken by the OAU council of ministers at its tenth session, held at Addis Ababa in February 1968. In a strongly worded resolution, it branded Israel as the aggressor in the Middle East and demanded the unconditional withdrawal of Israeli troops from the occupied territories. This resolution was, however, rejected by the summit conference of 1968 at Algiers. Instead, a 'Resolution on the Aggression against the United Arab Republic' was adopted which merely took note of the statement made by the UAR minister for foreign affairs; reaffirmed the OAU's support for the UAR; called for the withdrawal of foreign troops from all Arab territories occupied since 5 June 1967, in accordance with the UN Security Council resolution of 22 November 1967; and appealed to all OAU member states to use their influence to ensure a strict implementation of the resolution. In 1970 another resolution on the issue was adopted almost unanimously by the summit (with the Ivory Coast and Gabon expressing reservations). In 1971, however, the OAU council of ministers endorsed an Israeli donation of $2,800 towards the activities of the African liberation movements. Not only did the liberation movements unanimously reject the Israeli donation, but certain delegates even proposed that the donation should be transferred to the Palestine liberation movements.

The acceptance of the Israeli donation demonstrated the indecision of most OAU member states on the Middle East crisis. Israel has not only established diplomatic relations with most of them, but has continually assisted them in their development projects. Although it would be unrealistic to expect them to break off relations with Israel and forgo the assistance they receive from her, they must realize that, as long as the crisis continues, it will continue to bedevil Pan-Africanism. They must, therefore, concert their efforts to bridge the gap between the two sides in the Middle East crisis. If they remain complacent they will be condoning aggression against a fellow OAU state. The realization of this led the OAU summit of 1971 to set up the OAU Commission of Ten on the Middle East crisis. This commission, mandated to get in touch with both Israel and the United Arab Republic, in order to study the issue objectively and enable the OAU to use its good offices in bringing about a peaceful settlement, held its first meeting at Kinshasa in September 1971. As a result of its deliberations, a sub-committee of four was set up under the chairmanship of President Léopold Senghor of Senegal, with President Ahidjo of Cameroon, General Gowon of Nigeria, and President Mobutu of Zaire – formerly Congo (Kinshasa) – as the other members. The sub-committee was empowered to visit Cairo and Tel-Aviv, to discuss 'concrete proposals' worked out by the OAU. At the same time the OAU Commission of Ten authorized President Moktar Ould Daddah of Mauritania, the current OAU chairman, to communicate with both the UN secretary-general, U Thant, and the UN Middle East mediator, Dr Gunnar Jarring, on the OAU proposals.

Although it is too early to speculate on what the OAU efforts will achieve, they are nonetheless commendable. If Israel finally refuses to cooperate she will lose the sympathy of many African states which have so far been lukewarm towards the UAR standpoint. This must lead to a united front among OAU members, and the failure of Israeli efforts in Africa. If, however, Israel cooperates and withdraws her troops in accordance with the UN Security Council resolution of November 1967, then her stature

Progress and Problems

in Africa will be greatly enhanced, and the OAU enabled to press
on towards a final resolution of the crisis.

Notes to Chapter 6

1. For an account of the background to the crisis see Okoi Arikpo, *The Development of Modern Nigeria*, Penguin Books, Harmondsworth, 1967; Frederick Forsyth, *The Biafra Story*, Penguin Books, Harmondsworth, 1969; Klaus Stephan, *Der Krieg in Nigeria*, in *Europa Archiv* (Bonn), 23, Jahrgang Heft 4.
2. Decree No. 14, 27 May 1967.
3. Stephan, op. cit., p. 129.
4. A German Africanist at the Otto-Suhr-Institute of the Free University in West Berlin in 1968 tried to convince me of the need for Nigeria's becoming a Confederation as suggested by the Biafrans, and to lecture me on what he termed 'the root-causes' of the crisis in Nigeria. As he was wrong on matters of fact, I recommended some books on constitutional developments in Nigeria from 1914 to the beginning of the crisis in January 1966. Upon my asking him what he thought of the idea of Germany's becoming a Confederation in an attempt to unite the Federal Republic (West Germany) and the German Democratic Republic (East Germany), he retorted that it was impossible to compare a European case with an African one and that '*Nigeria ist zu gross für Afrikanische Verhältnisse*' ('Nigeria is too big for African standards'). This suggested that he and others of the same view were chiefly interested in balkanizing Nigeria under cover of what they termed 'humanitarian grounds'!
5. AHG/Res. 51 (IV), 14 September 1967.
6. *West Africa*, 23 September 1967, p. 1223.
7. The members of the committee who were in Lagos were Emperor Haile Selassie (chairman), presidents Ahidjo of Cameroon and Hamani Diori of Niger, and General Ankrah of Ghana. Presidents Tubman of Liberia and Mobutu of Congo (Kinshasa) did not attend, but the OAU secretary-general, Diallo Telli, was also present.
8. *West Africa*, 2 December 1967, p. 1561.
9. *African Research Bulletin*, Vol. 4, No. 11, p. 901 A.
10. *West Africa*, 2 December 1967.
11. *West Africa*, 28 January 1968.
12. The Kampala Peace Talks organized by the Commonwealth secretariat in May 1968 had broken down.
13. *United Nigeria*, No. 1, 30 July 1968, Federal Government of Nigeria, Nigeria House, London.
14. The Nigerian delegation, headed by chief Obafemi Awolowo, vice-chairman of the Federal Executive Council, included Dr T. O. Elias and Messrs Alhaji A. Baba Gana, Alhaji Ahmed Joda, A. A. Ayida, E. O. Sanu and A. Rufai as well as Alhaji Ali Akilu.

15. The Biafran delegation included Drs Nnamdi Azikiwe and Michael Okpara, Sir Louis Mbanefo, Dr Eni Njoku, Professor Eyo Bassey Ndem, Dr Ignatius Kogbara and Messrs Matthew Mbu, N. U. Akpan and C. C. Mojekwu.

16. *West Africa*, 27 July 1968, p. 853.

17. See above the communiqué issued by the OAU Consultative Mission at Niamey, on 26 July 1968, for the items.

18. *West Africa*, 3 August 1968, p. 885.

19. For a discussion on France's role in the Nigerian civil war, see 'France and the Nigerian Civil War', a preliminary statement made at a Press conference held in the Nigerian High Commission in London on 22 December 1969, by the Rt Hon. Dr Nnamdi Azikiwe, P.C., former president of Nigeria.

20. *United Nigeria*, No. 2, 20 August 1968.

21. *West Africa*, 10 August 1968, p. 937.

22. ibid.

23. *Africa Research Bulletin*, Vol. 5, No. 8, p. 1152.

24. *West Africa*, 7 September 1968, p. 1057.

25. See *West Africa*, 7 September 1968, p. 1055; also 14 September 1968, p. 1063.

26. *West Africa*, 21 September 1968, p. 1091.

27. *West Africa*, 26 April 1969, p. 485; also Auberon Waugh and Susanne Cronje, *Biafra – Britain's Shame*, Michael Joseph, London, 1969, p. 91.

28. The idea of 'others' taking the initiative on the Nigerian crisis was first put forward by Dr Nnamdi Azikiwe at a lecture on the Nigerian civil war at Oxford in February 1969. For a condensed version, see *West Africa*, 22 February 1969, p. 225.

29. See note 27 above.

30. *West Africa*, 27 September 1969, p. 1165.

31. *The Times*, 13 January 1970, p. 7; *Guardian*, 13 January 1970.

32. As far back as October 1965 I learnt from a reliable source in West Berlin that Eastern Nigeria had already finalized plans to secede from Nigeria.

33. Anybody interested in this topic should trace the history of 'revenue allocation' in the course of Nigerian constitutional developments from 1945 till the outbreak of the Nigerian crisis – see Okoi Arikpo, *The Development of Modern Nigeria*.

34. See *The Times*, 30 December 1970, and the *East African Standard*, 20 September 1967 – '*Amnesty for Six*'.

35. See note 31 above.

36. Beshir Mohammed Said, *The Sudan: Crossroads of Africa*, The Bodley Head, London, 1965, p. 74.

37. ibid., p. 81.

38. Quoted from Ronald Segal, *African Profiles*, p. 177.

39. *East African Standard*, 21 January 1965, p. 4.

40. *East African Standard*, 21 July 1969, p. 5.

41. *East African Standard*, 30 June 1969.

42. *West Africa*, 6 April 1968, p. 399.
43. *West Africa*, 28 February 1970, p. 219.
44. ibid.
45. See note 13 of Chapter 5.
46. For a detailed account of the organization of the UDE, see 'Economic Integration in Equatorial Africa', in *African Integration and Disintegration*, ed. A. D. Hazlewood, Oxford University Press, London, 1967.
47. ibid., p. 55.
48. See *West Africa*, 28 December 1968, pp. 1553–4; also 11 January 1969, p. 52.
49. *Economic Co-operation and Integration in Africa: Three Case Studies*, ST/ECA/109, p. 131.
50. ibid.
51. Report of the ECA/OAU Conference of Ministers of Industry (Addis Ababa, 3–7 May 1971), ECA Doc. E/CN/525; E/CN/INR/194; OAU/ CMI/W/9, 8 May 1971, Annex II – Joint Statement by the Member States of the Central African Customs and Economic Union (UDEAC) which participated in the proceedings of the conference of ministers of industry in Addis Ababa, 3–7 May 1971, p. 1.
52. ibid.
53. op. cit., p. 3.
54. See *The Times* and the *Financial Times*, 27 January 1971.
55. See Colin Legum's article in the *Observer*, 25 July 1971, p. 5.
56. See *The Times*, 1 February 1971.
57. See Colin Legum's article in the *Observer*, 18 July 1971, p. 2.
58. See Paul W. Blackstock, *The Strategy of Subversion*, Quadrangle Books, Chicago, 1964, pp. 207–17, on the use of border incidents to manipulate the politics of other nations.
59. See the *Guardian*, 28 July 1971.

Part Three: Any Need for Pan-Africanism?

7. Is Pan-Africanism Really Necessary?

To put Africa in motion, to co-operate in its organization, in its regrouping, behind revolutionary principles, to participate in the ordered movement of a continent – this was really the work I had chosen . . .

FRANTZ FANON*

(a) The Case against Pan-Africanism

Arguments have been advanced against the cause of Pan-Africanism. It would be wrong to dismiss them without any effort to consider their merits. The most significant argument holds that Pan-Africanism is a movement of the African élite; and that, as such, its ideals are not and cannot be understood by the masses on the African continent. It is, the argument goes, 'a movement among governments rather than peoples'. Pan-Africanists must not dismiss this out of hand. It is, indeed, the African élite that is chiefly concerned with Pan-Africanism. There are, however, two reasons. The first is that many Africans are illiterates. Only a very thin layer of the African community has been to any school or institution of higher learning. But this apparent weakness of Pan-Africanism is, at the same time, its source of strength. The élite, which is at the helm of African governments, administration, civil service, as well as in the professions, has the opportunity to meet and take decisions which affect the course of events in the whole continent.

And then, surely, every ideal has an avant-garde. It has always been so in history. In particular, proposals for wider unity have always been propounded by a hard core of determined and dedicated believers. This was how Pan-Germanism, Pan-Islamism, Pan-Slavism and Pan-Arabism came into existence and played significant roles in the areas where they were proclaimed. Other major historical events have been dreamt of and brought to reality, by dedicated élites. Among them was the

* *Toward the African Revolution*, Penguin Books, Harmondsworth, 1970, pp. 187-8.

319

Russian Revolution of 1917, which the Bolsheviks achieved despite the smallness of their numbers in comparison with the total Russian population and other evident odds. The Chinese Revolution of 1949 is another case in point. The French Resistance during the Second World War, and the Franco-German Rapprochement which led to the Franco–German Treaty of January 1963, are concrete examples of how élites of one sort or another have acted to produce new climates of popular opinion. Even the phenomenon of decolonization was headed by an élite. The drive for European unity which resulted in the establishment of the European Economic Community, at a time when most inhabitants of the EEC member states still had fresh memories of the German atrocities in the Second World War, was led by the élites of the countries concerned. Why, then, should it be an argument against Pan-Africanism itself, that its ideals should be advocated by an African élite? It would, it is true, be even better if the African masses were more directly and devotedly involved. But meanwhile the élite can at least show the light.

Other people have argued that Pan-African ideals cannot be attained because Africans have, as a result of colonialism, inherited different parliamentary, legal and cultural systems. Yet precisely: these so-called inheritances are not African, but foreign. The same applies to the official languages in many countries. It may be a burden; but it is not a block to Pan-Africanism. It is, indeed, a challenge to the Africans to develop their own systems along African lines. Copying European or other norms and trying to translate them into an African context can only lead to disaster. Africans cannot for ever use the former colonial medium of expression as their lingua franca, especially when it is remembered that fewer than one per cent of all Africans understand these foreign languages. Pan-Africanism provides the forum where such challenges can be tackled on a continental scale.

There is no doubt that the former colonial powers tried to impose their own culture on the colonies. But there is no proof that such cultures have *taken root* in the African states. African culture is more concerned than Western with human relations. This is manifest in the strong family relations and the communal way of life. The advantages of such cultural norms over the Western systems of the nuclear family, and rigid individualism, if not downright egocentricism, are more and more manifest, as discontent rises within the West itself. It is, therefore, self-deception to believe that imported Western cultures have such an impact on the Africans as to deny the validity of Pan-Africanism.

Even if the difference in language, and in legal parliamentary and cultural systems were accepted as a strong factor, it would still not be self-evidently strong enough to stand against Pan-Africanism. The European experience, at least in the EEC, has clearly demonstrated this. The parliamentary systems of many EEC members are quite different from one another. The language and cultural heritage of member states have not acted as an impediment to unity.

It has also been argued that African states should concentrate all their efforts on nation-building, rather than on the attainment of African unity. They face, it is claimed, a massive problem already, in forging many tribes together, so as to create a sense of common nationhood. It is true that the process of nation-building is at present confined to Africa. But why should it not be set in motion at a continental level? There is nothing to hinder such a move as long as the political will to that end is present. Nation-building can be transformed into the attainment of Pan-African ideals.

Economic reasons have also been put forward. It has been argued that African countries are so poor and their economies so competitive that they have nothing to offer one another. Consequently, so the argument goes, Pan-Africanism can only lead to economic suicide. Certainly African countries are poor. Certainly most of them produce identical items and their economies thus compete. But it is totally wrong to conclude that if these countries combined their economic and human resources, they would achieve nothing worthwhile. Experience in other parts of the world does not support such an argument. Europe, after the Second World War, was divided and weak. But with increasing cooperation among them, European states enormously raised their economic strength and their living-standards. The adage

321

'unity is strength' has at least as much significance in the economic as in other fields. Since the need for economic cooperation in Africa is fully considered in the next section, it will suffice here to state that the economic arguments advanced so far against Pan-Africanism are untenable.

Some may come to the conclusion that those who so fervently oppose Pan-Africanism have other, ulterior motives, which are only camouflaged by such arguments; and that the latter are mere verbal attempts to thwart the progress of the movement.

(b) The Case for Pan-Africanism

What do the proponents of Pan-Africanism advance as reasons for its necessity? What possibilities does it offer? Pan-Africanists have always argued that it creates the suitable atmosphere for economic cooperation; provides the medium whereby the foreign policies of independent African states may be coordinated, so as to make the African presence a force to be reckoned with in world politics; and promotes effective action to rid the continent of colonialism and racialism.

Is this mere wishful thinking; or does Pan-Africanism offer a real hope for the achievement of these ideals?

(i) *Economic Field*

It has already been pointed out that most African states attained political, without significant economic, independence. And those who doubt the seriousness of the consequences should examine what has happened in countries in which political independence has been enjoyed for more than a century, but which still rank with the underdeveloped parts of the world.

How economically dependent were the African states when they achieved political independence? As has been mentioned, agriculture formed the backbone of the African economy. There was also a dire shortage of that most important factor in economic development – a skilled, educated, highly-productive labour force; and in those colonies where some sort of economic development had taken place, it was orientated to the metropolitan countries, which provided the markets for export products and in return sold manufactured goods. The metropolitan interests naturally took precedence over the colonial ones. Most colonies were economically developed to produce much the same goods and services; so that there was competition among the African countries themselves. As their economy depended on their export earnings, more attention was paid to the oversea than to the intra-African trade. And this led to poor or non-existent intra-African communications.

Another legacy of colonialism has been the small size of markets available in the balkanized African states. There are some forty states in Africa, and most of them have a population of less than four million each (see Appendix 9). During the colonial era this fact was disguised by such constitutional and economic groupings as the Federations of French West Africa and French Equatorial Africa. With independence the federations disintegrated and many small states emerged. It is well known that the creation of an integrated modern economy with high levels of productivity requires large markets. Without these, it is impossible to attain the economies of scale which can make most efficient use of modern technology.

What are the possibilities which Pan-Africanism offers for the solutions of these vast problems?

During the Addis Ababa Summit of 1963, President Nkrumah of Ghana said: 'Our continent is probably the richest in the world for minerals and industrial and agricultural materials. From the Congo alone, Western firms exported copper, rubber, cotton and other goods to the value of 2,773 billion dollars in the ten years between 1945 and 1955'.[1] Africa is indeed immensely rich in mineral resources. Copper, zinc, uranium, titanium, iron ore and bauxite are to be found in abundance. And about 90 per cent of the whole continent is yet to be geologically surveyed.[2] Massive reserves of oil exist, while hydro-electric power can be easily generated. The density of the population is not high; and land for development programmes is clearly available. An enormous reservoir of potentially far more productive manpower exists.

323

Any Need for Pan-Africanism?

What Africa lacks is skilled manpower, a good intra-African communications system, capital and technological know-how. Pan-Africanism offers the possibilities of joint action in economic planning; the development of large industrial complexes; multi-national river projects; joint research schemes to improve agriculture and fight pests; improvement in intra-African communications; continental monetary and financial institutions; and steps to reduce the dependence of the African economy on fluctuations in the price of raw materials. Let us briefly examine each of these possibilities.

Continental Economic Planning. The UN Economic Commission for Africa rightly declared in 1964 that 'if Africa is to achieve maximum rates of economic growth to enable her to catch up with other regions of the world in levels of living; if the economic distance between her and the other regions of the world is to be covered in five or six decades, planned economic development on a co-ordinated and integrated basis for all countries in the region is imperative'.[3] The need for economic planning has been recognized by every African state. What Pan-Africanism makes possible is the realization that it is necessary to coordinate such plans. As has already been noted, most African countries produced almost the same products and services during the colonial period; and competition continues to operate among them. A coordinated planning system would prevent duplication of industries. Products would have a much wider market than the present small states can offer. Industries would be developed where economic factors such as raw materials, energy, manpower and land advised it. Specialization could be promoted, probably on a regional basis; and in the long run this would have a very favourable effect on Africa's balance of payments.

Continental economic planning might be achieved through the joint efforts of the ECA and the economic and social commission of the OAU, in which every African state is represented. In order to supervise such programmes, already approved by the two institutions, a permanent continental planning body, with representatives of each African state as well as representatives of the ECA, could be set up under the auspices of the OAU.

Industrialization. If agreement were reached on how best continental economic planning could be achieved, the next moves would centre on how continental industrial development might be so integrated as to locate certain types of industry in different parts of the continent. Such an industrial integration, if effectively followed, would inevitably provoke productive reactions: horizontally by producing and spreading progressive structural changes; and vertically by stimulating even closer cooperation. The objectives of such integrated industrial development should be the following: expansion of production opportunities, including improved usage of production capacities; acceleration of industrial growth rates; advancement of the industrial structure; improved use of resources, reflected in increased efficiency and cost reduction; high rates of growth in the national income of each African state. To achieve these objectives the following methods might be applied: industrial specialization on a regional but coordinated basis; cooperation among certain sectors of industry; improvement in the technology and operational efficiency of business enterprises; enlargement of the market through intra-regional trade liberalization; fair and rational distribution of benefits derived from integration; and the formulation of a common strategy for industrial development.[4]

Heavy industries like iron and steel could be located in West, East, Central, South and North Africa. Other ancillary industries could be located in such territories as are not too far from the heavy-industry locations in the regions concerned. Other industries could be so placed that no country would feel neglected in the overall industrial plan of the continent. An African industrial coordination board might be set up to examine the availability of raw materials, and consider where best industrial complexes like iron and steel, heavy engineering industries, chemicals and fertilizers, cement and textiles could be situated. Branches of such complexes could, in certain cases, be located in other countries of the regions concerned.

There is now increasing evidence that African states are trying to coordinate their economic plans in order to speed up the overall process of industrialization. During the ECA/OAU

Conference of Ministers of Industry held at Addis Ababa in May 1971, several delegations stressed the importance of multi-national cooperation in this regard. Some delegates observed that the major problem hindering progress was inadequate political will and commitment on the part of the African countries. Realizing the damage done by this lack of adequate political will during the first decade of their political independence, and 'conscious of the economic and political disadvantages of small unco-ordinated national markets and weak unrelated national economies in meeting the challenge of industrial growth', the ministers reaffirmed their faith in industrialization as a strategic element in the structural transformation of African economies. They therefore adopted a programme of action on industrialization, requesting the administrative secretary-general of the OAU and the executive secretary of the ECA to convene similar conferences every two years during the 70s, in order to review progress towards the target set for the period; evaluate other aspects of industrial performance; and recommend policies and actions for sustaining industrial growth.[5]

Multi-national River Projects. Africa has many rivers and lakes which either run through or lie between states and could be developed for harnessing hydro-electric power, for transport, irrigation and even a fishing industry. Programmes would be integrated in the overall continental economic development plans.

The development of the Sahara desert, too, is no longer an impossibility.

Joint Research Schemes. Africa is short of scientists. But Pan-Africanism offers the possibility of pooling Africa's small resources so as to carry out research schemes of vital importance to the improvement of African agriculture. Even if foreign assistance would be needed, the costs of maintaining such assistance would be kept to the barest minimum if, instead of separate research schemes, joint actions were undertaken. Specialization could be encouraged at different centres.

Improvement in Intra-African Communications. As a result of the partition of Africa into colonial territories under several separate European powers, the communications system was confined to particular areas under the same colonial power. Roads, railways and so on were built only to facilitate the transportation of raw materials to the ports, for onward transmission to the metropolis. The need for bigger markets makes it imperative that roads and railways should be built across boundaries, to connect the different African states. The intra-African air services should be improved, and maritime transport coordinated and advanced. Telephone links between states must be given priority; and the postal services also need improvement.

Setting up Continental Monetary and Financial Institutions. All the projects mentioned above need much investment from local sources or from abroad. Channels for the mobilization and direction of such funds to productive sectors of the economy must be established. If intra-African trade is to expand an African clearing and payment mechanism must be developed; with African-controlled central banks established, and their policies coordinated. It should be possible in the long run to have a unified policy for the mobilization and allocation of investment funds, and the creation of an African monetary union with a common currency. A continental central bank or development bank is needed.

When all the above possibilities have been realized, there is no doubt that the African market would have been unified; and with a population of about 350 million, the chances of achieving an economically strong continent would be great. But as long as African states hesitate to unite and coordinate their economic policies, the living standards of their inhabitants will remain low. Africa will be unable even to begin closing the gap with the developed parts of the world. While the advanced industrial countries continue to grow richer, Africa will stagnate. As Tables 9 and 10 show, the achievements of the African countries during the first decade of political independence, when compared with European and other developed countries during the same period, leave much to be desired.

It is worth noting that in spite of the high *per capita* income in the four countries marked (c) in Table 9 – Denmark, Ireland,

Norway and the United Kingdom – these still decided to apply for EEC membership. The decision was dictated by the desire for European unity, and by economic necessity; two motives

Table 9. Gross Domestic Product[a] **of some developed economies, 1967**

Country	Total (millions of dollars)	*Per capita* (dollars)
Australia	27,100	2,295
Belgium (b)	19,340	2,019
Canada	58,372	2,856
Denmark (c)	12,188	2,519
France (b)	115,860	2,338
Germany (West) (b)	124,000	2,149
Ireland (c)	3,052	1,053
Italy (b)	69,688	1,331
Japan	120,008	1,201
Luxembourg (b)	714	2,131
Netherlands (b)	22,735	1,805
Norway (c)	8,540	2,257
Sweden	24,143	3,069
Switzerland	15,481	2,550
United Kingdom (c)	108,791	1,976
United States	804,000	4,038
U.S.S.R.	278,856	1,184

Source: *World Economic Survey, 1969–70* (U.N. Publication Sales No.: E.71.II.C.1 E/4942; ST/ECA/141)

    (a) at market prices;
    (b) members of the EEC;
    (c) applicant members of the EEC.

expressed in the British Government White Paper on 'The United Kingdom and the European Communities'[6] which argued that an enlarged and united Europe would be able to play 'in world affairs the part which Europe of to-day is not at present playing. For a Europe that fails to put forward its full economic strength will never have political influences'.[7]

On economic necessity, the Paper declared: 'In particular, the development and exploitation of modern industrial technology upon which so much of our employment and income increasingly depends requires greater resources for research and development and wider markets than any one Western European nation can provide.'[8] It continued: 'If we enter the Communities we shall be able to profit from the general advantages of a larger market and, in particular, to play a full part in the development of industries based on advanced technology',[9] and concluded:

Together with the other members of the enlarged Community we could do more and better than any of us could do alone. Together we could tackle problems of technological innovation and development which would be too big for any one of us ... And together the members of the enlarged Community would be able to help each other.[10]

If such industrialized countries of Europe are uniting their resources and technological skills in order to step up further the living standards of their people, why should not African countries cooperate to conquer misery, poverty, ignorance and disease? There is no justifiable reason for delay. Those African leaders who cannot even breathe without approval from their former colonial masters should bear in mind that even the leaders of France and the United Kingdom accept the need for European unity. Why should African unity be less urgent?

(ii) Intra-African Politics

Pan-Africanists have always expressed their desire to liberate the African continent from colonialism and racial discrimination, and create conditions where people of all races, creeds, sexes, and religions would live together peaceably. They want all disputes, disagreements, and misunderstandings, which have so damaging an effect on interstate relations in Africa, to be settled within an African context. Opposed to any foreign interference in internal affairs, they strongly resist any armed aggression against any part of Africa. Does Pan-Africanism make their hopes possible?

Decolonization. Since the Pan-African congress of 1945, Pan-Africanism has made decolonization one of its objectives. That congress demanded autonomy and independence for Africa, affirmed the right of all colonial peoples to control their own destiny, and called for the establishment of nationalist movements

329

Table 10. Africa's Economy, 1960–68

Country	Gross domestic product (a) 1967 Total (millions) of dollars	Gross domestic product (a) 1967 Per capita (dollars)	Average annual rate of growth (percentage) (b) 1960–67	Average annual rate of growth (percentage) (b) 1967–8	Planned rate of growth Period of plan	Planned rate of growth Percentage per annum	Actual rate of growth from beginning of plan until 1968
Algeria	3,192	255	−1·5	6·1	1967–69	—	6·1
Botswana	59	99	5·5	3·9	1968–73	6·0	—
Burundi	174	52	2·7	1·5	1968–72	—	—
Cameroon	891	163	6·0	3·1	1966–71	5·8	4·0
Central African Republic	178	122	1·8	4·1	1967–70	7·0	4·1
Chad	241	70	2·0	2·9	1966–70	5·9	−0·2
Congo (Brazzaville)	228	265	7·7	7·0	1964–68	7·2	9·1
Congo (Kinshasa)	1,353	83	2·4	7·8	1965–69	—	4·5
Dahomey	208	83	1·2	9·9	1966–70	4·0	4·5
Equatorial Guinea	28	100					
Ethiopia	1,486	63	4·6	2·9	1968–72	6·0	—
Gabon	238	504 (c)	5·6	3·7	1966–70	7·5	4·4
Gambia	42	122	6·8	6·5	1967–70	4·2	6·5
Ghana	2,063	253	2·5	1·9	1968–70	6·0	—
Guinea	323	87	5·0	5·8	1964–70	—	4·6
Ivory Coast	1,117	279 (c)	6·9	11·6	1960–70	7·5	7·5
Kenya	1,209	122 .	4·5	6·7	1966–70	6·3	4·9
Lesotho	75	85	7·9	−1·3	1967–71	5·0	−1·3
Liberia	330	297	4·8	4·9	1967–70	—	4·9

Libya	2,218	1,276	30·0	36·4	1963–68	—	27·0
Madagascar	737	116	2·1	2·9	1964–69	4·9	1·7
Malawi	274	66	3·3	−0·5	1965–69	5·0	4·6
Mali	414	88	2·2	0·9	1961–66	5·0	2·0
Mauritania	178	162	10·3	5·8	1968–71	—	—
Mauritius	200	258	5·4	−0·5	1966–70	—	1·8
Morocco	2,688	190	2·9	13·0	1965–67	3·7	4·2
Niger	350	95	5·7	1·3	1967–70	4·7	1·3
Nigeria	4,321	70	1·3	−6·5	1962–68	4·0	−0·5
Rwanda	151	46	2·7	2·1	1965–69	—	2·7
Senegal	787	217	1·8	9·1	1965–69	5·5	3·7
Sierra Leone	393	161	3·8	12·6	1966–71	—	8·1
Somalia	159	61	3·5	4·4	1968–70	—	—
Sudan	1,568	109	4·1	8·8	1961–70	5·0	3·1
Swaziland	75	194	8·8	4·4	1965–68	—	1·4
Tanzania	874	73	3·4	3·5	1964–69	6·7	3·8
Togo	229	133	7·1	7·2	1966–70	5·6	3·7
Tunisia	1,011	210	3·7	6·8	1965–68	6·5	2·1
United Arab Republic	5,773	187	3·9	1·0	1960–70	—	3·5
Uganda	774	98	4·3	2·5	1966–71	6·3	3·8
Upper Volta	246	49	2·4	5·0	1967–70	4·0	5·0
Zambia	1,248	316	7·1	4·4	1966–70	11·7	4·7

Source: *World Economic Survey, 1969–70*

(a) at market prices;

(b) compound rate between terminal years, based on gross domestic product at market prices;

(c) this figure is distorted, since a large part of the income is expatriated.

to fight for independence. Pan-Africanism has, since then, acted as a lever towards the ultimate achievement of independence. At every subsequent Pan-African gathering, colonialism has been severely condemned, and its eradication advocated. Pan-Africanism has served as a platform from which to appeal to public opinion across the world. It has had an immense influence on events.

By 1963 it had become clear that the remaining dependent territories in Africa would not be liberated except by the use of force. And therefore it was decided at the Addis Ababa conference that united effort and support was needed for the fighting nationalist movements in the territories concerned. A liberation committee was set up to coordinate aid.

The situation has not changed. In spite of the noises made by the waverers, the dialoguers; those who either received their independence on a 'platter of gold' or had it thrust on them even against their personal belief and conviction, no attempt should be made to sell out those fighting for their birthright. Concessions and compromises should be made only if they would bring about the desired end. For this reason united action is still required; and only Pan-Africanism makes it possible.

DISPUTE SETTLEMENT

The settlement of disputes among African states within an African context has always been one of the targets of Pan-Africanism. In his opening address to the First Conference of Independent African States at Accra in April 1958, Nkrumah declared that 'if we can as independent African States show by our own efforts that we can settle our own problems in Africa, then we shall be setting an example to others'.[11] The experience of the Congo crisis demonstrated the need for such action to the Pan-Africanists, and also clearly showed that any external involvement in African affairs would create disunity among the African states, causing untold harm.

CONTINENTAL GOVERNMENT

Pan-Africanism also offers the possibility of a continental government, to be based either on a unitary or federal constitution. But because of the long estrangement caused by colonialism and lack of communications, a federal system of government might best suit shorter-term African needs.

How, then, should Africa be rearranged into the component parts of the Federation? Assuming that by then the Portuguese colonies had been liberated; that there was a change of heart or policy or government in South Africa; and that both

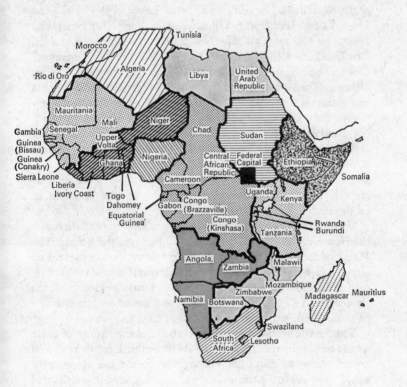

8. Federal Republic of Africa: Component Parts

Zimbabwe (Rhodesia) and Namibia (South-West Africa) had also achieved independence: there would be no reason why the Federation should not extend from Cairo to Cape Town, as well as from the Atlantic to the Indian Ocean; including, of course, all the off-shore islands. The chief criteria in determining the parts would be population and resources. If the present boundaries were used as a basis, the Federation could be made of the following fourteen states (see Map 8): (1) Algeria, Morocco, Tunisia and Rio di Oro; (2) Libya and the United Arab Republic; (3) Sudan; (4) Gambia, Guinea (Bissau), Guinea (Conakry), Mali, Mauritania, Senegal and Sierra Leone; (5) Liberia, the Ivory Coast, the Upper Volta, Ghana, Togo, Dahomey and Niger; (6) Nigeria; (7) Cameroon, the Central African Republic, Chad, Congo (Brazzaville), Congo (Kinshasa), Equatorial Guinea and Gabon; (8) Ethiopia and Somalia; (9) Kenya, Uganda, Tanzania, Burundi and Rwanda; (10) Angola, Zambia and Namibia; (11) Malawi, Zimbabwe, Mozambique and Botswana; (12) the Republic of South Africa, Lesotho and Swaziland; (13) Madagascar and Mauritius; (14) Federal territory (capital), to be carved out of Central Africa, where the Central African Republic, the Sudan and Congo (Kinshasa) meet. Other off-shore islands would have special federal status. This division should, however, be amended according to the situation in existence.

The constitution would provide for two Houses of parliament: the House of the People (the Lower House) and the Senate. The House of the People would have 700 members, each representing about half-a-million citizens. Direct elections would be held on the same day throughout the continent to the House of the People; with all citizens above eighteen years of age, irrespective of race, creed, sex or religion, entitled to vote.

The Senate would have 150 members. Some twenty of these would be nominated by the Federal Government for their special contributions to education, culture, commerce and so on: provided that such contributions were of significant continental value. Others would be elected by the state legislatures in accordance with the agreed quota based on population. A state like the one made up of Madagascar and Mauritius might be entitled to three; while a state like Nigeria would be entitled to ten.

There would be subjects which came exclusively within the federal prerogative (federal exclusive list); those which belonged to the States; and those to be concurrently handled by both the Federal and State Governments (concurrent list). Where there was any clash between the Federal and any State Government over a subject on the concurrent list, the decision of the Federal Government would take precedence.

The federal exclusive list would comprise defence, foreign affairs, overall internal security (including the police force), communications, all ports; higher education, the judiciary, economic planning, mineral resources, foreign trade, currency and monetary policies, and extradition.

There would be a federal president, elected at a joint session of both Houses of parliament for a five-year term. He might be eligible for another term, but not more.

The federal cabinet would be headed by the federal prime minister, and include not more than twenty ministers. There should be a minister for state affairs in the cabinet. The State governments would, of course, be subordinated to the Federal Government in all matters.

Every African would be entitled to equal rights and privileges, as well as being required to render the same obligations in accordance with the citizenship regulations. There would be freedom of movement, worship, and other fundamental human rights, in accordance with the Universal Declaration of Human Rights adopted by the United Nations. Yet there should not be more than two political parties; and those must be organized on a continental basis, thus making it difficult for self-seeking opportunists, who, in an effort to achieve inordinate ambitions, indulge in whipping up sectional and tribal sentiments.

The federal civil service would be composed on a quota basis: with each state having a certain number of the clerical, administrative, executive, technical and 'senior service' posts allocated to it, as now happens at certain levels in the secretariat of the OAU.

As external affairs would be on the federal exclusive list, the

335

staff of many embassies would be pruned, and the best diplomats chosen to man the African diplomatic missions abroad. In this way a large sum of money would be saved; and much mis-representation, caused abroad by incompetent diplomats appointed not on merit but through nepotism or political jobbery, would be eradicated, or at least severely reduced. Foreign representation in Africa, too, would come under scrutiny. A ceiling on the number of officials at the foreign embassies in Africa would have to be fixed, and, during the first twenty-five years of the continental government, efforts be made to prevent foreign agents from trying to undermine Africa's unity. This would necessitate thorough scrutiny of consular agreements with foreign governments before their signature. Other details of the federal constitution would be worked out by the experts. The secretariats, office blocks, presidential palaces and government quarters of the present régimes would be taken over by the federal authorities. Part would be given to the state governments, while others would be turned into living quarters for ordinary citizens. Thus the value of the rule of law and social justice would be demonstrated by the Federal Government; for such is the only basis on which a united African continent could really thrive.

(iii) World Politics

What are the chances for a United States of Africa, with a strong federal government to compete in world politics? Apart from the rapid economic development, the industrial capacity, the human resources and the unity of purpose which Pan-Africanism has provided, there are 'subjective' factors in world politics, such as social elements, nationalism, imperialism, anti-colonialism and the search for security, as well as 'objective' ones like technology, physical environment, population and economics. Interactions between these factors and the type of leadership combine to determine a nation's foreign policy.

Most of the 'subjective' factors, as we have seen, come within the orbit of Pan-Africanism. Are the 'objective' factors also within the reach of Pan-Africanism? Pan-Africanism best utilizes the available qualified human resources in science and technology, as well as training more personnel through joint efforts. Africa has many untapped mineral resources and is majestically situated between East and West. With a population of 350 million, it exceeds those of the United States of America and the Union of Soviet Socialist Republics. There is therefore nothing to prevent a united, stable, economically strong and highly-industrialized Africa from competing with them in world politics.

Pan-Africanism offers this possibility, which can be achieved, however long it may take. What is needed is selfless leadership. An African lingua franca should be adopted. This would be a long-term project; but while Arabic, English and French remained as official languages Hausa and Swahili would be taught in all schools. Such a move would facilitate the adoption of a lingua franca, while the European languages would be relegated to the background.

(c) Pan-African Congresses and African Unity

There is every reason to hope that African unity will eventually be attained. Started in America and the West Indies, the movement came over to Africa through Europe. In Africa it has faced many problems, diversions and tribulations. But instead of fading away it emerged in the shape of the OAU in May 1963. This may be regarded as the beginning of its second phase, in which it has overcome many difficulties. It would be unrealistic to expect every Pan-Africanist to hold the same view on every topic. If that were so, Pan-Africanism would be dull and uncreative. The most significant thing about Pan-Africanism is that it comes out stronger from every difficult situation it faces. If one compares the OAU with similar bodies, such as the EEC or the Organization of American States (OAS), one may see how it has never failed through the fear of any member state's whipping a big stick. The attempt by the Ivory Coast foreign minister, Arsène Assouan-Usher, during the 1971 summit conference, to hold the OAU to ransom over the issue of a dialogue with South

337

Africa[12] not only flopped, but caused others to come closer together in rejecting such a dialogue.

All Pan-Africanists realize that African unity has not yet been achieved. Many young Pan-Africanists have therefore concluded that the drive towards the goal has been made impossible by the OAU itself, where only the heads of state and ministers meet to find an acceptable formula. They are disillusioned by the attitude of very many African leaders. Although there is some justification for this attitude it is ultimately unacceptable. What we have to ask ourselves is whether or not that much-desired African unity can be achieved through the present system of annual summit conferences. If not, what *could* be done to achieve it?

The answer to the first question is not easy. It depends on the type and quality of the leaders concerned. If the leaders are of a kind who in their own countries indulge (overtly or covertly) in 'tribal politics' and may thereby be regarded as men of limited horizon, or are easily manipulated by foreign powers, then nothing much is to be expected from them. If, however, they are dedicated Pan-Africanists, who actually carry the masses with them and do not merely coerce them to accept their policies, something worthwhile could emerge. Even then a few changes should be introduced. National conventions of political parties, professional bodies, students' unions, farmers' unions, cooperative unions, women's and youth organizations, could be held annually in every OAU member state before the annual OAU summit conference takes place. These national conventions would deal with some of the topics to be discussed at the summit, such as 'Should a dialogue be held with South Africa by the member states, in order to solve the present problem in South Africa? If so, in what ways?' Those attending the OAU summit would be present at these annual conventions. In this way Pan-Africanism would be brought close to everyone. The need for continental rather than petty tribal or sectional unity would be implanted in every African; for African unity requires the efforts of every African.

(d) African Youth and Pan-Africanism

It may well be unrealistic to expect the present leaders to achieve African unity soon or speedily. Many will always be reluctant to surrender the sovereignty of their mini-states, because of fear that they would fall from the pinnacle of power if a continental government were to be established. Only youth may reasonably be expected to work towards the achievement of real African unity, through the establishment of a continental government.

Is there any cause for hoping that African youth will prove worthy of this task? Or are they concerned only with blindly copying foreign customs, whether or not these are in line with Pan-African ideals? Will they be able to analyse objectively the role of the present Pan-African leaders, in order to find out where these have gone wrong? Might they, too, allow themselves to be plagued by the disastrous 'get-rich-quick' mania, knowing full well that it has not only led to the ruin of many, but has had damaging and destructive effects on the course of Pan-Africanism itself?

Time will tell. One can only judge from what the youth have done so far. And the evidence is not discouraging.

The demonstration by Nigerian students in November 1960 against the Anglo-Nigerian defence pact sparked off a series of actions which subsequently led to the abrogation of the pact by the Nigerian Federal Government.

In April 1963, delegates from twenty-six African student unions in Europe and America met in London. Among the resolutions passed were the following:

Instruments giving expression to African Unity [should] be created as a matter of urgency. A method of political co-ordination [should] be worked in the consolidating of African Unity. A Political Constitution applying throughout the continent [should] be formulated and accepted. This Political Constitution should make provision for the establishment of a Pan-African Parliament, a Pan-African Executive and Public Service. A Pan-African Army under joint high command [should] be created from national contingents in order to safeguard the integrity of the African continent.

This Pan-African Army is urgently needed in order to defend Africa

against continuing aggression in South Africa, Angola, Portuguese
Guinea, Moçambique and other areas temporarily under colonial
subjection.

Africa should be free of all foreign military bases, nuclea and
atomic testing facilities, and foreign military missions or pacts The
foreign policy of African countries should in any case be guided only
by the principles of a most rigorous positive neutralism. African
countries must therefore free themselves from partnership in any
foreign national groupings which are not compatible with African
positive neutralism.[13]

That was before the Organization of African Unity was
founded. Shortly after the Kenyatta Conciliation Commission of
the OAU had failed to bring peace to the Congo in 1964, the
seventh congress of the Fédération des Étudiants d'Afrique
Noire en France (FEANF) – Federation of African Students in
France – was held. At that congress the students not only condemned the OAU's failure but also accused the organization of
being 'under the dominant influence of international imperialism
and reactionary African states'. A few weeks afterwards the
executive committee of the Pan-African Students' Movement,
meeting at Algiers, 'stigmatized the appeal of the OAU for
national reconciliation [in the Congo] as playing the imperialist
game and tending to demobilize Congolese patriots'.[14]

The third annual conference of the Pan-African Students
Movement, held at Nairobi in August 1967, adopted a constitution, whose preamble advocated the following as pre-conditions
for the achievement of African Unity: (a) the rupture of all
organic and institutional links with the former colonial and other
imperialist powers; (b) the liquidation of all foreign bases in
Africa; (c) the winding-up of foreign monopolies in African
countries; (d) the organization of democratic institutions,
assuring control by the popular masses of national construction
to the full satisfaction of their aspirations and their rights.[15]

Immediately after the Portuguese invasion of Guinea in
November 1970, students and other intellectuals throughout
Pan-Africa engaged themselves in strong protest actions. Even in
the Ivory Coast, students came out in support of Guinea.[16]

Such activities show that African youth are not prepared to

340

accept the lukewarm attitude shown by many leaders towards Pan-Africanism. They are more dynamic, and prefer continental unity to sectional or inordinate personal ambitions. This, however, entails much sacrifice, since some of the present leaders have reacted with anxiety and anger.

In August 1959, President Maurice Yameogo of the Upper Volta thought it his duty to address the Voltaic students thus, after they had made a series of 'militant and critical' speeches at their annual congress:

During the whole of this conference you have behaved like spoiled children. I was perfectly well aware what was said every day upon this platform, but I have held back and allowed this congress to go on to its end, to prove first that democracy is not an empty word in Upper Volta, then to know exactly what is biting you. I have this to say to you: you have amused yourselves nicely, you have spat well on everybody, but now the fun and games are over, for your brothers of the Volta labour daily to pay for your studies and not to launch you upon a criminal enterprise of demolition. Even if you have discovered the word liberty you do not yet know what it means; you take your ideas from the newspaper *L'Humanité*;[17] you are soaked in everything which cannot be said to men, for you are only children. I will not take your insults; if you have no self-respect at least respect your elders.[18]

Others have taken severe measures against youth. Student leaders have been expelled from the universities. In July 1961 the Ivory Coast Government of Félix Houphouet-Boigny imprisoned eight students expelled from France for their 'left-wing activities', and then offered to release them in January 1962, if they would acknowledge the sole authority of the National Union, which it had hurriedly set up itself to displace the real Students' National Union. At the end of 1963 the same government announced that in future Ivory Coast students in France or the Ivory Coast would have to belong to a single students' union, with headquarters in Abidjan. The announcement made it clear that students who did not belong to the union would neither receive state aid for their education nor be offered jobs by the state on completion of their studies. Addressing student representatives early in 1965, President Houphouet-Boigny declared: 'You are either with us in the bosom of the party . . . or you are against us and we will fight you.'[19] When, in November 1970, students at the University of Abidjan demonstrated in support of Guinea, shortly after the Portuguese invasion of that country, the Ivory Coast Government expelled many of them.[20] Many other African governments have been guilty of such high-handedness during the last decade. Others have tried to placate the young by buying them off with posts and other enticements.

And there is another source of trouble for youth. If they study abroad, every effort is made to brainwash them; and if that fails they are usually described as 'communists', with certain organ-izations compiling dossiers on them.[21] Some foreign govern-ments have been so used to manipulating African leaders that they and their nationals have come to believe that every African is vulnerable to easy manipulation. Disappointment at being unable to turn youth into educated imbeciles leads to calling them 'communists'. But the matter does not end there. Reports upon them are prepared and submitted to their home governments under the guise of 'technical assistance'. Sometimes those African leaders who want to maintain their position of authority and who, in any case, are used to accepting any form of 'foreign advice', take such reports at their face value.

As a result of these pressures, some of the young determined Pan-Africanists may well fall by the wayside. Some may be bought off by their governments through special inducements. But there will always remain a hard core who will grow to become:

> Men whom the lust of office does not kill,
> Men whom the spoils of office cannot buy,
> Men who possess opinions and a will
> Men who have honour . . .[22]

It is this core of dedicated Pan-Africanists who will show the light, so that the people may find the way. It is this group that will, in the end, lead Pan-Africanism to its final objective: African unity, with the establishment of a United States of Africa.

Notes to Chapter 7

1. 'United We Stand' – address delivered by Osagyefo, Dr Kwame Nkrumah, president of the Republic of Ghana, at the Conference of African Heads of State and Government in Addis Ababa on 24 May 1963 (supplement to *Ghana To-day* of 5 June 1963, p. 3).
2. See Economic Commission for Africa, *Industrial Growth in Africa – A Survey and Outlook* (E/CN.14/INR/1), December 1962, Appendix III.
3. ECA, *Co-ordination of Development Plans in Africa* (E/CN.14/239 B), 1964, p. 29.
4. See UNIDO Monographs on Industrial Development, especially UN Publication Sales No. E.69 II.B.39, Vol. 18, ID/40/18 – 'Regional Co-operation in Industry'.
5. For the report of the conference, and the declaration on industrialization in the 1970s adopted, see ECA: *Report of the ECA/OAU Conference of Ministers of Industry*, Addis Ababa, 3–7 May 1971 (E/CN/525, E/CN.14/INR/194; OAU/CM1/W/9), 8 May 1971.
6. 'The United Kingdom and the European Communities', Government White Paper Cmnd. 4715, 7 July 1971.
7. ibid., paragraph 33.
8. ibid., paragraph 47.
9. ibid., paragraph 48.
10. ibid., paragraph 60.
11. *Ghana Daily Graphic*, 16 April 1958.
12. For an account of Assouan-Usher's actions, see the *Financial Times*, 16 June 1971.
13. Quoted from Basil Davidson, *Which Way Africa?*, Penguin Books, Harmondsworth, 1967, pp. 65–6.
14. Immanuel Wallerstein, *Africa and the Politics of Unity*, Pall Mall Press, London, 1968, p. 216.
15. ibid.
16. For inside knowledge of Ivory Coast politics under President Houphouet-Boigny, see *East African Standard*, 2 October 1964, p. 9, and 3 December 1970, p. 12; also Michael Wolfer's article, 'Future of the Ivory Coast – Post-colonial dilemma', *The Times*, 19 May 1971.
17. *L'Humanité* is the French Communist newspaper.
18. Quoted from Ken Post, *The New States of West Africa*, Penguin Books, Harmondsworth, 1964, pp. 80–1.
19. *West Africa*, 9 January 1965, p. 39.
20. See *West Africa*, 12–18 December 1970, p. 1451; and 26 December 1970 to 1 January 1971, p. 1520.
21. The CIA, which arrogates to itself the right to tell African students in Western Germany what they should or should not do, has kept a complete dossier in both Frankfurt/Main and West Berlin (Dahlem) on all the officers of the African Students' League (Afrikanischer Studenten-

bund e.V.) in Germany at both local and federal levels ever since that organization was founded in 1962. The reason is that the League does not allow itself to be easily manipulated and is regarded as too 'Nkrumah-istic' (Pan-African) in outlook and objectives.

22. Josiah Gilbert Holland, *The Complete Poetical Writings*, 1879, p. 472.

Appendix I. Declaration of Rights of the Negro Peoples of the World

drafted and adopted at the convention held in New York, 1920, over which Marcus Garvey presided as chairman, and at which he was elected Provisional President of Africa

(Preamble)

Be it Resolved, That the Negro people of the world, through their chosen representatives in convention assembled in Liberty Hall, in the City of New York, and the United States of America, from August 1 to August 31, in the year of our Lord, one thousand nine hundred and twenty, protest against the wrongs and injustices they are suffering at the hands of their white brethren, and state what they deem their fair and just rights, as well as the treatment they propose to demand of all men in the future.

We complain:

I. That nowhere in the world, with few exceptions, are black men accorded equal treatment with white men, although in the same situation and circumstances, but, on the contrary, are discriminated against and denied the common rights due to human beings for no other reason than their race and color.

We are not willingly accepted as guests in the public hotels and inns of the world for no other reason than our race and color.

II. In certain parts of the United States of America our race is denied the right of public trial accorded to other races when accused of crime, but are lynched and burned by mobs, and such brutal and inhuman treatment is even practised upon our women.

III. That European nations have parcelled out among themselves and taken possession of nearly all of the continent of Africa, and the natives are compelled to surrender their lands to aliens and are treated in most instances like slaves.

IV. In the southern portion of the United States of America, although citizens under the Federal Constitution, and in some states almost equal to the whites in population and are qualified land owners and taxpayers, we are, nevertheless denied all voice in the making and administration of the laws and are taxed without representation by the state governments, and at the same time compelled to do military service in defense of the country.

V. On the public conveyances and common carriers in the Southern portion of the United States we are jim-crowed and compelled to accept separate and inferior accommodations and made to pay the same fare charged for first-class accommodations, and our families are often humiliated and insulted by drunken white men who habitually pass through the jim-crow cars going to the smoking car.

VI. The physicians of our race are denied the right to attend their patients while in the public hospitals of the cities and states where they reside in certain parts of the United States.

Our children are forced to attend inferior separate schools for shorter terms than white children, and the public school funds are unequally divided between the white and colored schools.

VII. We are discriminated against and denied an equal chance to earn wages for the support of our families, and in many instances are refused admission into labor unions, and nearly everywhere are paid smaller wages than white men.

VIII. In Civil Service and departmental offices we are everywhere discriminated against and made to feel that to be a black man in Europe, America and the West Indies is equivalent to being an outcast and a leper among the races of men, no matter what the character and attainments of the black man may be.

IX. In the British and other West Indian Islands and colonies, Negroes are secretly and cunningly discriminated against, and denied those fuller rights in governments to which white citizens are appointed, nominated and elected.

X. That our people in those parts are forced to work for lower wages than the average standard of white men and are kept in conditions repugnant to good civilized tastes and customs.

XI. That the many acts of injustice against members of our race before the courts of law in the respective islands and colonies are of such a nature as to create disgust and disrespect for the white man's sense of justice.

XII. Against all such inhuman, unchristian and uncivilized treatment we here and now emphatically protest, and invoke the condemnation of all mankind.

In order to encourage our race all over the world and to

stimulate it to a higher and grander destiny, we demand and insist on the following Declaration of Rights:

1. 'Be it known to all men that whereas, all men are created equal and entitled to the rights of life, liberty and the pursuit of happiness, and because of this we, the duly elected representatives of the Negro peoples of the world, invoking the aid of the just and Almighty God, do declare all men, women, and children of our blood throughout the world free citizens, and do claim them as free citizens of Africa, the Motherland of all Negroes.

2. 'That we believe in the supreme authority of our race in all things racial; that all things are created and given to man as a common possession; that there should be an equitable distribution and apportionment of all such things, and in consideration of the fact that as a race we are now deprived of those things that are morally and legally ours, we believe it right that all such things should be acquired and held by whatsoever means possible.

3. 'That we believe the Negro, like any other race, should be governed by those rights or privileges common to other human beings.

4. 'We declare that Negroes, wheresoever they form a community among themselves, should be given the right to elect their own representatives to represent them in legislatures, courts of law, or such institutions as may exercise control over that particular community.

5. 'We assert that the Negro is entitled to even-handed justice before all courts of law and equity in whatever country he may be found, and when this is denied him on account of his race or color such a denial is an insult to the race as a whole and should be resented by the entire body of Negroes.

6. 'We declare it unfair and prejudicial to the rights of Negroes in communities where they exist in considerable numbers to be tried by a judge and jury composed entirely of an alien race, but in all such cases members of our race are entitled to representation on the jury.

7. 'We believe that any law or practice that tends to deprive any African of his land or the privileges of free citizenship within his country is unjust and immoral, and no native should respect any such law or practice.

8. 'We declare taxation without representation unjust and tyrannous, and there should be no obligation on the part of the Negro to obey the levy of a tax by any law-making body from which he is excluded and denied representation on account of his race and color.

9. 'We believe that any law especially directed against the Negro to

his detriment and singling him out because of his race or color is unfair and immoral, and should not be respected.

10. 'We believe all men entitled to common human respect and that our race should in no way tolerate any insults that may be interpreted to mean disrespect to our color.

11. 'We deprecate the use of the term "nigger" as applied to Negroes, and demand that the word "Negro" be written with a capital "N".

12. 'We believe that the Negro should adopt every means to protect himself against barbarous practices inflicted upon him because of color.

13. 'We believe in the freedom of Africa for the Negro people of the world, and by the principle of Europe for the Europeans and Asia for the Asiatics; we also demand Africa for the Africans at home and abroad.

14. 'We believe in the inherent right of the Negro to possess himself of Africa, and that his possession of same shall not be regarded as infringement on any claim or purchase made by any race or nation.

15. 'We strongly condemn the cupidity of those nations of the world who, by open aggression or secret schemes, have seized the territories and inexhaustible wealth of Africa, and we place on record our most solemn determination to reclaim the treasures and possessions of the vast continent of our forefathers.

16. 'We believe that all men should live in peace one with the other, but when races and nations provoke the ire of other races and nations by attempting to infringe upon their rights, war becomes inevitable, and the attempt in any way to free one's self or protect one's rights or heritage becomes justifiable.

17. 'Whereas, the lynching, by burning, hanging or any other means, of human beings is a barbarous practice, and a shame and disgrace to civilization, we therefore declare any country guilty of such atrocities outside the pale of civilization.

18. 'We protest against the atrocious crime of whipping, flogging and over-working of the native tribes of Africa and Negroes everywhere. These are methods that should be abolished, and all means should be taken to prevent a continuance of such brutal practices.

19. 'We protest against the atrocious practice of shaving the heads of Africans, especially of African women or individuals of Negro blood, when placed in prison as a punishment for a crime by an alien race.

20. 'We protest against segregated districts, separate public conveyances, industrial discrimination, lynchings and limitations of politi-

cal privileges of any Negro citizen in any part of the world on account of race, color or creed, and will exert our full influence and power against all such.

21. 'We protest against any punishment inflicted upon a Negro with severity, as against lighter punishment inflicted upon another of an alien race for like offense, as an act of prejudice and injustice, and it should be resented by the entire race.

22. 'We protest against the system of education in any country where Negroes are denied the same privileges and advantages as other races.

23. 'We declare it inhuman and unfair to boycott Negroes from industries and labor in any part of the world.

24. 'We believe in the doctrine of the freedom of the press, and we therefore emphatically protest against the suppression of Negro newspapers and periodicals in various parts of the world, and call upon Negroes everywhere to employ all available means to prevent such suppression.

25. 'We further demand free speech universally for all men.

26. 'We hereby protest against the publication of scandalous and inflammatory articles by an alien press tending to create racial strife and the exhibition of picture films showing the Negro as a cannibal.

27. 'We believe in the self-determination of all peoples.

28. 'We declare for the freedom of religious worship.

29. 'With the help of Almighty God, we declare ourselves the sworn protectors of the honor and virtue of our women and children, and pledge our lives for their protection and defense everywhere, and under all circumstances from wrongs and outrages.

30. 'We demand the right of unlimited and unprejudiced education for ourselves and our posterity forever.

31. 'We declare that the teaching in any school by alien teachers to our boys and girls, that the alien race is superior to the Negro race, is an insult to the Negro people of the world.

32. 'Where Negroes form a part of citizenry of any country, and pass the civil service examination of such country, we declare them entitled to the same consideration as other citizens as to appointments in such civil service.

33. 'We vigorously protest against the increasingly unfair and unjust treatment accorded Negro travelers on land and sea by the agents and employees of railroad and steamship companies and insist that for equal fare we receive equal privileges with travelers of other races.

Appendix 1

34. 'We declare it unjust for any country, state or nation to enact laws tending to hinder and obstruct the free immigration of Negroes on account of their race and color.

35. 'That the right of the Negro to travel unmolested throughout the world be not abridged by any person or persons, and all Negroes are called upon to give aid to a fellow Negro when thus molested.

36. 'We declare that all Negroes are entitled to the same right to travel over the world as other men.

37. 'We hereby demand that the governments of the world recognize our leader and his representatives chosen by the race to look after the welfare under such governments.

38. 'We demand complete control of our social institutions without interference by any alien race or races.

39. 'That the colors, Red, Black and Green, be the colors of the Negro race.

40. 'Resolved, That the anthem "Ethiopia, Thou Land of Our Fathers," etc., shall be the anthem of the Negro race.

THE UNIVERSAL ETHIOPIAN ANTHEM
(Poem by Burrell and Ford)

I

Ethiopia, thou land of our fathers,
Thou land where the gods loved to be,
As storm cloud at night suddenly gathers
Our armies come rushing to thee.
We must in the fight be victorious
When swords are thrust outward to gleam;
For us will the vict'ry be glorious
When led by the red, black and green.

Chorus:

Advance, advance to victory,
Let Africa be free;
Advance to meet the foe
With the might
Of the red, the black and the green.

II

Ethiopia, the tyrant's falling,
Who smote thee upon the knees,
And thy children are lustily calling
From over the distant seas.
Jehovah, the Great One, has heard us,
Has noted our sighs and our tears,
With His spirit of Love He has stirred us
To be One through the coming years.

Chorus – Advance, advance, etc.

III

O, Jehovah, thou God of the ages,
Grant unto our sons that lead
The wisdom Thou gave to Thy sages,
When Israel was sore in need.
Thy voice thro' the dim past has spoken,
Ethiopia shall stretch forth her hand,
By Thee shall all fetters be broken,
And Heav'n bless our dear fatherland.

Chorus – Advance, advance, etc.

41. 'We believe that any limited liberty which deprives one of the complete rights and prerogatives of full citizenship is but a modified form of slavery.

42. 'We declare it an injustice to our people and a serious impediment to the health of the race to deny to competent licensed Negro physicians the right to practise in the public hospitals of the communities in which they reside, for no other reason than their race and color.

43. 'We call upon the various governments of the world to accept and acknowledge Negro representatives who shall be sent to the said governments to represent the general welfare of the Negro peoples of the world.

44. 'We deplore and protest against the practice of confining juvenile prisoners in prisons with adults, and we recommend that such youthful prisoners be taught gainful trades under humane supervision.

45. 'Be it further resolved, that we as a race of people declare the

351

League of Nations null and void as far as the Negro is concerned, in that it seeks to deprive Negroes of their liberty.

46. 'We demand of all men to do unto us as we would do unto them, in the name of justice; and we cheerfully accord to all men all the rights we claim herein for ourselves.

47. 'We declare that no Negro shall engage himself in battle for an alien race without first obtaining the consent of the leader of the Negro people of the world, except in a matter of national self-defense.

48. 'We protest against the practice of drafting Negroes and sending them to war with alien forces without proper training, and demand in all cases that Negro soldiers be given the same training as the aliens.

49. 'We demand that instructions given Negro children in schools include the subject of "Negro History", to their benefit.

50. 'We demand a free and unfettered commercial intercourse with all the Negro people of the world.

51. 'We declare for the absolute freedom of the seas for all peoples.

52. 'We demand that our duly accredited representatives be given proper recognition in all leagues, conferences, conventions or courts of international arbitration wherever human rights are discussed.

53. 'We proclaim the 31st day of August of each year to be an international holiday observed by all Negroes.

54. 'We want all men to know we shall maintain and contend for the freedom and equality of every man, woman and child of our race with our lives, our fortunes and our sacred honor.

'These rights we believe to be justly ours and proper for the protection of the Negro race at large, and because of this belief we, on behalf of the four hundred million Negroes of the world, do pledge herein the sacred blood of the race in defense, and we hereby subscribe our names as a guarantee of the truthfulness and faithfulness hereof in the presence of Almighty God, on the 13th day of August, in the year of our Lord, one thousand nine hundred and twenty.'

Appendix 2. The Casablanca Conference
3–7 January 1961

I. THE AFRICAN CHARTER OF CASABLANCA

We, the Heads of the African States, meeting in Casablanca from January 3 to January 7, 1961, conscious of our responsibilities towards the African Continent, proclaim our determination to promote the triumph of liberty all over Africa and to achieve its unity,

Affirm our will to preserve and consolidate our identity of views and unity of action in international affairs, to safeguard our hard won independence, the sovereignty and territorial integrity of our States, to reinforce peace in the world by adopting a policy of non alignment,

Proclaim our determination to liberate the African territories still under foreign domination, by giving them aid and assistance, to liquidate colonialism and neo-colonialism in all their forms, to discourage the maintenance of foreign troops and the establishment of bases which endanger the liberation of Africa and to strive equally to rid the African Continent of political and economic interventions and pressures,

Proclaim the necessity for the Independent African States to direct their political, economic and social policies to the exploitation of the national wealth for the benefit of their peoples and to ensuring an equitable distribution of that wealth among all nationals,

Affirm our will to intensify our efforts for the creation of an effective form of co-operation among the African States in the economic, social and cultural domains,

Aiming at the consolidation of liberty in Africa and building up its unity and security, decide:

1. The creation of an African Consultative Assembly, as soon as conditions permit, composed of the representatives of every African State, having a permanent seat and holding periodical sessions,

2. The creation of the following four committees:

(a) The African Political Committee, comprising Heads of State, or their duly accredited representatives, will meet periodically with a view to co-ordinating and unifying the general policy of the various African States;

353

(b) The African Economic Committee, comprising the Ministers of Economic Affairs of the Independent African States, will meet periodically with a view to taking decisions with regard to African Economic Co-operation. One of the most urgent tasks of this Committee will be to establish postal and telecommunication links among the various African Capitals;

(c) The African Cultural Committee, comprising the Ministers of Education of the Independent African States, will meet periodically with a view to preserving and developing African culture and civilisation and intensifying African cultural co-operation and assistance;

(d) A Joint African High Command, comprising the Chiefs of Staff of the Independent African States, will meet periodically with a view to ensuring the common defence of Africa in case of aggression against any part of this Continent, and with a view to safeguarding the independence of African States,

3. The creation of a liaison office for establishing effective co-operation among the different organisations mentioned above and particularly for the holding within three months of a meeting of experts charged with defining the practical procedure concerning the functioning of the organisations in question.

We, the Heads of African States, convened in Casablanca from the 3rd January to the 7th January, 1961, reaffirm our faith in the Conferences of the Independent African States, held in Accra in 1958 and in Addis Ababa in 1960, and appeal to all Independent African States to associate themselves with our common action for the consolidation of liberty in Africa and the building up of its unity and security.

We solemnly reaffirm our unshakeable adherence to the United Nations Charter and to the Declaration of the Afro–Asian Conference held in Bandung, with the aim of promoting co-operation among all the peoples of the world and of consolidating international peace.

2. RESOLUTIONS

RESOLUTION ON PALESTINE

The Conference at Casablanca,

Having examined the important problem of Palestine, and deeply concerned about the situation created in Palestine by depriving the Arabs of Palestine of their legitimate rights:

1. Warns against the menace which this situation presents to the peace and security of the Middle East and the international tension which results therefrom.

2. Insists on the necessity to have a just solution to this problem in conformity with the United Nations resolutions and the Asian African resolution of Bandung to restore to the Arabs of Palestine all their legitimate rights.

3. Notes with indignation that Israel has always taken the side of the imperialists each time an important position had to be taken concerning vital problems about Africa, notably Algeria, the Congo and the nuclear tests in Africa, and the Conference, therefore, denounces Israel as an instrument in the service of imperialism and neo-colonialism not only in the Middle East but also in Africa and Asia.

4. Calls upon all the States of Africa and Asia to oppose this new policy which imperialism is carrying out to create bases for itself.

RESOLUTION ON MAURITANIA
The Conference,

Considering the colonialist intrigues aimed at dividing the territories of the African States in order to weaken them;

Considering that France, in order to strengthen her domination over the Sahara, exploits its wealth and secures for herself an outlet on the Atlantic, has severed from Morocco the southern portion of her territory, in Mauritania;

Considering that the setting up of a puppet State, the said Mauritania, against the will of the people concerned, and in disregard of the solemn undertakings given by France, is a violation of international treaties and agreements;

Considering that the setting up of Mauritania as a puppet State is merely a means for France to encircle the African countries, secure for herself bases to which she can retreat, and increase the number of her satellites;

Considering that, in general, the increase in the number of artificial States in Africa is a permanent threat to the security of the African Continent, and, at the same time, a strengthening of the forces of imperialism;

Considering that the objective aimed at by France in Mauritania is the economic exploitation and strategic use of this area, particularly against the African countries, as well as the maintenance of artificial barriers in Africa;

Considering that the defence of the unity and territorial integrity of all African States is, at the same time, the defence of the freedom of Africa;

Solemnly denounces and condemns all forms of economic, political and military exploitation in Africa;

355

Appendix 2

Declares its determination to oppose, by all possible means, every attempt to partition and create satellite States in certain parts of the African Continent;

Approves any action taken by Morocco on Mauritania for the restitution of her legitimate rights.

RESOLUTION ON RUANDA–URUNDI

With regard to the Trust Territory of Ruanda–Urundi, the Conference denounces Belgium's attempts to divide this country by creating two pseudo-independent States established by a policy of organised repression against the nationalist elements of this country.

The Conference supports unreservedly the cause of the people of Ruanda–Urundi in their struggle for real independence and urges the implementation of the resolutions passed by the General Assembly of the United Nations at its Fifteenth Session concerning the future of Ruanda–Urundi and the constitutional regime of Ruanda–Urundi, namely:

> A general and unconditional amnesty for all those involved in the incidents which occurred in November, 1959;
> The lifting of the state of emergency and the restoration of democratic liberties and fundamental human rights;
> The immediate return of all political refugees;
> A national reconciliation;
> The safeguard of the national unity and the protection of the territorial integrity of this country.

The Conference denounces the use of the territory of Ruanda–Urundi as a base for aggression against African peoples and the Congo in particular.

The Conference demands the immediate evacuation of all Belgian forces stationed in this territory and the restoration of an atmosphere of peace and security.

RESOLUTION ON APARTHEID AND RACIAL DISCRIMINATION

The Casablanca Conference,

Recalling the resolutions of the United Nations Organisation which denounced the Apartheid policy and the racial discrimination practised by the Government of the Union of South Africa, and

Recalling in particular the resolution of the Security Council of the 1st of April, 1960, which considers the policy of racial discrimination

pursued by the Government of the Union of South Africa as a threat
to world peace and security,

1. Denounces the Government of the Union of South Africa for
its contempt of the decisions taken by the United Nations Organisation and by the African and Asian Conferences and condemns its
obstinacy in pursuing a policy which affects human dignity and
constitutes a flagrant violation of human rights;
2. Denounces the imperialist Powers who continue to lend moral,
political and military support to the racialist Government of the
Union of South Africa;
3. Reaffirms and undertakes to implement the decisions taken at
the Bandung, Accra, Monrovia and Addis Ababa Conferences on this
subject and urges all African States to implement these decisions;
4. Calls upon the United Nations Organisation to invoke the
sanctions provided for in Articles 40 and 41 of the United Nations
Charter should the Government of the Union of South Africa not
put an end to its policy of racial discrimination.

RESOLUTION ON NUCLEAR TESTS

The Conference,

Vigorously opposes the carrying out of nuclear tests by France on
the African continent, in spite of the outraged conscience of the world,
the disapproval of African countries, and the recommendations of the
United Nations;

Strongly denounces this act of provocation directed against the
African peoples, with a view to intimidating them and hindering their
march towards the attainment of freedom and unity, and is a permanent danger for the African peoples and a constant threat to world peace;

Denounces and condemns the collusion between France and Israel
in regard to nuclear tests, a collusion which threatens peace in the
world and particularly in Africa;

Appeals to all peoples and in particular to the peoples of Africa who
are most directly threatened, to do everything in their power to prevent
these tests from taking place, and oppose the use of African territories
for purposes of political domination;

Having noted with satisfaction the refusal by the people of France to
allow these tests to take place on their own soil;

Invites all African countries to reconsider their relations with France,
faced as they are with France's obstinate insistence on carrying out
atomic explosions in Africa.

Appendix 2

RESOLUTION ON ALGERIA

The Conference,

Considering that the fifteenth session of the United Nations has recognised the right of the Algerian people to Independence and Self-Determination on the basis of the unity and territorial integrity of Algeria, as well as the responsibility of the United Nations in the implementation of the right in Algeria;

Considering that all political, diplomatic and material aid given to the Algerian people represents a contribution to the liberation of Africa;

Considering that every assistance given to France in her war in Algeria constitutes an act of hostility directed against Africa as a whole;

Considering that the Provisional Government of the Algerian Republic is the only authority qualified to represent and speak on behalf of Algeria;

Considering that the war pursued by France in Algeria constitutes an increasing threat to peace and security in Africa and the world;

Considering that the events and demonstrations which are taking place and developing in Algeria constitute the unequivocal affirmation of the will of the Algerian people to realise their Independence, and of their unanimity in support of the Provisional Government of the Algerian Republic;

Declares its determination to support by all means the Algerian people and the Provisional Government of the Algerian Republic in their struggle for the Independence of Algeria;

Calls upon all the countries which support the Algerian people in their struggle for national liberation to re-enforce their political, diplomatic and material aid to the Provisional Government of the Algerian Republic;

Denounces the assistance given by NATO to France in her war of colonial reconquest in Algeria;

Invites all countries to take steps forthwith to prevent their territories from being used directly or indirectly for operations against the Algerian people;

Calls for the immediate withdrawal of all African troops serving under French command in Algeria;

Approves the enlistment of African and other volunteers in the Army of National Liberation;

Invites all the Governments which have not done so to recognise the Provisional Government of the Algerian Republic;

358

Declares that the continuation of the war in Algeria is of such nature that it impels the participating countries to reconsider their relations with France;

Opposes the partition of Algeria and rejects any unilateral solution and any constitution either imposed or granted.

DECLARATION

The Conference denounces and condemns all consultations and references unilaterally organised by France in Algeria, and the results thereof can in no way commit the Algerian people.

3. COMMUNIQUÉ

CONCERNING THE SITUATION IN THE CONGO

The Conference at Casablanca convened by His Majesty King Mohammed V of the Kingdom of Morocco, and constituted by the following Heads of States, namely His Majesty King Mohammed V of the Kingdom of Morocco, His Excellency Gamal Abdel Nasser, President of the United Arab Republic, His Excellency Kwame Nkrumah, President of the Republic of Ghana, His Excellency Sékou Touré, President of the Republic of Guinea, His Excellency Modibo Keita, President of the Republic of Mali, His Excellency Ferhat Abbas, Prime Minister of the Provisional Government of Algeria representing the Provisional Government of Algeria, His Excellency Abdelkader El Allam, Minister of Foreign Affairs representing His Majesty King Idris I of the Kingdom of Libya and His Excellency Alwin B. Perera, Ambassador Extraordinary and Plenipotentiary representing the Prime Minister of Ceylon, having considered the situation in the Congo:

1. Declares the intention and determination of the respective Governments represented to withdraw their troops and other military personnel placed under the United Nations Operational Command in the Congo.

2. Reaffirms their recognition of the elected Parliament and legally constituted Government of the Republic of the Congo which came into being on 30th of June, 1960.

3. Convinced that the only justification for the presence of the United Nations troops in the Congo is:

(i) To answer the appeals of the legitimate Government of the Republic of the Congo at whose request the United Nations decided to create its Operational Command;

(ii) To implement the decisions of the Security Council in respect of the situation in the Congo;

(iii) To safeguard the unity and independence of the Republic of the Congo and preserve its territorial integrity;

Urges the United Nations to act immediately to:

(a) Disarm and disband the lawless bands of Mobutu;

(b) Release from prison and detention all members of the Parliament and legitimate Government of the Republic of the Congo;

(c) Reconvene the Parliament of the Republic of the Congo;

(d) Eliminate from the Congo all Belgian and other foreign military and para-military personnel not belonging to the United Nations Operational Command whether operating as such or in disguise;

(e) Release to the legitimate Government of the Congo all civil and military airports, radio-stations and other establishments, now unlawfully withheld from that Government;

(f) Prevent the Belgians from using the United Nations Trust Territory of Ruanda–Urundi as a base to commit aggression – direct or indirect – to launch armed attacks against the Congolese Republic.

4. Decides that if the purposes and principles which justified the presence of the United Nations Operational Command in the Republic of the Congo are not realised and respected then the States here represented reserve the right to take appropriate action.

Appendix 3. The Monrovia Conference
8–12 May 1961

The means of promoting better understanding and co-operation
towards achieving unity in Africa and Madagascar

The Conference of Heads of States and Governments of Africa and
Malagasy meeting at Monrovia from 8th to 12th May, 1961:

RECOGNIZING the historic importance of the Monrovia Conference, because of the number of participating states;

NOTING with deep regret the absence of some of our sister states;

CONFIDENT in their intense desire for African solidarity and
expressing the hope that they may find it convenient to attend subsequent meetings;

ANXIOUS to promote henceforth a full and brotherly co-operation
between Independent Africa and Malagasy States;

CONSIDERING the need for pooling resources and co-ordinating
efforts in order to overcome the barriers of growth which confront all
African and Malagasy countries on their way to development;

A. Solemnly affirms and adopts the following principles which shall
govern the relationship between the African and Malagasy States:

(i) Absolute equality of African and Malagasy States whatever may
be the size of their territories, the density of their populations, or
the value of their possessions;
(ii) Non-interference in the internal affairs of other states;
(iii) Respect for the sovereignty of each state and inalienable right to
existence and development of its personality;
(iv) Unqualified condemnation of outside subversive action by
neighbouring states;
(v) Promotion of co-operation throughout Africa, based upon
tolerance, solidarity and good-neighbour relations, periodical
exchange of views, and non-acceptance of any leadership;
(vi) The unity that is aimed to be achieved at the moment is not the
political integration of sovereign African States, but unity of
aspirations and of action considered from the point of view of
African social solidarity and political identity;

B. Urges that all African and Malagasy States shall refrain from encouraging, directly or indirectly, dissident groups or individuals of other states in subversive activities by permitting their own states to be used as bases from which such dissidents may operate, or by financing dissidents in other countries or otherwise;

C. Accepts, in principle, that an inter-African and Malagasy Advisory Organization shall be created, the essential purpose of which shall be to put into effect the above-mentioned principles and to establish this organization at the next conference;

D. Decides that a technical commission of experts designated by the respective states shall be created and that these experts shall meet in Dakar, Senegal within three months after the close of this conference for the purpose of working out detailed plans for economic, educational, cultural, scientific and technical co-operation, as well as for communications and transportation among African and Malagasy States;

And that the existing research and technical institutions should constitute effective machinery for the collection of data and the dissemination of the results of research among African and Malagasy States, and that all states shall so direct;

And that all African and Malagasy States shall recognize the desire to promote the revival of African culture and traditions in the interest of preserving the real African heritage;

And that all African and Malagasy States shall make a special effort to include in addition to their respective national and official languages the teaching of the French and English languages;

E. Decides, finally, that the next Conference of Heads of African and Malagasy States shall be held in Lagos, Nigeria.

RESOLUTION II

Threats to Peace and Stability in Africa and the World

The Conference was profoundly disturbed by the serious threats which hang over peace and stability in Africa and the world.

Considering that the principle of non-interference in the domestic affairs of African States applies only to States already independent and sovereign, the conference affirms its unanimous determination to give material and moral assistance to all dependent territories of colonial powers with a view to accelerating their accession to independence.

The conference, as concerns the Algerian question, welcomes the improvement of the situation in Algeria and the decision of the two parties to open negotiations on 20th May, 1961; and appeals to the Government of France and the Provisional Government of the Algerian Republic to conclude at the earliest moment an agreement putting an end to the war and accord to Algeria its independence and territorial integrity.

The conference, as concerns the Congo, re-affirms its faith in the United Nations as the only organisation which, in spite of past weaknesses and mistakes in its work, is best adapted to achieve a real solution of the Congo problem;

CALLS on all African States to desist from such activities as the hasty recognition of break-away regimes in the Republic of the Congo, and generally from taking sides with rival groups in any form or manner;

CONDEMNS assassinations as a means to attain political power;

CONDEMNS the action of certain non-African States which encourage subversion in other African States.

The conference, as concerns Angola, calls on all African and Malagasy States to pledge their whole-hearted material and moral support to the Africans in Angola in their struggle for autonomy;

APPEALS to the universal conscience against the atrocities and the bloody repression of the Angolan population.

The conference, as regards the Union of South Africa, condemns unreservedly the theory and practice of apartheid by the Government of the Union of South Africa;

CALLS on all African and Malagasy States to apply immediately political and economic sanctions, collectively and individually, against the Government of the Union of South Africa, not only to demonstrate our resentment of the ruthless degradation of the non-whites there, but also ultimately to compel the Government of the Union of South Africa to abandon the iniquitous practice of apartheid;

CALLS on all African and Malagasy States to take all necessary steps to give all material and moral support to the Africans and Asians of South Africa in their struggle to regain the stature of man;

AFFIRMS that all the participating African States strongly support the reiterated decision of the Trusteeship Council of the United Nations that the Government of the Union of South Africa must acknowledge the authority of the council as guardian of the mandate over the Territory of South-West Africa.

The conference, as concerns disarmament, appeals to all the nuclear powers to stop the manufacture and stock-piling of nuclear weapons and all further nuclear explosions anywhere in the world;

DECIDES that the chairman should make a written appeal in the name of the conference to the Commission on Nuclear Disarmament, now in session in Geneva, to use their best endeavours to secure the objective stated in the preceding paragraph;

NOTES the assurances given by the French Government that they will cease all further explosions in Africa.

The conference, as concerns the United Nations, urges the members of the United Nations to assure a more equitable geographical distribution of the seats of the Security and the Economic and Social Council and also to work for the expansion of the councils;

Decides to send a cablegram to members of the Security Council asking them to take a decision in favour of the admission of Mauritania in the United Nations Organisation in conformity with the last resolution of the General Assembly;

CONDEMNS all attempts to weaken or undermine the authority of the United Nations;

RECORDS the intention of all African and Malagasy States to present a united front in the future, to all world problems with which Africa might be faced at the United Nations.

RESOLUTION III

Settlement of Conflicts which may arise between African States

This Conference of Heads of African and Malagasy States and Governments, meeting at Monrovia from 8th to 12th May, 1961, recommends:

(i) That the settlement of disputes shall be by peaceful means;
(ii) That a commission shall be created which shall be attached to the Organization of Co-operation of the African and Malagasy States;
(iii) That this conference unanimously resolve that a written appeal be made through the executive authority of the present conference to His Imperial Majesty the Emperor of Ethiopia and His Excellency the President of Somalia to make renewed efforts toward a sincere and early solution of all their existing frontier and any other disputes.

Appendix 4. The Protocol of the African Charter 5 May 1961

In compliance with their determination to implement the African Charter issued at the Casablanca conference, which was held between 3rd and 7th January, 1961, and in accordance with the provisions of the said Charter; the Governments of the African States which signed the Charter agree to this protocol:

Article 1. Co-operation among the member States of the Charter shall be conducted through the following bodies: (a) an African Political Committee; (b) an African Economic Committee; (c) an African Cultural Committee; (d) an African Joint High Command; and (e) a Liaison Office. These bodies which carry out the provisions of the Charter shall have a permanent character.

Article 2. The African Political Committee. The African Political Committee shall be the highest body for the co-ordination and unification of the general policy of the member States, and shall be composed of the Heads of States, or their accredited representatives. At its first meeting, the Committee shall lay down the provisions of its by-laws.

Article 3. Meetings of the African Political Committee. The African Political Committee shall hold an ordinary meeting ONCE a year and may hold a number of extraordinary meetings at the request of one member State, upon the approval of the majority of the member States.

Article 4. The African Economic Committee. The African Economic Committee shall consist of the Ministers of Finance of the member States or their representatives. The Committee shall hold periodic meetings and shall submit a report on the problems it is tackling and an annual report on its activities to the African Political Committee. At its first meeting, the Committee shall decide its by-laws.

Article 5. The African Cultural Committee. The African Cultural Committee shall consist of the Ministers of Education of the member States or their representatives. The Committee shall hold periodic meetings, and shall submit a report on the problems it is tackling and an annual report on its activities to the African Political Committee. At its first meeting, the Committee shall decide its by-laws.

Article 6. The African Joint High Command. The African Joint High Command shall consist of the Chiefs of Staffs of the member States or their representatives. The Committee shall hold periodic meetings and shall report to the African Political Committee immediately after every meeting.

Article 7. Recommendations of the African Joint High Command. Recommendations of the African Joint High Command shall become valid as soon as they are approved by the African Political Committee.

Article 8. The Liaison Office. The headquarters of the Liaison Office shall be at Bamako, the capital of the Republic of Mali. It may be transferred to any other place by a decision of the African Political Committee. It shall be headed by a secretary to be appointed by the African Political Committee for a renewable term of three years. He will be assisted by a number of assistant secretaries appointed by the African Political Committee. The secretary of the Liaison Office is the highest administrative official of this body.

Article 9. Officials of the Liaison Office. The secretary of the Liaison Office shall appoint the officials required for the smooth functioning of the various committees and shall submit to the African Political Committee drafts of the by-laws governing the conditions of their appointments.

Article 10. Co-ordination of the Committees' Work. The secretary of the Liaison Office shall submit to the African Political Committee an annual report on the measures which ensure the best possible co-ordination of work among the various bodies provided for in the Casablanca African Charter.

Article 11. The Committees' Secretariat. The secretary or his representative shall carry out the secretarial work during the meetings of the afore-mentioned bodies.

Article 12. The Budget. The secretary shall prepare the draft budget and shall submit it to the African Political Committee before the beginning of the financial year. The African Political Committee shall then determine the shares to be paid by each of the member States.

Article 13. The Status of the Secretariat Officials. The secretary and the officials of the Liaison Office shall be considered international officials and shall receive no instructions from any member State during the exercise of their duties and tasks. All their actions must be in line with their position as international officials. The member States shall pledge to refrain from any action which would affect the officials while they are carrying out their responsibilities.

Article 14. Privileges and Immunities. The secretary of the Liaison Office, his assistants, his technical officials, the special envoys, and the representatives of the member States shall enjoy the privileges and immunities customarily granted to members of the diplomatic corps during the performance of their duties in the member States.

Article 15. The Liaison Office Building. The building of the Liaison Office shall enjoy all the privileges and immunities agreed upon. The secretary shall conclude an agreement for this purpose with the host State. The committees shall enjoy the same privileges and immunities when they meet outside the Liaison Office.

Article 16. Applications for Membership. Any African State accepting the provisions of the African Charter and this protocol may apply for membership to the president of the African Political Committee and shall become a member upon the approval of the African Political Committee.

Article 17. General Provisions. (a) The member States declare that the obligations and commitments they incur by virtue of their international undertakings shall not contradict their obligations and commitments under the Casablanca African Charter and this protocol and, in particular, the policy of non-alignment provided for in the aforementioned Charter. (b) The member States undertake to inform the secretary of any agreements and treaties they become party to. (c) The Casablanca African Charter and this protocol shall be registered with the UN Secretariat-General in accordance with Para. 1 of Art. No. 102 of the UN Charter.

367

Appendix 4

Article 18. Amendments. At the request of one of the member States and the approval of two-thirds of the member States, this protocol may be amended with a view to strengthening the relations among these States. The proposed amendments shall be submitted to the secretary of the Liaison Office two months before the meeting of the African Political Committee.

Article 19. Signing and Validity of the Protocol. This protocol shall become effective as soon as it is approved by at least two of the member States.

Done at Cairo, UAR, this day Friday 5th May 1961, in three original copies, in Arabic, English, and French, which have equal validity.

MUHAMMAD YAZID, for the Provisional Government of the Algerian Republic; AKO ADJEI, for the Republic of Ghana; LOUIS LANSANA BEAVOGUI, for the Republic of Guinea; BAREMA COCOUM, for the Republic of Mali; IDRISS MUHAMMADI, for the Kingdom of Morocco; MAHMUD FAWZI, for the United Arab Republic.

Appendix 5. The Charter of the Organization of African Unity

We, the Heads of African States and Governments assembled in the City of Addis Ababa, Ethiopia;

CONVINCED that it is the inalienable right of all people to control their own destiny;

CONSCIOUS of the fact that freedom, equality, justice and dignity are essential objectives for the achievement of the legitimate aspirations of the African peoples;

CONSCIOUS of our responsibility to harness the natural and human resources of our continent for the total advancement of our peoples in spheres of human endeavour;

INSPIRED by a common determination to promote understanding among our peoples and co-operation among our States in response to the aspirations of our peoples for brotherhood and solidarity, in a larger unity transcending ethnic and national differences;

CONVINCED that, in order to translate this determination into a dynamic force in the cause of human progress, conditions for peace and security must be established and maintained;

DETERMINED to safeguard and consolidate the hard-won independence as well as the sovereignty and territorial integrity of our States, and to fight against neo-colonialism in all its forms;

DEDICATED to the general progress of Africa;

PERSUADED that the Charter of the United Nations and the Universal Declaration of Human Rights, to the principles of which we reaffirm our adherence, provide a solid foundation for peaceful and positive co-operation among states;

DESIROUS that all African States should henceforth unite so that the welfare and well-being of their peoples can be assured;

RESOLVED to reinforce the links between our states by establishing and strengthening common institutions;

HAVE agreed to the present Charter.

Appendix 5

ESTABLISHMENT
Article I

1. The High Contracting Parties do by the present Charter establish an Organization to be known as the ORGANIZATION OF AFRICAN UNITY.

2. The Organization shall include the Continental African States, Madagascar and other Islands surrounding Africa.

PURPOSES
Article II

1. The Organization shall have the following purposes:

    a. to promote the unity and solidarity of the African States;

    b. to co-ordinate and intensify their co-operation and efforts to achieve a better life for the peoples of Africa;

    c. to defend their sovereignty, their territorial integrity and independence;

    d. to eradicate all forms of colonialism from Africa; and

    e. to promote international co-operation, having due regard to the Charter of the United Nations and the Universal Declaration of Human Rights.

2. To these ends, the Member States shall co-ordinate and harmonize their general policies, especially in the following fields:

    a. political and diplomatic co-operation;

    b. economic co-operation, including transport and communications;

    c. educational and cultural co-operation;

    d. health, sanitation, and nutritional co-operation;

    e. scientific and technical co-operation; and

    f. co-operation for defence and security.

PRINCIPLES
Article III

The Member States, in pursuit of the purposes stated in Article II, solemnly affirm and declare their adherence to the following principles:

1. the sovereign equality of all Member States;

2. non-interference in the internal affairs of States;

3. respect for the sovereignty and territorial integrity of each State and for its inalienable right to independent existence;

4. peaceful settlement of disputes by negotiation, mediation, conciliation or arbitration;

5. unreserved condemnation, in all its forms, of political assassination as well as of subversive activities on the part of neighbouring States or any other State;

6. absolute dedication to the total emancipation of the African territories which are still dependent;

7. affirmation of a policy of non-alignment with regard to all blocs.

MEMBERSHIP
Article IV

Each independent sovereign African State shall be entitled to become a Member of the Organization.

RIGHTS AND DUTIES OF MEMBER STATES
Article V

All Member States shall enjoy equal rights and have equal duties.

Article VI

The Member States pledge themselves to observe scrupulously the principles enumerated in Article III of the present Charter.

INSTITUTIONS
Article VII

The Organization shall accomplish its purposes through the following principal institutions:

1. the Assembly of Heads of State and Government;
2. the Council of Ministers;
3. the General Secretariat;
4. the Commission of Mediation, Conciliation and Arbitration.

THE ASSEMBLY OF HEADS OF STATE AND GOVERNMENT
Article VIII

The Assembly of Heads of State and Government shall be the supreme organ of the Organization. It shall, subject to the provisions of this Charter, discuss matters of common concern to Africa with a view to co-ordinating and harmonizing the general policy of the Organization. It may in addition review the structure, functions and acts of all the organs and any specialized agencies which may be created in accordance with the present Charter.

Appendix 5

Article IX

The Assembly shall be composed of the Heads of State and Government or their duly accredited representatives and it shall meet at least once a year. At the request of any Member State and on approval by a two-thirds majority of the Member States, the Assembly shall meet in extraordinary session.

Article X

1. Each Member State shall have one vote.
2. All resolutions shall be determined by a two-thirds majority of the Members of the Organization.
3. Questions of procedure shall require a simple majority. Whether or not a question is one of procedure shall be determined by a simple majority of all Member States of the Organization.
4. Two-thirds of the total membership of the Organization shall form a quorum at any meeting of the Assembly.

Article XI

The Assembly shall have the power to determine its own rules of procedure.

THE COUNCIL OF MINISTERS
Article XII

1. The Council of Ministers shall consist of Foreign Ministers or such other Ministers as are designated by the Governments of Member States.
2. The Council of Ministers shall meet at least twice a year. When requested by any Member State and approved by two-thirds of all Member States, it shall meet in extraordinary session.

Article XIII

1. The Council of Ministers shall be responsible to the Assembly of Heads of State and Government. It shall be entrusted with the responsibility of preparing conferences of the Assembly.
2. It shall take cognizance of any matter referred to it by the Assembly. It shall be entrusted with the implementation of the decision of the Assembly of Heads of State and Government. It shall co-ordinate inter-African co-operation in accordance with the instructions of the Assembly and in conformity with Article II(2) of the present Charter.

Article XIV

1. Each Member State shall have one vote.
2. All resolutions shall be determined by a simple majority of the members of the Council of Ministers.
3. Two-thirds of the total membership of the Council of Ministers shall form a quorum for any meeting of the Council.

Article XV

The Council shall have the power to determine its own rules of procedure.

GENERAL SECRETARIAT

Article XVI

There shall be an Administrative Secretary-General of the Organization, who shall be appointed by the Assembly of Heads of State and Government. The Administrative Secretary-General shall direct the affairs of the Secretariat.

Article XVII

There shall be one or more Assistant Secretaries-General of the Organization, who shall be appointed by the Assembly of Heads of State and Government.

Article XVIII

The functions and conditions of services of the Secretary-General, of the Assistant Secretaries-General and other employees of the Secretariat shall be governed by the provisions of this Charter and the regulations approved by the Assembly of Heads of State and Government.

1. In the performance of their duties the Administrative Secretary-General and the staff shall not seek or receive instructions from any government or from any other authority external to the Organization. They shall refrain from any action which might reflect on their position as international officials responsible only to the Organization.
2. Each member of the Organization undertakes to respect the exclusive character of the responsibilities of the Administrative Secretary-General and the Staff and not to seek to influence them in the discharge of their responsibilities.

Appendix 5

COMMISSION OF MEDIATION, CONCILIATION AND
ARBITRATION

Article XIX

Member States pledge to settle all disputes among themselves by
peaceful means and, to this end, to decide to establish a Commission of
Mediation, Conciliation and Arbitration, the composition of which and
conditions of service shall be defined by a separate Protocol to be
approved by the Assembly of Heads of State and Government. Said
Protocol shall be regarded as forming an integral part of the present
Charter.

SPECIALIZED COMMISSIONS

Article XX

The Assembly shall establish such Specialized Commissions as it
may deem necessary, including the following:

1. Economic and Social Commission;
2. Educational and Cultural Commission;
3. Health, Sanitation and Nutrition Commission;
4. Defence Commission;
5. Scientific, Technical and Research Commission.

Article XXI

Each Specialized Commission referred to in Article XX shall be
composed of the Ministers concerned or other Ministers or Plenipotentiaries designated by the Governments of the Member States.

Article XXII

The functions of the Specialized Commissions shall be carried out
in accordance with the provisions of the present Charter and of the
regulations approved by the Council of Ministers.

THE BUDGET

Article XXIII

The budget of the Organization prepared by the Administrative
Secretary-General shall be approved by the Council of Ministers. The
budget shall be provided by contributions from Member States in
accordance with the scale of assessment of the United Nations; provided, however, that no Member State shall be assessed an amount
exceeding twenty percent of the yearly regular budget of the Organization. The Member States agree to pay their respective contributions
regularly.

374

SIGNATURE AND RATIFICATION OF CHARTER

Article XXIV

1. This Charter shall be open for signature to all independent sovereign African States and shall be ratified by the signatory States in accordance with their respective constitutional processes.

2. The original instrument, done if possible in African languages, in English and French, all texts being equally authentic, shall be deposited with the Government of Ethiopia which shall transmit certified copies thereof to all independent sovereign African States.

3. Instruments of ratification shall be deposited with the Government of Ethiopia, which shall notify all signatories of each such deposit.

ENTRY INTO FORCE

Article XXV

This Charter shall enter into force immediately upon receipt by the Government of Ethiopia of the instruments of ratification from two-thirds of the signatory States.

REGISTRATION OF THE CHARTER

Article XXVI

This Charter shall, after due ratification, be registered with the Secretariat of the United Nations through the Government of Ethiopia in conformity with Article 102 of the Charter of the United Nations.

INTERPRETATION OF THE CHARTER

Article XXVII

Any question which may arise concerning the interpretation of this Charter shall be decided by a vote of two-thirds of the Assembly of Heads of State and Government of the Organization.

ADHESION AND ACCESSION

Article XXVIII

1. Any independent sovereign African State may at any time notify the Administrative Secretary-General of its intention to adhere or accede to this Charter.

2. The Administrative Secretary-General shall, on receipt of such notification, communicate a copy of it to all the Member States. Admission shall be decided by a simple majority of the Member States. The decision of each Member State shall be transmitted to the Administrative Secretary-General, who shall, upon receipt of the

required number of votes, communicate the decision to the State concerned.

MISCELLANEOUS
Article XXIX
The working languages of the Organization and all its institutions shall be, if possible, African languages, [or, if not, then] English and French.

Article XXX
The Administrative Secretary-General may accept on behalf of the Organization gifts, bequests and other donations made to the Organization, provided that this is approved by the Council of Ministers.

Article XXXI
The Council of Ministers shall decide on the privileges and immunities to be accorded to the personnel of the Secretariat in the respective territories of the Member States.

CESSATION OF MEMBERSHIP
Article XXXII
Any State which desires to renounce its membership shall forward a written notification to the Administrative Secretary-General. At the end of one year from the date of such notification, if not withdrawn, the Charter shall cease to apply with respect to the renouncing State, which shall thereby cease to belong to the Organization.

AMENDMENT OF THE CHARTER
Article XXXIII
This Charter may be amended or revised if any Member State makes a written request to the Administrative Secretary-General to this effect; provided, however, that the proposed amendment is not submitted to the Assembly for consideration until all the Member States have been duly notified of it and a period of one year has elapsed.

Such an amendment shall not be effective unless approved by at least two-thirds of all the Member States.

IN FAITH WHEREOF, We, the Heads of African State and Government, have signed this Charter.

Done in the City of Addis Ababa, Ethiopia, this 25th day of May, 1963.

Algeria	President Ben Bella
Burundi	King Mwambutsa

376

Cameroon	President Ahmadou Ahidjo
Central African Republic	President David Dacko
Chad	President François Tombalbaye
Congo (Brazzaville)	President Fulbert Youlou
Congo (Kinshasa)	President Joseph Kasavubu
Dahomey	President Hubert Maga
Ethiopia	Emperor Haile Selassie
Gabon	President Leon M'ba
Ghana	President Kwame Nkrumah
Guinea	President Sékou Touré
Ivory Coast	President Félix Houphouet-Boigny
Liberia	President William V. S. Tubman
Libya	King Idris I
Malagasy Republic	President Philibert Tsiranana
Mali	President Modibo Keita
Mauritania	President Makhtar Ould Daddah
Niger	President Hamani Diori
Nigeria	Prime Minister Alhaji Sir Abubakar Tafawa Balewa
Rwanda	Foreign Minister Callixte Habamenshi
Senegal	President Léopold Sédar Senghor
Sierra Leone	Prime Minister Sir Milton Margai
Somalia	President Abdullah Osman
Sudan	President Ibrahim Abboud
Tanganyika	President Julius Nyerere
Tunisia	President Habib Bourguiba
Uganda	Prime Minister Milton Obote
United Arab Republic	President Gamal Abdul Nasser
Upper Volta	President Maurice Yameogo

377

Appendix 6. Resolutions Adopted at the Addis Ababa Summit of May 1963

I. DECOLONIZATION

The Summit Conference of Independent African States meeting in Addis Ababa, Ethiopia, from 22 May to 25 May 1963; *having considered* all aspects of the questions of decolonization; *unanimously convinced* of the imperious and urgent necessity of coordinating and intensifying their efforts to accelerate the unconditional attainment of national independence by all African territories still under foreign domination; *reaffirming* that it is the duty of all African independent states to support dependent people in Africa in their struggle for freedom and independence; *noting* with deep concern that most of the remaining dependent territories in Africa are dominated by foreign settlers; *convinced* that the colonial powers by their forcible imposition of the settlers to control the governments and administration of those territories are thus establishing colonial bases in the heart of Africa; *have agreed* unanimously to concert and coordinate their efforts and action in this field, and to this end have decided on the following measures:

(1) *Declares* that the forcible imposition by the colonial powers of the settlers to control the governments and administration of the dependent territories is a flagrant violation of the inalienable right of the legitimate inhabitants of the territories concerned;

(2) *Invites* the colonial powers to take the necessary measures for the immediate application of the declaration on the granting of independence to colonial countries and peoples by insisting on the fact that their determination to maintain colonies or semi-colonies in Africa constitutes a menace to the peace of the continent;

(3) *Invites* further the colonial powers, particularly the United Kingdom with regard to Southern Rhodesia, not to transfer the powers and attributes of sovereignty to foreign minority governments imposed on African peoples by the use of force and under cover of

racial legislation. A transfer of this kind would amount to a violation of the provisions of United Nations resolution 1514 on independence;

(4) *Reaffirms* its support of African nationalists of Southern Rhodesia and solemnly declares that if power in Southern Rhodesia were to be usurped by a racial white minority government, the states members of the Conference would lend their effective moral and practical support to any legitimate measures which the African nationalist leaders may devise for the purpose of recovering such power and restoring it to the African majority. The Conference undertakes henceforth to concert the efforts of its members to take such measures as the situation demands against any state according to such recognition;

(5) *Reaffirms* that the territory of South-West Africa is an African territory under international mandate and that any attempt by the Republic of South Africa to annex it would be regarded as an act of aggression; *Reaffirms* also its determination to render all necessary support to the second phase of the South-West Africa case before the International Court of Justice; *Reaffirms*, further, the inalienable right of the people of South-West Africa to self-determination and independence;

(6) *Intervenes* expressly with the great powers so that they cease without exception to lend directly or indirectly any support or assistance to all those colonialist governments which might use such assistance to suppress African national liberation movements, particularly the Portuguese Government, which is conducting a real war of genocide in Africa. *Informs* the allies of colonial powers that they must choose between their friendship for the African peoples, and their support of powers that oppress African peoples;

(7) *Sends* a delegation of Ministers of Foreign Affairs to speak on behalf of all African states at the meeting of the Security Council which will be called to examine the report of the United Nations Committee of 26 on the situation in African territories under Portuguese domination;

(8) *Demands* the breaking off of diplomatic and consular relations between all African states and the Governments of Portugal and South Africa so long as they persist in their present attitude towards decolonization;

(9) *Asks for an effective boycott* of the foreign trade of Portugal and South Africa by (a) prohibiting the import of goods from those two countries; (b) closing African ports and airports to their ships and planes; (c) forbidding the planes of those two countries to overfly the territories of all African states;

379

(10) *Earnestly invites* all national liberation movements to coordinate their efforts by establishing common action fronts wherever necessary so as to strengthen the effectiveness of their struggle and the rational use of the concerted assistance given them;

(11) *Establishes* a coordinating committee consisting of Ethiopia, Algeria, Uganda, UAR, Tanganyika, Congo-Leopoldville, Guinea, Senegal, and Nigeria, with headquarters in Dar-es-Salaam, responsible for harmonizing the assistance from African states and for managing the special fund to be set up for that purpose;

(12) *Establishes* a special fund to be contributed by member states with the deadline (15 July) to supply the necessary practical and financial aid to the various African national liberation movements;

(13) *Appoints* the day of 25 May 1963, as African Liberation Day and will organize popular demonstrations on that day to disseminate the recommendations of the Heads of State Conference and to collect sums, over and above the national contributions, for the special fund;

(14) *Receives*, on the territories of independent African states, nationalists from liberation movements in order to give them training in all sectors, and afford young people all the assistance they need for their education and vocational training;

(15) *Promotes*, in each state, the establishment of a body of volunteers in various fields, with a view to providing the various African national liberation movements with the assistance they need in the various sectors;

(16) *Fixes* a deadline for the accession of all African territories to independence.

II. APARTHEID AND RACIAL DISCRIMINATION

The Summit Conference of Independent African States, *having considered* all aspects of the questions of apartheid and racial discrimination; *unanimously convinced* of the imperious and urgent necessity of coordinating and intensifying their efforts to put an end to the South African Government's criminal policy of apartheid and wipe out racial discrimination in all its forms; *have agreed unanimously* to concert and coordinate their efforts and action in this field, and to this end have decided on the following measures:

(1) Creation of a fund for concerted financial assistance to the anti-apartheid movement in South Africa.

(2) Effective assistance of every kind to anti-apartheid movements in South Africa to help them carry out their struggle for freedom efficiently.

(3) The immediate release of Mr Mandela, Mr Sobukwe, and all other political prisoners in South Africa.

(4) Granting of scholarships, educational facilities, and possibilities of employment in African government service to refugees from South Africa.

(5) Supporting the recommendations presented to the Security Council and the General Assembly by the Special Committee of the United Nations on the apartheid policies of the South African Government.

(6) Despatch of a delegation of Foreign Ministers to inform the Security Council of the explosive situation existing in South Africa.

(7) Coordination of concrete measures of sanction against the Government of South Africa.

(8) Appeal to all states, and more particularly to those which have traditional relations and cooperate with the Government of South Africa, strictly to apply UN resolution 1761 of 6 November 1962, concerning apartheid.

(9) Appeal to all governments who still have diplomatic, consular, and economic relations with the Government of South Africa to break off those relations and to cease any other form of encouragement for the policy of apartheid.

(10) Stress the great responsibility incurred by the colonial authorities of territories neighbouring on South Africa for the pursuit of the policy of apartheid.

(11) Condemnation of racial discrimination in all its forms in Africa and all over the world.

(12) Expression of the deep concern aroused in all African peoples and governments by the measures of racial discrimination taken against communities of African origin living outside the continent and particularly in the United States of America. Expression of appreciation for the efforts of the Federal Government of the United States of America to put an end to these intolerable malpractices which are likely seriously to deteriorate relations between the African peoples and governments on the one hand and the people and government of the United States of America on the other.

III. AFRICA, NON-ALIGNMENT, AND THE UNITED NATIONS

The Summit Conference, *believing* that the United Nations is an important instrument for the maintenance of peace and security among nations and for the promotion of the economic and social advancement of all peoples; *reiterating* its desire to strengthen and support the United Nations; *noting* with regret that Africa as a region is not equitably represented in the principal organs of the United Nations; *convinced* of the need for closer cooperation and coordination among the African states members of the United Nations:

(1) *Reaffirms* its dedication to the purposes and principles of the United Nations Charter, and its acceptance of all obligations contained in the Charter, including financial obligations;

(2) *Insists* that Africa as a geographical region should have equitable representation in the principal organs of the United Nations, particularly the Security Council and the Economic and Social Council and its Specialized Agencies;

(3) *Invites* African governments to instruct their representatives in the United Nations to take all possible steps to achieve a more equitable representation of the African region;

(4) *Further invites* African governments to instruct their representatives in the United Nations, without prejudice to their membership in and collaboration with the African–Asian group, to constitute a more effective African Group to bring about closer cooperation and better coordination in matters of common concern.

IV· GENERAL DISARMAMENT

The Summit Conference, *having considered* all aspects of the question of general disarmament; *unanimously convinced* of the imperious and urgent necessity of coordinating and intensifying their efforts to contribute to the achievement of a realistic disarmament programme through the signing, by all states concerned, of a Treaty on general and complete disarmament under strict and effective international control; *have agreed* unanimously to concert and coordinate their efforts and action in these various fields, and to this end have decided on the following measures;

382

(1) To declare and accept Africa as a denuclearized zone, the banning of nuclear and thermonuclear tests; the peaceful use of nuclear energy and the banning of the manufacture of nuclear weapons.

(2) The destruction of existing nuclear weapons.

(3) The removal of military bases from Africa and disentanglement of African countries from military pacts with foreign powers.

(4) To appeal to the great powers to: (a) reduce conventional weapons; (b) put an end to the arms race; and (c) sign a general and complete disarmament agreement under strict and effective international control.

(5) To appeal to the great powers, in particular to the Soviet Union and the United States of America, to use their best endeavours to secure the objectives stated above.

(6) To undertake to bring about by means of negotiation the end of military occupation in the African continent, the elimination of military bases and nuclear tests which constitute an essential element of African independence and unity.

V. ECONOMIC PROBLEMS

The Summit Conference, *concerned* with the active share of the developing countries in world trade and at the persistent deterioration of the terms of trade in these external commercial relationships; *conscious* of the fact that owing to its extreme dependence on the export of primary products, Africa and Madagascar more than any other developing region are adversely affected by persistent deteriorations in export earnings; *convinced* of the necessity for concerted action by the African countries and Madagascar in order to ensure a much more remunerative price from the sale of their primary products; *mindful* of the need to eliminate the barriers to trade between the African states and thereby to strengthen their economies; *considering* that economic development, including the expansion of trade on the basis of fair and remunerative prices, should tend to eliminate the need for external economic aid, and that such external economic aid should be unconditional and should not prejudice the independence of African states; *considering* the imperative necessity for African countries to pool their resources and harmonize their activities in the economic field; *aware of* the necessity for the joint utilization of river basin resources, the study of the use of Saharan zones, the coordination of means of transport and communication systems, and the provision of research facilities, all of which serve to stimulate economic growth and expansion of trade, both regionally and inter-regionally; *convinced* that the acceleration of the rate of economic and social development of the various African countries lies in the industrialization of these countries and the diversification of their production; *considering* the serious problems arising from the great shortage of trained and skilled personnel, the lack of qualified staff, scarce capital resources, grossly inadequate infra-structure, limited outlets for industrial products and the far too inadequate participation of Africans in the economic construction of their countries; *desiring* to explore the effects of regional economic groupings of the African economy; *noting* with satisfaction that the Executive Secretary of the Economic Commission for Africa has decided to convene a Conference of African Ministers of Finance, to be held in Khartoum (Sudan) in July 1963, with a view to setting up an African Development Bank; *resolves to*:

(1) Appoint a preparatory economic committee to study, in collaboration with governments and in consultation with the Economic Commission for Africa, *inter alia*, the following questions and submit their findings to member states; (a) the possibility of establishing a free trade area between the various African countries; (b) the establishment of a common external tariff to protect the emergent industries and the setting up of a raw material price stabilization fund; (c) the restructuralization of international trade; (d) means for developing trade between African countries by the organization of and participation in African trade fairs and exhibitions and by the granting of transport and transit facilities; (e) the coordination of means of transport and the establishment of road, air, and maritime companies; (f) the establishment of an African Payments and Clearing Union; (g) a progressive freeing of national currencies from all non-technical external attachments and the establishment of a Pan-African monetary zone; (h) ways and means of effecting the harmonization of existing and future national development plans;

(2) Invite the Economic Commission for Africa to request their Executive Secretary to give the Commission of Experts all the necessary support and assistance which it may require in the fulfilment of its assignment;

(3) Welcome the forthcoming Conference of African Ministers of Finance and give the respective Ministers of Finance instructions to take the necessary measures for the rapid establishment of the African Development Bank;

(4) The Summit Conference of Independent African States note with satisfaction the progress achieved by the Economic Commission for Africa in establishing the Dakar Institute of Economic Development and Planning and affirm their profound interest in that Institute and their intention of giving it appropriate financial and other support;

(5) Welcome the forthcoming World Conference on Trade and Development which is to examine international trade problems in relation to the economic development of emerging countries;

(6) *Urge* all states concerned to conduct negotiations, in concert, with a view to obtaining from the consumer countries real price stabilization and guaranteed outlets on the world market so that the developing countries may derive considerably greater revenue from international trade.

VI. THE FUTURE OF THE CCTA

The Summit Conference, considering that at the last CCTA session in Dar-es-Salaam in January to February 1963, the final adoption of the new CCTA convention was deferred until the Heads of African States had had an opportunity to consider and direct on the role of the CCTA within the overall context of Pan-African cooperation, *and in view* of the fact that Article 23 of this new convention lays down as follows: 'Pending the signature and the ratification of this convention as provided in Article 16, the Parties having initialled this convention agree to apply it provisionally as if it had entered into force as from the date of initialling, subject to any decision which may be taken by the Heads of African States at the Conference at Addis Ababa or at any subsequent conference on the role of the CCTA within the overall context of Pan-African cooperation'; decides to reconsider its role in order to bring it eventually within the scope of the organization of African states which will have, as one of its arms, an organ for technical, scientific, and cultural cooperation.

Appendix 7. Protocol of Mediation, Conciliation and Arbitration

PART I

ESTABLISHMENT AND ORGANISATION

Article I

The Commission of Mediation, Conciliation and Arbitration established by Article XIX of the Charter of the Organisation of African Unity shall be governed by the provisions of the present Protocol.

Article II

1. The Commission shall consist of twenty-one members elected by the Assembly of Heads of State and Government.

2. No two members shall be nationals of the same State.

3. The Members of the Commission shall be persons with recognised professional qualifications.

4. Each Member State of the Organisation of African Unity shall be entitled to nominate two candidates.

5. The Administrative Secretary-General shall prepare a list of the candidates nominated by Member States and shall submit it to the Assembly of Heads of State and Government.

Article III

1. Members of the Commission shall be elected for a term of five years and shall be eligible for re-election.

2. Members of the Commission whose terms of office have expired shall remain in office until the election of a new Commission.

3. Notwithstanding the expiry of their terms of office, members shall complete any proceedings in which they are already engaged.

Article IV

Members of the Commission shall not be removed from office except by decision of the Assembly of Heads of State and Government, by a two-thirds majority of the total membership, on the grounds of inability to perform the function of their office or of proved misconduct.

Article V

1. Whenever a vacancy occurs in the Commission, it shall be filled in conformity with the provisions of Article II.

2. A member of the Commission elected to fill a vacancy shall hold office for the unexpired term of the member he has replaced.

Article VI

1. A President and two Vice-Presidents shall be elected by the Assembly of Heads of State and Government from among the members of the Commission who shall each hold office for five years. The President and the two Vice-Presidents shall not be eligible for re-election as such officers.

2. The President and the two Vice-Presidents shall be full-time members of the Commission, while the remaining eighteen shall be part-time members.

Article VII

The President and the two Vice-Presidents shall constitute the Bureau of the Commission and shall have the responsibility of consulting with the parties as regards the appropriate mode of settling the dispute in accordance with this Protocol.

Article VIII

The salaries and allowances of the members of the Bureau and the remuneration of the other members of the Commission shall be determined in accordance with provisions of the Charter of the Organisation of African Unity.

Article IX

1. The Commission shall appoint a Registrar and may provide for such other officers as may be deemed necessary.

2. The terms and conditions of service of the Registrar and other administrative officers of the Commission shall be governed by the Commission's Staff Regulations.

Article X

The Administrative expenses of the Commission shall be borne by the Organisation of African Unity. All other expenses incurred in connection with the proceedings before the Commission shall be met in accordance with the rules of procedure of the Commission.

Article XI

The Seat of the Commission shall be at Addis Ababa.

Appendix 7

PART II
GENERAL PROVISIONS

Article XII

The Commission shall have jurisdiction over disputes between States only.

Article XIII

1. A dispute may be referred to the Commission jointly by the parties concerned, by a party to the dispute, by the Council of Ministers or by the Assembly of Heads of State and Government.

2. Where a dispute has been referred to the Commission as provided in paragraph 1, and one or more of the parties have refused to submit to the jurisdiction of the Commission, the Bureau shall refer the matter to the Council of Ministers for consideration.

Article XIV

The consent of any party to a dispute to submit to the jurisdiction of the Commission may be evidenced by:

(a) a prior written undertaking by such party that there shall be recourse to Mediation, Conciliation or Arbitration;

(b) reference of a dispute by such party to the Commission; or

(c) submission by such party to the jurisdiction in respect of a dispute referred to the Commission by another State, by the Council of Ministers, or by the Assembly of Heads of State and Government.

Article XV

Member States shall refrain from any act or commission that is likely to aggravate a situation which has been referred to the Commission.

Article XVI

Subject to the Provisions of this Protocol and any special agreement between the parties, the Commission shall be entitled to adopt such working methods as it deems to be necessary and expedient and shall establish appropriate rules of procedure.

Article XVII

The members of the Commission, when engaged in the business of the Commission, shall enjoy diplomatic privileges and immunities as provided for in the Convention on Privileges and Immunities of the Organisation of African Unity.

Article XVIII

Where, in the course of Mediation, Conciliation or Arbitration, it is deemed necessary to conduct an investigation or inquiry for the purpose of elucidating facts or circumstances relating to a matter in dispute, the parties concerned and all other Member States shall extend to those engaged in any such proceedings the fullest cooperation in the conduct of such investigation or inquiry.

Article XIX

In case of a dispute between Member States, the parties may agree to resort to any one of these modes of settlement: Mediation, Conciliation and Arbitration.

PART III
MEDIATION

Article XX

When a dispute between Member States is referred to the Commission for Mediation the President shall, with the consent of the parties, appoint one or more members of the Commission to mediate the dispute.

Article XXI

1. The role of the mediator shall be confined to reconciling the views and claims of the parties.

2. The mediator shall make written proposals to the parties as expeditiously as possible.

3. If the means of reconciliation proposed by the mediator are accepted, they shall become the basis of a protocol of arrangement between the parties.

PART IV
CONCILIATION

Article XXII

1. A request for the settlement of a dispute by conciliation may be submitted to the Commission by means of a petition addressed to the President by one or more of the parties to the dispute.

2. If the request is made by only one of the parties, that party shall indicate that prior written notice has been given to the other party.

Appendix 7

3. The petition shall include a summary explanation of the grounds of the dispute.

Article XXIII

1. Upon receipt of the petition, the President shall, in agreement with the parties, establish a Board of Conciliators, of whom three shall be appointed by the President from among the members of the Commission, and one each by the parties.

2. The Chairman of the Board shall be a person designated by the President from among the three members of the Commission.

3. In nominating persons to serve as members of the Board, the parties to the dispute shall designate persons in such a way that no two members of it shall be nationals of the same State.

Article XXIV

1. It shall be the duty of the Board of Conciliators to clarify the issues in dispute and to endeavour to bring about an agreement between the parties upon mutually acceptable terms.

2. The Board shall consider all questions submitted to it and may undertake any inquiry or hear any person capable of giving relevant information concerning the dispute.

3. In the absence of agreement to the contrary between the parties, the Board shall determine its own procedure.

Article XXV

The parties shall be represented by agents, whose duty shall be to act as intermediaries between them and the Board. They may moreover be assisted by counsel and experts and may request that all persons whose evidence appears to the Board to be relevant shall be heard.

Article XXVI

1. At the close of the proceedings, the Board shall draw up a report stating either:

(a) that the parties have come to an agreement and, if the need arises, the terms of the agreement and any recommendations for settlement by the Board; or
(b) that it has been impossible to effect a settlement.

2. The report of the Board of Conciliators shall be communicated to the parties and to the President of the Commission without delay and may be published only with the consent of the parties.

390

PART V

ARBITRATION

Article XXVII

1. Where it is agreed that arbitration should be resorted to, the Arbitral Tribunal shall be established in the following manner:

(a) each party shall designate one arbitrator from among the members of the Commission having legal qualifications;

(b) the two arbitrators thus designated shall, by common agreement, designate from among the members of the Commission a third person who shall act as Chairman of the Tribunal.

(c) Where the two arbitrators fail to agree on the choice of the person to be Chairman of the Tribunal, the Bureau shall designate the Chairman.

2. The President may, with the agreement of the parties, appoint to the Arbitral Tribunal two additional members who need not be members of the Commission but who shall have the same powers as the other members of the Tribunal.

3. The arbitrators shall not be nationals of the parties nor may they have their domicile in the territories of the parties or be employed in their service. They shall all be of different nationalities.

Article XXVIII

Recourse to arbitration shall be regarded as submission in good faith to the award of the Arbitral Tribunal.

Article XXIX

1. The parties shall, in each case, conclude a *compromise* which shall specify:

(a) the undertaking of the parties to go to arbitration, and to accept as legally binding, the decision of the Tribunal,

(b) the subject matter of the controversy, and

(c) the Seat of the Tribunal.

2. The *compromise* may specify the law to be applied by the Tribunal and the power, if the parties so agree, to adjudicate *ex aequo et bono*, the time limit within which the award shall be rendered, and the appointment of agents and Counsel to take part in the proceedings before the Tribunal.

Appendix 7

Article XXX

In the absence of any provision in the *compromise* regarding the applicable law, the Arbitral Tribunal shall decide the dispute according to treaties concluded between the parties, International Law, the Charter of the Organisation of African Unity, the Charter of the United Nations and, if the parties agree, *ex aequo et bono*.

Article XXXI

1. Hearings shall be held *in camera* unless the arbitrators decide otherwise.

2. The record of the proceedings signed by the arbitrators and the Registrar shall alone be authoritative.

3. The arbitral award shall be in writing and shall, in respect of every point decided, state the reasons on which it is based.

PART VI
FINAL PROVISIONS

Article XXXII

The present Protocol shall, upon approval by the Assembly of Heads of State and Government, be an integral part of the Charter of the Organisation of African Unity.

Article XXXIII

This Protocol may be amended or revised in accordance with the provisions of Article XXXIII of the Charter of the Organisation of African Unity.

In *Faith Whereof*, *We*, the Heads of African State and Government, have signed this Protocol.

Appendix 8. The Lusaka Manifesto

The Future of Southern Africa

1. When the purpose and the basis of States' international policies are misunderstood, there is introduced into the world a new and unnecessary disharmony. Disagreements, conflicts of interest, or different assessments of human priorities, which already provoke an excess of tension in the world, disastrously divide mankind at a time when united action is necessary to control modern technology and put it to the service of man. It is for this reason, that discovering widespread misapprehension of our attitudes and purposes in relation to Southern Africa, we the leaders of East and Central African States meeting at Lusaka, 16th April, 1969 have agreed to issue this Manifesto.

2. By this Manifesto we wish to make clear, beyond all shadow of doubt, our acceptance of the belief that all men are equal, and have equal rights to human dignity and respect, regardless of colour, race, religion, or sex. We believe that all men have the right and the duty to participate, as equal members of the society, in their own government. We do not accept that any individual or group has any right to govern any other group of sane adults, without their consent, and we affirm that only the people of a society, acting together as equals, can determine what is, for them, a good society and a good social, economic, or political organization.

3. On the basis of these beliefs we do not accept that any one group within a society has the right to rule any society without the continuing consent of all the citizens. We recognize that for the sake of order in human affairs there may be transitional arrangements while a transformation from group inequalities to individual equality is being effected. But we affirm that without an acceptance of these ideals – without a commitment to these principles of human equality and self-determination – there can be no basis for peace and justice in the world.

4. None of us would claim that within our own States we have achieved that perfect social, economic, and political organization which would ensure a reasonable standard of living for all our people and establish individual security against avoidable hardship or miscarriage of justice. On the contrary, we acknowledge that within our

393

own States the struggle towards human brotherhood and unchallenged human dignity is only beginning. It is on the basis of our commitment to human equality and human dignity, not on the basis of achieved perfection, that we take our stand of hostility towards the colonialism and racial discrimination which is being practised in Southern Africa. It is on the basis of their commitment to these universal principles that we appeal to other members of the human race for support.

5. If the commitment to these principles existed among the States holding power in Southern Africa, any disagreements we might have about the rate of implementation, or about isolated acts of policy, would be matters affecting only our individual relationships with the States concerned. If these commitments existed, our States would not be justified in the expressed and active hostility towards the regimes of Southern Africa such as we have proclaimed and continue to propagate.

6. The truth is, however, that in Mozambique, Angola, Rhodesia, South West Africa, and the Republic of South Africa, there is an open and continued denial of the principles of human equality and national self-determination. This is not a matter of failure in the implementation of accepted human principles. The effective Administrations in all these territories are not struggling towards these difficult goals. They are fighting the principles; they are deliberately organizing their societies so as to try to destroy the hold of these principles in the minds of men. It is for this reason that we believe the rest of the world must be interested. For the principle of human equality, and all that flows from it, is either universal or it does not exist. The dignity of all men is destroyed when the manhood of any human being is denied.

7. Our objectives in Southern Africa stem from our commitment to this principle of human equality. We are not hostile to the Administrations of these States because they are manned and controlled by white people. We are hostile to them because they are systems of minority control which exist as a result of, and in the pursuance of, doctrines of human inequality. What we are working for is the right of self-determination for the people of those territories. We are working for a rule in those countries which is based on the will of all the people, and an acceptance of the equality of every citizen.

8. Our stand towards Southern Africa thus involves a rejection of racialism, not a reversal of the existing racial domination. We believe that all the peoples who have made their homes in the countries of Southern Africa are Africans, regardless of the colour of their skins; and we would oppose a racialist majority government which adopted a

philosophy of deliberate and permanent discrimination between its citizens on grounds of racial origin. We are not talking racialism when we reject the colonialism and apartheid policies now operating in those areas; we are demanding an opportunity for all the people of these States, working together as equal individual citizens, to work out for themselves the institutions and the system of government under which they will, by general consent, live together and work together to build a harmonious society.

9. As an aftermath of the present policies it is likely that different groups within these societies will be self-conscious and fearful. The initial political and economic organizations may well take account of these fears, and this group self-consciousness. But how this is to be done must be a matter exclusively for the peoples of the country concerned, working together. No other nation will have a right to interfere in such affairs. All that the rest of the world has a right to demand is just what we are now asserting – that the arrangements within any State which wishes to be accepted into the community of nations must be based on an acceptance of the principles of human dignity and equality.

10. To talk of the liberation of Africa is thus to say two things: First, that the peoples in the territories still under colonial rule shall be free to determine for themselves their own institutions of self-government. Secondly, that the individuals in Southern Africa shall be freed from an environment poisoned by the propaganda of racialism, and given an opportunity to be men – not white men, brown men, yellow men, or black men.

11. Thus the liberation of Africa for which we are struggling does not mean a reverse racialism. Nor is it an aspect of African Imperialism. As far as we are concerned the present boundaries of the States of Southern Africa are the boundaries of what will be free and independent African States. There is no question of our seeking or accepting any alterations to our own boundaries at the expense of these future free African nations.

12. On the objective of liberation as thus defined, we can neither surrender nor compromise. We have always preferred and we still prefer to achieve it without physical violence. We would prefer to negotiate rather than destroy, to talk rather than kill. We do not advocate violence; we advocate an end to the violence against human dignity which is now being perpetrated by the oppressors of Africa. If peaceful progress to emancipation were possible, or if changed circumstances were to make it possible in the future, we would urge our

brothers in the resistance movements to use peaceful methods of struggle even at the cost of some compromise on the timing of change. But while peaceful progress is blocked by actions of those at present in power in the States of Southern Africa, we have no choice but to give to the peoples of those territories all the support of which we are capable in their struggle against their oppressors. This is why the signatory states participate in the movement for the liberation of Africa, under the aegis of the Organisation of African Unity. However, the obstacle to change is not the same in all the countries of Southern Africa, and it follows, therefore, that the possibility of continuing the struggle through peaceful means varies from one country to another.

13. In MOZAMBIQUE and ANGOLA, and in so-called PORTUGUESE GUINEA, the basic problem is not racialism but a pretence that Portugal exists in Africa. Portugal is situated in Europe; the fact that it is a dictatorship is a matter for the Portuguese to settle. But no decree of the Portuguese dictator, nor legislation passed by any Parliament in Portugal, can make Africa part of Europe. The only thing which could convert a part of Africa into a constituent unit in a union which also includes a European State would be the freely expressed will of the people of that part of Africa. There is no such popular will in the Portuguese colonies. On the contrary, in the absence of any opportunity to negotiate a road to freedom, the peoples of all three territories have taken up arms against the colonial power. They have done this despite the heavy odds against them, and despite the great suffering they know to be involved.

14. Portugal, as a European State, has naturally its own allies in the context of the ideological conflict between West and East. However, in our context, the effect of this is that Portugal is enabled to use her resources to pursue the most heinous war and degradation of man in Africa. The present Manifesto must, therefore, lay bare the fact that the inhuman commitment of Portugal in Africa and her ruthless subjugation of the people of Mozambique, Angola and the so-called Portuguese Guinea, is not only irrelevant to the ideological conflict of power-politics, but it is also diametrically opposed to the politics, the philosophies and the doctrines practised by her Allies in the conduct of their own affairs at home. The peoples of Mozambique, Angola, and Portuguese Guinea are not interested in Communism or Capitalism; they are interested in their freedom. They are demanding an acceptance of the principles of independence on the basis of majority rule, and for many years they called for discussions on this issue. Only when their demand for talks was continually ignored did they begin to

fight. Even now, if Portugal should change her policy and accept the principle of self-determination, we would urge the Liberation Movements to desist from their armed struggle and to cooperate in the mechanics of a peaceful transfer of power from Portugal to the peoples of the African territories.

15. The fact that many Portuguese citizens have immigrated to these African countries does not affect this issue. Future immigration policy will be a matter for the independent Governments when these are established. In the meantime we would urge the Liberation Movements to reiterate their statements that all those Portuguese people who have made their homes in Mozambique, Angola, or Portuguese Guinea, and who are willing to give their future loyalty to those States will be accepted as citizens. And an independent Mozambique, Angola, or Portuguese Guinea may choose to be as friendly with Portugal as Brazil is. That would be the free choice of a free people.

16. In Rhodesia the situation is different in so far as the metropolitan power has acknowledged the colonial status of the territory. Unfortunately, however, it has failed to take adequate measures to re-assert its authority against the minority which has seized power with the declared intention of maintaining white domination. The matter cannot rest there. Rhodesia, like the rest of Africa, must be free, and its independence must be on the basis of majority rule. If the colonial power is unwilling or unable to affect such a transfer of power to the people, then the people themselves will have no alternative but to capture it as and when they can. And Africa has no alternative but to support them. The question which remains in Rhodesia is therefore whether Britain will re-assert her authority in Rhodesia and then negotiate the peaceful progress to majority rule before independence. In so far as Britain is willing to make the second commitment, Africa will co-operate in her attempts to re-assert her authority. This is the method of progress which we would prefer; it would involve less suffering for all the people of Rhodesia, both black and white. But until there is some firm evidence that Britain accepts the principle of independence on the basis of majority rule and is prepared to take whatever steps are necessary to make it a reality, then Africa has no choice but to support the struggle for the people's freedom by whatever means are open.

17. Just as a settlement of the Rhodesian problem with a minimum of violence is a British responsibility, so a settlement in SOUTH WEST AFRICA with a minimum of violence is a United Nations responsibility. By every canon of international law, and by every precedent,

397

Appendix 8

South West Africa should by now have been a sovereign Independent State with a Government based on majority rule. South West Africa was a German colony until 1919, just as Tanganyika, Rwanda and Burundi, Togoland, and Cameroon were German colonies.

It was a matter of European Politics that when the Mandatory System was established after Germany had been defeated, the administration of South West Africa was given to the white minority Government of South Africa, while the other ex-German colonies in Africa were put into the hands of the British, Belgian, or French Governments. After the Second World War every mandated territory except South West Africa was converted into a Trusteeship Territory and has subsequently gained independence. South Africa, on the other hand, has persistently refused to honour even the international obligation it accepted in 1919, and has increasingly applied to South West Africa the inhuman doctrines and organization of apartheid.

18. The United Nations General Assembly has ruled against this action and in 1966 terminated the Mandate under which South Africa had a legal basis for its occupation and domination of South West Africa.

The General Assembly declared that the territory is now the direct responsibility of the United Nations and set up an ad hoc Committee to recommend practical means by which South West Africa would be administered, and the people enabled to exercise self-determination and to achieve independence.

19. Nothing could be clearer than this decision – which no permanent member of the Security Council voted against. Yet, since that time no effective measures have been taken to enforce it. South West Africa remains in the clutches of the most ruthless minority government in Africa. Its people continue to be oppressed and those who advocate even peaceful progress to independence continue to be persecuted. The world has an obligation to use its strength to enforce the decision which all the countries cooperate in making. If they do this there is hope that change can be effected without great violence. If they fail, then sooner or later the people of South West Africa will take the law into their own hands. The people have been patient beyond belief, but one day their patience will be exhausted. Africa, at least, will then be unable to deny their call for help.

20. THE REPUBLIC OF SOUTH AFRICA is itself an independent Sovereign state and a member of the United Nations. It is more highly developed and richer than any other nation in Africa. On every legal basis its internal affairs are a matter exclusively for the people of

398

South Africa. Yet the purpose of law is people and we assert that the actions of the South African Government are such that the rest of the world has a responsibility to take some action in defence of humanity.

21. There is one thing about South African oppression which distinguishes it from other oppressive regimes. The apartheid policy adopted by its Government and supported to a greater or lesser extent by almost all its white citizens, is based on a rejection of man's humanity. A position of privilege or the experience of oppression in the South African society depends on the one thing which it is beyond the power of any man to change. It depends upon a man's colour, his parentage, and his ancestors. If you are black you cannot escape this categorization; nor can you escape it if you are white. If you are a black millionaire and a brilliant political scientist, you are still subject to the pass laws and still excluded from political activity. If you are white, even protests against the system and an attempt to reject segregation, will lead you only to the segregation and the comparative comfort of a white jail. Beliefs, abilities, and behaviour are all irrelevant to a man's status; everything depends upon race. Manhood is irrelevant. The whole system of government and society in South Africa is based on the denial of human equality. And the system is maintained by a ruthless denial of the human rights of the majority of the population and thus, inevitably of all.

22. These things are known and are regularly condemned in the Councils of the United Nations and elsewhere. But it appears that to many countries international law takes precedence over humanity; therefore no action follows the words. Yet even if international law is held to exclude active assistance to the South African opponents of apartheid, it does not demand that the comfort and support of human and commercial intercourse should be given to a government which rejects the manhood of most of humanity. South Africa should be excluded from the United Nations Agencies, and even from the United Nations itself. It should be ostracized by the world community. It should be isolated from world trade patterns and left to be self-sufficient if it can. The South African Government cannot be allowed both to reject the very concept of mankind's unity, and to benefit by the strength given through friendly international relations. And certainly Africa cannot acquiesce in the maintenance of the present policies against people of African descent.

23. The signatories of this Manifesto assert that the validity of the principles of human equality and dignity extend to the Republic of South Africa just as they extend to the colonial territories of Southern

Africa. Before a basis for peaceful development can be established in this continent, these principles must be acknowledged by every nation, and in every State there must be a deliberate attempt to implement them.

24. We re-affirm our commitment to these principles of human equality and human dignity, and to the doctrines of self-determination and non-racialism. We shall work for their extension within our own nations and throughout the continent of Africa.

Appendix 9. OAU Member States: December 1971

State	Capital	Area (in square miles)	Population	Date of independence
1. Algeria	Algiers	952,000	13,349,000	3 July 1962
2. Botswana	Gaberones	275,000	629,000	30 September 1966
3. Burundi	Bujumbura	11,000	3,475,000	1 July 1962
4. Cameroon	Yaounde	182,000	5,680,000	1 January 1960
5. Central African Republic	Bangui	238,000	1,518,000	13 August 1960
6. Chad	Fort Lamy	496,000	3,510,000	11 August 1960
7. Congo (Brazzaville)	Brazzaville	132,000	880,000	15 August 1960
8. Congo (Kinshasa)	Kinshasa	905,000	17,100,000	30 June 1960
9. Dahomey	Porto Novo	45,000	2,640,000	1 August 1960
10. Ethiopia	Addis Ababa	460,000	24,769,000	Independent throughout its history
11. Equatorial Guinea	Santa Isabel	10,785	286,000	12 October 1968
12. Gabon	Libreville	103,000	485,000	17 August 1960
13. Gambia	Bathurst	4,000	357,000	18 February 1965
14. Ghana	Accra	92,000	8,600,000	6 March 1957
15. Guinea	Conakry	95,000	3,890,000	2 October 1958
16. Ivory Coast	Abidjan	124,000	4,195,000	7 August 1960
17. Kenya	Nairobi	220,000	10,506,000	12 December 1963
18. Lesotho	Maseru	12,000	930,000	4 October 1966

No.	Country	Capital	Area	Population	Date of Independence
19.	Liberia	Monrovia	43,000	1,150,000	26 July 1847
20.	Libya	Benghazi and Tripoli	679,000	1,869,000	24 December 1951
21.	Malagasy Republic	Tananarive	230,000	6,643,000	26 June 1960
22.	Malawi	Zomba	37,000	4,398,000	6 July 1964
23.	Mali	Bamako	465,000	4,881,000	22 September 1960
24.	Mauritania	Nouakchott	419,000	1,140,000	28 November 1960
25.	Mauritius	Port Louis	720	799,000	12 March 1968
26.	Morocco	Rabat	171,000	15,050,000	2 March 1956
27.	Niger	Niamey	459,000	3,909,000	3 August 1960
28.	Nigeria	Lagos	357,000	63,870,000	1 October 1960
29.	Rwanda	Kigali	10,000	3,500,000	1 July 1962
30.	Senegal	Dakar	76,000	3,780,000	25 August 1960
31.	Sierra Leone	Freetown	28,000	2,512,000	27 April 1961
32.	Somali Republic	Mogadishu	246,000	2,730,000	1 July 1960
33.	Sudan	Khartoum	967,000	15,186,000	1 January 1956
34.	Swaziland	Mbabone	6,705	410,000	6 September 1968
35.	Tanzania	Dar es Salaam	342,000	12,926,000	9 December 1961
36.	Togo	Lome	22,000	1,815,000	27 April 1960
37.	Tunisia	Tunis	63,078	5,027,000	20 March 1956
38.	Uganda	Kampala	80,000	9,500,000	9 October 1962
39.	United Arab Republic	Cairo	386,000	32,501,000	28 February 1922
40.	Upper Volta	Ouagadougou	106,000	5,278,000	5 August 1960
41.	Zambia	Lusaka	290,000	4,208,000	24 October 1964

Source: *Demographic Yearbook of the United Nations*, 1969.

Abbreviations

AAPO	All African Peoples' Organization
AATUF	All African Trade Union Federation
ABAKO	Association des Bakongo pour l'Unification, la Conservation et l'Expansion de la Langue Kikongo
AEF	L'Afrique Équatoriale Française
ANC	Armée Nationale Congolaise
AOF	L'Afrique Occidentale Française
BCEAEC	Banque Centrale des États de l'Afrique Équatoriale et du Caméroun
BDS	Bloc Démocratique Sénégalais
CA	Convention Africain
CAR	Central African Republic
CIA	Central Intelligence Agency
CIAS	Conference of Independent African States
CONAKAT	Confederation des Associations des Katangaises
CONCP	Conference of the Nationalist Organizations of the Portuguese Territories
COSERU	Comite Secreto de Restauraçao da UDENAMO
CPP	Convention People's Party
EAC	East African Community
ECA	Economic Commission for Africa
EEC	European Economic Community
ELF	Eritrean Liberation Front
FLING	Frente Libertação de l'Independencia Nationale de Guiné
FLN	Front de Libération Nationale
FLNA	National Front for the Liberation of Angola
FRELIMO	Frente de Libertaçao de Moçambique
GRAE	Angolan Revolutionary Government-in-Exile
ICFTU	International Confederation of Free Trade Unions
MANU	Mozambique African National Union
MNC	Mouvement National Congolais
MORECO	Mozambican Revolutionary Council

404

MPLA	Movimento Popular de Libertação de Angola
MSA	Mouvement Socialiste Africain
MVD	Mouvement Démocratique Voltaïque
NAACP	National Association for the Advancement of Coloured People
NATO	North Atlantic Treaty Organization
NESAM	Núcleo dos Estudantes Africanos Secundarios de Moçambique
NIBMAR	No Independence Before Majority African Rule
NPC	Northern People's Congress
NUP	National Unionist Party
OAU	Organization of African Unity
OCAM	L'Organisation Commune Africaine et Malgache
OERS	L'Organisation des États Riverains du Sénégal
ONUC	Opération des Nations Unies au Congo
PAFMECA	Pan-African Freedom Movement of East and Central Africa
PAFMECSA	Pan-African Freedom Movement of Eastern, Central and Southern Africa
PAIGC	Partido Africano de Independencia de Guiné e Cabo Verde
PDA	Angolan Democratic Party
PDCI	Parti Démocratique de la Côte d'Ivoire
PFA	Parti Fédéraliste Africain
PIDE	Policia Internacional e de Defesa do Estado
RDA	Rassemblement Démocratique Africain
SANU	Sudan African National Union
UAM	L'Union Africaine et Malgache
UDE	L'Union Douanière Équatoriale
UDEAC	L'Union Douanière et Économique de l'Afrique Centrale
UDENAMO	União Nacional Democrática de Moçambique
UEAC	L'Union des États d'Afrique Centrale
UGTAN	Union Générale des Travailleurs d'Afrique Noire
UNAMI	União Africana de Moçambique Independente
UNAR	União Nacional Africana da Rombézia
UNCTAD	United Nations Conference on Trade and Development
UNGA	United Nations General Assembly
UNIA	Universal Negro Improvement Association
UN(O)	United Nations (Organization)

Abbreviations

UPA	União das Populacaoes de Angola
URGP	Union of Portuguese Guinea Nationals
USA	United States of America
USSR	Union of the Soviet Socialist Republics
WASU	West African Students' Union
WFTU	World Federation of Trade Unions
ZANU	Zimbabwe African National Union
ZAPU	Zimbabwe African People's Union

Bibliography

(a) Books

Addis Ababa Summit, 1963, Publications and Foreign Language Press Department, Ministry of Information, Addis Ababa, 1963

African Summit in Monrovia, Federal Ministry of Information, Lagos, 1961

AMIN, SAMIR, *The Maghreb in the Modern World*, Penguin Books, Harmondsworth, 1970

ANSPRENGER, FRANZ, *Auflösung der Kolonialreiche*, Deutscher Taschenbuch Verlag, Munich, 1966

ARIKPO, OKOI, *The Development of Modern Nigeria*, Penguin Books, Harmondsworth, 1967

AUSTIN, DENNIS, and WEILER, HANS, *Inter-State Relations in Africa*, Freiburg, 1965

BING, GEOFFREY, *Reap the Whirlwind – An Account of Kwame Nkrumah's Ghana from 1950–1966*, MacGibbon & Kee, London, 1968

BLACKSTOCK, PAUL W., *The Strategy of Subversion – Manipulating the Politics of Other Nations*, Quadrangle Books, Chicago, 1964

BRODERICK, FRANCIS L., *W.E.B. DuBois: Negro Leader in a Time of Crisis*, Stanford University Press, Stanford, 1959

CERVENKA, ZDENEK, *The Organisation of African Unity and its Charter*, Hurst, London, 1969

COX, RICHARD, *Pan-Africanism in Practice*, Oxford University Press, London, 1964

CRONON, EDMUND DAVID, *Black Moses: The Story of Marcus Garvey and the Universal Negro Improvement Association*, University of Wisconsin Press, Madison, 1955

DAVIDSON, BASIL, *Which Way Africa?*, Penguin Books, Harmondsworth, 1967

DAVIDSON, BASIL, *The Liberation of Guiné*, Penguin Books, Harmondsworth, 1969

DOOB, LEONARD W. (ed.), *Resolving Conflict in Africa*, Yale University Press, London, 1970

Bibliography

DRYSDALE, JOHN, *The Somali Dispute*, Pall Mall Press, London, 1964

DUBOIS, W. E. B., *Color and Democracy: Colonies and Peace*, Harcourt Brace, New York, 1945

DUBOIS, W. E. B., *The Souls of Black Folk – Essays and Sketches*, Premier Americana, Fawcett Publications, Greenwich, Connecticut, 1961

DUBOIS, W. E. B., *The World and Africa*, Viking Press, New York, 1947

DUFFY, JAMES, *Portugal in Africa*, Penguin Books, Harmondsworth, 1963

DUVE, FREIMUT (ed.), *Kap ohne Hoffnung: oder Die Politik der Apartheid*, Rowohlt Taschenbuch Verlag, Rheinbeck, 1965

ECA, *Report of the ECA/OAU Conference of Ministers of Industry* (Addis Ababa, 3–7 May, 1971), E/CN. 14/INR/194; OAU/CMI/W/9, 8 May 1971

ECA Doc. E/CN. 14/ADB/36, 1964 – 'Agreement Establishing the African Development Bank'

ECA Doc. ADB/1/BG/5 – 'Committee of Nine, African Development Bank: Its Functions and Purposes'

Economic Co-operation and Integration in Africa – Three Case Studies, UN Publication E.6911.K.7, ST/ECA/109

FANON, FRANTZ, *Die Verdammten dieser Erde*, Suhrkamp Verlag, Frankfurt, 1966

FANON, FRANTZ, *Toward the African Revolution*, Penguin Books, Harmondsworth, 1970

FIRST, RUTH, *The Barrel of a Gun: Political Power in Africa and the Coup d'État*, Allen Lane The Penguin Press, London, 1970

FOLTZ, WILLIAM, *From French West Africa to the Mali Federation*, Yale University Press, London and New Haven, 1965

FORSYTH, FREDERICK, *The Biafra Story*, Penguin Books, Harmondsworth, 1969

GERMANI, HANS, *Weisse Söldner im schwarzen Land – ein Erlebnisbericht*, Ullstein, Frankfurt, 1966

GRAMONT, SANCHE DE, *Der geheime Krieg*, Deutscher Taschenbuch Verlag, Munich, 1964

GREEN, REGINALD H., and SEIDMAN, ANN, *Unity or Poverty? – The Economics of Pan-Africanism*, Penguin Books, Harmondsworth, 1968

HAZLEWOOD, ARTHUR (ed.), *African Integration and Disintegration*, Oxford University Press, 1967

HODGKIN, THOMAS, and SCHACHTER, RUTH, *French-Speaking West Africa in Transition* (International Conciliation – Carnegie Endowment for International Peace, No. 528, May 1960)

HOLT, P. M., *A Modern History of the Sudan*, Weidenfeld & Nicolson, London, 1961

HOSKYNS, CATHERINE, *The Congo since Independence*, Oxford University Press, London, 1965

HOVET, THOMAS, Jr, *Africa in the United Nations*, Faber & Faber, London, 1963

HOWE, RUSSELL WARREN, *Black Africa: From the Colonial Era to Modern Times*, Parts 3 and 4, New African Library, London, 1967

HUGHES, A. J., *East Africa: The Search for Unity*, Penguin Books, Harmondsworth, 1963

ITALIAANDER, ROLF, *The New Leaders of Africa*, Prentice-Hall, London, 1961

JACQUES-GARVEY, A. (ed.), *Philosophy and Opinions of Marcus Garvey*, Vol. I, Universal Publishing House, New York, 1923

JACQUES-GARVEY, A. (ed.), *Philosophy and Opinions of Marcus Garvey*, Vol. II, Universal Publishing House, New York, 1926

KEATLEY, PATRICK, *The Politics of Partnership; the Federation of Rhodesia and Nyasaland*, Penguin Books, Harmondsworth, 1963

LEGUM, COLIN, *Pan-Africanism: A Short Political Guide*, Pall Mall Press, London, 1962

LEGUM, COLIN (ed.), *Africa: A Handbook* (revised and enlarged edition), Anthony Blond, London, 1965

LLOYD, P. C., *Africa in Social Change*, Penguin Books, Harmondsworth, 1967

LUSIGNAN, GUY DE, *French-Speaking Africa since Independence*, Pall Mall Press, London, 1969

LUTHULI, A., *Africa's Freedom*, Allen & Unwin, London, 1964

MAZRUI, ALI A., *Towards a Pax Africana*, Weidenfeld & Nicholson, London, 1967

McKAY, VERNON (ed)., *African Diplomacy – Studies in the Determinants of Foreign Policy*, Praeger Publishers, New York, 1964

MEZU, S. OKECHUKWU (ed.), *The Philosophy of Pan-Africanism*, Washington, 1965

MONDLANE, EDUARDO, *The Struggle for Mozambique*, Penguin Books, Harmondsworth, 1969

Mr Prime Minister – A Selection of Speeches made by Alhaji the Rt Hon. Sir Abubakar Tafawa Balewa, KBE, MP, Prime Minister of the Federal Republic of Nigeria, Federal Ministry of Information, Lagos, 1964

NAETHER, CLAUS MICHAEL, *Ein Kontinent sucht die Freiheit*, Fisher Bücherei, Frankfurt, 1968

NKRUMAH, KWAME, *Ghana – The Autobiography of Kwame Nkrumah*, Nelson, London, 1959

NKRUMAH, KWAME, *I speak of Freedom*, Heinemann, London, 1961

Bibliography

NKRUMAH, KWAME, *Africa Must Unite*, Heinemann, London, 1963
NOGUEIRA, FRANCO, *The United Nations and Portugal – A Study of Anti-Colonialism*, Sidgwick & Jackson, London, 1963
PADELFORD, NORMAN J., and LINCOLN, GEORGE A., *The Dynamics of International Politics* (second edition), Macmillan, London and New York, 1967
PADMORE, GEORGE, *Pan-Africanism or Communism ?*, Dennis Dobson, London, 1956
PHILLIPS, JOHN, *Kwame Nkrumah and the Future of Africa*, Faber & Faber, London, 1960
POST, KEN, *The New States Of West Africa*, Penguin Books, Harmondsworth, 1964
SAID, BESHIR MOHAMMED, *The Sudan: Crossroads of Africa*, The Bodley Head, London, 1965
SEGAL, RONALD, *Political Africa*, Stevens, London, 1961
SEGAL, RONALD, *African Profiles*, Penguin Books, Harmondsworth, 1963
The Growth of World Industry, UN Publication, 1969 edn
The Somali Republic and the Organization of African Unity, Public Relations Section of the Ministry of Foreign Affairs, Mogadiscio, 1965
THIAM, DOUDOU, *The Foreign Policy of African States*, Phoenix House, London, 1965
THOMPSON, V. BAKPETU, *Africa and Unity: The Evolution of Pan-Africanism*, Longmans, London, 1969
THOMPSON, W. SCOTT, *Ghana's Foreign Policy, 1957–1966: Diplomacy, Ideology and the New State*, Princeton University Press, New Jersey, 1969
UNIDO Monograph No. 17, *Industrial Planning and Regional Co-operation*, UN Publication, ID/40/17
UNIDO Monograph No. 18, *Industrialization of Developing Countries: Problems and Prospects*, UN Publication ID/40/18, April 1970
WALLERSTEIN, IMMANUEL, *Africa – The Politics of Independence*, Random House, New York, 1961
WALLERSTEIN, IMMANUEL, *Africa and the Politics of Unity*, Pall Mall Press, London, 1968
WAUGH, AUBERON, and CRONJE, SUSANNE, *Biafra: Britain's Shame*, Michael Joseph, London, 1969
WELCH, CLAUDE E., Jr, *Dream of Unity: Pan-Africanism and Political Unification in West Africa*, Cornell University Press, Ithaca, New York, 1966
WISE, DAVID, and ROSS, THOMAS B., *The Invisible Government*, Jonathan Cape, London, 1965

World Economic Survey, 1969–1970: The developing countries in the 1960s, UN Publication Sales No. E.71.II.C.1, E.4942; ST/ECA/141

ZARTMAN, I. WILLIAM, *International Relations in the New Africa*, Prentice-Hall, Englewood Cliffs, 1966

(b) Articles

BALFOUR, CAMPBELL, 'Rhodesien – eine Herausforderung für Grossbritannien und die Vereinten Nationen', *Europa Archiv*, Frankfurt, Heft 4, 1967

BECHTOLDT, HEINRICH, 'Weisser Süden im schwarzen Afrika', *Aussenpolitik*, Freiburg, Heft 1, 1966

ETINGER, V., 'Attacks on African Unity', *International Affairs*, Moscow, July 1965

FRANCKE, ROLFJÜRGEN, 'Komplexe Kombinationen um Portugiesisch–Angola', *Aussenpolitik*, Heft 10, 1962

HAFTENDORN, HELGA, 'Stabilität und Unsicherheit im Horn von Afrika', *Europa Archiv*, Heft 19, 1967

HUNCK, JOSEPH MARIA, 'Portugal und das dritte Afrika', *Aussenpolitik*, Heft 9, 1969

JANTZEN, GÜNTHER, 'Konstellationen und Spannungen in Ostafrika', *Aussenpolitik*, Heft 2, 1964

KUDRYAVTSEV, V., 'Neo-Colonialism and African Reality', *International Affairs*, Moscow, April 1965

MARKAKIS, JOHN, 'The Organization of African Unity: A Progress Report', *Journal of Modern African Studies*, Cambridge, Vol. 4, No. 2, 1966

MCKEON, NORA, 'The African States and the OAU', *International Affairs*, London, Vol. 42, No. 3, 1966

NEWMANN, HEINZGEORG, 'Portugal's Policy in Africa: A Study of the four years since the beginning of the Uprising in Angola', *International Affairs*, London, Vol. 41, No. 4, 1965

OGANISYAN, Y., 'Colonialism's Agony in Africa', *International Affairs*, Moscow, February 1966

PANTER-BRICK, S. K., 'The Right to Self-determination: Its application to Nigeria', *International Affairs*, London, Vol. 44, No. 2, 1968

PERHAM, MARGERY, 'The Rhodesian Crisis: the Background', *International Affairs*, London, Vol. 42, No. 1, 1966

POST, K. W. J., 'Is there a case for Biafra?', *International Affairs*, London, Vol. 44, No. 1, 1968

Bibliography

REYNER, A. S., 'Morocco's International Boundaries – A Factual Background', *Journal of Modern African Studies*, Vol. I, No. 3, October 1963

ROSHCHIN, K., 'Imperialism, Congo and Africa', *International Affairs*, Moscow, March 1965

SCHOLL-LATOUR, PETER, 'Afrikanische Schlichtung im Maghreb', *Aussenpolitik*, Heft 12, 1963

SPENCE, J. E., 'Südafrika und seine Nachbarn', *Europa Archiv*, Heft 8, 1968

STAHN, EBERHARD, 'Die Isolierung Kwame Nkrumahs in Afrika', *Aussenpolitik*, Heft 6, 1964

STEPHAN, KLAUS, 'Der Krieg in Nigeria: Seine Hintergründe und seine möglichen Folgen', *Europa Archiv*, Heft 4, 1968

STEPHAN, KLAUS, 'Der nigerianische Sezessionskrieg – Verlauf der Kämpfe und Verhandlungen', *Europa Archiv*, Heft 11, 1969

TIMMLER, MARKUS, 'Das grosse Palaver von Addis Abeba', *Aussenpolitik*, Heft 8, 1963

TIMMLER, MARKUS, 'Afrika seit dem Gipfeltreffen von Addis Abeba', *Aussenpolitik*, Heft 12, 1964

TIMMLER, MARKUS, 'Accra – die Konferenz der Besinnung', *Aussenpolitik*, Heft 12, 1965

TIMMLER, MARKUS, 'OCAM – die Organisation des frankophonen Schwarzafrika', *Aussenpolitik*, Heft 10, 1966

TIMMLER, MARKUS, 'Nigeria – Erdöl sprengt die Föderation', *Aussenpolitik*, Heft 7, 1967

TOUVAL, SAADIA, 'Africa's Frontiers – Reactions to a Colonial Legacy', *International Affairs*, London, Vol. 42, No. 4, 1966

ZARTMAN, I. WILLIAM, 'The Politics of Boundaries in North and West Africa', *Journal of Modern African Studies*, Vol. 3, No. 2, 1965

(c) **Magazines and Newspapers**

African Research Bulletin

African World

Pan-Africanist Review, Vol. 1, No. 2, 1964

West Africa, various dates from January 1958 to January 1971

East African Standard, Nairobi, various dates from 26 September 1958 to 31 December 1970

Ghana Daily Graphic, Accra, various dates from 5 April 1958 to 9 November 1966

Neue Zürcher Zeitung, various dates from 1 July 1960 to 31 December 1968
New York Times, various dates from 16 April 1958 to 31 December 1969
Nigerian Daily Times, Lagos, 2 May 1961; 8 May 1961 to 10 May 1961; 22 January–February 1962
Tanganyika Standard, Dar es Salaam, 15 October 1960 to 28 October 1960
Financial Times, various dates from 17 October 1970 to 30 June 1971
Guardian, various dates from 24 October 1960 to November 1971
Observer, various dates from January 1969 to November 1971
Sunday Telegraph, 29 June 1969
The Times, various dates from 2 January 1969 to November 1971
West African Pilot, Lagos, 6–10 May, 1961; 22 January to February 1962

(d) Other Sources

ARMSTRONG, R. G., *The Issues at Stake, Nigeria 1967*, Ibadan, At the University Press, 1967
CORNIDES, WILHELM, and MENDE, DIETRICH, *Die Internationale Politik, 1961*, Oldenbourg Verlag, Munich, 1964
Demographic Yearbook of the United Nations
EUROPÄISCHE WIRTSCHAFTS GEMEINSCHAFT; *Das Abkommen von Jaunde (Die Assoziierung der Überseeischen Länder mit der EWG): Dazugehörige Dokumente*, 1965
Fifty Facts about the East African Economic Community, Information Division of the East African Economic Community, 1968
STEPHAN, KLAUS W., 'Das nigerianische Missverständnis – Ein Kommentar im Bayerischen Rundfunk, Programme I', 11 September 1967
The Rise and Fall of Kwame Nkrumah and its Impact on the Rest of Africa – speech by H.E. Mr Justice William Bedford van Lare, GMG, Ghana High Commissioner to Canada, to the United Nations Club, Queen's University, Kingston, Ontario, 1 March 1967
United We Stand – address delivered by Osagyefo Dr Kwame Nkrumah, President of the Republic of Ghana at the Conference of African Heads of State and Government on Addis Ababa, Ethiopia, 24 May 1963 (supplement to *Ghana To-day*, of 5 June 1963)
Yearbooks of the United Nations, 1960–62

Index

Index

Algerian: National Liberation Front (FLNA), 16, 19, 25; provisional government, 26–7 *p.*, 30, 35, 38–9 *p.*, 120; War of Independence, 16, 17, 25–9 *p.*, 38 *p.*, 120, 131

Algiers, 71, 145–6 *p.*; at OAU Summit (1968), 80, 89, 136, 142, 226, 273–5, 312; OAU Scientific, Technical and Research Commission's first meeting at (1964), 86–7

All African Peoples' Conferences (*see also* AAPO *and* Conference of Independent African States), 26, 110: I (1945), 9–12 *p.*: II (1958), 40–2; III (1960), 24–5; IV (1968), 164

All African Peoples' Organization (AAPO), 19, 24 *p.*; constitution and objectives, 24; conferences, *see* All-African Peoples' Conferences (*above*)

All African Trade Union Federation (AATUF), 25

America: *see* Central America, South America *and* United States

American: Intelligence Agency (CIA), 172, 173, 201, 209, 214 *p.*; Government, *see* United States; Negro Academy (1897), 102; Negroes, *see* Negroes

Americans of African descent (*see also* Africans), 3–6 *p.*

Amin, General Idi (of Uganda), 248, 310–11

Anglo-Egyptian: Condominion Agreement (1899–1953), 283, 285; Sudan, *see* Sudan (E)

Anglo-Nigerian defence pact, 339

Anglo-Rhodesian talks (condemned by OAU), 225

Angola, 210–11 *p.*, 212–15, 217; People's Union of (UPA), 212–13

Angolan: Democratic Party (PDA), 213; Popular Liberation Movement (MPLA), 212–14 *p.*; Revo-

lutionary Government in Exile (GRAE), 213–15 *p.*

Ankrah, General Joseph (of Ghana), 170, 261–3 *p.*

anti-Garveyism, 95–101

Antilles, the, 9

Anya'nyas (Sudanese guerrillas), 287, 289, 290

apartheid in South Africa, 17, 26, 38, 53, 66, 121, 124, 177, 220, 227, **230–6**, 240; *see also next below*

'Apartheid and Racial Discrimination': Casablanca resolution, (1961), 356–7; OAU Summit resolution (May 1963), 231, 240, 380–2; *ditto* (1967), 233

Apithy, President Sorou Migan (of Dahomey), 107, 184, 185

Arab: League, 148; States, 282

Arabs: and other Africans, 14; of the Sudan, *see* Sudan (E)

Armah, Kwesi, 145

Armattoe, Dr Raphael (of Togo), 11

Arusha (Tanzania), 158, 305 *p.*; meeting of Somali and Kenyan representatives (1967), 158–60

Asmara (Ethiopia): meeting (June 1962), 49

assimilados: in French colonies, 114; in Portuguese colonies, 210

Assouan-Usher, Arsène (of Ivory Coast), 337

atomic and nuclear tests in Africa, *see* nuclear (and atomic) tests

Awolowo, Chief Obafemi, 13, 260

Ayida, Allison (of Nigeria), 264

Azikiwe, Dr Nnamdi ('Zik'), 13, 14, 23, 269, 272

BCEAEC, *see* Banque Centrale des États de l'Afrique Équatoriale et du Caméroun

BDS, *see* Bloc Démocratique Sénégalais

Baako, Kofi, 13

Backe, Falilou M. (Grand Khalif of Senegal), 189

Index

Congo (Brazzaville) – *cont.*
1963–4 and 1968), 170, **170–3**;
titles of, 292
Congo crisis (1960 ff.), 29–32, 38,
75, 120, 141, 181, **198–210**, 244,
247, 280, 282, 289, 332, 340; and
African groups at UN, 199;
Congolese delegations to UN,
200–1; three centres of power,
201; UN Security Council resolutions (Feb. 1961), 202–4; government of national reconciliation,
204, 205; rebellion, 204–6; OAU
and, 204–8 (Council of Foreign
Ministers (1964), 207–8); 'Committee of Seven', 207; Special
Conciliation Commission, 207–8,
208–10; Casablanca communiqué
on (1961), 359–60
Congo, French, *see* Congo (Brazzaville)
Congo (Kinshasa) (Democratic Republic of the Congo, *formerly*
Congo Léopoldville, *and earlier*
Belgian Congo; now Zaire, *q.v.*),
25, 26, 49, 68, 141, 142, 229, 230,
260, 267, 271, 291, 296, 298, 300,
302–3 *p.*; and Katanga, *q.v.*, 170;
titles, 292
Congo (Kinshasa) and her neighbours, 167, **170–4**, 206; and
Congo (Brazzaville) (1963–4 and
1968), **170–3**, 302; and Rwanda
(1967), 173; and Uganda (1964),
173–4; and CAR, 302
Congo (Léopoldville) (republic,
formerly Belgian Congo, *q.v.*; *later*
Congo (Kinshasa), *q.v.*; *now* Zaire
Republic, *q.v.*), 25, 27–30 *p.*, 42,
207, 208; crisis in, *see* Congo
crisis; independent (1960), 27;
UN operational command in, 31;
and Congo (Brazzaville) and
Burundi, 206
Congo, River, 172
Congolese: Central Government, 27
p., 29, 198–200 *p.*, 208–9 *p.*, 212;

mineral wealth (*see also* Katanga),
27; National Army (ANC), 27,
171, 173, 205, 206 (and white
mercenaries, 171, 206–7 *p.*, 209);
National Liberation Committee,
171, 205, 206; rebels, 170, 171,
204–6 *p.*, 208–9 *p.*; Republic
(*formerly* Belgian Congo, *q.v.*; *see
also* Congo (Léopoldville) *and*
Congo (Kinshasa)), 198, 204
Conseil de l'Entente, 70
Conseils, Grands (of AEF and
AOF), 114, 119 *p.*, 183
continental (African) government,
proposals for a, 332–6, 339
Convention Africain (CA), 182, 183
Convention People's Party (CPP,
Nkrumah's, 1949), 108–9 *p.*
Co-ordinating Freedom Council, 43
corrupt practices in administration
and government in Africa – and
elsewhere, 252
Cotonou (Dahomey), 113, 161, 182;
UAM meeting (1963), 139
Coulibaly, Ouezzin (PM of Upper
Volta), 249
coups d'état (military) in African
independent states, 247–8, 258,
280, 286, 293–4, 310–11
Coussey Report (GC, 1949), 108
Crisis (NAACP magazine), 5, 98,
100, 101, 102
Cubans, anti-Castro, 209

Daddah, Moktar Ahmed Ould
(President of Mauritania), 49, 292,
293, 313
Dahir, Muktal (of Somalia), 154
Dahomey, 70, 136, 140, 141, 153,
183, 185, 194, 195, 197, 199, 243,
248, 249; and Niger (dispute),
143, 160–1; and federation, 183–5
p.
Dakar (Ghana), 79, 116, 118, 119,
182, 183, 189–90 *p.*, 194, 196, 216,
250, 292–5 *p.*; Declaration (recommendations of Monrovian

Fall, Colonel (of Mali), 190

Fanon, Frantz, *quoted*, 319

Federal Constituent Assembly and Conference (French West Africa), 183, 185

Fédération des Étudiants d'Afrique Noire en France (FEANF), 340

federation in French West Africa (proposed), **181–90**

federation of *all* African states (proposed), **332–6**

Federation of the Rhodesias and Nyasaland, *see* Central African Federation

Figuig (Algeria), 149 *p.*

financial institutions, *see* monetary

Finland, 135

Firestone Rubber Coy., 99

Foccart, Jacques, 300

Forna, Dr Mohammed (of SL), 165 *p.*

Fort Lamy, 298

France, 173, 212, 228–9 *p.*; and Algeria, 38 (*see also* Algerian War of Independence); and former African colonies (continued ties with), 98, 137–8, 199; and Ethiopia, 150; and Morocco, 143–4; and Ethiopia (treaty, 1897), 150; and Mali Federation, *q.v.*, 184, 185, 249–50 *p.*; and Congo crisis, *q.v.* (at UN), 202; supplies arms to South Africa and Portugal, 229; and Biafra, 238; and Malagasy Republic and South Africa, 241–2; and Upper Volta, 249–50; ethnic variety in, 251; and Nigerian crisis, *q.v.*, 268, 279; and UEAC, 300

Franco–Malian military pact, 188 *p.*

'Freedom Charter' (of PAFMECA, *q.v.*), 42

Freetown (SL), 166 *p.*, 262

French, the (*see also* France), and Algeria, 16; and Guinea, 20; and Mali Federation, 181–90 *p.*

French: Academy, 119; atomic and

nuclear tests in the Sahara, 21, 23, 120, 124; colonial policy after the Second World War, 181

French African colonies and overseas empire, 20, 25, 26, 112 *p.*, 117–20 *p.*, 132 *p.*, 135–7 *p.*, 181, 199; de Gaulle's alternative offer to, 114; continued ties with France, 98, 137, 137–8, 199

French colonies in Africa: *see* Cameroon, Central African Republic, Chad, Congo (Brazzaville), Dahomey, Gabon, Ivory Coast, Madagascar, Niger, Senegal, Sudan (W), *and* Upper Volta

French Communist Party (CP), 113, 118

French community, African states members of (*see also* French colonies in Africa), 20, 22, 39, 98, 114, 119, 185, 199, 243, 244–6; African leaders in, 26–8 *p.*; and UN, 243–4; and West Africa, 244–5; and Portuguese invasion of Guinea, 245; and French atomic-bomb tests in the Sahara, *q.v.*, 245; and French sale of arms to South Africa, 245; and OAU, 245; and a 'dialogue' with South Africa, 245–6

French: Equatorial Africa (AEF), 28, 113, 114, 117, 119, 296–7, 323; Government, 7, 38, 98, 118, 119, 234, 242; National Assembly, 7, 113, 117–18 *p.* (African members of, 107, 109, 117, 118); Socialist Party (SFIO), 116, 117; West Africa (AOF), 28, 113, 114 *p.*, 117, 119 *p.*, 181–4 *p.*, 196 *p.*, 323

Frente de Libertaçao de Moçambique (FRELIMO), 218 *p.*

Frente Libertação de l'Independençia Nationale de Guiné (FLING, Liberation front for the National Independence of Portuguese Guinea), 215–16 *p.*

Index

429

Index

Nur, Dr Mohammed (of Sudan (E)), 288, 290

Nyasaland (*now* Malawi, *q.v.*), 219 *p.*

Nyerere, President Julius (of Tanzania), 41, 42, 62, 106, 152, 163, 164, 218, 277 *p.*, 305, 310–11 *p.*; *quoted*, 47

OAMCE, *see* Organisation Africaine et Malgache de Coopération Économique

OAS, *see* Organization of American States

OAU, *see* Organization of African Unity

OCAM, *see* Organisation Commune Africaine et Malgache

OERS, *see* Organisation des États Riverains du Sénégal

ONUC, *see* Opération des Nations Unies au Congo

Obote, Dr Milton (PM *and later* President of Uganda), 61, 174, 221, 305; and sale of arms to South Africa, 248; his overthrow, 248, 310

Odesanya, Justice M. A. (of Nigeria), 82

Odinga, Oginga (of Kenya), 151

Ogaden province (Ethiopia), 150, 151 *p.*, 154

oil, *see* petroleum

Ojukwu, Lieutenant-Colonel C. Odumegwa (of Biafra), 258–9 *p.*, 262, 264, 269 *p.*, 276, 278; *quoted*, 265

Okunnu, Femi (of Nigeria), 275

Olympio, President Sylvanus (of Togo), 34, 124; assassinated, 51, 67

'Operation Big Bill' (CIA), 173

Opération des Nations Unies au Congo (ONUC), 31, 199, 204 *p.*

Organisation Africaine et Malgache de Coopération Économique (OAMCE), 137, 139, 140

Organisation Commune Africaine et Malgache (OCAM), 135, 136, 140–2

Organisation des États Riverains du Sénégal (OERS), 136, 216, 291, **291–6**; organs and officials, 292; activities, 293–6 *p.*; its needs, 296

Organization of African Unity (OAU; *formation, constitution etc.*), **47–89**; steps leading to, **47–51**; foreign ministers' preliminary conference, **51–3**; discussion of title, 51–2, 63; draft Charter, 52, 54–6, 58; the Charter, 63, 64, 67, 76–7, 81–3 *p.*, 122, 139 *p.*, 157, 162 *p.*, 174, 282, 289, **369–77** (Preamble, 65, **369**); inception, 63; aims and principles, 65–7; membership and admission, 67–9; structure, **69–89**

Organs: General Assembly of Heads of State and Government, 68, 69, **69–72**, 72, 73, 76, 79, 82, 86–8 *p.*, 221–7 *p.*; (meetings, 69–72; rules of procedure, 71–2; functions and powers, 72); *see also* OAU Summit Conferences

Council of Ministers, 68–71 *p.*, **72–6**, 77, 83 *p.*, 86–7 *p.*, 215, 221–6 *p.* (meetings, 73–4; functions and powers, 74–6); first ordinary session (1963), 51–3, 150 (agenda and resolutions for Summit, 52–3); second ordinary session (1964), 80, 83, 232–3; sixth ordinary session (1966), 168–9; tenth ordinary session (1968), 233–4, 273–4, 312; extraordinary (special) sessions, 70, 73, 75–6, 149, 152–3, 157, 164, 207, 222

Secretary-General and Secretariat (*see also* Telli, D.), 69, 73, **76–81**, 88, 157, 175, 222–4 *p.*, 230 ('Functions and Regulations of the General Secretariat', **77–8**; candidates for post of Secretary-General, 80)

Index

Parti (du) Regroupement Africain (PRA = CA *plus* MSA, *qq.v.*), 183, 185, 249

Partido Africano de Independençia de Guiné e Cabo Verde (PAIGC: African Party for the Independence of Portuguese Guinea and Cape Verde), 215–16 *p.*

peace and stability, threats to: Monrovia resolution (May 1961), 362–4

Pearson, Donald (of Malawi), 241

Peking (seat of Chinese communist government), 209

People's Democratic Party (Sudanese (E)), 288

People's Revolutionary Armed Forces (FARP – the PAIGC (*q.v.*) army in Guinea (Bissau)), 216

petroleum (oil): in Africa generally, 323; in Nigeria, 197, 280

Philosophy and Opinions (Garvey), 107

Pickens, William, 95

Pierre, Lieutenant-Colonel, 189–90 *p.*

Pognon, M. Augustin (of Dahomey), 80

Polícia Internaçional e de Defesa do Estado (PIDE: Portuguese secret police), 212, 217 *p.*

political instability in, and foreign manipulation of, African dependent states, 247–50

politics, intra-African: and Pan-Africanism, 329

Port Gentil meeting (1968), 300

Port Harcourt (Nigeria), 264

Portugal and the Portuguese, 177, 214–18, 228, 229, 231, 244, 245, 295; Gestapo (secret police), *see* PIDE; supply of arms to (for use in colonial wars), 228

Portuguese colonies in Africa, liberation of, 210–18, 219: Ang-

ola, 212–15; Guinea (Bissau), 215–17; Mozambique, 217–18

Présence africaine (magazine), 116

Pretoria trade agreement (South Africa–Malawi, 1967), 241 *p.*

RDA, *see* Rassemblement Démocratique Africain

RF, *see* Rhodesian Front

Rabat (Morocco), 145 *p.*, 149

Rabemananjara, Jacques (of Malagasy), 242

racial discrimination and racism (*see also* apartheid, DuBois *and* Garvey), 10, 21, 132–3, 177 *p.*, 322, 329; in Portuguese African colonies, 210–18, 219; in Rhodesia, 219–26, 229; in South Africa, 220, 229, 230–6; in South-West Africa (Namibia), 226–8, 229 *p.*

Radio Ghana, 49

Rassemblement Démocratique Africain (RDA, 1946), 113–14 *p.*, 119–20 *p.*; special congress of (1959), 119; and Mali Federation, 249–50 *p.*

refugee problem, 167, 174–6; agreement on (Uganda and Sudan, Dec. 1964) – 'a model', 175

regional economic groupings, 291–310: OERS, *q.v.*, 291–6; UDEAC and UEAC, *qq.v.*, 296–304; EAEC, *q.v.*, 305–10

Renner, Awooner, 12

research schemes, joint, 326

Rhodesia (*formerly* Southern Rhodesia, *q.v.*; *see also* Smith, Ian, *and* Zimbabwe), 4, 76, 177, 214, 228, 229, 231, 248; UDI (Unilateral Declaration of Independence, 1965), 69, 74, 75, 124, 220–6 *p.*, 230, 246; British Government's five principles, 219; sanctions against, 220

Rhodesian Front (RF), 219–20

river projects, multi-national, 326

436

Index

Slimane, Major (of Algeria), 145

Smith, Ian (PM of Rhodesia, *q.v.*) and his régime, 220 *p.*, 225, 226 *p.*, 229

Sobukwe (political prisoner in South Africa), 232

Société Ivoriène d'Engrais (Ivory Coast), 135

Soglo, Colonel (of Dahomey), 160

Solanke, Ladipo, 8

Somali–Ethiopian dispute (1963–4), 73, 75, 143, **150–6**; settlement, 154–6

Somali–Kenyan dispute (1967), 73, 143, 150–1 *p.*, 156–60; Kinshasa Communiqué (declaration), 1967, 158; Arusha Memorandum, 159–60

Somali Republic, *see* Somalia

Somali 'shiftas' (guerrillas), 151–2, 154, 157

Somalia (*see also* Somali–Ethiopian *and* Somali–Kenyan disputes), 33, 39, 42, 82, 153, 199, 208, 223, 229, 230, 311, 312; Great, 152

Soumialot, Craston (of Congo), 206

Soumare, Colonel (of Mali Federation), 189–90 *p.*

South Africa, Union (*now* Republic) of (*see also* PAFMECSA), 4, 21, 42, 66, 67, 73, 177, 206 *p.*, 214, 220, 228, 229; apartheid in, *see* apartheid; African National Congress of, 19; sale of arms to, 177, 220, 228, 234 *p.*, 242, 245, 246, 248; self-governing (1910), 220; and South-West Africa (Namibia, *q.v.*), 42, **226–8**, 229; liberation of black and coloured peoples of, **230–6**; and independent African states, 235–6; and OAU, 235, 236; and Malawi, 240–1; and Malagasy Republic, 241–2; and Gabon, 242; and Ivory Coast, 242; and Ghana, 242; 'dialogue' with, 338

South African: Industrial Develop-

ment Corporation, 241, 242; Liberal Party, 19; racist régimes (*see also* apartheid *and* Namibia), 124, 227; Treaty Organization, 228

South Africans, white, 19

South America, 6, 96

Southern Africa: three racist régimes, 229; future of, 229–30 (Lusaka Manifesto (1969), **393–400**)

Southern Front (Sudanese (E)), 288

Southern Hotel Group (South Africa), 242

Southern Rhodesia (*now* Rhodesia, *q.v.*; *see also* Zimbabwe), 206, 219 *p.*, 221

South-West Africa (Namibia, *q.v.*), 42, **226–8**

Soviet Union (USSR), *see* Russia

Springfield (USA) lynching (1908, *see also* lynching), 102

Stanleyville (in Congo, *now* Kisangani, *q.v.*), 29, 201, 206

Steiner, Rolf (mercenary), 290

Stevens, Dr Siaka (of SL), 164–6 *p.*

'Stop the Tour' campaign (Great Britain, 1970), 177

students (African) and Pan-Africanism, 339–42 *p.*

Sudan (E) (*sometime* Anglo-Egyptian Sudan) and Sudanese, 156, 281, 282; and Uganda (agreement on refugees, 1964), 175–6; secessionist movement, **283–91**; after independence (1956), 284–7; coup d'état (Nov. 1958), 286; Southern Front, 288; seeking a solution, 287–9; OAU and Southern Sudan, 289–91; and Ethiopia, 282; provisional government in exile (*see also* 'Nile Republic'), 288–91 *p.*; and Chad (relations, 1965–6), 167, 167–8

Sudan (E): African National Union (SANU), 287; National Unionist Party (SNUP), 282; Revolutionary Council (El-Nimeiry's), 288

438